MONTANA AND THE WEST SERIES
VOLUME NINE

Gathered together on the porch of the Custer's home at Ft. Lincoln in this 1875 view, an assembly of officers, ladies and guests included George Custer on the far right and Tom Custer on the far left. Keogh sits in the center, holding a fan from one of the Wadsworth girls. *Courtesy of North Dakota Historical Society.*

MYLES KEOGH

Edited and Compiled by
JOHN P. LANGELLIER, KURT HAMILTON COX, AND BRIAN C. POHANKA

UPTON AND SONS
El Segundo, California, 1998

Copyright, 1991
Gene Autry Western Heritage Museum
Second printing, 1998

All rights reserved including the rights
to translate or reproduce this work or parts
thereof in any form or by any media.

Library of Congress Catalog Card Number 91-65910
ISBN 0-912783-21-4

Designed and produced under the direction of
Robert A. Clark, The Arthur H. Clark Company,
Spokane, Washington

(On the title page) This portrait of Keogh was taken in Louisville, Kentucky, between 1871 and 1873. Although Keogh had complained to his brother that he was "getting too fat" and had "plenty of grey hairs," he still projects a youthful image. *Courtesy of Gene Autry Western Heritage Museum.*

In Memory of
JOHN M. CARROLL
and
LAWRENCE A. FROST

Vivas to those who have failed!
And to those whose war-vessels sank in the sea!
And to those themselves who sank in the sea!
And to all generals who have lost engagements,
   and all overcome heroes!
And to the numberless unknown heroes equal
   to the greatest heroes known!

Walt Whitman

Contents

FOREWORD, *by Lawrence Frost* 11
ACKNOWLEDGMENTS 13
INTRODUCTION, *by Kurt Hamilton Cox* . . . 15

1. THE LEGEND BEGINS: Comanche—The Horse Who Conferred Fame On His Rider, *by Elizabeth A. Lawrence* 21

2. THE WEARING OF THE BLUE: The Irish in the U.S. Army, 1776-1876 *by Kevin Mulroy* 29

Reconnaissance—Custer's Theme Song: Keogh and "Garry Owen," *by Peggy Champlin*. . 45

3. HEARTH AND HOME: Keogh's Early Years In Ireland and Italy *by John S. Manion*. . 49

Reconnaissance—John Joseph Coppinger, 1834-1909 64

4. "UNSURPASSED IN DASH:" Keogh in the American Civil War *by Brian C. Pohanka* . 67

5. THE GIRL I LEFT BEHIND: Keogh and the Martin Family *by Lenora A. Snedeker*. 87

Reconnaissance—Myles Keogh: A Graphological Perspective, *by P.D. Gleason*. . . . 100

6. TO GARRY OWEN AND GLORY: Keogh and the Seventh Cavalry, 1866-1876 *by Kurt Hamilton Cox*. 103

Reconnaissance—The Warren Favor Affair. . 124
Reconnaissance—William Averill Comstock, 1842-1868 126
Reconnaissance—A Matter of Drink *by Kurt Hamilton Cox and John S. Manion*. 128

7. INTO THE VALLEY OF DEATH: The Historiography of Keogh's Role at the Little Big Horn *by John Phillip Langellier* . 131

8. THE KEOGH EPISODE: Archaeology and the Historical Record *by Richard A. Fox, Jr.* . 143

9. TAPS: Keogh's Burial and Memorials *by Francis B. Taunton*. 155

Reconnaissance—Captain Keogh's Medals . . 162

10. THE LEGEND CONTINUES: A Checklist of Keogh in Fiction, Poetry, and Film *by Rev. Vincent Heier*. 165

Reconnaissance—Henry Inman's Keogh: Fact or Fiction 187
AFTERWORD, *by Gary Keogh* 189
CONTRIBUTERS 191
BIBLIOGRAPHY 193
INDEX 199

Illustrations

Officers, Ladies and Guests at Ft. Lincoln	*frontispiece*
Keogh in the early 1870s	*title page*
Comanche with Gustave Korn	20
Comanche with Capt. Charles S. Ilsley	25
Lithograph of the Irish soldier, 1846	30
Col. Corcoran and the N.Y. Sixty Ninth at Bull Run	37
"Enlisting Irish and German Emigrants"	38
Sgt. Robert Hughes	41
Cpl. Thomas Eagen	42
Pvt. Thomas O'Neill	43
The Score of "Garry Owen"	45
Keogh and the Company of St. Patrick, c. 1861	48
Keogh in his Papal Uniform	54
Keogh Wearing His Papal Campaign Medal	55
Keogh's Family	61
John Joseph Coppinger	64
Keogh in 1862 and 1863	66
Gen. James Shields	68
Andrew J. Alexander and Keogh	72
Lincoln Reviews the Army of the Potomac	73
George Stoneman and His Officers	74
Keogh Astride His Horse	74
John Buford and His Staff	75
Daniel J. Kelly	78
Keogh Atop Lookout Mountain in Tennessee	82
Joseph O'Keefe	84
Keogh and Comrade, 1865	85
Enos Thompson Throop	88
Upper House at Willowbrook	89
Keogh with Emily, Cornelia, and Lylie Martin	91
Andrew Alexander and Evy Martin Alexander	92
Emory Upton and Emily Martin Upton	93
Nelly Martin	95
Nelly Martin after 1878	97
Nelly Martin in the late 1870s	98
Keogh in Dress Uniform, c. 1870	102
James Bell, Myles Moylan, and Henry J. Nowland	102
Keogh in the Uniform of a Lieutenant-Colonel	111
Keogh in Civilian Garb	116
Keogh in Suit and Bowler Hat	118
Keogh in the New Uniform Issued in 1872	120
Emma and Nellie Wadsworth	122
The "Hunting Party" at Ft. Lincoln, 1875	123
Dr. John Arvid Ouchterlony	123
John Carland, Stephen Baker, and Charles Henry Ingalls	130
James Porter	133
Henry Bailey	135
Red Horse and Two Moon	141
Archaeology Figure 1-1 and Legend	142
Archaeology Figure 1-2	145
Archaeology Figure 1-3	148
Edwin Bobo and Frank Varden	149
Archaeology Figure 1-4	150
Archaeology Figure 1-5	151
Archaeology Figures 1-6 and 1-7	153
Keogh's Company I Guidon	154
The New Marker for Keogh, 1879	156
The New Marker for Keogh, c. 1890	158
Monuments at the Fort Hill Cemetery	159
Philip Carey in *Tonka*	164
Grant Woods as Keogh in "The Legend of Custer"	184

Foreword

Over the decades, Myles Walter Keogh has come to play an ever increasing role in the literature of the Little Big Horn. At first, much of Keogh's fame stemmed from the survival of his hardy mount, Comanche. As years passed, Keogh took on importance in his own right for historians and fiction writers as well. Alternately portrayed in many previous depictions as the epitome of the Victorian cavalier *sans peur et sans reproche* or, conversely as a caricature of the hard-drinking, boorish, brutal Irish stereotype complete with heavy brogue, he remains a misunderstood figure. Unraveling who this man really was and why he would become such a noteworthy part of the Little Big Horn lore offered a challenge to a number of scholars. Devoting considerable time and energy to the reconstruction of Keogh's story, they have conducted research in international collections in order to unearth clues about the historical figure, as well as to trace the symbolic stature Keogh has assumed over the years.

This group of specialists has reached a number of interesting conclusions. The results of their combined work indicate an extremely complex character, and a man of many contradictions. At times, Keogh is romantic, humorous, and well liked by those around him. Dashing in his uniform, he was outwardly the model of the "Irish Dragoon," his hero. Inwardly, however, he seems to have fallen short of his romantic ideal. Over time, his shortcomings weighed heavily upon him. A loyal son, brother, and friend, Keogh appears to have felt that he had not lived up to his potential. At the same time, he was deeply wounded by deaths or other misfortunes which separated him again and again from those he loved. As an outgrowth of many disappointments, he increasingly became isolated, and perhaps even distanced himself in a form of self-imposed exile on occasions. Introspection during this period seems to have evolved into brooding and an ever-increasing self-consciousness. He even may have developed a problem with alcohol, a common disease among frontier soldiers, although this is not conclusive. In turn, medical problems cropped up, which may have been induced just as much by psychological causes as they were by physical factors.

This book offers new and varied approaches and insights, the combined chapters fitting together as an intricate, fascinating mosaic. The scholarship points to some new directions as well. Since there is considerable food for thought within this volume, I welcome the anthology and believe it will become a standard text in the future. In this way, it serves as a fitting recognition for the 150th anniversary of Myles Keogh's birth.

Lawrence A. Frost
March 25, 1990
Monroe, Michigan

Acknowledgments

The authors and editors wish to express their indebtedness to the numerous persons who generously have assisted in making this project possible. First, thanks is due to the Gene Autry Western Heritage Museum for nurturing this publication through hosting a conference on the topic in the summer of 1990. The Museum's Executive Director, Joanne D. Hale; the Director of Education, Cynthia Harnish; and the Chief Curator, James Nottage, all contributed greatly to this project. Robert Coontz, the Museum's Director of Development likewise made his knowledge of computers available, thereby making the project much easier for all the participants. In addition, Andrew Belanger and Mercedes Delaney, both volunteers at the Museum, provided many types of important assistance. Dr. Peggy Champlin and Dr. Kevin Mulroy, of the Museum's Research Center, also spent numerous hours undertaking additional research for this project and providing editorial assistance. Dr. Champlin prepared the bibliography for the publication.

At the Custer Battlefield, Historian Douglas McChristian and Curator Mark Nelson offered considerable services. John Drayton and Susanne Harrell of the University of Oklahoma Press cooperated in allowing segments of Dr. Richard Fox's forthcoming archaeological study of the Custer Battlefield to be reprinted here.

Many individuals and institutions gave various additional support and deserve thanks. These include: the late Ross Kehoe, of Clifden, Kilkenny, Ireland for permission to use the papers in his possession relating to Myles Keogh; the Keogh family, who made it possible for the Gene Autry Western Heritage Museum to obtain this material for its collections; The Irish National Library for providing microform copies of the Keogh correspondence it preserved in its collections; David Scollan, of Auburn, New York, for sending various photographs of Keogh's grave and relevant matters; the late John A. Carroll for permission to use photographs from his excellent collection; the Fort Hill Cemetery Association for providing details of interments at the Enos Throop Martin lot; George W. Martin of Kennett Square, Pennsylvania for use of several photographs in his family's collection and many other kindnesses; Hugh Shick of Burbank, California who generously shared his fine library and time; and the late Dr. Lawrence A. Frost of Monroe, Michigan for permission to quote from matarials in his collection.

Thanks also are due to the following: Michael Knapp and Michael Musick, National Archives, Washington, D.C.; Barbara Flanary, Archivist, Memphis Public Library and Information Center, Memphis, Tennessee; Mellissa Thompson, Amon Carter Museum, Ft. Worth, Texas; Dr. Douglas Scott, Lincoln, Nebraska; James Wadsworth Symington, Washington, D.C.; Mrs. John L. Morrison, New Roads, Louisiana; Clark B. Hall, Fairfax, Virginia; David Evans, Athens, Georgia; Roger B. Hunt, Rockville, Maryland; Walter Damrosch Littell, New Haven, Connecticut; Ella Pozell, The Oak Hill Cemetery, Georgetown, D.C.; Phil Martin, Long Beach, California; John Monahan, Carlow, Ireland; Arnold Blumberg, Baltimore, Maryland; John Hennessy, Selkirk, New York; Richard A. Sauers, Harrisburg, Pennsylvania; Paul Kallina, Silver Spring, Maryland; Rebecca F. Peek, Alexandria, Virginia; Fred W. Hunter, American Medical Association, Chicago, Illinois; The English Society of the Westerners; The Filson Club, Louisville, Kentucky; The Music Library, UCLA; the Auburn *Citizen*; Phyllis Bryant of Auburn, New York; Jim Court of the Custer Battlefield Preservation Committee; Ann Loomis and JoAnn Newell of Oxford, New York; the Norwich, New York, Civil War Roundtable; the United States Military Academy, West Point; Peter J. Lysy, The Archives of the

ACKNOWLEDGMENTS

University of Notre Dame, Notre Dame, Indiana; and Fr. Barry Hagan, The Archives of the University of Portland, Portland, Oregon.

Finally, Robert Clark of The Arthur H. Clark Company is to be recognized for transforming the original manuscript into the present volume, while Richard and Frankie Upton of Upton & Sons, who kindly agreed to publish the results of many years of work by the contributors and editors, deserve special appreciation for publishing this study.

Introduction

Of the men who died at the Battle of the Little Big Horn, Myles Keogh has taken on an importance second only to George Custer. Although Custer may be portrayed as either hero or fool, authors almost always depict Keogh in an heroic light. Often, he is accorded the position of the last man alive or, in many cases, is held up as "the Bravest Man" based upon Indian oral tradition.

Edward Luce, the first of the serious Keogh biographers, envisioned his glorious subject's death and then assembled a past that properly would clothe such a titan. That most of his "history" was conjured of whole cloth never seemed to bother him or the legion of followers who have accepted his larger-than-life characterization. For half a century, Luce's flawed biography has stood as the basis for countless other Keogh depictions, thereby amplifying not only the mistakes but also the legend.

Luce's supposition, which others echoed, that the Keogh legend was born in the midst of battle, is incorrect. The genesis of Keogh's stature in the Little Big Horn saga does begin on a battlefield, but long after the trumpets had been silenced. Ironically, Keogh's actions on the field of death that day in June 1876 had little impact on his transcendence to a legendary figure. The instrument of Myles Keogh's transformation from mortal to legend was a horse.

Today, few individuals believe the popular notion that the only living thing to survive the Battle of the Little Big Horn was Myles Keogh's steed, Comanche. Most of the Indian participants also lived to fight another day, while other horses also remained alive, as reportedly did at least one dog. But to belabor that point is to miss the greater idea.

During an age that took its romantic inspirations from the writing of Sir Thomas Malory, Sir Walter Scott, and Lord Tennyson, the ideal of chivalry was held as both a perceivable and attainable reality. In a world that was rushing headlong into the modern era, the image of the cavalry officer represented the very embodiment of the chivalric sensibility.

This association was not lost on the men and officers of the cavalry, and there was a conscious effort on their part to perpetuate that image, particularly within the Seventh, led by its flamboyant field commander, George Armstrong Custer. In the wake of Little Big Horn, there arose a need for a symbol to preserve and honor this romantic ideal. Comanche, being the mount of a dashing cavalry officer, was best suited to shoulder this burden. By association, his rider would carry it as well.

Understanding Comanche's symbolic transcendence of death, and the perpetuation of this 19th-century ideal is essential to an appreciation of the way in which Myles Keogh would be remembered after his passing. In Chapter 1, veterinarian and anthropologist Elizabeth Atwood Lawrence examines the role played by Comanche in the creation of the legend of Myles Keogh. Her conclusions pave the way for the remainder of this volume.

But the connection to Comanche alone cannot account for the enormous popularity of Keogh to both readers and writers of the Little Big Horn story. There

MYLES KEOGH

exists beyond the legend an intangible persona—a rarely glimpsed character whose very elusiveness has attracted and fascinated many who then are drawn into the realm of this Irish soldier's life. The authors of this work count themselves in such company.

Part of the mystery that surrounds Keogh results from the lack of reliable information. Early references to Keogh are few. In 1909, Sergeant John Ryan, writing of his experiences in the Seventh Cavalry, remembered the commander of Company I as, "The brave and dashing Captain Myles Keogh, probably as fine a looking officer as was in the United States Cavalry at the time. . . ." Though written over three decades after the fact, Ryan's description probably comes closest to how Keogh's contemporaries saw him—and how he wished to be seen. There is indication that the image of the devil-may-care Irish cavalier, which has come down to the present day, consciously was cultivated by Keogh in an effort to fulfill his romantic dreams.

Keogh's posturing, to some degree, also may have resulted from an effort to put his origins behind him. In modern times, it is difficult to imagine the way in which the Irish were viewed by much of the American population in the 19th-century. They were seen as rude and uncivilized, ready to brawl at a moment's notice, and habitually under the influence of strong drink. Discrimination was open and omnipresent, because the Irishman was both a foreigner and a Catholic.

In Chapter 2 of this work, Kevin Mulroy explores the history of the Irish in the U.S. Army from the American Revolution to the Little Big Horn. With a clear understanding of the common perception of the Irish soldier, it becomes easier to see how Myles Keogh was, in fact, the exception to the Irish experience in America. Unlike many of his fellow countrymen who had fled their homes to escape famine and economic woes, Keogh seems to have left in search of adventure. Additionally, a long tradition existed of the "wild geese," or gentlemen who freely took up the profession of arms abroad as a way of life. For the rank and file who hailed from Ireland, donning a uniform was merely "a job of work" which had to be taken out of necessity. Finally, Keogh became an officer, which allowed him to move in different social circles than the enlisted personnel from his former homeland. His commission gave him access to areas which the average Irish soldier never could hope to reach.

This divergence between the expectation of the common Irishman and the image of the Irish gentleman began for Myles at an early age. In Chapter 3, John Manion recounts the life of Keogh from his birth in Carlow until his voyage to America. What emerges is a picture of Keogh as a member of the landed gentry, with the opportunities of education afforded few of his contemporaries. But even with the benefits of land ownership, Myles' family could not escape the realities of life in mid 19th-century Ireland. To the Keoghs, land was a double-edged sword which gave privilege but also brought privation. They were tied to the land and what opportunities there were grew out of the land. As the youngest son of a large family, Myles would have played a lesser role in the scheme of things as his older brothers took charge of the property as part of a long-standing tradition. Besides, to a boy raised on Charles Lever's *Charles O'Malley: The Irish Dragoon*, the life of a gentleman farmer paled in comparison with the glory and excitement of the battlefield. Nevertheless, he would contemplate his self-imposed exile from time to time and, recalling his family, feel homesick.

Yearning to live out his fantasy, Keogh pledged his sword to the Pope and set out for Italy. This initiation to the military fell short of the young man's expectations. After his first exposure to combat in the brief Papal Wars, Keogh soon found himself as a parade ground soldier in peacetime. Tiring of this situation in Rome, he then journeyed to America in search of another cause. In Chapter 4, Brian Pohanka examines the career of Keogh in the Union Army. While not achieving the same sort of meteoric success as George Custer, Keogh nevertheless distinguished himself, both in battle and as a man of responsibility. More importantly, he was able to form friendships and acquaintances which would be of lasting benefit to his career as well as to his assimilation into American society.

By and large, the body of the commissioned officers' corps was composed of West Pointers and those with political influence. Keogh's associates, Emory Upton and Andrew Alexander, were typical of the men chosen to lead the army. That Keogh was able to move into this elite society is remarkable given that he was an Irish Catholic. In large measure, an understanding of Myles Keogh is enhanced by a knowledge of the people with whom he associated. In Chapter 5, Lenora Snedeker reveals his relationship with people from the upper classes who impacted most upon him. As an officer and gentleman, Keogh felt drawn to these people and their way of life.

That the Martin family of Willowbrook and its circle took Myles Keogh into their homes and hearts is certain, yet there was always the implication that Keogh remained the outsider. Myles was not the typical Irish immigrant, nor was he really of that genteel New York society of which he seemingly longed to be a part. This situation must have been frustrating for the young man who sought status within the United States. Keogh's contention that, "He could often have married for money," may have indicated his desire for independence, but it more likely was the sort of idle boast that he was prone to make when trying to mask an unpleasant truth. This attitude, religious differences, and other factors may have kept Myles and Nelly Martin apart but still tales of unrequited love remain a part of the story, whether true or not.

Keogh's post-Civil War years were marked by what has come to be characterized as "melancholia." In his letters of this period there is an ever present aura of sadness. He speaks often of his loneliness. In the Civil War Myles had been caught up in the spectacle of 19th-century warfare, "like in a dream," with its pomp and glory. The reality of Indian warfare was far different. A soldier of fortune might not take to this situation with the same enthusiasm. Thus, Chapter 6 details this last period of Myles' life. Duty in the frontier army was filled with hardships of all sorts. The posts usually were far beyond the pale of even the most rude civilization. The enemy was elusive and ill defined. Supplies were limited and at times nonexistent, as was the support of the American public. Though he was determined to remain in the army, despite the constant threat of a reduced service, there is every indication that Keogh was content to rest on his laurels. Contrary to the popular conception of Keogh being one of Custer's most experienced Indian fighters, Myles had little background in that area, preferring staff duty to the rigors of plains warfare. In fact, Keogh missed every major expedition that Custer led—save the last, when the chivalric ideal was shot to pieces at the Little Big Horn.

When the time came to mount the campaign that would culminate in the Battle of the Little Big Horn, Myles Keogh was just coming off a long period of illness and inactivity. Even as he rejoined his command to begin the march, he hoped for yet another leave of absence on his return. But, once back in the saddle, Keogh's characteristic competence as an officer again came to the fore.

In Chapter 7, John Langellier recounts the last days of Myles Keogh and delves into an investigation of the various theories advanced over the years as to what happened to the Irish officer at the Little Big Horn. The opinions about Keogh's role in the fight along the Greasy Grass are as varied as the conclusions reached about the course of the battle itself. Indeed, an entire "industry" has grown up around the battle and Keogh usually is found at its very heart. Solving the mystery of exactly what transpired has fueled the interest of several generations of historians. With the passage of time, Keogh gained considerable prominence in the literature. In almost all instances, these conclusions are drawn from thin evidence and considerable supposition.

Chapter 8 reveals the work done by archaeologist Richard Fox and others on the site of Custer's last stand. Fox attempts to avoid preconceptions about the battle. He uses evidence from archaeology, the tactics of the period, and contemporary accounts to piece together troop movements and present a plausible scenario for what happened to Custer and his five companies. A portrait is painted of unit disintegration, which suggests that Myles Keogh and his command died quickly and with little opportunity to mount effective resistance. According to Fox, Keogh's death was less than glorious.

In Chapter 9, Francis Taunton takes the Keogh story from the discovery of his body on the Custer battlefield to his internment in Auburn, New York. It is appropriate that this author should close the life of Myles Keogh, for in a very real sense he was instrumental in introducing this story to those who have come after him. Building upon his efforts through their own prolific research, John Manion and Brian Pohanka have devoted decades to the pursuit of the real Myles Walter Keogh.

This work ends where it began—with the legend of Myles Keogh. Vincent Heier devotes Chapter 10 to the portrayal of Keogh in fiction, poetry, film, and television. This chapter relates strongly to Bruce A. Rosenberg's *Custer and the Epic of Defeat,* a study which places the Battle of the Little Big Horn in the context of other "last stands." Rosenberg suggests that fiction writers and 19th-century chroniclers alike had the same goal of dramatization. Fascinated with the "few against many" theme, the fine line between fact and fiction often was crossed in early works on the battle, as can be seen in the examples Heier presents. Just as Saul had his armor bearer at Mt. Gilboa, Leonidas his Dioneces at Thermopylae, Byrthnoth his Aelfwine at Maldon, Arthur his Gawain at Viterbo, and Roland his Oliver at Roncesvalles, so Custer had Keogh at the Little Big Horn. Thus, the Irishman joined a company of truly legendary figures. This doubtless would have appealed to Keogh's romantic Victorian sensibilities.

Between several of the chapters the reader will be taken on a short "Reconnaissance," a survey of related incidents and anecdotes concerning Keogh prepared by the editors.

Perhaps the essential lesson to be learned from these studies of Myles Keogh is how well the life of an enigmatic individual serves as a blank sheet to be written upon in whatever form suits the artistic will of the author. Keogh, Custer, and the Seventh Cavalry would be elevated to the very pinnacle of American manhood as the United States began to reflect more upon its history in the wake of the First World War and the Depression. Keogh made a perfect choice, for his mystique contains the very stuff of which legends are made.

Somewhere between that artistic license and this book lies the reality of a man named Myles Walter Keogh. We may be no nearer to that reality now than when we began, but I trust our efforts may illuminate some of the darkness. More questions may have been raised than have been answered, but the questions will be better informed, and more complex. Hopefully, too, the concept of a multi-disciplinary anthology has merit for those who might explore this type of biographical approach in the future.

KURT HAMILTON COX
March 29, 1990
Los Angeles, California

MYLES KEOGH:

The Life and Legend of an "Irish Dragoon" in the Seventh Cavalry

Gustave Korn of Company I, who served as one of Comanche's attendants after the Little Big Horn fight, would be killed at Wounded Knee in 1890. *Courtesy of Custer Battlefield National Monument.*

Chapter 1

THE LEGEND BEGINS: Comanche—The Horse Who Conferred Fame On His Rider

by Elizabeth A. Lawrence, VMD, Ph.D.

> . . .as I pressed into the canter, that secret sympathy between the horse and his rider shot suddenly through me. . . .
>
> Charles Lever, *Charles O'Malley*

No man of the immediate command of Lieutenant Colonel (Brevet Major General) George Armstrong Custer survived to describe the dramatic clash between the Seventh United States Cavalry and the Sioux and Cheyenne warriors which came to be known as "Custer's Last Stand." Fought on a Montana hillside on June 25, 1876, the conflict in which approximately 210 men with Custer's command lost their lives has evoked extraordinary interest not only in the minds of Americans but even on a worldwide scale. Although the Custer battle was part of a larger two-day military engagement, the Battle of the Little Big Horn, it is the "Last Stand" that has exerted such profound influence on people's imagination. The image of Custer's men, outnumbered and surrounded, fighting to the death against overwhelming odds is a perennially fascinating image deeply etched into human consciousness.

Much of the appeal of Custer's Last Stand is rooted in the mystery that surrounds the event and the many questions about it that even a single soldier who lived through the battle might have clarified. But the one being who became famous as a survivor was mute. Almost incredibly, two days following the fighting a cavalry horse from Custer's command was found alive— Comanche, the mount who had belonged to Captain Myles W. Keogh of Company I. Seldom in history have people wished so fervently that an animal could speak and illuminate the unknown elements of the battle and the actions and motivations of its controversial leader. Although other Seventh Cavalry horses survived, and, of course, the men of the Seventh Cavalry not detailed with Custer as well as great numbers of victorious Indians lived through the engagement, Comanche became widely known as the "only survivor" of Custer's Last Stand. This designation has been an inextricable part of his fame—molding his life and legend from the time of the battle even through the present day.

The courage and hardiness that enabled him to live through the battle not only marked the beginning of Comanche's renown as the "lone survivor" but also initiated the legend of his rider—the dashing and valorous Irish "soldier of fortune," Myles Keogh. By means of Comanche's feat of endurance and the unusual

MYLES KEOGH

1. Elizabeth Atwood Lawrence, *His Very Silence Speaks: Comanche—The Horse who Survived Custer's Last Stand* (Detroit, MI: Wayne State University Press, 1989), 82-93 and 183-184.

faithfulness and fortitude attributed to him, the horse endowed his master with immortality and imbued him with a romantic aura. Most of the celebrated horses in history have achieved hero status primarily through the fame of their owner-riders. Although mounts such as Alexander the Great's Bucephalus and Robert E. Lee's Traveller possessed splendid and admired qualities in their own right and contributed immeasurably to their masters' accomplishments, they would not be remembered as they are without the secure place accorded their riders in history. Comanche is different in this regard, because the intense interest centered around his rider, Captain Myles Keogh, results mainly from his being the man who rode Comanche. A handsome, gallant, and bold military figure, Keogh would be noted, even without his mount, as one of the bravest and most honored officers who fought with Custer and would have achieved fame in dying with his comrades at the Last Stand. But it cannot be denied that Keogh is known and recollected primarily as the rider of the remarkable horse who lived through the Custer Battle.[1]

Following his discovery, the badly wounded horse was rescued from the battlefield, nursed back to health, and maintained as an honored member of the Seventh Cavalry until his death in 1891. Though he did not have the capacity for speech, Comanche communicated in other ways. For, as a heroic survivor, he was invested with deep significance, and he assumed a powerful symbolic role in American culture. When he died, his body was preserved and mounted as a museum specimen that continues to be a very popular exhibit at the University of Kansas in Lawrence. Over the years, Comanche has become even more articulate as he has taken on diverse meanings at different times and for various groups of people.

Seldom in history has there been a more cherished battle survivor than Comanche—both in life and after his death. Great value was attributed to the wounded mount from the very moment of his discovery following the battle. As a living creature found by soldiers at the scene of so much death and destruction, Comanche represented the only element of hope in the face of shock and despair. Viewed as the last living tie to Custer and his men, Comanche became a surrogate for the annihilated command. Instantaneous sentiments on the part of the men who found him spared Comanche the merciful death routinely meted out to suffering war horses. Against the dictates of practicality and custom, the mount was treated for his injuries and conveyed back to Fort Abraham Lincoln with the same care due a wounded soldier.

News of the Seventh Cavalry's overwhelming defeat at the hands of Indians was felt keenly by the young country celebrating its one-hundredth anniversary as a nation in July of 1876. Not only was the victory of an untrained and so-called "savage" foe at the Little Big Horn perceived as a national disgrace, but there was also a sense of loss and grief for the death of the flamboyant General Custer and his command of soldiers who reportedly had been "massacred" to the last man. These cavalrymen, most of whom had been killed in the prime of life in this unexpected defeat, generally were regarded as heroes who died bravely fighting for their country. When Comanche was discovered among the dead near the battle site, his wounds had made him a comrade-in-arms of the fallen troopers. From the cavalrymen he represented, Comanche took on the mantle of heroism. The horse soon became a link between the living and the dead. His endurance and invincibility became symbols for survival in the face of overwhelming odds. The wounded horse became the focus for various emotions—the bitter anger of defeat, sorrow for the dead troopers, and vengeance toward the Indians.

Comanche lived for fifteen-and-a-half years following the Little Big Horn battle, and became the most famous of American military horses. Designated as the "lone survivor," he earned his own place in history through fortitude, and endowed his rider with glory. The strong bond between Captain Keogh and his horse, which may well have actually existed, soon took on legendary proportions and was purported to be the reason for the animal's unlikely survival. Accounts of Comanche during the two days prior to his rescue depicted the wounded horse standing guard over the dead Keogh, trying to awaken the beloved master he hoped was only sleeping.[2] A wide-spread belief exists that Keogh was unwilling to shoot his mount for use as breastworks as the other cavalrymen did. This view is upheld by Indian testimony that Keogh (or someone fitting his description) did indeed remain with his horse until the end, kneeling between the animal's front legs and shooting from under his breast. Little Soldier, a Sioux who fought in the Battle of the Little Big Horn, explained Comanche's survival by reference to the relationship between horse and rider. Keogh, he said, died gripping his mount's bridle reins tightly in his hands. No matter how badly in need of a horse, no Indian would take the mount of a dead man who still held the horse's reins.[3] Reality and legend are often inextricable, for men of the burial party determined from the nature of Keogh's and Comanche's wounds that the same bullet hit them both and man and horse went down together.[4] Thus Comanche became known not only as a paragon of endurance, but of faithfulness as well. The horse's bond to his rider became a symbolic expression of humankind's ancient dream of unity with the animal world.

Although direct evidence of an affectionate bond between Keogh and Comanche is lacking, it is likely that they experienced a close relationship. Keogh, who, it is said, "rode like a centaur,"[5] seems to have been a skilled and concerned horseman. In his letters, he wrote about horses with more than routine interest and once described with strong feelings his appreciation for a particular cavalry horse who had saved his life. Keogh undoubtedly spent long periods of time with Comanche, sharing many hardships and adventures with his mount. The Captain, generally known as a gallant cavalry officer, also has been characterized as a rather lonely, brooding, sometimes melancholy person, and individuals of that temperament often show a tendency to form strong attachments with animals.[6]

Caretakers and others who interacted with Comanche during his life indicated he was a fine horse. Evidently he was intelligent, tractable, dependable, and hardy—the kind of mount an expert horseman like Keogh would admire and find especially valuable for cavalry duty. Horses' actions are not determined strictly by habit and instinct, as one writer recently claimed.[7] Rather, scientific studies have shown that horses possess some cognitive abilities and exhibit a degree of behavioral plasticity that may allow them to adapt to specific circumstances. Moreover, horses do demonstrate an unmistakable fondness for people who interact with them over long periods of time. Recorded feats of devotion and heroism on the part of war horses are legion, and some cavalrymen had deep feeling for their equine partners. Judging from the sort of man Keogh seems to have been and the kind of horse Comanche was, it can be inferred, though never proven, that man and mount shared an affectionate relationship.[8]

Because of Comanche's association with Keogh, from the first moment of the wounded mount's discovery, he was revered as a representative of the dead. Under the assiduous care of the Seventh Cavalry, Comanche ultimately regained his health. He is undoubtedly unique among horses as the subject of a remarkable set of military injunctions known as "General Orders No. 7." Proclaimed by Colonel Samuel D. Sturgis at Fort Lincoln on April 10, 1878, these orders clearly documented the symbolic meaning of the horse whose "very silence speaks in terms more eloquent than words of the desperate struggle against overwhelming odds, of the hopeless conflict, and heroic manner in which all went down that day." The horse's special care, retirement status, and ceremonial role within the regiment were established.[9] To understand the genesis of these orders, it is necessary to acknowledge not only the significance of the horse to the nation but also his special meaning to Colonel Sturgis, commander of the regiment. That officer's only son, a lieutenant newly graduated from West Point, had been killed with Custer's battalion. Recent studies by scholars from various disciplines have shown that animals can play a healing role for people in times of grief, and the veteran war horse who had been present with

2. Edward S. Luce, *Keogh, Comanche and Custer* (St. Louis, MO: J. S. Swift, 1939), 64.
3. Tom Charles, "Why Comanche Survived," *The Graduate Magazine* (December 4, 1941), 4.
4. Luce, *Keogh, Comanche and Custer*, 60.
5. Theodore F. Allen, "Yesterday, The Reminiscences of Theodore F. Allen," *Journal of the United States Cavalry Association* (March, 1898), 227-228.
6. Lawrence, *His Very Silence Speaks*, 87-89, and 289.
7. Lawrence A. Frost, *General Custer's Thoroughbreds* (Mattituck, NJ: J. M. Carroll Company, 1986), 28.
8. Lawrence, *His Very Silence Speaks*, 285-306.
9. Luce, *Keogh, Comanche and Custer*, 67.

10. Ibid., 66.

11. "Old Comanche Dead," *Junction City Union* (November 14, 1891), 3.

12. Barron Brown, Archives of the University of Kansas.

13. Barron Brown, *Comanche: The Sole Survivor of All the Forces in Custer's Last Stand, The Battle of the Little Big Horn* (Kansas City, MO: Burton Publishing Company, 1935), 16 and 77.

14. Sister M. Perpetua, R.S.M., Mary Synon, L.L.D., and Katherine Rankin, *These Are Our Freedoms* (Boston, MA: Ginn & Company, 1959), 173-179.

15. "More of the Story of Comanche, Survivor of Custer Battle," *Lawrence Journal-World* (January 13, 1932).

Custer's men, had suffered with them, and somehow survived to become their surrogate, served as an instrument of solace for a father's sorrow and a nation's pain.

During his retirement, Comanche was not only an honored soldier referred to as the "second commanding officer" of his regiment but also a pampered pet. Reportedly, he was allowed to roam free on the grounds of his assigned post to "graze and frolic as he wished."¹⁰ Many visitors traveled to see the celebrated equine veteran who often was regarded with near veneration and whose fame became widespread. Comanche remained with his regiment during his lifetime and following his recuperation at Fort Lincoln he was stationed at various military posts, including Forts Totten, Meade, and Riley. On solemn occasions, especially on the anniversary of the Battle of the Little Big Horn, Comanche, draped in mourning with a pair of boots facing backward in the saddle, represented the honored dead in ceremonial parades.

Throughout his life, Comanche stood for the honor of the defeated cavalrymen who died for their country and for the shame and anger the nation felt at the Indians' victory. As the years unfolded, the horse also was imbued with broader meanings, for the United States was undergoing an era of dramatic change. Comanche's life as an Indian fighter came full circle, spanning the time from the great Indian victory at the Little Big Horn through the Indians' total defeat at Wounded Knee in 1890 (an engagement often referred to as "the Seventh's revenge"). In that same year, the American frontier had been declared officially closed by the Census Bureau. For all practical purposes, the wild continent, including the Indians who had attempted to resist white encroachment upon their land, was now tamed, and "Manifest Destiny" was fulfilled. Honor and glory accrued to those who had played a part in the "winning of the West," and foremost among these were frontier heroes like Custer and his Seventh Cavalrymen, including Keogh—and their mounts. Horses indeed were the instruments that had made possible the conquest and settlement of the new continent, and it was fitting that the courageous and enduring mount, Comanche, who had participated in the struggle, receive the honor due his kind.

For many people, Comanche was a symbol of patriotism. One writer noted of the "gallant steed" that he served his country well, and "from his back many brave blows were struck for the preservation of the lives and homes of frontier settlers."¹¹ Barron Brown, the earliest biographer of the horse, expressed the idea that "Comanche belongs . . . to the whole country and is identified with all that is best in our military annals and the conquest of our West." He revealed that, "My researches, and the long and close study of the famous horse . . . have made a better man and a better American of me. I wish that I and a lot of other people had the same self-possession, devotion to duty, courage, sense of obedience, and as few faults as had the noble animal."¹² Brown extols Comanche as a "personification of faithfulness and fearlessness, a symbol of the conquest of a great continent," who "will always live as long as valor and the dreams of high achievement live in the hearts of men."¹³ Comanche's image as a teacher of patriotic values is sustained by the inclusion of the horse's story, along with other national heroes, in a seventh grade reader on American freedom used for moral instruction of Catholic school children in the recent past.¹⁴

When Comanche died at Fort Riley in 1891, his deep meaning to his regiment and to the nation was recognized. His remains were preserved and mounted by Lewis L. Dyche of the Natural History Museum at the University of Kansas, where he is still displayed. One of the conditions of Dyche's agreement with the Seventh Cavalry was that he could exhibit the stuffed horse along with his other zoological specimens at the World's Columbian Exposition at Chicago in 1893. Thus Comanche's posthumous role began as an oddity—a domestic animal standing among wild species—an incongruous attraction for throngs of people who attended the fair. As one source reported, "The period saw no harm in mixing the scientific with the purely sentimental and historic."¹⁵ The purpose of the Exposition was to commemorate the 400th anniversary of the landing of

Columbus by celebrating American progress. Yankee ingenuity and hard work had carved a nation out of the wilderness, and 1893 was a time to take pride in the accomplishments of expansion and the final conquest of a once wild continent, which many people construed as the victory of "civilization over savagery." The ambience of the Exposition was dominated by the evolutionary view of humanity that presumed progression upward from the barbarity of native life to the lofty achievements of Euro-American culture.[16]

America was entering the machine age, and the end of the horse era that was represented by the cavalry mount was fast approaching. Comanche was an extremely popular attraction at the Chicago Fair, and it was reported that "thousands of people came to the Kansas building for the express purpose of seeing what is still in existence of this memorable and historic horse." In describing Dyche's display of wild fauna among which the horse stood, anthropomorphism and racism were often combined. For example, two wolverines were said to be "meditating upon some kind of meanness," and so were referred to as "Indian devils." It is noteworthy that Comanche, "the old war horse," was designated as "the only surviving horse of the Custer massacre."[17] Comanche, like other elements associated with Custer's Last Stand, became inextricably identified with the term "massacre," an inappropriate word since the battle involved armed fighting forces on both sides. Well into the middle of the 20th-century, the designation "Custer massacre" was routine. It is still used. For instance, in 1987, a Kansas newspaper referred to the famous horse as the "survivor of the Little Big Horn Massacre."[18] Incredibly, the 1989 Spring and Summer University of Oklahoma Press catalog began its description of one new book with the phrase, "Ever since the Custer massacre."

Little information has been found regarding Comanche's first few decades as a museum specimen, which presumably began in 1902 when he was placed in the newly constructed Dyche Hall at the University of Kansas. In 1931, Major General Hugh Scott, who remembered caring for the wounded horse after the battle, paid a visit

Captain Charles S. Ilsley (right), an enlisted man of Troop E, and a gray horse (which may be Ilsley's mount) appeared in this 1880s picture attributed to photographer W. Scott of Deadwood, South Dakota.
Courtesy of Custer Battlefield National Monument.

to him in the museum.[19] From 1934 until 1941, the building which housed him was closed and Comanche was stored in the basement of the university auditorium. There, neglect of the stuffed mount allegedly caused deterioration—a factor which was used later by those who wished to transfer the specimen elsewhere.

Comanche's significance and the value he embodies for many people are reflected by the numerous requests to obtain him—either as a loan or permanent possession—that have been and still are received by the University of Kansas. For example, a movement spearheaded by General Jonathan Wainwright in 1947 sought to transfer Comanche to the U.S. Cavalry Museum at Fort Riley. Later, South Dakota claimed the horse for Fort Meade, and North Dakota also put in a bid. Numerous owners of museums in the West sought to purchase him, and

16. Robert W. Rydell, *All the World's A Fair* (Chicago, IL: University of Chicago Press, 1984), 38-71.

17. *Report of the Kansas Board of World's Fair Managers* (Topeka, KS: Hamilton Printing Company, 1894), 36.

18. "Lawrence's Year in Review," *Lawrence Journal-World* (January 1, 1987), C1.

19. "An Old Friend of Comanche Finds Him in K. U. Museum," *Kansas City Star* (April 30, 1931).

20. Archives of the University of Kansas.
21. Custer Battlefield National Monument Files, Crow Agency, Montana.
22. Lawrence, *His Very Silence Speaks*, 168.
23. Archives of the University of Kansas.
24. Ibid.

Comanche was in demand for a publisher's autograph party, for various frontier day and state anniversary celebrations, and for display at a race track.[20]

Beginning about 1938, and continuing sporadically through the Little Big Horn Centennial in 1976 and into the present, the greatest number of requests have involved relocating Comanche at the Custer Battlefield National Monument Museum. Edward S. Luce, one of the horse's main biographers, who was the first superintendent of the Custer Battlefield, was an active proponent of this transfer, and many present day Little Big Horn buffs still favor the move. In general, National Park officials and Custer Battlefield personnel have opposed transferring Comanche to the site (even if it were possible), arguing that the horse would overshadow other exhibits used to interpret the battle. Their responses reveal much about the horse's image and popularity as a relic and their failure to take into account some of the most meaningful factors underlying the profound appeal of the Last Stand and Comanche's role in it. One regional director, for example, considered the horse "not essential to the proper interpretation of the battle," stating that, "If we retrieved the horse, it would be entirely on sentimental grounds." He added that, though the horse would exert "a potent spell" upon students of the battle as well as the average visitor, it would not "enlighten him on the historical background, the tactics and maneuvers which make the story so fascinating." Thus, the horse would make the visitor "goggle and exclaim" rather than understand. One official even asserted that Comanche's main value was as "an interesting example of the techniques of taxidermy in transition," and was not among the "genuine historical objects interpreting the Custer Battlefield story."[21] Recently, a Custer Battlefield employee summed up the objections more succinctly: "We don't want Comanche here. The horse would become more important than the battle."[22]

Undoubtedly, many visitors would disagree with the National Park Service officials' position, but the argument is purely philosophical. For, from the beginning and with increasing vehemence, the University of Kansas has resisted all proposals for transfer of its prized possession. As pointed out by the exhibits director at the Dyche Museum, after his death "Comanche has been the object of more battles than he was in." Verbal wars waged between the university and those agencies that claim Comanche, though often tinged with humor, have consistently evidenced the university's absolute unwillingness to part with its famous exhibit, whose value only grows greater with time. Whereas for those who want him at Fort Riley, Comanche epitomizes the glory of cavalry life, and for those who would move him to Montana he is an inseparable part of the battle that made him immortal, for the University of Kansas he represents cherished tradition. It is noteworthy that virtually never in the university community (or elsewhere) has Comanche been referred to as "it." He is fondly personified by students, alumni, and all who are associated with the institution. As the university chancellor who resisted the Army's onslaught explained, Comanche is "quite unconcerned and calm about the hullabaloo which has been blowing about his ears. He seems to want to stay right where he is very much indeed and I am confident that he will remain there."[23] Later, during one of the arguments over returning the horse to the battlefield, letters were published purportedly written by Comanche and another mount expressing preference for the climate and conditions in either Kansas or Montana.

To insure Comanche's retention at the university, graduates wrote letters insisting that their alma mater "hold that line" against any attempt to remove him, for they remembered the horse as an essential part of college life, the "battle-scarred old 'Faithful' " who "was 'our silent partner' and in our hearts became a real part of the University." Because of Comanche's courage and endurance, students would rub Comanche's nose or steal a strand of his tail hair to bring luck in exams (before he was encased in glass). As alumni, they looked forward to returning to be greeted by "the old boy" in the museum. An alumnus who referred to Comanche as a "stout hearted hero" was "sure he would prefer to remain [in] his present 'Happy Hunting Grounds'."[24]

And so Comanche stayed, secure in his special

humidified glass "stall" at the University of Kansas. Prior to 1970, there was a brief label outlining the horse's history beside the exhibit. The first sentence stated: "Comanche was the sole survivor of the Custer Massacre at the Battle of the Little Big Horn on June 25, 1876." Over the years, no one seems to have objected to this wording, but in 1970, the idea of Comanche as "sole survivor" and the inaccuracy of "massacre" for what was in reality a battle, took on new significance. Times were favorable in that year not only for questioning of time-honored assumptions but for action as well. American Indian students at the university took up the challenge that, for them, was embodied by the display and interpretation of the cavalry horse in the museum. As a result of this different kind of onslaught, Comanche's image would be transformed to accommodate new meanings for the modern era.

Calling the Comanche exhibit a "racist symbol," a group of native American university students protested that the horse perpetuated the stereotype of Custer and his troops being "massacred" by "savage" Indians who were in the wrong. And since, in reality, large numbers of Indians lived through the battle, the students were distressed over the designation of the horse as the sole survivor of the Little Big Horn. As a faculty member who championed their cause wrote in the university newspaper:

> What does this make of the Indians who won the battle—sticks? rocks? vegetables? non-persons? The children of those Indians are today's American citizens, and the Battle of the Little Big Horn is part of their history and ours . . . . The Sioux that he [Custer] pursued were acting lawfully and peaceably, but he was intent on a battle and he got one. History does not offer many such simple stories in which evil receives its just desserts, but the Battle of the Little Big Horn was such an instance, and if the Museum of Natural History is to display an exhibit about that battle, then the history should be full and accurate.

As a cavalry mount, Comanche was not responsible for Custer's morals; and as a symbol of a great battle, he merits the popular attention that he receives. But a university museum should exhibit truth rather than comfortable prejudice.[25]

Even the protesting Indians, with their tradition of profound respect for horses, placed no blame on Comanche himself, but rather expressed anger at the way the display had been used and interpreted. A committee representing the native American students met with the museum director and asked that the Comanche exhibit be closed until a more accurate label was written. The director and other officials complied, listened to the Indians' grievances, provided total cooperation, and came to understand feelings and viewpoints they had never before considered. Recalling those events, the museum director stated, "Comanche was one of the greatest learning experiences of my life."[26] In November 1971, a celebration sponsored by both Indians and whites accompanied the reopening of the Comanche exhibit. There was now a long text which began by explaining that the horse stands "as a symbol of the conflict between the United States Army and the Indian tribes of the Great Plains that resulted from the government's policy of confinement of Indians on reservations and extermination of those Indians who refused to be confined," and detailed the Indians' struggle to retain their land and way of life. The Battle of the Little Big Horn was designated as an Indian victory, and the 1890 engagement was accurately termed "the Massacre of Wounded Knee Creek."

Although the Indians had first wanted the horse permanently removed from the museum, they compromised and wisely decided Comanche could be a "learning tool" for both sides. Thus he was transformed from an object representing a federal defeat to a subject articulating the Indian peoples' way of life and struggle for existence. As a museum official related:

> The protest over Comanche was a sign of the times, and similar events occurred throughout the country. The original label was misleading, anyway. It was slanted toward the army's viewpoint and didn't tell the real story. The Comanche display has great value to the museum, but it was misrepresented for a long time, and was used to idealize cavalry life.

25. Murray Wax, "Comanche's Stand: To the Editor," *University Daily Kansan* (October 15, 1971).

26. Personal Communication with the author, 1980.

27. Personal Communication with the author, 1980.
28. "Comanche Once Angered Indians," Olathe *Daily News* (January 10, 1978).
29. Lawrence, *His Very Silence Speaks*, 205.
30. See David Dary, *Comanche* (Lawrence, KS: University of Kansas Museum of Natural History, 1976).

Comanche once symbolized a terrible loss to Americans, but now he stands for the conflict between Indians and whites. The horse symbolizes one of the few and the greatest of all victories the Indians ever had, and the terrible mistake made by the whites. For Indians, he's a symbol of victory; everyone likes to ride a winner.[27]

The Kansas University protest accomplished a great deal, representing "a victory for the Indians seeking to tell their viewpoint of American history." One writer explained, "The horse that once angered Indians" now "allows them to raise their heads in the pride of telling their side of the story . . . . They were able to change the horse Comanche from the battle's 'lone survivor' into a symbol of the Indians' perseverance against government policy that sought to push them from their ancestral lands." Now, the horse was not just "a symbol of the Indians' past victories," but also "what modern Indians can accomplish."[28]

Indeed Comanche, in his new role, led the way for further beneficial changes within the museum. To dispel implications that angered the native Americans, Indian exhibits were disassociated from those dealing with so-called "primitive man." Native American religious objects, previously appearing as "curios," were labeled in a more respectful manner or removed. The whole idea of how best to exhibit cultural relics and artifacts for educational purposes was re-examined and addressed. Indians themselves realized they needed to know more about their heritage in order to interpret it for others. Comanche's influence in raising consciousness about Indians took on even broader aspects, as courses in native American studies were established at the university and Indian students were recruited for admission. One of Comanche's most astounding accomplishments was to give the Indians at the University of Kansas and in neighboring communities a sense of solidarity. As the protestors expressed this unique phenomenon:

> Comanche helped in uniting us. He was a positive thing that gave us hope. Although it's generally hard to get Indians to agree, they agreed on Comanche. We were all from different backgrounds. I thought we would all go our own way and not get organized; I expected we would be factionalized and individualistic, but I was thrilled when we acted together. It was one of the few times different Indian people agreed.[29]

During the last two decades, Comanche has continued to be a highlight for the 120,000 annual visitors to the Dyche Museum, many of whom travel long distances specifically to see him. He attracted increased attention at the time of the Little Big Horn Centennial in 1976, when some new interpretive displays about the battle were added and a pamphlet about him was published by the university.[30] In 1986, when Comanche was damaged by flooding, news of the disaster was flashed nationwide. No effort was spared in his repair, and museum experts agree he is now in better shape than ever.

As a once living creature whose posthumous existence is even more meaningful than his cavalry career, and as a member of a species with a long history of close alliance with humankind, Comanche has an image of courage, stamina, and fidelity with which people continue to identify, adapting it to their own ethos and times. Beyond his capacity to represent the Seventh Cavalry troopers who died in battle, lending a sense of immediacy to Custer's Last Stand, Comanche is a focus for the empathetic responses commonly evoked by that event.

As the celebrated survivor who conferred fame upon his rider, Myles Keogh's enduring war mount faces the twenty-first century appearing peaceful, as horses are known to be except when ridden into battles not of their making. He stands as a symbolic bridge between the living and the dead, between Indian and white, between civilization and the untamed, and between humankind and the animal world, and links the horse era with the machine age. Freed now from any label identifying him in time and place, Comanche continues to instruct in silence and hopefully will come to be seen within a larger context than Custer's Last Stand. More than a battle relic from a bygone era, "his very silence speaks in terms more eloquent than words," articulating a timeless message protesting humankind's aggressive domination of nature, the oppression of the weak by the strong, and even the universal barbarity of war.

Chapter 2

Wearing of the Blue:
The Irish in the U.S. Army, 1776-1876

by Kevin Mulroy, Ph.D.

'Captain, darlin', will you tell me what we're doing ten thousand miles from Ireland, where the rain damps the dust and there's Englishmen to be shot at instead of naked heathens. . . ?'

Wendell Mayes, "The Day Custer Fell."

The question of what flashed through the minds of Custer's troops once they found themselves surrounded and hopelessly outnumbered by their Indian adversaries at the Little Big Horn, and finally realized help would not be forthcoming, is a fascinating one. For the Irish present, the Emerald Isle must have seemed all of 10,000 miles away and the most wonderful place on earth, during those final few terrible moments. The opening quotation, taken from the script of a proposed 1965 movie, has Private Archibald McIlhargey putting that very question to his company commander, Captain Myles Walter Keogh, both immigrants from Ireland.[1] Though Keogh provides a somewhat curt and simplistic answer in the script, the strong Irish presence at the Little Big Horn was, in fact, the culmination of complex developments that had been taking place since the American Revolution—developments that included a massive migration from Ireland to America, and the accompanying growth of a strong Irish tradition within the U.S. Army.

The Irishman was no stranger to soldiering abroad. During the 18th-Century, Irish brigades had fought in France, Spain, Austria, and other Catholic countries. Recruiting for the brigades had gone on steadily in Ireland throughout the century and young soldiers of fortune, barred from a military career by their religion, left regularly for the continent. The image of the flight of the "wild geese" was already a potent one by the time of the American Revolution. From the Treaty of Limerick in 1691 to the fall of the French monarchy in 1792, the Irish brigades had served in the royal armies of France. These famous regiments—Dillon's, Mountcashel's, O'Brien's, Clanricarde's, Walsh's, and a dozen others —fought the English in Flanders, Germany, Spain, France, India, and the Antilles, and over half a million Irishmen died for the cause. Irish officers rose to high rank, not only in France but also in Spain, Austria, and other Roman Catholic countries.[2] Keogh's later participation in the Italian Papal Wars, with some 1400 of his fellow countrymen, therefore, had long-established precedents and was part of a deep tradition.

At the outbreak of the American Revolution, some four million white people were living in the thirteen Colonies that declared independence. Of these, perhaps 2.4 million, or 60%, were of British origin. A decline in the linen trade and high rents had spurred a wave of emigration from the north of Ireland in the five years before the Revolution. During that period, some 30,000 people from Ulster made their way across the Atlantic.

[1]. Wendell Mayes, "The Day Custer Died," Draft script for proposed David Weisbert production, April 1965, 68. Copy in possession of Father Vincent A. Heier.

[2]. The best book-length study of Irish troops serving in foreign armies thus far is Maurice N. Hennessy, *The Wild Geese: The Irish Soldier in Exile* (Old Greenwich, CT: Devin-Adair Co., 1973). See also, James E. McGee, *Sketches of Irish Soldiers in Every Land* (New York: J.A. McGee, 1873).

The first census of the United States, taken in 1790, recorded 44,000 Irish-born residents but this estimate is, clearly, far too low and the actual figure may have been three times that number. The highest projection of the total number of Irish birth or descent in the colonies by 1776 is 400,000, or 10%.[3]

Of those of British origin, only a minority supported the Revolution. New York furnished more soldiers to George III, for example, than to George Washington. It is not surprising, therefore, that the Irish gave strong support to the American cause. Service also brought the possibility of connections, a land grant in the West, or termination of servitude for those still indentured. Servants, farmers, laborers, and urban workers were included among the Irish under arms as were large numbers of second generation immigrants. Michael J. O'Brien estimated that the Irish supplied as many as 38% of Washington's soldiers and the British and Loyalists claimed the figure to be still higher at 50%. The authoritative David Noel Doyle attacked O'Brien for his "grotesquely exaggerated" estimates, but concurred with the basic premise that the Irish supported the American cause in numbers disproportionate to their total population.[4]

During the Revolution, regiments of the Irish Brigade distinguished themselves in the West Indies and were landed in support of the American troops at the unsuccessful siege of Savannah, in 1780. But most of the Irish served with the regular forces, or Continental Line, the most mobile and reliable section of Washington's forces. The best known unit was the Pennsylvania Line which, General Henry Lee observed, "might with more propriety have been called the Line of Ireland." The Irish

---

Edward W. Clay, "One of the Californian Bo-Hoys Taking Leave of His Gal." Lithograph by Henry R. Robinson, 1846. Popular at the time of the Mexican War, this cartoon, rich in detail of the period, caricatured Irish immigrant members of the New York Volunteers hoping to find opportunity in "Californy." *Courtesy of Amon Carter Museum.*

became noted for their fighting qualities and hostility to the English. General Sir Henry Clinton reported to London that, "The emigrants from Ireland are in general to be looked upon as our most serious antagonists," and another contemporary noted, "On more than one occasion Congress owed its existence and America possibly its preservation to the fidelity and firmness of the Irish."[5]

By the end of the war, the foreign-born officers in the American forces who had made brigadier-general or higher numbered twenty-six, of whom sixteen were Irish. Several were Irish Catholics who overcame prejudice through natural ability and proven success. Based on his choices of aides-de-camp, Washington, clearly, did not discriminate on these grounds. His ADCs included, in succession, Joseph Reed, Joseph Carey, Stephen Moylan, John Fitzgerald, and James McHenry, all of Irish birth or descent. General Moylan, born in Cork, went on to become the Quartermaster General and eventually served as the Chief of Cavalry for the whole American Army. Edward Hand, adjutant general for the army, hailed from King's County and Generals John Sullivan and Anthony Wayne, arguably the most successful generals of the American Revolution, were both of Irish extraction. General Henry Knox, born of Irish parents in Boston, became the commander of the Continental artillery and Washington subsequently appointed him the first secretary of war. James McHenry of Ballymena succeeded Knox, and went on to fill the same office under Adams.[6]

The Irish also actively supported the Revolutionary cause through the naval service, the bulk of which was a freelance, privateering navy which proffered officerships. There were large numbers of Irish sailors in the trans-Atlantic, inter-colonial coastal, and West Indies trades. Many rose to be ships' captains and officers and made a substantial contribution to the war effort. The Irish also would play an important role in the Union and Confederate navies during the Civil War.[7]

Precious little is known about the Irish enlisted men between the Revolutionary War and the War of 1812. A list of sixty deserters from Harmar's Pennsylvania contingent, 1784, showed nineteen Irish among the thirty foreign-born and, of those giving a birthplace, twelve of thirty deserters from the First Regiment of Infantry listed in 1792 were Irish. All of the latter had deserted in their first year of enlistment and the army, recognizing the majority contingent, offered pardons to any who would surrender before the next Saint Patrick's Day. Around 18% of enlisted men during the decade 1799-1809 were immigrants.[8]

During the War of 1812, Andrew Jackson became a major-general, captured Pensacola, and inflicted a crushing defeat on Packenham's British army at New Orleans —America's only victory on land during the war. Jackson, whose father was born in Carrickfergus, County Antrim, went on to become the seventh president of the United States, serving from 1828-1836. Commodore John Shore, who emigrated from Ireland in 1790, commanded the U.S. naval squadron in the Mediterranean during the war. Other officers of Irish descent who made notable contributions to the American war effort in 1812 included Major-General John Coffee, Major-General William Carroll, and Commodore Thomas Macdonough.[9]

The native-born American population would answer the call to arms in time of war but in peacetime the army had little appeal and it proved impossible to fill the ranks with U.S. citizens. As a result, the military was forced to adopt a very flexible approach towards recruitment. *The General Regulations for the Army*, drawn up by Major General Winfield Scott in 1820, described acceptable recruits as "all free white male persons, above eighteen and under thirty-five years, who are able-bodied, active, and free from disease."[10] In short, any healthy young Irishman could enter military service without provision, and many chose to do so. The nation was still young and defining itself. A land of immigrants, the profile of its armed forces reflected the United States' multi-national composition.

The prospect of regular pay, and the security of the military, attracted many new arrivals. A five year enlistment offered a quick and easy escape from poverty,

3. U.S. Bureau of the Census, *Historical Statistics of the United States, 1789-1945* (Washington, D.C.: Government Printing Office, 1949), 1168-1170; Michael J. Costello, "The Irish and the American Military Tradition," in David Noel Doyle and Owen Dudley Edwards, eds., *America and Ireland, 1776-1976: The American Identity and the Irish Connection* (Westport, CT: Greenwood Press, 1980), 219; William D. Griffin, ed., *The Irish in America, 550-1972: A Chronology and Fact Book* (Dobbs Ferry, NY: Oceana Pubs., 1973), 8, 11.

4. David Noel Doyle, *Ireland, Irishmen and Revolutionary America, 1760-1820* (Dublin and Cork: Mercier Press, 1981), 137-144.

5. Quoted in Costello, "Irish and American Military," 220. See also W.S. Murphy, "The Irish Brigade of France at the Seige of Savannah, 1779," *Georgia Historical Quarterly* (1954), 307-321.

6. Costello, "Irish and American Military," 222; W.S. Murphy, "Four Soldiers of the American Revolution," *Irish Sword* (1962), 164-174. On leading individuals see: Thomas C. Amory, *Military Services and Public Life of Major-General John Sullivan, of the American Revolutionary Army* (Boston, MA: Wiggin and Lunt, 1868); North Callahan, *Henry Knox, General Washington's General* (New York, NY: Rinehart, 1958); Paul David Nelson, *Anthony Wayne, Soldier of the Early Republic* (Bloomington, IN: Indiana University Press, 1985); and Bernard Christian Steiner, *Life and Correspondence of James McHenry, Secretary of War under Washington and Adams* (Cleveland, OH: Burrows Brothers Co., 1907).

7. Doyle, *Ireland, Irishmen*, 144; John B. Heffernan, "Ireland's Contribution to the Navies of the American Civil War, 1861-1865," *Irish Sword* (1957), 81-87; John de Courcy Ireland, "The Confederate States at Sea in the American Civil War: The Irish Contribution," *Irish Sword* (1980), 73-94.

8. Edward M. Coffman, *The Old Army: A Portrait of the American Army in Peacetime, 1784-1898* (NY: Oxford University Press, 1986), 17.

9. W.S. Murphy, "Four American Officers of the War of 1812," *Irish Sword* (1963), 1-12.

10. United States. War Department. *General Regulations for the Army; or, Military Institutes* (Philadelphia, PA: M. Carey and Sons, 1821), Art. 74, Par. 13.

11. Richard H. Coolidge, *Statistical Report on the Sickness and Mortality in the Army of the United States Compiled from Records of the Surgeon General's Office Embracing a Period of Sixteen Years from January, 1839 to January, 1855* (Washington, D.C.: Government Printing Office, 1856). 34 Congress, 1 Session, Senate Executive Document 96, 627. Useful work still needs to be done on the comparative strengths of national blocs, and the relations between various immigrant groups, within the U.S. military.

12. Coffman, *Old Army*, 17; Francis Paul Prucha, *The Sword of the Republic: The United States Army on the Frontier, 1783-1846* (Bloomington, IN: Indiana University Press, 1969), 327.

13. United States. War Department. *General Regulations for the Army; or, Military Institutes* (Washington D.C.: Davis and Force, 1825), Art. 74, Par 1287; 27 Congress, 3 Session, Senate Document 1, 180.

14. John K. Mahon, ed., *Letters From the Frontiers by Major General George A. McCall* (Gainesville, FL: University of Florida Press, 1974. Facsimile of 1868 ed.), 334; Francis Paul Prucha, *Broadax and Bayonet: The Role of the United States Army in the Development of the Northwest 1815-1860* (Lincoln, NE: University of Nebraska Press, 1967), 36; Prucha, *Sword of the Republic*, 327; Francis Paul Prucha, "The United States Army as Viewed by British Travellers, 1825-1860," *Military Affairs* (Fall, 1953), 115.

15. *Army and Navy Chronicle* (May 5, 1836), 287-288; Woodburne Potter, *The War in Florida, Being an Exposition of its Causes and an Accurate History of the Campaigns of General Clinch, Gaines and Scott* (Baltimore, MD: Lewis and Coleman Publishers, 1836), 106. On the black guide see Kenneth Wiggins Porter, "Louis Pachecho: The Man and the Myth," *Journal of Negro History* (January, 1943), 65-72;

ignorance, and squalor. Some saw enlisting as a means of avoiding discrimination through assimilation; a means of gaining respect. It was attractive to immigrants to put themselves in a situation in which uniformity was considered one of the great virtues. The army also offered the opportunity to serve with other immigrant compatriots, and fostered camaraderie. Still others looked to the military as simply a free ticket to new opportunities. As Dr. Richard H. Coolidge put it in 1856, "A large proportion of the immigrants who are landed at our seaport cities, where the army is principally recruited, are extremely destitute; and to those not finding immediate employment, the army . . . offers a temporary resource of which many avail themselves."[11] Proportionately few Irish became officers, the great majority remaining in the ranks, but many went on to make non-commissioned officer. During the antebellum period, the American Regular Army scarcely could have survived without this heavy infusion of Irishmen into the ranks.

Of the men enlisting between June 1821 and December 1823, some 25% were of foreign birth whereas earlier, from 1810-1819, only 15% had been immigrants.[12] This development was responsible for the restriction appearing in the *General Regulations* of 1825 that "no foreigner shall be enlisted in the army without special permission from general head-quarters." The reduction in enlistments in 1825 and 1826 was blamed, in part, upon this restriction. In consequence, beginning in 1828, all citizens were accepted no matter what their place of birth, and in 1842 the secretary of war proposed taking immigrants who had taken the first step towards naturalization. Finally, in 1847 the prohibition on recruiting immigrants was dropped altogether, providing only that recruits had competency in the English language.[13] It seems clear, moreover, that foreigners continued to enlist in large numbers even when the regulations made no provision for them.

Contemporary reports leave no doubt that army officers and civilian observers were acutely aware of the deficiencies in the character and circumstances of the average recruit. Travellers from abroad were struck by the fact that the ranks of the U.S. Army were filled either with "worthless" Irish, English, and German recruits or native-born Americans representative of undesirable elements from the older states who had joined the military only as a last resort. Army officers also bemoaned the lack of solid native-born stock. Captain George A. McCall, while serving as a recruiting officer in Philadelphia in 1837, poured contempt upon "the unsophisticated, untutored, and intractable sons of Erin" who made up almost all of his recruits. McCall noted that many of the Irish falsified their place of birth in the belief that foreign origin would exclude them from enlisting. Yet the answers to a special questionnaire sent to officers superintending the recruiting service in 1827 suggest that foreign-born soldiers were no less efficient in military duties than the Americans and were less likely to desert.[14] Though some were of turbulent character and intemperate habits, many were decent men and proved a strong asset to the service.

In something of a preview of events that would take place in Montana a little over forty years later, a contingent of Irish recruits in Florida found themselves in the wrong place at the wrong time on December 28, 1835. Seminole and black depredations in the north of the peninsula led the military to dispatch a relief column of regular infantry under Major Francis L. Dade. North of the Withlacoochee River, near the Great Wahoo swamp, the column was led into an ambush by Louis Pachecho, a black guide, and annihilated by Indians and blacks, the blacks returning later to mutilate the bodies of the victims. This incident, subsequently termed the "Dade Massacre," marked the beginning of the Second Seminole War, the most expensive Indian war in American history. Among the ninety-six dead listed for the Dade command were forty-six foreign born, with thirty Irishmen making up the largest contingent.[15]

In 1840, Inspector General George Croghan visited Fort Leavenworth and discovered that 20 out of 110 recruits there could neither speak nor understand English. Croghan suggested that such men not be allowed to enlist in the future and suggested "a like interdict against the Irish, who (a few honorable exceptions to the contrary) are the very bane of our garrisons."[16] The army commanders were quick to realize, however, that the military needed the Irish and Croghan's recommendations went unheeded.

Many of the new immigrant recruits would see action on the western frontier during the Mexican War of 1846-1848. There was a problem for Irish and other Roman Catholic soldiers in the military in that most officers and, prior to the war, all chaplains, were Protestant. No one knew how many Catholics were in the ranks and few cared. Suddenly, however, an army which included a sizeable Catholic population was about to do battle with a Catholic country. The fear of desertion and defection ran high and President James K. Polk was quick to recognize this possibility. During the first month of the war, he had two Jesuits sent out to join General Zachary Taylor's troops in northern Mexico. This gesture was one of several attempts made to thwart Mexican efforts at labelling the conflict a religious war.[17]

Such efforts were not completely successful in preventing defection and the Mexicans managed to recruit a number of American deserters from Taylor's army. Religion probably was not the prime motive—if it constituted a motive at all. Maltreatment by officers, drink, boredom, and Mexican promises of land and money seem to have been much stronger reasons. The Mexicans organized the deserters into a separate corps called the San Patricio Battalion.[18] John Reilly, an Irish former Fifth Infantry sergeant who had served as a drill instructor at West Point and in a New York City recruiting station, became the ranking defector and Patrick Dalton, from County Mayo, his second in command. The San Patricios were assumed to consist mostly of Irish Catholics but, in actuality, a mixture of American and other European-born deserters outnumbered the Irish. Reilly's leadership, the name of the unit, and its utilization of symbols of Ireland, however, have served to link forever the San Patricios with the Emerald Isle in popular legend.

Though termed a battalion, the San Patricios never numbered more than two companies strong. They first saw action as a unit at Buena Vista where they carried their distinctive green flag, decorated with a shamrock, a figure of Saint Patrick, and the harp of Erin, into battle. The battalion fought valiantly in the engagement and was cited for bravery. Their impact was greatest, however, at the battle of Churubusco. It is said that, each time the two Mexican units there tried to raise it, the San Patricios tore down the white flag of surrender knowing that, for them, capture meant death. They made an heroic stand in a losing cause, and the green flag was the last left flying.

The American forces took around seventy of the San Patricios prisoner after Churubusco. The prisoners were court-martialled, and eventually fifty were hanged. The execution of thirty prisoners was attended with an unusual act of cruelty. The San Patricios were made to sit on mule carts with nooses around their necks and watch the storming of Chapultepec, the last Mexican bastion before Mexico City, by the American forces. For the Irish contingent at that moment, as later for Keogh's compatriots at the Little Big Horn, thoughts of the old country must have been prominent. As soon as the American flag went aloft over the captured castle, the prisoners were hanged. Today, a plaque in the Plaza San Jacinto in San Angel, Mexico City, honors seventy Irishmen who chose to oppose American manifest destiny as members of the legendary San Patricio Battalion.

The Irish presence in the Mexican Army was minute when compared with the numbers they put into the field for the American cause. General Winfield Scott was quick to come to the defense of the loyalty and conduct of Irish Catholics as a whole within the U.S. forces. On July 2, 1850, he wrote to William E. Robinson:

> In Mexico, we estimated the number of persons in the army, foreigners *by birth*, at about 3500, and of these more than 2000 were Irish... Of our Irish soldiers—save a few who deserted from General Taylor, and who had never taken the naturalization oath—not one ever turned his back upon the enemy or faltered in advancing to the charge.

16. Francis Paul Prucha, ed., *Army Life on the Western Frontier: Selections from the Official Reports Made Between 1826 and 1845 by Colonel George Croghan* (Norman, OK: University of Oklahoma Press, 1958), 148.

17. Coffman, *Old Army*, 179.

18. For a good recent study of the activities of the San Patricios see Robert Ryal Miller, *Shamrock and Sword: Saint Patrick's Battalion in the U.S.-Mexican War* (Norman, OK: University of Oklahoma Press, 1989). See also Blanche Marie McEniry, *American Catholics in the War with Mexico* (Washington, D.C.: n.p. 1937), Chapter 5; K. Hatch, "Saint Patrick's Battalion: Unlikely Victims of a Mexican War," *Ireland of the Welcomes* (1977), 32-35; Wally Power, "The Enigma of the Patricios," *Eire-Ireland* (1969), 7-12; and Walter Power, "Facets of the Mexican War," *Recorder* (1975), 135-143.

19. William M. Sweeny, "The Irish Soldier in the War with Mexico," *Journal of the American Irish Historical Society* (1927), 256-259.

20. The best study of Shields remains William H. Condon's *Life of Major-General James Shields, Hero of Three Wars and Senator from Three States* (Chicago, IL: Blakely Printing Company, 1900). See also William W. Hassler, "The Irrepressible James Shields," *Lincoln Herald* (1979), 187-191; and R.J. Purcell, "James Shields: Soldier and Statesman," *Studies: An Irish Quarterly Review* (1932), 73-87.

21. U.S. Bureau of the Census, *Historical Statistics*, 106, 118. By far the best study to date of Irish emigration to the U.S. is Kerby A. Miller's monumental *Emigrants and Exiles: Ireland and the Irish Exodus to North America* (New York, NY: Oxford University Press, 1985). See also William F. Adams, *Ireland and the Irish Emigration to the New World from 1815 to the Famine* (New Haven, CT: Yale University Press, 1932); S.H. Cousens, "The Regional Variations in Emigration from Ireland Between 1821 and 1841," *Transactions of the Institute of British Geographers* (1965), 15-29; S.H. Cousens, "The Regional Pattern of Emigration during the Great Famine, 1846-1851," *Transactions of the Institute of British Geographers* (1960), 119-134; and Philip Taylor, *The Distant Magnet: European Emigration to the United States* (New York, NY: Harper and Row, 1971), 32-36.

22. Allan Nevins and Milton H. Thomas, eds., *The Diary of George Templeton Strong* (New York, NY: Macmillan, 1952), vol. 2, 348; Henry J. Browne, ed., "A Memoir of Archbishop Hughes, 1838-1858," *U.S. Catholic Historical Society, Historical Records and Studies* (1952), 164-168.

23. Robert Ernst, *Immigrant Life in New York City, 1825-1863* (New York, NY: King's Crown Press, 1949), 56, 58; Florence E. Gibson, *The Attitudes of the New York Irish Toward State and National Affairs, 1848-1892* (New York, NY: Columbia University Press, 1951), 16-18; Carl Frederick Wittke, *The Irish in America* (Baton Rouge, LA: Louisiana State University Press, 1956), 45.

William. M. Sweeny, in fact, listed as many as 133 officers of Irish birth or descent who served the American forces with credit during the war. Noteworthy among these were General William O. Butler, who succeeded Scott as commander-in-chief in Mexico, and General S.W. Kearny, who directed the conquest of California.[19]

The most notable Irish officer to take part in the Mexican War was James Shields, brigadier-general of Volunteers, who was born in Dungannon, County Tyrone. Shields fought valiantly in the campaigns before a severe wound, received at Cerro Gordo, put an end to his Mexican war service. He later would hold the same rank during the American Civil War and be Keogh's commanding officer. During the course of his lifetime, the remarkable Shields would serve as governor of the Oregon Territory, and be the only man ever to represent three different states—Illinois, Minnesota, and Missouri—in the U.S. Senate.[20]

Foreign immigration had grown from around 151,000 in the 1820s to 2,314,000 in the 1850s. Throughout this period the Irish were by far the most numerous element. The problems in Ireland were massive and all-encompassing. Widespread poverty and unemployment, and the efforts of absentee landlords to rationalize an outdated and problematic system of land tenure, led to evictions, displacement, and pauperism. In consequence, the Irish found it necessary to cross the Atlantic in large numbers, as many as 850,000 leaving for America between 1815-1845. Most of these emigrants came from the northern counties, or from Keogh's native southeast. Then came the failures of the staple potato crops, famine, and disease—a disaster so complete that there was no prospect of recovery. A vast migration followed. In the eight year period after 1846, 1,250,000 citizens of Ireland fled to America and by 1854 the Irish contributed 25% of all European emigrants to the U.S.[21]

Many perceived the latest Irish immigrants to be poverty-stricken, filthy, ignorant, drunken and disorderly, lawless, slum-dwellers—dangerous, and alien. New York diarist George Templeton Strong commented, "Our Celtic fellow citizens are almost as remote from us in temperament and constitution as the Chinese." Bishop John Hughes described the utter destitution of the Irish who arrived in New York in 1847-1848, the high rate of disease and mortality within the group, and the tragic state of their children. Hughes referred to a sinister underclass among them, "the scattered debris of the Irish nation," and recommended stopping immigration for at least a decade.[22] Throughout the 1850s employers posted signs stating simply, "No Irish Need Apply."

A disproportionate number of Irish also languished in almshouses, which meant higher taxes for property holders and a heavy burden for private charities. Even before 1845, 25% to 33% of the 40,000 foreign-born paupers in New York City and 37% of the inmates in Boston's House of Industry came from Ireland. In the 1850s, the number of destitute Irish in New York City almshouses grew out of all proportion. Half the needy in 1852 were Irish and German immigrants, with the Irish far in the lead. From 1849-1891, the proportion of Irish in these establishments ran as high as 60% and dropped below that figure only twice during the period. Fifty-five per cent of all arrests made in New York City during 1859 were Irish, compared to 23% native-born Americans.[23] Small surprise, then, that this profile gave rise to the stereotype of the down-at-heel, pug-faced, red-nosed, quarrelsome "thick Mick." The image of the Irish suffered terribly under this handicap, and many of the most proud sought to disassociate themselves from it by proving their worth in the military.

As immigration increased, so did the number of foreign-born recruits entering the army, from roughly 25% in the early 1820s, through 40% in the late 1830s, to 66% in the 1850s. In keeping with their place among the most destitute of immigrants, the Irish volunteered in ever greater numbers. In 1842, Dr. Daniel Drake found that of the 316 men he examined at three northern posts 161 were immigrants, the Irish being in the majority with 82. The dominance of the Irish was even more striking in 1850 and 1851, in the wake of the exodus ushered in by the famine. Of the 5000 men accepted by the army during those two years, 2113 of the total 3516 foreigners, or more than 42% of the whole, were from Ireland.[24]

Largely in response to the massive Irish immigration of the late 1840s and early 1850s, anti-foreign parties arose in New York City and elsewhere and evolved into the powerful and violent "Know-Nothing" agitation of the 1850s. Members of the self-styled "American party" saw Roman Catholicism as an un-American activity and viewed the Irish with deep distrust. They feared an invasion of pauper Catholic laborers and supported stiff naturalization laws and the exclusion of foreigners from public office. Under this pressure, the Irish became ever more insular and clannish. The conflict reached a climax in 1855 with riots and pitched battles between Irish and Know-Nothings in Philadelphia; Chelsea and Lawrence, Massachusetts; Newark; Baltimore; Brooklyn; and Saint Louis. The nativist movement would die out quickly and almost completely during the Civil War with the enlistment of foreign immigrants for the Union. As John Higham noted, "The war completed the ruin of organized nativism by absorbing xenophobes and immigrants in a common cause. Now the foreigner had a new prestige; he was a comrade-at-arms. The clash that alienated sections reconciled their component nationalities."[25]

Prior to the Civil War, every foreign-born group of any size in America's largest cities raised its own militia company. Because they were not made welcome in the military organizations of native-born Americans, the immigrants had no choice but to form their own units. In fact, such units filled a deep psychological and emotional need, providing links with the former homeland and fostering pride in a common heritage. The Irish traditionally loved uniforms, parades, and ceremony, and they derived a strong sense of pride from their military history. Consequently, their leaders urged the organization of militia companies to help eliminate factional rivalries and gain respect. Several of these would be subjected to blatant discrimination and abuse, particularly during the nativist fervor of the 1850s, when attempts were made either to disband Irish units or create "pure" American companies.[26]

By 1853, the Irish militia of New York numbered 2600 men. The Irish units' names included the Jasper Greens, the Hibernian Greens, the Napper Tandy Light Artillery, the Emmet Guards, the Irish Rifles, the Irish-American Guards, and the Mitchel Light Guards. They wore bright and striking uniforms, generally featuring the traditional emerald green and gold. The Montgomery Guards dated from 1836 when the New York Cadets excluded all foreign-born from their ranks and forced the Irish to create their own organization. By the 1850s, they formed part of the regular New York militia but still wore their own distinctive uniforms. The first Irish regiment in the United States appears to have been the Sixty-Ninth New York State Militia, which came into being in 1846.[27]

The huge influx of refugees following the potato famine led to the establishment of the first American organization, with mass appeal, dedicated to freeing Ireland from English oppression through military means. Named after a mythical band of Irish warriors, the Fenians were founded in 1857 by John O'Mahony from New York and James Stephens from Dublin. O'Mahony hardly had begun to recruit Irish militia members for the organization when the Civil War broke out. The Fenians saw the conflict as an opportunity to gain the military experience they felt was necessary to free Ireland at a later date while, at the same time, striking a blow at British interests in America. Throughout the war, the Fenians operated openly in the Union army, publicly stating their intention to wage war eventually against Britain. Their strength grew rapidly and peaked at around 50,000 members in 1865. By the end of the war, Fenianism had become the most popular and powerful ethnic organization in Irish-American history. But Fenian attempts to free Ireland ultimately would prove anti-climactic, undermined by a split in the organization that took place in 1865. One faction arranged an abortive rising in Ireland in 1867, and the other made several raids into Canada before the U.S. put a stop to them. By 1870, the power of the Fenians had declined and they came to be overshadowed by other Irish nationalist groups.[28]

In 1869, the U.S. Sanitary Commission reported that

24. Coffman, *Old Army*, 141; Coolidge, *Statistical Report*, 627; Prucha, *Army Life*, 142 n.11.

25. John Higham, *Strangers in the Land: Patterns of American Nativism 1860-1925* (New York, NY: Atheneum, 1971), 13.

26. Marcus Cunliffe, *Soldiers and Civilians: The Martial Spirit in America, 1775-1865* (New York, NY: Macmillan, 1973), 227-230.

27. Ibid, 224; Ernst, *Immigrant Life*, 128; Thomas J. Mullen, "The Fighting Sixty-Ninth," *Eire-Ireland* (1969), 13; Wittke, *Irish in America*, 52-53.

28. The best book-length study of the Fenians in the U.S. thus far is W.S. Neidhardt's *Fenianism in North America* (University Park, PA: Pennsylvania State University Press, 1975). See also William D'Arcy, *The Fenian Movement in the United States, 1858-1886* (Washington, D.C.: Catholic University of America Press, 1947), 180-181, 210; and Miller, *Emigrants and Exiles*, 336-343.

29. Wittke, *Irish in America*, 135-136. On Irish participation in the Civil War see Robert F. Athearn, *Thomas Francis Meagher* (Boulder, CO: University of Colorado Press, 1949), 89-142; William L. Burton, "Irish Regiments in the Union Army: The Massachussetts Experience," *Historical Journal of Massachussetts* (1983), 104-119; D.P. Conyngham, *The Irish Brigade and Its Campaigns* (New York, NY: W. McSorley and Co., 1867); J.L. Garland, "Irish Soldiers of the American Confederacy," *Irish Sword* (1949-1952), 174-180; Joseph M. Hernon, *Celts, Catholics and Copperheads: Ireland Views the American Civil War* (Columbus, OH: Ohio State University Press, 1968); Paul John Jones, *The Irish Brigade* (Washington D.C.: Robert Luce Inc., 1969); Ella Lonn, *Foreigners in the Confederacy* (Chapel Hill, NC: University of North Carolina Press, 1940); Ella Lonn, *Foreigners in the Union Army and Navy* (Baton Rouge, LA: Louisiana State University Press, 1951); and James F. Maguire, *The Irish in America* (London: Longmans, Green and Co., 1868), 545-589.

30. Quoted in Jones, *Irish Brigade*, 35.

31. Quoted in Ibid, 53-54.

32. Quoted in Wittke, *Irish in America*, 136.

144,221 Irish-born Americans had served on the side of the Union during the Civil War, and probably three times that many of Irish descent had taken up the Northern cause.[29] Some three dozen of the Irish-born, men like Thomas William Sweeny, St. Clair Augustin Mulholland, Thomas Alfred Smyth, James Shields, Michael Corcoran, Patrick Robert Guiney, and Thomas Francis Meagher, received the full or brevet rank of general with the North. Besides those already resident in the U.S., the Irish were recruited directly for the Union forces in Ireland and elsewhere by federal agents and clergymen. Indeed, Irish envoys played a large part in recruiting Keogh and his fellow Irishmen while they were fighting for the Pope in Italy. Other Irish immigrants were enlisted as soon as they arrived on American soil. Recruiting tents, complete with banners and stocked with whisky and food, were situated conveniently within twenty yards of the famous Castle Garden point of entry, and here Union officers offered liberal bounties to immigrant volunteers.

There came to be a number of Union regiments and brigades that were predominantly Irish, Catholic chaplains, known to the soldiers as "Holy Joes," being attached to some of them. Such units were raised in Ohio, Michigan, Indiana, Illinois, and Iowa, for example. But the familiar term "Irish Brigade" usually is used in reference to the New York, Boston, and Philadelphia regiments of the Army of the Potomac. These were commanded first by the renowned Meagher, an exile from Ireland in the wake of the abortive rising of 1848, and an escapee from the prison colony of Tasmania. Following Lincoln's call to arms, Colonel Michael Corcoran, of the predominantly Irish Sixty-Ninth New York Militia, gave Meagher permission to raise a company in New York and incorporate it into the Sixty-Ninth at Washington. Meagher's advertisement read:

> Young Irishmen to arms! To arms young Irishmen! Irish zouaves. One hundred young Irishmen—healthy, intelligent and active—wanted at once to form a company under command of Thomas Francis Meagher. To be attached to the 69th Regiment, N.Y.S.M. No applicant under eighteen or above thirty-five will be enrolled in the company.[30]

Within a week the rolls were complete and Meagher was drilling his company in New York City. The early career of the famous Irish Brigade had begun.

On April 20, 1861, the influential weekly newspaper the *Irish-American* published an appeal to its readership that stressed history, tradition, and the future of the new homeland while undermining the basic premises behind Know-Nothingism:

> Irish-Americans, we call on you by the sacred memories of the past, by your remembrance of the succor extended to your suffering brethren, by the future hope of your native land here taking root and springing toward a vigorous maturity, to be true to the land of your adoption in this crisis of her fate.[31]

In October, the *Boston Transcript* struck the same note, "You have fought nobly for the Harp and Shamrock, fight now for the stars and stripes... Your adopted country wants you."[32] The Irish proved both their loyalty and worth to the Union during the campaigns. Their first major action came at the Battle of Bull Run in July when the Sixty-Ninth New York Regiment, led by Corcoran, carried its emerald green regimental standard into combat as part of Sherman's brigade. During the battle, the unit lost thirty-eight killed, fifty-nine wounded, and ninety-five missing, or around 15% of its strength. The Irish fought bravely and left the field in better order than most of the units engaged. From then on, they frequently were referred to as the "Fighting Sixty-Ninth," the "Bloody Sixty-Ninth," or the "Fighting Irish."

The overriding wish was to commence recruitment for an Irish brigade, in the tradition of those of the past. A separate unit, it was felt, would foster pride and easier identification, and would lead to greater recognition. Two weeks after Bull Run, the Sixty-Ninth Regiment, New York State Militia, was mustered out of service. More than 500 of its members immediately reenlisted for three years in a new regiment, the Sixty-Ninth New York Volunteers, which became the core of the Irish

Brigade. Most of the remainder joined other Irish-American units forming in New York. In Philadelphia, many Irish-Americans had enlisted earlier with the California Brigade, later renamed the Philadelphia Brigade, while in Massachusetts the Irish were recruited into the Ninth and Twenty-Eighth. The Twenty-Eighth carried its own green flag into battle under the command of Colonel Richard Byrnes, before joining the Irish Brigade just prior to the Battle of Fredericksburg.

Three units, the Sixty-Third, Sixty-Ninth, and Eighty-Eighth New York Volunteers, had joined the brigade by mid November and by early the next year Meagher boasted a tough infantry brigade of 2500, including veterans who had seen action in the Crimea, India, and Italy. The Twenty-Eighth and Twenty-Ninth Massachusetts, the 116th Pennsylvania, and the Seventh New York Heavy Artillery also would serve with the brigade at various times during the campaigns. The brigade's green colors featured favorite and time-honored symbols—a golden sunburst, the Irish harp, and a wreath of shamrocks. The officers wore green hat plumes and men in the ranks sported green cockades to emphasize further the unit's Irish character. Meagher described his troops as, "A rough and tumble, drive-ahead, rollicking, devil-may-care set of fellows."[33] This recklessness later would cost them dearly in terms of casualties.

33. Quoted in Jones, *Irish Brigade*, 102.

Colonel Michael Corcoran leading the Sixty-Ninth New York regiment against the Confederate forces at the Battle of Bull Run, July 21, 1861. Behind Corcoran flies the emerald green regimental standard, bearing the golden harp of Erin. *Courtesy of Anne S.K. Brown Military Collection, Brown University Library.*

"Enlisting Irish and German Emigrants on the Battery at New York." This scene, at Castle Garden, New York, depicted Union Army recruiting efforts in September of 1864. *Courtesy of Radio Times Hulton Picture Library, London.*

During 1862, the brigade saw action at the Peninsula and Seven Days campaigns, Antietam, and Fredericksburg, and never would be as numerous again. The brigade lost around 20% of its strength—killed, wounded, and missing—during the Seven Days campaign, incurred heavy losses at Fredericksburg, and was shot to pieces at Chancellorsville. By the spring of 1863, when Meagher resigned his command, only around 520 men remained of the five regiments of the original brigade. The Irish again distinguished themselves through their bravery and endurance on the bloody battlefields of Gettysburg, Bristoe Station, and Mine Run. By the end of the war, the loyal Irish troops had built a proud record and proven themselves equal to the best.

The Confederacy, like the Union, dispatched emissaries to Ireland to recruit for the Southern cause. Lieutenant James L. Capston, Bishop Patrick Lynch of Charleston, and Father John Bannon, a former Confederate army chaplain, spoke in Ireland on behalf of the South in an attempt to stop the flow of Irish immigration into the Union army. In 1864, Confederate President Jefferson Davis even appointed Bishop Lynch as Southern commissioner to the Papal States in an attempt to gain Pius IX's support for the cause, but the Vatican was careful to receive him as a bishop only and not as a representative of the Confederacy.

Of the 85,000 Irish estimated to be living in the South at the outbreak of the Civil War, most tended to adopt the Confederate point of view, seeing it as a states' rights issue and similar to the grievances of the old country. Accurate figures are not available but the Irish clearly provided the largest proportion of foreign-born Confederate troops and made a substantial contribution to the Southern cause. Alabama, Georgia, Missouri, North Carolina, South Carolina, Tennessee, Texas, and Virginia all raised Irish units. The ranking Irish officer of the provisional army of the Confederate states was Major General Patrick Ronayne Cleburne, from County Cork, and other Irish generals included Joseph Finnegan, James Hagan, Walter Paye Lane, and Patrick Theodore Moore. Lane, who earlier had served in the Mexican War, came also from Cork, while Moore was from Galway. On several occasions, Union and Confederate Irish met face-to-face in combat, most notably at Fredericksburg where Georgia Irishmen defended Marye's Heights against Meagher's Irish Brigade.

Typically, Confederate Irish units comprised occasional companies within regiments, though there were some larger formations. One of the better known units was the Emerald Guards from Mobile, which later became Company I of the Eighth Alabama Infantry. Almost all the personnel in this company, including the officers, were born in Ireland. The uniform was dark green, and the company colors displayed a harp encircled with a wreath of shamrocks with the words "Erin-go-bragh" and the Gaelic war cry "Faugh-a-ballagh" on the one side, and the stars and bars, together with a full-length figure of George Washington, on the other. Louisiana furnished more Irish troops to the Southern cause than any other state. Most famous were the Louisiana Tigers, or "Irish Tartars" known officially as the Second Louisiana Battalion of Infantry, or the First Louisiana Special Battalion. Other Irish Confederate units of note included the Irish Jasper Greens from Savannah, who formed Companies A and B of the First Georgia Volunteers; the South Carolina Irish Artillery, active at the bombardment of Fort Sumter in 1861; and the First Irish Battalion from Virginia.

After the Civil War, the Irish continued to immigrate in large numbers, though now they were less numerous than the Germans or British.[34] Most were concentrated in the northeastern states where they either lived in poverty or performed most of the common labor. Prejudice, resulting largely from distrust of Catholicism or social criticism, again became prevalent for a time. Once more, the Irish were pictured as rowdy ne'er-do-wells—poverty-stricken, drunken roughnecks. Henry Seidel Canby thus recalled clashes between American and Irish youth, "No relations except combat were possible or thought of between our gangs and the 'micks'. . . They were still the alien, and had to be shown their place." Impoverished Irish immigrants still squatted in shanties on the edges of cities and indignant property owners continued to petition against this "low and squalid class of people," who left the surrounding neighborhoods "in a filthy and disgusting condition."[35]

It was to be expected then that the recruiting patterns of the antebellum period would reemerge after the war. The army offered no more attractions to young Americans than it had before the war. Pay was poor, ranging from thirteen dollars a month for privates to twenty-two dollars for first sergeants, and superior performance brought few rewards. Atrocious living conditions, harsh discipline, and the possibility of disease, injury, or even death in combat reduced still further the incentives to enlist. Most civilians looked upon soldiers with condescension, if not contempt. American postwar recruits were often of lower intelligence or in poor shape physically, the New York *Sun* charging that, "The Regular Army is composed of bummers, loafers, and foreign paupers."[36] To the Irish and other immigrants, however, the military again presented a means of escape from poverty and prejudice, and a source of secure employment. As it began to expand in size and extend its operations ever further into the trans-Mississippi West, moreover, the military offered recent arrivals the pros-

34. Miller, *Emigrants and Exiles*, 346-353, 569; C.O. Grada, "A Note on Nineteenth-Century Irish Emigration Statistics," *Population Studies* (1975), 143-144.

35. Quoted in Higham, *Strangers in the Land*, 26.

36. Quoted in *Army and Navy Journal* (October 20, 1877), 170. See also Robert M. Utley, *Frontier Regulars: The United States Army and the Indian, 1866-1891* (New York, NY: Macmillan, 1973), 23-25.

37. On the activities of the Buffalo Soldiers in the frontier military see John M. Carroll, ed., *The Black Military Experience in the American West* (New York, NY: Liveright, 1971); Jack D. Foner, *Blacks and the Military in American History* (New York, NY: Praeger Publishers, 1974); Arlen L. Fowler, *The Black Infantry in the West, 1869-1891* (Westport, CT: Greenwood Press, 1971); and William H. Leckie, *The Buffalo Soldiers: A Narrative of the Negro Cavalry in the West* (Norman, OK: University of Oklahoma Press, 1967).

38. Statement Showing the Nationality of Men Enlisted in the United States Army, from January 1, 1865 to December 31, 1874. 44 Congress, 1 Session, House Miscellaneous Document 105.

39. Vern D. Campbell, "Armor and Cavalry Music," *Armor* (March-April 1971), 30-34; Michael J. Mooney, "From Garry Owen in Glory," *Army* (February, 1989), 58-64.

40. William A. Graham, *The Story of the Little Big Horn* (New York, NY: Century Co., 1926), xx.

41. William A. Graham, *The Custer Myth: A Source Book of Custeriana* (Harrisburg, PA: Stackpole Co., 1953), jacket notes.

42. John S. Gray, *Centennial Campaign: The Sioux War of 1876* (Fort Collins, CO: Old Army Press, 1976, 2nd ed.), 284-297, 346-357.

---

pect of land and opportunity beyond the frontier. In consequence, large numbers of Irish and Germans once more entered the ranks.

The same incentives appealed to blacks. After the war, former slaves and freedmen joined the newly-organized Ninth and Tenth Cavalry and Twenty-Fourth and Twenty-Fifth Infantry Regiments in large numbers. These segregated units, led by white officers, came to be called "Buffalo Soldiers" by their Indian adversaries. Like the Irish and other immigrant troops, they contributed significantly to the Indian campaigns and the settlement of the West, and the exploits of the Buffalo Soldiers remain one of the most dramatic and colorful sagas in the annals of the frontier military.[37]

During the decade following the Civil War, January 1865 to December 1875, 183,659 men enlisted for army service. Of these, 86,593, were not American citizens but foreign nationals. The Irish provided the largest contingent with 38,649, followed by Germany with 23,127, and England with 9,037. Other nationalities with over a thousand enlistees included Canada with 4,703, Scotland with 2,456, France with 1,593, and Switzerland with 1,562. Among the others were five Africans, three Arabs, three Chinese, two Sandwich Islanders, an Egyptian, and a Turk. The frontier military had become a rich and colorful ethnic mosaic. A full 47% of the men recruited by the Regular Army during the period just prior to the Battle of the Little Big Horn were foreign-born. Next to the Americans, the Irish were easily the largest group, constituting 21% of all enlistees, and almost 45% of all non-citizen recruits.[38]

A strong Irish contingent was present in the Seventh Cavalry from its organization under the act of July 28, 1866, until the Battle of the Little Big Horn a decade later. During that period, the Irish in the regiment contributed to the pacification and settlement of the plains. They participated in the defeat of Black Kettle's Cheyenne at the Battle of the Washita, Indian Territory, on November 28, 1868. In 1873 they took part in General David S. Stanley's Yellowstone campaign and in the summer of 1874 they helped lead an exploring expedition through the Black Hills that resulted in the discovery of gold and brought a flood of prospectors into the area. By the spring of 1876, when the Seventh joined the campaign being mounted against the Sioux and Cheyenne, the Irish had become an established and integral part of the regiment. The Seventh had assumed an unmistakably Irish flavor, also. "Garry Owen," "The Girl I Left Behind Me," and "Thaddy O'Brien," the songs and marches most closely associated with the regiment, for example, had originated in Ireland.[39]

Just how many Irish were present with Custer at the Little Big Horn on that fateful Sunday in June 1876 has been a bone of contention. In 1926, Colonel William A. Graham wrote in his *Story of the Little Big Horn*:

> Custer became the magnet that lured to his standard hundreds of daring young Americans; for when the Seventh Cavalry took the field against the hostiles of the southern plains, Custer at the head of the column, it was practically an American regiment, one in which the soldier of foreign birth was almost a stranger. The roster of the Seventh Cavalry was made up in greater number —probably far greater—than any other in the army of the United States, of eager young troopers, American to the core.[40]

By 1953, Graham felt it necessary to try to debunk the Custer myth that he himself had helped create by presenting "original source material, unbiased by interpretations and misconstructions."[41] By then, however, the image of the all-American Seventh had been portrayed in film, TV, and fiction. The idea was appealing to Americans during a period of rapid and fundamental change and it gained a strong footing in the popular imagination. The reality, of course, was far more complex.

The best statistical work on the participants at the Little Big Horn to date has been conducted by John S. Gray in his *Centennial Campaign*.[42] In this important study, the author has provided informed and intelligent estimates not only of Custer's forces that day but also of his Indian adversaries. Unfortunately, Gray did not break down the Seventh Cavalry by ethnic groups. John McCormack recently completed an in-depth study of the subject in his, "The Irish at the Little Big Horn." McCormack, defining "Irish" as "men actually born in Ireland, as well as those of Irish descent born elsewhere," used surnames to establish a link with the Emerald Isle. Based on this, he concludes that, "Approximately one out of every three men in the regiment was either Irish or of Irish descent."[43] Robert M. Utley, in his recent biography of Custer, *Cavalier in Buckskin*, also adhered to this figure.[44]

Assigning the term "Irish" to someone merely with a Celtic-sounding surname is dubious at best, but to count the Custer brothers as being Irish merely because their mother may have been of Irish descent is misleading and confusing. Categorizing George Armstrong Custer with Myles Keogh in terms of ethnic background simply undermines the entire argument. A much more sound and useful approach is to look at men who admitted being born in Ireland—the premise being that the total represents the absolute minimum, for there was nothing for a soldier to gain by pretending to be Irish. It is much more likely that a number coming from Ireland would have claimed to have been born in the U.S., and the figures for the Irish-born probably should be much higher. Nevertheless, the numbers of Irish at the Little Big Horn that day were considerable. Serving beside them were many other Irish-Americans, the sons and grandsons of earlier emigrants from Ireland.

There were men from at least twenty-nine of the thirty-two Irish counties with the Seventh that day, some stating simply that they were born in Ireland but not specifying where.[45] Soldiers of Irish birth accounted for 103, or 16%, of the 637 enlisted men present at the battle, and 33, or 14%, of the 237 enlisted men killed. Twenty-five of the 171 enlisted men who could or should have been at the battle but dodged the bullet because of detached service, sickness, or other reasons, had been born in Ireland. Lieutenant Henry Nowlan often is cited as being Irish but in fact he was born in the British protectorate of Corfu and Keogh was the only officer born in Ireland present that day. The Irish did provide a good number of NCOs, however, the two highest-ranking being First Sergeants Michael Kenney from Galway and Michael Martin from Dublin. There were also fifteen Irish sergeants present at the battle—James Akers, James Bustard, Patrick Carey, William Cashan, Patrick Conelly, Martin Considine, Jeremiah Finley, James Flanagan, Thomas W. Harrison, Robert H. Hughes, George M. McDermott, John McGlone, Matthew Maroney, Lawrence Murphy, and Thomas Murray—as well as three corporals—Thomas P. Eagan, George Loyd, and James Martin. Of these twenty Irish NCOs, eight were killed at the battle.

Keogh's own Company I reflected the diversity of ethnic backgrounds present in the Seventh Cavalry. Sixty-seven members of the company could or should have been present, or were at the Little Big Horn. In addition to the thirty-three who claimed to have been born in the U.S., fifteen were Irish, nine Germans, four English, and three Canadian, with Hungary, Switzerland, and Wales being represented by one man each. Three of the company's five sergeants—Bustard, Michael C. Caddle and George Gaffney—were Irish. Caddle and Gaffney were both on detached service at the time of the campaign and only Bustard was present. In fact, only forty-nine of the sixty-seven members of the company actually took part in the battle. Of these, twenty-one, or 43%, were foreign-born, with the eleven Irish representing a large majority and constituting 23% of the entire company. Eight of the eleven—Keogh, Bustard, and Privates John Barry, Thomas Patrick Downing, Edward C. Driscoll, Patrick Kelley, McIlhargey, and John E. Mitchell—died in battle with just three—Privates David Cooney, James P. McNally, and Eugene Owens—surviving.

Several interesting stories concerning Irish participants at the battle emerged. Two Irishmen—Sergeant Thomas Murray from Managhan and Private Thomas J. Callan from Louth—received Medals of Honor for their roles in the battle. Murray was honored for bringing in the pack train on June 25, carrying rations to the firing

Sergeant Robert Hughes, from Dublin, carried Custer's personal flag before being killed at "the last stand." *Courtesy of John M. Carroll Collection, Custer Battlefield National Monument.*

---

43. Jack McCormack, "The Irish at the Little Big Horn," *Research Review* (June, 1986), 3. McCormack has not been alone in basing his calculations on "unmistakably Irish names." See also e.g. "Irish in the 7th U.S. Cavalry," *Irish Sword* (1949-1952), 336-338 (also 211).

44. Robert M. Utley, *Cavalier in Buckskin: George Armstrong Custer and the Western Military Frontier* (Norman, OK: University of Oklahoma Press, 1989), 168.

45. The following figures are based on John M. Carroll, ed., *They Rode with Custer: A Biographical Directory of the Men that Rode with General George A. Custer* (Mattituck, NJ, and Bryan, TX: John M. Carroll and Co., 1987). This has replaced Kenneth M. Hammer's *Men with Custer: Biographies of the 7th Cavalry* (Fort Collins, CO: Old Army Press, 1972) as the standard reference work utilized by the staff at the Custer Battlefield National Monument.

Corporal Thomas Eagen unwittingly predicted his demise just months before the Battle of the Little Big Horn. *Courtesy of John M. Carroll Collection, Custer Battlefield National Monument.*

line on June 26, and fetching water for the wounded. Callan received his medal for showing conspicuous gallantry as a member of the water party in the Little Big Horn River fight.[46]

Some Irishmen had narrow escapes in the wake of the Reno retreat. One of these was Private Thomas O'Neill from Dublin who was left stranded in the river bottom with First Lieutenant Charles DeRudio, the interpreter F.F. Girard and the mixed blood Blackfoot scout William Jackson. The three tried to rejoin the command at night but found the approaches guarded by Indians and so concealed themselves in the brush further up the valley, Girard relating that, "The retreating warriors passed by hundreds close to where we lay hid in the willows." O'Neal and his companions subsequently managed to rejoin the Reno battalion on the hilltop and the three escaped unscathed. DeRudio later noted:

> ... The fidelity and bravery of Private O'Neill. He faithfully obeyed me and stood by me like a brother. I shall never cease to remember him and his service to me during our dangerous companionship. This brave soldier is highly thought of by his company commander and of course ever will be by me and mine.

Benteen shared in the admiration, describing O'Neill as a "cool, level-headed fellow," qualities vital in such a situation.[47]

Reno's orderly, Private Edward Davern from Limerick, was another who was lucky to escape. Lieutenant Edward Godfrey related that Davern found himself alone and suddenly engaged in "hand-to-hand conflict with an Indian; his horse was killed; he then shot the Indian, caught the Indian's pony, and rode to the command." Sergeant Carey from Tipperary also became separated from the command with several others and had to hide in the woods or under the river embankment to escape the enemy before rejoining the regiment after dark.[48]

Others were not so fortunate. For example, Sergeant Robert Hughes from Dublin, who carried Custer's personal standard into action, was killed at the "last stand," and Private Mitchell from Galway took the second message from Reno before being killed with the Custer battalion. Corporal Eagan made an unwitting prediction in his last letter to his sister, March 5, 1876, when he wrote that he would contact her next when he returned from the campaign, "That is if I do not get my hair lifted by some Indian. . . ." Eagan died in combat on June 25. Still others survived but were wounded or lost limbs. One of these was Saddler Michael P. Madden from Galcony. Madden was shot below the right knee in the hilltop fight on June 26 and later lost his leg through amputation. He received a promotion to sergeant on the field for his gallantry during the campaign.[49]

Sergeant Finley from Tipperary served as a tailor for the regiment and made the buckskin jacket that Custer wore during the Sioux expedition. Finley was killed during the battle, his body being found with twelve arrows shot into it. His widow later married Private John Donahue from Galway, who also was present at the battle but survived, the couple making their home in Oberon, North Dakota. A similar circumstance occurred with the widow of McIlhargey. The private was a close friend of Sergeant Caddle, both being in Company I. As Caddle was to be on detached service during the Sioux campaign, McIlhargey asked him to take care of his family in the event of his demise. McIlhargey carried the first message from Reno before being killed with the Custer battalion on June 25. Caddle rode with his company when it returned to the battlefield to remove the remains of the officers and rebury the enlisted men. He later married McIlhargey's widow Josie, became a father to her children, and in time the couple had children of their own, the family also settling in North Dakota.[50] The Irish took care of their own and, as women were in short supply on the frontier, such matches tended to be well-made.

Several Irish survivors of the Little Big Horn took part in later Indian campaigns as part of the Seventh Cavalry. First Sergeant Martin and Sergeant George M. McDermott were killed and Sergeant James Flanagan, Corporal John Nolan, and Private Michael Murphy were wounded during the Snake Creek engagement with

---

46. Earl A. Brininstool, *Troopers with Custer: Historic Incidents of the Battle of the Little Big Horn* (New York, NY: Bonanza Press, 1957), 264, 266-267.

47. Statements of Edward S. Godfrey, Charles C. DeRudio, F.F. Girard, and Frederick William Benteen in Graham, *Custer Myth*, 145-146, 251, 253-256, 300.

48. Statements of Godfrey and Theodore W. Goldin in Ibid, 140, 270, 346; Statement of John Ryan in the Hardin *Tribune* (June 22, 1923), quoted in Carroll, *They Rode with Custer*, entry for Sergeant Patrick Carey. For two accounts of the battle by other Irish survivors see Private John Dolan's statement in the New York *Herald* (July 23, 1876), 4; and Private Daniel Newell's piece "The Story of the Little Big Horn Campaign of 1876," *Sunshine Magazine*, (September 30, 1930).

49. Statements of Godfrey and Goldin in Graham, *Custer Myth*, 146, 270, 346; Carroll, *They Rode with Custer*, entry for Corporal Thomas P. Eagen; Statement of William C. Slaper in Brininstool, *Troopers with Custer*, 57-59.

50. Statement of Daniel Alexander Kanipe in Graham, *Custer Myth*, 248, 250, 364; Carroll, *They Rode with Custer*, entries for Sergeant Jeremiah Finley, Sergeant Michael C. Caddle, and Private Archibald McIlhargey; Annie R. Gwyther, "Pioneer Days on Fort Rice Military Reserve," *North Dakota History* (1959), 128-131.

Chief Joseph's Nez Perce band in Montana Territory on September 30, 1877. A number were present at Wounded Knee, December 29, 1890, which finally put an end to the long history of the Indian wars and sealed the tragic fate of the Sioux. Most notable was Corporal George Loyd who, by then, had become a sergeant in Keogh's old Company I. Loyd displayed conspicuous gallantry during the exchange after having received a fatal lung wound, and received a posthumous Medal of Honor.[51]

By the centennial of the American Revolution, the Irish had established a long-standing and proud tradition in the U.S. Army. They had made a substantial contribution to the American war effort in every major conflict affecting the U.S.—including the War of Independence, the War of 1812, the Mexican War, the Civil War, and the various Indian wars. Following the great migrations from Ireland to America in the late 1840s, the Irish presence within the military increased to dramatic proportions until, by 1850, they constituted fully 42% of all enlisted men. By the decade following the Civil War, the figures had declined but remained high, the Irish-born constituting one in five of all enlistees. At the Battle of the Little Big Horn, around one in six of the enlisted men present and one in seven of those who died in combat had been born in Ireland. The story did not end there, of course. Irish soldiers fought for the U.S. in the Spanish-American War, both World Wars, Korea, and Vietnam. Between 1863-1963, 194 Medals of Honor went to men of Irish birth; twice as many as the number awarded to nationals of any other foreign country.[52]

Though the percentage of Irish in the military was consistently high, the number of Irish officers remained relatively low. Between 1789-1903, Ireland provided more officers for the U.S. Army than any other foreign country, 188 in all, including 32 for the cavalry. Germany came in second with 115, England third with 85, and Canada fourth with 52.[53] But the Irish total constitutes less than 1% of the overall number of officers who served in the U.S. military during these years—a massive reduction from the figures for Irish enlisted men. Relatively few Irish made officer, but many made NCO. Seventeen, or more than one in four, of the Seventh' sixty sergeants at the time of the Little Big Horn were Irish, for example. The typical Irish NCO has been portrayed by Hollywood as tough and aggressive, with the characteristics of a frontiersman. In fact, most of the Regular Army's campaigns during this period were frontier wars in one sense or another and the use of this image, brought out time and again in the movies of John Ford and recently epitomized in the character of Sergeant Mulcahey in the epic *Glory*, has some merit, based on the record.

This raises the interesting question, how typical of the Irish at the Little Big Horn, or indeed of the Irish in the U.S. military generally, was Myles Walter Keogh? There can be no doubt that he was untypical, if not atypical, of the Irish immigrant soldier. Unlike most of his compatriots, Keogh had not been born into poverty and was not ignorant or illiterate. The family was large, he being one of thirteen children, but the Keoghs had money, land, and servants. Myles went on to receive a good education at St. Patrick's College, a Jesuit school in Carlow, some accounts even suggesting that he attended university in Dublin.[54] While he grew up in a time in which many around him were forced to emigrate from their native homeland, Keogh chose to leave.

In addition to being a gentleman, Keogh was also an officer—a rarity among the Irish within the military. Irish-birth was considered a handicap to a successful military career. There is a strong suggestion, for instance, that Phil Sheridan, probably the most important general to serve in the U.S. Army during the 19th-Century, felt it necessary to play down his Irish heritage in order to further his military career.[55] Keogh was the sole Irish-born officer at the Little Big Horn and among the small elite that constituted Ireland's contribution to the U.S. officer corps during the period under consideration. As has been indicated, the vast majority of Irish nationals became enlisted men, and hoped to make corporal or sergeant.

Keogh clearly pictured himself in the role of the romantic, charismatic Irish soldier of fortune, the

Private Thomas O'Neill, from Dublin, narrowly escaped with his life from the Battle of the Little Big Horn. *Courtesy of John M. Carroll Collection, Custer Battlefield National Monument.*

IRISH IN THE ARMY

51. Carroll, *They Rode with Custer*, entries for First Sergeant Michael Martin, Sergeants James Flanagan and George M. McDermott, Corporals John Nolan and George Loyd, and Private Michael Murphy.

52. William D. O'Ryan and Robert M. Gaynor, "Irish Recipients of Awards for Bravery in the United States Armed Forces, 1863-1963," *Irish Sword* (1967-1968), 274-275; "Irish-Born Recipients of the U.S. Congressional Medal of Honor," *Irish Sword* (1975), 149.

53. Figures drawn from Francis B. Heitman, *Historical Register and Dictionary of the United States Army, From its Organization, September 29, 1789, to March 2, 1903* (Washington, D.C.: Government Printing Office, 1903), vol. 1, pt. 2, 149-1069. My thanks to John P. Langellier for providing this information.

54. Brian C. Pohanka, "Myles Walter Keogh (1840-1876)," *Greasy Grass* (May, 1988), 5.

55. Joseph Hergesheimer, *Sheridan: A Military Narrative* (Boston and New York: Houghton-Mifflin, 1931), 9-12; Paul Andrew Hutton, *Phil Sheridan and His Army* (Lincoln, NE: University of Nebraska Press, 1985), 2, 375 n.2; Richard O'Connor, *Sheridan the Inevitable* (Indianapolis, IN and New York, NY: Bobbs-Merrill Co., 1953), 18-20, 361.

MYLES KEOGH

56. Charles James Lever, *Charles O'Malley, The Irish Dragoon* (Dublin: W. Curry, 1841).

57. Myles Keogh to Tom Keogh, November 30, 1867, Mircofilm Copy Manuscript No. 3885, National Library of Ireland, Dublin. Unless otherwise noted, these letters were sent by Myles to his brother Tom. Hereafter referred to as National Library Microfilm. Another member of the Irish educated elite to express similar sentiments around this time was Windham Thomas Wyndham-Quin, the 4th Earl of Dunraven. In his autobiography *Past Times and Pastimes* (1922) he had this to say of his feelings during the passage to New York in the summer of 1869:

> I was young—not twenty-eight years of age; and my boyish brain-cells were stored to bursting with tales of Red Indians and grizzly b'ars; caballeros and haciendas, prairies and buffalos, Texans and Mexicans, cowboys and voyageurs, and had not yet discharged their cargo. I was in search of such sport and adventure as, under the circumstances, were to be found.

The words could have come from Myles himself. Quoted in Marshall Sprague, "The Dude from Limerick," *American West* (Fall, 1966), 53.

58. Costello, "Irish and the American Military," 227.

59. Robert M. Utley, *Frontiersmen in Blue: The United States Army and the Indian, 1848-1865* (New York, NY: Macmillan, 1967), 40.

60. Herbert A. Croly, *The Promise of American Life* (New York, NY: Macmillan, 1909).

61. David Noel Doyle, *Irish Americans, Native Rights and National Empires: The Structure, Divisions, and Attitudes of the Catholic Minority in the Decade of Expansion, 1890-1901* (New York, NY: Arno Press, 1976), 40-42, 59-60, 74-75; David M. Emmons, *The Butte Irish: Class and Ethnicity in an American Mining Town* (Urbana, IL: University of Illinois Press, 1989), 13. For Butte City the figures were 8,026 immigrant or second generation Irish in a total population of 30,470, or 26%. See also Catherine Dowling, "Irish-American Nationalism in Butte, 1900-1916," *Montana* (Spring, 1989), 51; and George Wesley Davis, *Sketches of Butte: From Vigilante Days to Prohibition* (Boston, MA: Cornhill Co., 1921), 64.

living embodiment of Lever's *Charles O'Malley, the Irish Dragoon*.[56] Raised during a period that saw a tremendous resurgence of interest among the educated in Britain and Ireland in the Arthurian legends, the crusades, and ancient rites of chivalry, Keogh became influenced deeply by these epic tales. While others left Ireland because they could not find enough potatoes to eat, young Myles went in search of the Holy Grail. By late 1867, he felt he had arrived. In a letter to his brother Tom he expressed his belief that, by receiving the Order of Saint Gregory and becoming a brevet lieutenant-colonel in the regular U.S. Army, he had received "a full reward" and was satisfied that he had "carried out some at least of the rather visionary fancies we as boys indulged of long ago."[57] Most of the Irish in the military were not looking for a cause, but for food and clothing. The army promised an escape from poverty and discrimination and a hope for the future. The need for massive doses of adventure in epic proportions was missing from the priority lists of most of the Irish serving in the ranks.

The old adage about losing the battle but winning the war certainly applies to the Irish experience at the Little Big Horn. Through their efforts, they dramatized in the public imagination the role played by the Irish in the "winning of the West." As Michael J. Costello pointed out, this, "Helped to establish the respectability of successive generations of Irishmen in the mind of America, a mind which, despite its inconstancy to the value of military tradition, has always admired the integrity of soldierly courage."[58] The battle was merely a temporary setback to the inevitable surge of white westward expansion. Many of the Little Big Horn survivors went on to make their homes on the northern plains. As Utley remarked, the army took new immigrants and "distributed them at the close of their enlistment along the sparsely populated frontier."[59] Other settlers—immigrant and American-born miners, farmers, ranchers, and homesteaders—followed the frontier military at a massive rate and peopled the western states. Within fifteen years of the battle, Montana, Wyoming, and the Dakotas had entered the Union.

Though McIlhargey and Keogh had different reasons for being at the Little Big Horn that day, both were in search of what Herbert Croly later termed "the promise of American life."[60] It would elude them but many of their compatriots would take up the search where they had left off. By 1900, more than one in three of the Irish-born and the children of Irish-born were living in the midwestern and plains states, or the far West, and the copper mining town of Butte, Montana, just 250 miles west of the Custer battlefield, was found to contain a higher percentage of immigrant and second generation Irish in its population than any other community in the United States.[61]

Sergeant Jeremiah Finley, from Tipperary, served as a tailor for the Seventh Cavalry and made the buckskin shirt worn by Custer during the Sioux campaign. Finley, who was killed with the Custer battalion at the Little Big Horn, stands with this horse. *Courtesy of John M. Carroll Collection, Custer Battlefield National Monument.*

"Reconnaissance"

Custer's Theme Song:
Keogh and "Garry Owen"

by Peggy Champlin, Ph.D.

> Now I like Garryowen,
> When I hear it at home,
> But it's not half so sweet when you're going to be kilt.
> Charles Lever, *Charles O'Malley*

Because of its connection with Custer, "Garry Owen," the Seventh Cavalry's spirited theme song, has been called the most famous of all American Army regimental marches.[1] A legend has persisted that gives Myles Keogh credit for introducing the song to Custer. The link to Keogh may have begun with Elizabeth Custer's remark to Keogh's biographer, Edward S. Luce, that she first heard Custer hum and whistle the tune shortly after the regiment was organized at Fort Riley in 1866, and that she thought Keogh "was in some way connected" with Custer's adopting the song.[2] It now seems certain that Custer had known the song long before 1866, but the association with Keogh is understandable, since "Garry Owen" has its roots in Keogh's native Ireland.

It is a traditional Irish tune, appearing in a collection of old songs to the words "The Bosom that Beats to a Brother's Distress."[3] Its more famous career, however, is as a rowdy drinking song. "Garryowen" is Gaelic for Owen's Garden, a tavern in Limerick which was a gathering place for the Fifth Royal Irish Lancers who were stationed there. By the late 18th-century, some unknown author had written words to the air that urged "Bacchus' sons" to "booze and sing and lend your aid" in wreaking general havoc in the Limerick streets.

Although an Irish tune, "Garry Owen" achieved much of its fame due to the song's association with the United States Seventh Cavalry Regiment. *Courtesy of Custer Battlefield National Monument.*

1. Edward A. Dolph, *"Sound Off"; Soldier Songs from the Revolution to World War II,* (New York, NY: Farrar and Rinehart, 1942, 2nd. ed.), 510-511.
2. Luce, *Keogh, Comanche and Custer,* Appendix J, 123. Luce's Appendix is reprinted in Melbourne C. Chandler, *Of Garryowen in Glory: The History of the 7th U.S. Cavalry* (Annandale, VA: Turnpike Press, 1960), Appendix E, 412-414.
3. Letter from William Martin Hobkirk to Edward S. Luce, October 14, 1938, in *Keogh, Comanche and Custer,* Appendix J, 126.

4. Michael J. Mooney, "From 'Garry Owen' in Glory," *Army*, (February, 1989), 60.

5. Luce, *Keogh, Comanche and Custer*, 123; Brian C. Pohanka, "Myles Walter Keogh (1840-1876), *Greasy Grass* (May, 1988), 5. Mooney, "From Garry Owen in Glory," 60, repeats the Luce error and has Keogh himself a member of the Fifth Royal Irish Lancers as well.

6. Elias Van Arsdale Andruss to Elizabeth Custer, May 8, 1887 (Elizabeth B. Custer Collection, Roll 5, frames 4863-4868, Custer Battlefield National Monument). This collection consists of approximately 8000 frames microfilmed in 1971 on 8 rolls of 35 mm film under the auspices of the Custer Battlefield Historical and Museum Association, Inc. The Andruss letter is found in part in Ernest Lisle Reedstrom, *Bugles, Banners and War Bonnets* (Caldwell, ID: Caxton Printers, 1977).

7. Elizabeth Custer, *Tenting on the Plains, or General Custer in Kansas and Texas* (New York, NY: Charles L. Webster, 1889), 323.

8. Evan S. Connell, *Son of the Morning Star* (San Francisco, CA: North Point Press, 1984), 293.

9. Fairfax Downey, *Fife, Drum and Bugle* (Fort. Collins, CO: Old Army Press, 1971), 119-122.

The tune is a lilting one and according to Luce was adopted as a quick march by the Royal Lancers, although there is little evidence to support this statement. It was used by other regiments as well, being played in battles where Irish units fought, from Spain to Waterloo. In America, where many immigrants from Ireland served as soldiers both in the Revolution and the Civil War, "Garry Owen" was adopted by an Irish unit of what later became the New York Sixty-Ninth Regiment, and may have been played as early as 1775 when the unit marched to Quebec under Irish-born Major General Richard Montgomery. It was later the official marching tune of the Sixty-Ninth New York Regiment, which saw action in many Civil War campaigns."[4]

It is interesting to speculate about where or when Keogh first heard "Garry Owen." Luce suggested that he might have learned it from his father who served with the Fifth Irish Lancers, but Keogh's father was never a member of that regiment.[5] He might have become familiar with the song after he entered the Papal service, since by the 1860s the tune was being used by Irish regiments and might well have been known to some of Keogh's fellow Irish soldiers who were defending the Papal States. He also undoubtedly would have heard it played or sung during his service in the Civil War, by army bands or in saloons, much as Custer was pictured hearing it in a scene from the film *They Died with Their Boots On*. Keogh, with his reputation for drinking, was no doubt more of a frequenter of barrooms than was Custer, and it is not difficult to imagine his joining other soldiers in singing the words of the rousing drinking song.

Custer already was familiar with "Garry Owen" before he first met Keogh during the Antietam campaign. According to an 1887 letter to Mrs. Elizabeth Custer from one of her husband's former classmates, "Garry Owen" was known to Custer while he was still at West Point. "General Custer and myself were members of the same Cadet Company," her correspondent wrote:

> On entering West Point every plebe is supposed to be gifted with some accomplishment. Mine was to hum and drum by ear on the guitar and I was always sure of an attentive listener in General Custer, which was very flattering to this 'plebe.'
> I remember his asking me if I played 'Garry Owen' or 'The Girl I Left Behind Me,' they seemed to be his favorite airs. I could not gratify his wish as the tunes did not belong to my repertoire! If my memory serves me correctly he afterwards had Mr. Appeles, the leader of the band, to arrange the airs to different instruments and they were performed on appropriate occasions . . . .[6]

In *Tenting on the Plains*, Elizabeth Custer provides other evidence that Custer knew "Garry Owen" before 1866. At the end of the Civil War and before the Seventh Cavalry was organized, Custer often would attend reunions of veterans of his Michigan brigade and be asked to speak. She reported: "He tried on his return to give me a lucid account of the ceremonies, and how signally he failed in making a speech . . . and his subterfuge for hiding his confusion and getting off the scrape by proposing 'Garryowen' by the band, or three cheers for the old brigade."[7]

Keogh was assigned to Custer's newly-organized Seventh Cavalry in November, 1866, and it may have been about that time that Custer decided to have his own regimental band. Evan S. Connell suggests that it was either Keogh or Major Alfred Gibbs who proposed the idea of a band to him, and that Custer was so taken with the idea that he personally contributed fifty dollars for the purchase of instruments.[8] It is just as likely, however, that Custer himself first thought of having a band, since he had one with him as early as the fighting of October of 1863 in the Civil War.[9] Custer's subsequent use of the band, both in battle and other situations to boost morale and heighten the theatricality of an event, was another expression of his own flamboyant personality.

Whether it was Keogh or Custer himself who chose "Garry Owen" as the regimental theme song, it was a very appropriate choice. Not only was its lilting rhythm suited to the gallop of horses but also its Irish origin made it especially fitting for a regiment which included a high proportion of Irish immigrants.

There have been various reports of "Garry Owen"

being played by the band to accompany a dramatic moment, most of which occurred when Keogh was on other assignments. Keogh was serving with General Alfred Sully on the frosty morning of November 26, when Custer attacked the Cheyenne winter encampment on the banks of the Washita. The music adds drama to one of the most memorable scenes in the film *Little Big Man*, as the Indians first detect Custer's advance through the mist to the eerie music of "Garry Owen." It is easy to see why the Indians called it "the Devil's music." As Custer told it, he had previously instructed the band leader to be ready "to play Garry Owen as the opening piece," as the signal that the attack was to begin. When the time came,

> I directed him to give us 'Garry Owen.' At once the rollicking notes of that familiar marching and fighting air sounded forth through the valley, and in a moment were re-echoed back from the opposite sides by the loud and continued cheers of the men of the other detachments, who, true to their orders, were there and in readiness to pounce upon the Indians the moment the attack began.[10]

Custer's version of the attack has become part of the Custer legend. Other accounts are less heroic. One has it that it was so cold that morning that the musicians' saliva froze in the valves of their instruments and they were unable to play more than a few bars.[11] The leader of the band later told General Edward S. Godfrey that Custer had turned to him at the moment "Charge" was sounded and instructed him to "play something lively:"

> The Band leader (a little German) afterwards told me he was thinking of his revolver and not of his cornet and music. He quickly pulled out his music book and fortunately opened it at "Garry Owen." He called out the number of the piece and began to toot his cornet, and the rest soon chimed in.[12]

Whatever the circumstances surrounding its role in the battle, it was after the defeat of the Cheyennes at the Washita that "Garry Owen" became firmly identified with the Seventh Cavalry. Custer's carefully staged return to Camp Supply after the battle was witnessed by many, including a Kansas volunteer who noted the playing of "Gen. Custer's favorite" as the troops, scouts and Indian prisoners paraded into camp for review by General Sheridan.[13]

The last time Keogh would have heard the band playing "Garry Owen" was as he and his company left the Powder River Depot with Custer, headed for the Little Big Horn. The whole band did not go with them, but was "posted on a knoll overlooking the river," remembered a private of Company G:

> They played merrily while we were fording the river. After all were across . . . the band broke into the rollicking strains of "Garry Owen," which as usual brought a hearty cheer, and its notes were still ringing in our ears as we left the river bottoms and the band was lost to sight.[14]

---

10. George Armstrong Custer, *My Life on the Plains*, Centennial ed. (Norman, OK: University of Oklahoma Press, 1976), 240.
11. Downey, *Fife, Drum and Bugle*, 121.
12. General Edward F. Godfrey to Mr. Pratt, May 11, 1921 (Elizabeth B. Custer Collection, Roll 6, 6168ff).
13. David L. Spotts, *Campaigning with Custer*, E. A. Brininstool, ed. (Lincoln, NE: University of Nebraska Press, 1988), entry for December 1, 1868, 66.
14. Theodore W. Goldin to Chaplain George J. McMurry, n.d., quoted in Luce, *Keogh, Comanche and Custer*, 124.

In this *circa* 1861 photograph of the Company of St. Patrick, Keogh stands third from the left while his comrade, Daniel J. Keily, is fourth from the left. *Courtesy of Dr. Elizabeth Atwood Lawrence.*

Chapter 3

Hearth and Home:
Keogh's Early Years in Ireland and Italy

by John S. Manion

> A brooding melancholy gained daily more and more upon me. A wish to return to Ireland, a vague and indistinct feeling that my career was not destined for aught of great and good, crept upon me, and I longed to sink into oblivion, forgotten and forgot.
>
> Charles Lever, *Charles O'Malley*

Although known by many because of his horse Comanche, Myles Walter Keogh holds a special place in history in his own right. Born in County Carlow, Ireland near Leighlinbridge (more precisely in Orchard House, a stone dwelling that still exists and today is occupied by his collateral descendants) on March 25, 1840, he would grow up far from the site of his death and final resting place in America.[1] Myles was the son of John Keogh and Magarete Blanchfield. His father also hailed from Orchard, County Carlow according to John O'Hart's *Irish Pedigrees*, while his mother appears in this same reference as coming from Rathgarven, near Clifden in Kilkenny County, just west of Carlow.[2] Some accounts list his mother as Margarete Blanchville, an error which originated in records of the Papal army, copies of which Edward Luce received through John Francis Spellman in 1939. Little is known about the life spans of Myles' parents, however. Evidently, his father died while Myles was young and his mother passed away after he completed his service in Italy in 1862.

In contrast to this scant information, a great deal of supposition has arisen concerning John Keogh's association with the Fifth Royal Lancers, once stationed in a suburb of Limerick known as Garryowen. This tradition appeared in Luce's volume and became "gospel" for many people over the years.[3] Francis Taunton conducted extensive research on that unit in an effort to substantiate the validity of the statement. He ruled out the possibility that Myles' father served in this outfit since it had been deactivated from 1799 through 1858. Moreover, even after the Fifth Lancers were reactivated, in 1858, they did not serve in the Limerick area.[4] That would mean that Keogh's introduction of "Garry Owen" as the Seventh Cavalry's battle song, based on his allegedly having heard the tune as a child from his father, is virtually impossible.

But could Keogh's father have been with another unit of the British Army? Taunton did find a John Henry Keogh among the men of the Thirteenth (Duke of Cambridgeshire's) Regiment, an organization which had four depots stationed in Clonmel, comparatively near Carlow and Kilkenny Counties.[5] This same man later served with the Carlow militia and went on to enjoy a distinguished career as high sheriff (a lord lieutenant) of County Carlow. He also was "of the landlord type" and a Protestant. Consequently, he was not Myles' father,

1. Francis Taunton to David Scollan, April 1, 1964, David Scollan Papers in collection of the author. Scollan (1921-1976) lived in Auburn, New York and was a lifetime student of Myles Keogh.

2. John O'Hart, *Irish Pedigrees* vol. 1 (New York, NY: Murphy & McCarthy, 1923), 506-509.

3. Luce, *Keogh, Comanche and Custer*, 120-127.

4. Francis Taunton to David Scollan, February 18, 1964.

5. Ibid.

although the two men lived scarcely fifteen miles apart.[6] It seems, then, that John Keogh never took up arms, even temporarily.

Myles' mother belonged to the distinguished Blanchfield family of Clifden Castle in County Kilkenny.[7] Family members still live in Clifden, although the castle, which may date from Norman times, was in ruins even in Myles' day.[8] Generations of Blanchfields leased the lands of Rathgarvan (or Clifden), which includes the castle. In 1874 Miss Mary Blanchfield, Myles' aunt, held the lease. Dying in that year, she bequeathed it to her nephew.[9] The property had to be claimed within four months for him to take charge of the inheritance. Myles did return, and was able to give the land to his sister Margaret.[10]

Of Myles' ancestors, little can be said except that O'Hart refers to an uncle (John's older brother) named Patrick Keogh, "Who according to Cox's magazine, was on the 9th of June, 1798, hanged at the town of Carlow because of his connection with the United Irishmen of that period." O'Hart also gives Myles' paternal grandfather's name as James and indicates he lived from 1723 through 1779.[11]

In addition to his parents, Myles' immediate family consisted of twelve other brothers and sisters. There were five boys named, in order of their births, James, Patrick, Thomas, John, and Myles. The seven girls, also listed oldest to youngest, were Julia, Mary, Joanna, Bridget, Ellen, Margaret, and Fanny.[12] An eighth sister, Catherine, evidently died in infancy.[13] Myles' brothers James and John apparently died young, somewhat confirmed by O'Hart who listed them in 1887 as "died unmarried." Of the seven sisters, Julia was the only one listed in O'Hart as "died unmarried." Thus, of the thirteen children, nine evidently survived at least to young adulthood, though Joanna died in 1867, apparently after a long illness or some handicap. Myles seemed to hold a special place for her since he wrote:

> I often think that if Joanna had even a fair chance she would have raised very high the family she would have connected herself with. She started out in this world with a greater [?] body and spirit and God knows it often pains me to think of her now. Her life has been spent and nothing left but to groan over her countless limitations which stand out in an overwhelming dark . . . .[14]

Myles sent other letters to his family over the years after he left Ireland which tend to indicate that, as the youngest brother, he still felt very close to his brothers and sisters and the old home. This correspondence likewise suggested that Myles was closest to his brother Tom. Perhaps his relationship with his oldest brother was somewhat different since Patrick, as the eldest, may have taken the other children under his wing, disciplining them in the place of their deceased father. An excerpt from one letter to Tom hints of this: "Some way I always think now of the old family when we were together in Orchard—and do you remember old fellow how difficult Patrick found it to keep us from listening to the servants' stories in the kitchen . . . ."[15] Subsequent letters home revealed a continued longing for the warmth of his family since Myles had "a feeling that some time in the future" he would relate his experiences to the family in person "sitting all together by the fireside."[16]

From these letters one learns more than just Myles' feelings for his brothers and sisters. Another picture emerges of a relatively comfortable lifestyle complete with servants and the luxury of education. Given the hard times in Ireland, this financial stability was not shared widely by the country's population in the 19th-century. Indeed, it seems that fiscal problems struck the family later on, causing Myles to be concerned for the well-being of his sisters. Evidently, the possibility existed that they would have to leave their home.[17] For this reason, Myles hoped to be in a better position to help. He indicated:

> I am getting my money affairs in order and as soon as I get them straight I will open a banking account . . . , and as Congress proposes to raise our pay and one can live cheaply out here [in Kansas], I hope to be able easily and without any inconvenience in the least to fulfill anything and more that I have spoken of . . . [regarding financial assistance to the family].[18]

---

6. Francis Taunton to David Scollan, April 21, 1964; Francis Taunton to John S. Manion, July 16, 1967 and January 28, 1990; Francis Taunton to Robert Keogh, December 11, 1979.

7. Delores Kehoe to John S. Manion, June 21, 1968.

8. Francis Taunton to John S. Manion, April 11, 1979.

9. Francis Taunton to David Scollan, April 24, 1964; O'Hart, *Irish Pedigrees*, 507.

10. Service File, Myles Walter Keogh, Record Group 94, Document File K173 CB 1864; National Archives and Records Administration, Washington, D.C., hereinafter referred to as "Service File." Also see O'Hart, *Irish Pedigrees*, 507.

11. O'Hart, *Irish Pedigrees*, 507. This author's information about Keogh's uncle and grandfather may not be accurate. For instance, Edward MacLysaght, *Irish Families, Their Names, Arms And Origins* (Dublin: Hodges, Figges & Company, 1957), 115 mentioned one Captain Matthew Keogh (1744-1798) as being hanged "for a prominent part in the 1798 insurrection." It could be that confusion between Matthew Keogh and Patrick Keogh exists. If not, the year 1798 seems to have been a bad one for persons named Keogh! Also, upon examining Myles' grandfather's death (1779), it follows that the very latest his son John could have been born would be that year. Accordingly, Myles' father would have been at least sixty-one years-old in 1840. While not impossible, it seems that there is a missing generation or further confusion attributable to so many individuals with the name Keogh in Ireland.

12. Taken from "Register of Baptisms, 1827-1844," Microfilm Copy #928,118, Ireland, Carlow, Clonmelsh, Parish Church Leighlinbridge, Catholic Church, Dublin 1773-1880; Diocese: Kildare and Leighlin, Church of Jesus Christ, Latter-Day Saints Archives, Salt Lake City, Utah. Hereafter referred to as "Baptismal Record." This information was obtained through the research of Pat D. Gleason who went through the records from July 3, 1827 through November 16, 1844. He found that Myles' middle name was listed as "Tomas" in this document and his father's surname as "Kehoe."

13. Baptismal Records for January 28, 1838 list Catherine Keogh as being christened on that

Keogh voiced in another letter that he felt the United States provided opportunities not available in Ireland, which may allow him to leave the "next generation" at home in a "better fix than we found ourselves."[19] Subsequent exchanges with Tom followed a similar line, since it appeared that Myles continued to display concern for the family's support.[20]

In addition to his loyalty to the immediate family, Myles' maternal uncle, J. P. Blanchfield, assumed an important role. He exerted a steadying influence over Myles and his other nephews and nieces, providing a father figure for the children. Myles described his uncle as fat and once he himself began gaining weight he humorously wrote: "I shall rival, I fear, dear Uncle Blanchfield."[21] In addition, Keogh recalled his uncle as "a man of sound sense and from whom one could have valuable ideas."[22] When Myles learned of Tom's financial difficulties he asked him if he had spoken to Uncle Blanchfield about the situation.[23] Years after he left, Myles anticipated returning to Ireland to spend many happy hours with his uncle. He hoped to talk things over with him but, by February 1867, Myles began to hear reports of his uncle's declining health. He admonished Tom to "not fail to keep me posted about dear Uncle's health."[24] When Uncle Blanchfield was appointed a peace commissioner in late 1866, Myles commented that it gratified him very much but "I could not help feeling that he should have received it long ago—when he was able by good health to exercise the influence and power it confers upon him. I trust my dear brother that you will be given the same Commission in course of time. Catholic influence, however, is not very powerful in Carlow."[25] It can be inferred that Uncle Blanchfield, though a very influential man, did not possess considerable wealth. In fact, after he died sometime before September 30, 1867, Myles remarked in a letter to his sister Margaret: "My poor uncle's death grieved me but the debt has to be endured by all mortals. I am glad to think that he left what little there was to the family."[26]

Besides his uncle, Keogh left others behind in Eire. Though he departed his motherland at a tender age, Myles did develop an interest in girls before then. He would recall fondly on Christmas Eve, 1865, visiting "B-town" many years before ("B-town" was his short hand method of writing Bagenalstown, a community located a few miles south of Leighlinbridge):

> [Tom] your speaking of being at B-town reminded me of the happy evenings I spent there with you. You remember I went there frequently & was always so kindly treated. Dear Lizzy—how does she look—is she as sweet and amiable as ever. Do you know my dear fellow that outside of our own family, yourselves, the boys, etc., thinking back I take very little as fact now except in the Bagenalstown people. I feel somehow a great affection for Lizzy & Alice & Dick . . . . When you see the B-town girls, give them my regards . . . .[27]

Nor did he forget these fair friends as time passed. On his first leave to go back to Ireland in 1868, Keogh was thwarted by breaking his leg in Boston in February. While convalescing, he wrote of his disappointment in not being able to make the trip, "I did so want to see you all & then to see the girls I used to admire so much— Elizabeth [undoubtedly the previously mentioned Lizzy] and Alice—& Bessie Nowlan."[28] The next year Myles again remembered Lizzy, whom he, "always liked . . . and Alice at B-town and poor Bessie Nowlan. Fond love to all, Mag and Fan."[29]

This tenderness towards women had a special place that went beyond mere romance. Perhaps some of these feelings came from the time when young Myles suffered from typhus fever. He remembered particularly that his sister Margaret gave him excellent care while he was recovering. Recalling Margaret's ministrations, Myles, recovering from his broken leg at Willowbrook, near Auburn, New York noted on March 27, 1868: "I got Mag's kind letter & tell her that except the nursing I got when I had the Typhus fever in Orchard, I never was so well cared for since."[30]

Keogh was not just a man of the heart, however, for he had a good head on his shoulders. At least he enjoyed the benefits of considerable schooling for his era. Myles was educated at the St. Patrick's College in Carlow.[31]

HEARTH & HOME

day and gave her parents as John "Kohoe" and "Magaret" Blanchfield.

14. December 24, 1865, National Library Microfilm.

15. June 1, 1869, National Library Microfilm.

16. Ibid.

17. August 5, 1866, National Library Microfilm.

18. February 23, 1867, National Library Microfilm.

19. December 24, 1865, National Library Microfilm.

20. See for example letters of August 6, 1866; October 27, 1866 (to Myles' sister Ellen), and May 9, 1869, National Library Microfilm.

21. August 13, 1868, National Library Microfilm.

22. November 30, 1867, National Library Microfilm.

23. August 5, 1866, National Library Microfilm.

24. February 23, 1867 and September 30, 1867, National Library Microfilm.

25. February 23, 1867, National Library Microfilm.

26. Undated letter to Myles' sister Margaret Keogh (probably sent with the September 30, 1867 letter to Tom), National Library Microfilm.

27. December 25, 1865, National Library Microfilm.

28. March 29, 1868, National Library Microfilm.

29. May 5, 1869, National Library Microfilm.

30. March 27, 1868, National Library Microfilm.

31. Francis Taunton, *"Letter to the Editor," Montana, The Magazine of Western History* (Autumn, 1966), 92 and Francis Taunton to John S. Manion, June 27, 1967.

32. Marcus Bourke, *John O'Leary—A Study in Irish Separatism* (Dublin, Ireland: Harcourt Books, c. 1968), passim.
33. Service File, National Archives.
34. Hayes-McCoy, *Captain Myles Walter Keogh*, 118n.
35. Gene Autry Western Heritage Museum, Myles Keogh Collection.

He referred to it as Carlow College when he filled out his service record in 1866. Efforts to find records of Myles' school days thus far have been unsuccessful. It is known that Carlow College was described as Ireland's leading boarding school.[32] Although he made no claim to having graduated from this institution, Myles did underscore that he "was educated at Carlow Colleges and resided at my homes or colleges until I was sixteen years of age . . . ."[33]

While little can be determined about his educational background, more concrete evidence exists concerning his physical appearance. By 1860, Myles probably had reached his full height of six feet and a quarter inch. On his citizenship papers, issued in 1869, he was described as having blue eyes, brown hair, and a florid complexion.[34] From his photographs one observes he had very handsome features.[35] He particularly seemed dashing in portraits taken in uniform. Over his life, he would wear a number of martial styles. His first opportunity to don military finery would come in 1860 when he, along with some 1400 other young Irishmen, responded to a call referred to as "The Last Crusade." It was then that Pope Pius IX issued an appeal to Irishmen throughout the world to come to Italy to defend his temporal powers in the central Italian regions of Marches and Umbria. Unconfirmed family traditions indicate that Myles was employed in a bank at the time he left for Italy.

Italy was not a united country, in the first decades of the 1800s, being instead a number of independent city-states. These were easy prey for foreign countries such as France and Austria who, at various times, ruled parts of the peninsula. The city-states were often engaged in internecine warfare. There was an underlying belief that Italy could free itself from foreign rule. A movement to bring together all of the Italian peninsula was started, eventually resulting in the united Italy of today. This unification movement was known as the *Risorgimento*, and included among its leaders were Giuseppe Garibaldi and Giuseppe Mazzini.

By the late 1850s, the kingdom of Piedmont-Sardinia, ruled by King Victor Emmanuel II, controlled the north. Austria ruled the northeastern regions, including Venetia and Lombardy. War broke out between Piedmont-Sardinia and Austria in April 1859. France supported the Piedmontese and the Piedmontese, under Garibaldi, emerged victorious. As a result, Piedmont-Sardinia acquired the province of Lombardy from Austria. When peace returned, Garibaldi, now a popular figure, turned his attentions to the south to engage the armies of the Francis II, the King of Naples, and went on to free that part of Italy from foreign domination.

Meanwhile, King Victor Emmanuel II had ambitions on central Italy. Situated like a wide belt across the Italian boot were the Papal States, separating the forces of King Victor Emmanuel II in the north from Garibaldi's in the south. The States of the Church comprised the Patrimony of St. Peter, bordering on the Tyrrhenian Sea to the west; the inland state of Umbria, including the cities of Spoleto and Perugia; and the Marches on the Adriatic Sea, including the cities of Ancona and Castelfidardo. The Patrimony also included the City of Rome which, in 1860, was still occupied by the French to protect the temporal powers of Pius IX. This resulted from events in 1848 and 1849 when, threatened by liberal forces within the Papal States, Pius was forced to flee Rome. The city then was occupied by a group of volunteers under Garibaldi until April 1849, when a French army arrived to confront him. The French forces defeated Garibaldi causing his army to flee into central Italy. At that time, Pius returned to Rome and the French remained there to protect his government until 1860, the year Keogh would rally to the Pope's support.

It was the time for decisions for the Piedmontese. They could seize the initiative in the unification movement if they acted quickly to annex Parma, Modena, Tuscany, Romagna, and the Papal States. If they could accomplish these objectives before Garibaldi could defeat the King of Naples and invade those regions, King Victor Emmanuel would emerge as the reigning power when the unification was completed.

However, several obstacles lay in the path of King Victor Emmanuel and his Prime Minister, Count Camillo Benso di Cavour. If their army marched south, the Piedmontese risked another war with Austria, which might attack from the north. A Piedmontese invasion of these regions, particularly the Papal States, also might provoke a war with France whose armies were already in Rome protecting the Papal government.

Annexing Parma, Modena, Tuscany, and Romagna proved to be no problem. The people there, inspired by the Piedmontese victory over Austria and caught up with the spirit of unification, voted to unite with Sardinia-Piedmont. If it had been put to a popular vote, the peasants of Umbria and the Marches, weary of the outmoded methods of an ecclesiastical government, also might have voted to join the Sardinia-Piedmont State. But such a plebescite was unthinkable to Pope Pius. Even though his clerical government had proved to be an impractical anachronism by 1860, the Pope opposed any thought of relinquishing his temporal powers over these States of the Church, feeling it his holy duty to turn over to his successor the lands placed in his charge when he had assumed power.

It was apparent to Prime Minister Cavour that an invasion of the Papal lands was necessary if these states were to be annexed. But first, he must somehow convince Napoleon III of France not to interfere. Cavour used strong arguments. He agreed to cede the northwestern regions of Savoy and Nice, but France could well have demanded this territory anyway in return for the help it gave Piedmont-Sardinia in achieving its victory over Austria in 1859.[36] Cavour also could promise to leave the French occupied Patrimony of St. Peter out of his invasion plans.

But Cavour was able to give Napoleon III a further reason to remain neutral in the event of an invasion of the Papal states. Napoleon was not pleased particularly with the prospect of a unified Italy, a goal likely to be pursued more vigorsly by Garibaldi than by King Victor Emmanuel. It virtually was certain that Garibaldi would continue northward to invade the States of the Church, as soon as he completed freeing the south. If the Piedmontese could invade and annex the Papal States before Garibaldi, it would be to France's advantage.

Napoleon gave his passive consent for the invasion of the Papal States, saying "Faites viet"—what thou doest

do quickly."[37] So far as was possible, this decision was kept secret as Napoleon III did not wish to offend the Catholics in France. Publicly, he declared his opposition to the invasion, even breaking off relations with the Piedmontese to appease the Catholics. Napoleon was truly in a difficult diplomatic situation. Garibaldi was popular, as was his cause. For Napoleon to have been backed into a position of opposing either Garibaldi or the Piedmontese to protect the Papal States in order to block the unification process, would have put him in a bad light with non-Catholics everywhere.

The Piedmontese decided to go ahead with their plans even though Austria might intervene. Well aware of the discontent of the peasants of Umbria and the Marches, the Piedmontese preceded their main thrust by sending raiders into these areas to stir up an insurrection. They proposed to use the ensuing unrest as justification for the invasion. The raiders, entering Umbria and the Marches from newly-annexed Romagna and Tuscany to the north, could easily dash across the border to create havoc. One historian reported that the roving bands were organized, armed, and assisted by revolutionary committees. They would rush through several towns and "tear down the Papal emblems and hoist the tricolor and proclaim far and wide that the district was in revolt and had declared for a united Italy."[38] Brochures were distributed in an attempt to persuade the Pope to give up his sovereignty over the States of the Church "in return either for money or for some nominal vicariate which might save his face and perhaps salve his conscience."[39]

The Papal government was powerless to prevent these raids, which were subjecting the Pope to ridicule throughout the world. The army of the Papal States was too small to put an end to these forays. Besides, many of the Papal soldiers were divided in their loyalties, perhaps on the side of the Pope in spiritual matters but at the same time favoring Italian unification.

Due to this, the Papal government issued a call to Catholics throughout Europe for men and arms to be sent to Italy to aid in defending the Pope's temporal powers. Outwardly, it was a call to raise an army of sufficient size to bring order back to the Papal States and

36. G. F. H. Berkeley, *The Irish Battalion in the Papal Army* (Dublin & Cork, Ireland: The Talbot Press Limited, 1929), 4.
37. G. M. Trevelyan, *Garibaldi and the Making of Italy* (New York, NY: Longmans, Green & Company, 1928), 212.
38. Berkeley, *The Irish Battalion*, 6.
39. Ibid., 4.

This faded picture of Myles Keogh in his Papal uniform was copied from an original *carte de visite* which Henry Nowlan recovered some time after the Battle of the Little Big Horn. Nowlan had duplicates made and sent them to Keogh's family. *Courtesy of Gene Autry Western Heritage Museum.*

---

40. Ibid., 6.

41. Ampthill Odo William Leopald Russell, [ed. by Noel Blakiston], *The Roman Question* (London: Chapman & Hill, 1962), 44.

42. Mary Cryan Pancani, "The Last Crusade," *Cara*, the in-flight magazine of Aer Lingus (January, 1988), 1 and Berkeley, *The Irish Battalion*, 21.

43. Hayes-McCoy, *Captain Myles Walter Keogh*, 3.

44. Berkeley, *The Irish Battalion*, 21 and 35; Pancani, "Last Crusade," 1.

45. September 30, 1867, National Library Microfilm.

46. Berkeley, *The Irish Battalion*, 22,

to repel the raiders. The Papal government was under no illusion that it could repel a full scale invasion even if its army were augmented by Catholics from elsewhere in Europe. The Papal States, not yet aware of the pact made between Napoleon and Cavour, had reason to feel secure from such an invasion under the terms of the 1815 Treaty of Vienna, wherein Europe's leading powers guaranteed the sovereignty of the States of the Church.[40]

In early March 1860 Papal emissaries arrived in Dublin to negotiate sending an Irish battalion to Italy. Papal officials had felt some doubts at first as to whether they could raise an such a battalion. Knowing the cheapness of wine in Italy and believing the stereotype of the Irish tendency to over imbibe, some felt the Italian tour might prove fatal to many. Then there was the Foreign Enlistment Act, an English law forbidding the recruitment of British subjects to fight for other countries.[41]

But the situation in the Papal States had become so critical, by 1860, that the task of raising a battalion was begun. The Irish, because of the sympathetic support given by Pius IX during the great potato famine of 1848-1849, felt an extraordinary debt of gratitude to the Pope—even beyond their traditional loyalty to the Roman Catholic Church. Thus, the call for volunteers, despite the legal difficulties, was met with enthusiastic support. Throughout Ireland, speeches and sermons urged young men to join the crusade. Eventually, over 1400 responded and made the journey to Italy. Few knew or cared about the politics of Italy and most were making their first trip away from home.

Myles Keogh was one of those who answered the call. He just would have turned twenty in March 1860, though he states in his service record that he left for Italy when he was only sixteen years of age. Keogh was joined by Irishmen from all walks of life. There were peasants, farmers, men from the working-classes, lawyers, doctors, medical students, a graduate of Sandringham Military Academy, and some relatives of prelates, one being nineteen year-old Joseph O'Keeffe, a nephew of the Bishop of Cork. Twenty members of the Cork police force resigned their posts and gave up good salaries to join the crusade. Daniel J. Keily, from Waterford, more than ten years older than Myles, also rallied to the cause. Keogh, O'Keeffe, and Keily became close friends, a friendship which extended into their Civil War service, when all three joined the Union forces.[42]

Along with many fellow countrymen, Myles said goodbye to his family at Carlow's newly-constructed railway station in the spring of 1860, apparently being among the first of the Irish Volunteers. Keogh may have sacrificed a good position in his own country by answering this call during a critical year in his emerging career.[43]

Whatever the personal sacrifice, if any, he had charted a new course, but not one which all agreed upon. Because of divided sentiments in Britain, many opposed the formation of an Irish battalion and those who joined met with hostility when they returned—to the extent that they could not resume their former careers. Added to this, there were vocal anti-Papal and pro-Italian unity elements in Britain. The London newspapers were particularly vicious in their attacks on the battalion, accusing the Irish of being plunderers, ne'er-do-wells and, worst of all, mercenaries, when in fact they were paid a pittance and had no chance for advancement.[44]

Myles left without even consulting his Uncle Blanchfield, apparently fearing his disapproval. In 1867, when he learned that his uncle had died, Myles wrote:

> It is a great loss to you all, poor dear old fellow—I hoped to see him once more, but it is now too late. I always felt sorry that I did not acquaint him with my intentions of going to Italy. I trust he understood however that I never intended a slight to him by not asking his advice.[45]

It is not known how Myles traveled to Italy but it required some tricky maneuvering to circumvent the Foreign Enlistment Act. Stiff fines and imprisonment faced those guilty of helping foreign enlistees and any master of a ship who knowingly transported such persons was liable to a fine of fifty pounds. It was difficult for the government to enforce this law as there were some Garibaldians also leaving from the British Isles.[46]

Various loopholes enabled Irishmen to journey to Italy. Some signed enrollment letters in Belgium using names other than their own. When it was determined that men could legally enroll as policemen or "gendarmes" for the Papal States, groups of Irish volunteers used this to enter the service. Some resorted to traveling in groups of twenty to forty, accompanied by priests, and called themselves pilgrims, emigrants, or workmen.[47] Others took a route via Hull, Antwerp, Vienna, and Trieste, while still more journeyed through Marseilles and Civita Vecchia, a port city situated a few miles north of Rome.[48]

Referring to his journey, Myles wrote, "I then traveled over Europe & in six months afterwards entered service in Italy, where I served as 2nd Lt. in an Infantry Rgt. for two years and a half . . . ."[49] Myles did not leave a record of the route he took but, passage through Vienna seems the most likely, though Myles' recollection that it took six months seems two months too long. It appears that during this extended stay in Vienna (lasting from the spring months until a few days before July 5, 1860, when they arrived at Ancona), the Irish Volunteers having previous military experience were examined to select the four who later would be made captains and serve as the company commanders of the four Irish companies which were to be garrisoned at Ancona. At the same time, no doubt, those who were to become subalterns also were selected from among the raw recruits. The four captains were Irishmen who were veterans of the Austrian Army and, after they were gazetted as captains during the first week of August 1860, Myles Keogh was among those appointed second lieutenant on August 7. Since he had no previous military experience prior to leaving Ireland, one may surmise Myles demonstrated his potential as a military officer during his stay in Vienna. He was selected from among some 450 recruits at Ancona. Myles' friend, Joseph O'Keeffe, also received an appointment as second lieutenant, possibly on the same day as Myles. Daniel Keily, who had been a midshipman in the British navy, became a full lieutenant.[50] Another Irishman, John Joseph Coppinger, born in Cork in 1834, had spent five years in the British Army before obtaining his captain's commission with the Papacy.

Mere military titles do not make an army, however. The experience of the Irish in Italy proved to be a disaster, not only because the Pope's forces were defeated rather easily when the Piedmontese finally invaded the States of the Church on September 11, 1860 but also because of the conditions under which they had to train prior to the fighting. They had been led to believe that their pay would be much more than it was. They had been told they would receive two shillings a day but instead were paid "5 bajocchis" (about fourpence).[51]

Furthermore, the climate was hot and miserable during their training period. They were poorly armed, some never receiving weapons at all. Worst of all, the Irish never got to serve as a single national unit, being dispersed instead among the Italians, French, Austrians, Belgians, Swiss, Poles, and Bohemians (Czechs) who also came to the aid of Pius IX. Although conditions improved somewhat between the time the volunteers arrived and the start of the war in September, morale and discipline were initially at the lowest level imaginable. The Italians, natives of the Papal States and not particularly motivated towards the Pope's cause, usually were undisciplined and, for the most part, hated by the foreigners with whom they were to serve. They were suspected, in many instances, of being spies for the raiders from the north and not likely to fight as ardently as, say, the Irish who traveled thousands of miles to defend a cause they deeply believed in. The residents of Ancona, where the Irish who arrived with Myles were garrisoned, also were unaccomodating, shouting taunts at the foreigners. The men dared not walk through the streets alone at night, and no officer ventured out unarmed.

There are recorded instances of the Irish fighting among themselves, injuring at one time some of their

HEARTH & HOME

47. Pancani, "Last Crusade," 2 and Russell, *The Roman Question*, 101.

48. Berkeley, *The Irish Battalion*, 22. Russell, *The Roman Question*, 102 reported that the Pope expected 1000 Irish recruits to arrive at Ancona, Italy by way of Belgium and Trieste.

49. Service File, National Archives.

50. Berkeley, *The Irish Battalion*, 68ff, 70, 75, Appendices C & D.

51. Russell, *The Roman Question*, 112.

Lieutenant Keogh, as an officer of the Company of St. Patrick in Rome, wears his *Medaglia di Pro Petri Sede* (a Papal campaign medal) on his green uniform trimmed in gold. *Courtesy of John Monahan.*

52. Ibid, 112.
53. Berkeley, *The Irish Battalion*, Appendix E.
54. Ibid., 7 and 22.
55. Ibid., 68.
56. Pancani, "Last Crusade," 3.
57. Ibid, 2 and Berkeley, *The Irish Battalion*, 34, 36, 69, 110, and 221.
58. Ibid, 22 and Appendix E.
59. Trevelyan, *Garibaldi*, 208.
60. Berkeley, *The Irish Battalion*, 21 and 23; "Lamoriciére," *The New Encyclopedia Britannica* VII (Chicago, IL: Encyclopedia Britannica, 1988, 15th ed.), 124. See also John Keegan and Andrew Wheatcroft, *Who's Who in Military History* (New York, NY: William Morrow & Co. Inc., 1976), 188.
61. Berkeley, *The Irish Battalion*, 108.
62. Hennessy, *The Wild Geese*, Figure 12.
63. Ibid., 141ff and Berkeley, *The Irish Battalion*, 218.

own officers and an Austrian non-commissioned officer. Once the Irish even set fire to their barracks.[52] Some 1400 Irishmen arrived in Italy but, because of resignations, disgust, the weeding out of malcontents, and desertions, only around 1036 remained to help repel the invasion.[53]

In April 1860, Catholic recruits began to report for duty. The Irish were among the last to arrive, coming in from late May through the end of July.[54] In fact, a large contingent of 538 men and 5 officers from Ireland appeared in Ancona on July 5 having traveled via Vienna. Keogh very well might have been in this group.[55]

Once they had reported, the Irish, and all the other foreign volunteers, were exposed to propaganda urging them to desert the Papal Army. When British ships entered the harbor at Ancona, the crew invited some Irishmen aboard and tempted them with offers of jobs as stokers, paying four pounds a month, an enormous sum compared to pay in the Pope's service.[56]

Still other problems faced the new recruits. The Irish were poorly clothed, worse than any other nationality serving in the Papal Army. At the time of the invasion, some of the men evidently had to use the same clothes that they had worn when they arrived in Italy, six or eight weeks before. Some uniforms were available, these being worn and dirty leftovers from Austria, surplus from previous wars. They consisted of a blue tunic with wide tails, red breeches, and white canvas gaiters. Some were embarrassingly small. Once, for instance, an Irish volunteer measuring six foot three was compelled to squeeze into clothing made for a soldier five foot four. Their own green uniforms never arrived, in fact they were never issued and, as a result, those having uniforms so resembled the foreigners that they had no external sign of their national identity. The Irish were disappointed in the extreme at not being able to wear their own green and gold uniforms. Only a few of the officers had the time and the money to have a tailor make them the regulation pattern designed for the Irish Battalion and even then the gold and green colors were referred to derisively as "eggs and spinach."[57]

Uniforms or no uniforms, the Irish were divided into eight companies. Four of these, consisting of 456 officers and men, were stationed at Ancona and the other four, consisting of 580 officers and men, were posted to Spoleto, a fortress town located in the center of the peninsula in the province of Umbria. The men at Ancona and Spoleto, where Coppinger was stationed, never trained together. In fact, they saw nothing of each other.[58]

The entire Papal army consisted of some 18,300 men of ten nationalities. There were three official languages, English not being one, which added to the difficulties of the Irish soldiers. The Irish trained with the men of the nine other nationalities, mainly at Ancona and Spoleto. At Ancona, the Irish drilled with around 6000 Austrian veterans.[59] In command of the Irish unit, the Battalion of St. Patrick, was Irishman Major Myles O'Reilly. In overall command of the Papal Army was General Louis Christophe Léon Juchault de Lamoriciére, a Frenchman, considered by many to be one of finest generals in Europe.[60] When it began in September 11, 1860, the invasion was a fiasco for de Lamoriciére's unprepared Papal forces.[61] There were 33,000 Piedmontese facing the Papacy's 18,300. Almost immediately, Perugia and Spoleto fell, to the delight of the natives. Keogh did not participate in the defense of Spoleto, but the Irish who fought there were universally acclaimed for their fighting ability.

Although he took no part in this action, a medal was struck showing Myles standing before the Rocco at Spoleto. An illustration of this medal—the image does not look too much like him—is labeled *"Captain Myles Keogh at the Battle of Spoleto"* and appears in *The Wild Geese*. So much for historical accuracy and the origin of one of the many Keogh legends![62]

Coppinger, who held the rank of captain, played an important role at Spoleto, where he was wounded. In the 1890s he would become one of the better known generals in the United States Army, while earlier, his name was linked with Keogh in the Civil War.[63]

Meanwhile, General Lamoriciére, with a detachment of some 6500 men, including 108 members of the Battalion of St. Patrick, fled Umbria and headed northeast towards Ancona, hoping to hold out on the faint possibility that either France or Austria would intervene in the war.[64] Myles erroneously thought Lamoriciére had 8000 men with him when he wrote his mother on September 17 from Ancona.[65]

On September 16, 1860, Lamoriciére's force was intercepted by 16,500 Piedmontese at Castelfidardo, some eight miles southwest of Ancona.[66] The troops in Ancona anxiously were expecting the arrival of Lamoriciére. Part of the garrison marched out on more than one occasion to cooperate with Lamoriciére but, being carefully watched by the northern Italians, had to return to Ancona. One of these sorties occurred on Tuesday, September 18.[67] Myles wrote that he had participated in such a reconnaissance three days earlier, on Saturday, September 15:

> My dearest Mother
> We expect to have an engagement every day. Our 450 men with 200 others & 2 pieces of cannon made a reconnaissance [sic] on Saturday evening. We saw the enemy who keeps his outposts within 5 miles of this. Lamoriciére is reported today with 5000 men if so we may have an engagement tomorrow.[68]

Myles' forecast proved accurate. On September 18, the Papal forces were defeated decisively at Castelfidardo in the bloodiest engagement of the entire war. Lamoriciére managed to limp into Ancona but with only forty-five out of the 6500 men who had started out with him from Umbria, the rest being either killed or captured at Castelfidardo or along a seacoast track leading to Ancona. Many of Lamoriciére's command literally were driven into the Adriatic by the north Italians, who pursued them relentlessly.[69]

The siege of Ancona began almost immediately. The harbor city was bombarded intensely, with well placed artillery. The Papal artillery responded defiantly. Ancona then was garrisoned by around 3000 Papal troops housed mostly in Lazzareto barracks. Overlooking the town were massive fortifications.

But the real threat to Ancona came from the sea. On September 11, the day the invasion started, the Piedmontese fleet, under Admiral Persano, was dispatched from Naples and headed for Ancona's harbor. During the siege, which lasted until September 29, the Piedmontese stormed the outer works several times. Both sides showed great courage. The Governor of Ancona was impressed by the zeal of the small body of Irish defending the town, which included Myles Keogh. The Governor seems to have been intrigued by their eccentric conduct. When under fire, they would chant ballads and their officers would have great difficulty in restraining them from constantly leaping over the battlements to hurl defiance at the infidel, or to applaud the work of the Papal artillery.[70]

Father John McDermott, a chaplain to the troops in Ancona, told of how the men withstood the siege:

> Our poor fellows are in great heart, cheering, etc.
> I am really fatigued hearing their Confessions and preparing them to die happily but the fatigue of last night and a little freedom jug with hated liquor has (I fear) made a few of them forget themselves.[71]

Another account of the role the four companies of Irish troops played in the defense of Ancona is provided by Francis "Frank" Russell, Count of Killough, who commanded Irish Troop No. 4, the unit in which Keogh, Keily, and O'Keeffe may have served during the siege. Russell had been in the First Regiment of the French Legion in Rome when, on May 10, 1858, he became an officer in the Papal forces. Because the events described by Russell also were witnessed by Keogh, his observations shed light on the general activities of this portion of Myles' life.[72]

Russell maintained that 45,000 Piedmontese were in the force attacking Ancona, the vanguard being camped within a league of Ancona's outlying entrenchments. Upon the arrival of Persano's fleet, the Piedmontese were able to launch a simultaneous land and sea attack. Persano's fleet consisted of 400 gunships. On land, the Piedmontese had 200 siege guns and artillery pieces with

---

64. Trevelyan, *Garibaldi*, 219ff; Berkeley, *The Irish Brigade*, 108.
65. Service File, National Archives, and September 17, 1860, Myles Keogh to His Mother, National Library Microfilm.
66. Trevelyan, *Garibaldi*, 220.
67. Ibid., 223, footnote 1.
68. September 17, 1860, National Library Microfilm. The 450 men Keogh mentioned corresponded closely to the figure found in Berkeley, *The Irish Battalion*, Appendix E, which was 456 at Ancona.
69. Trevelyan, *Garibaldi*, 223.
70. Ibid., 224ff; Berkeley, *The Irish Battalion*, 71.
71. Pancani, "Last Crusade," 3.
72. Le Count Frank Russell-Killough, *Dix Annees Au Service Pontifical* (Paris: Victor Palme Libaire-Editeur, 1871) covers Russell's ten years in Papal service. The author is grateful to Brian Pohanka who translated extensive portions of this book for him.

a range double that of those of the Papal army. The Pope's artillery included only 149 assorted pieces. In turn, the Papal forces numbered 4,200 infantry with a truly international flavor, as indicated by Lamoriciére as follows:

> One native [Italian] regiment of the line; Two companies and a small detachment of the 1st Swiss Regiment which escaped from the disaster of Castelfidardo; Three and a half battalions of German chasseurs; Four companies of the regiment of St. Patrick (Irish); A few police; Four hundred artillerymen; A detachment of engineers . . . . [73]

Russell indicated that his company "occupied a middle-sized bastion situated at the extreme east of camp."[74] Without cover from the elements "during the first days" and encamped in the open on "ground, which had been freshly dug up to create the defenses ordered by the commander-in-chief," which, "at the first rain turned into thick mud," his men suffered terribly from the cold and fatigue. Although "without any shelter but the sky," these troops "did not complain, as their conduct in other circumstances had made me fear. All night long they rested on this sodden earth, under pouring rain, but without the slightest murmur of complaint." In fact, "The sight of the enemy had excited their ardor, and brought forth their military virtues." The harsh realities of war had brought out the fighting spirit in Keogh's comrades. Russell remarked further: "Strange thing! It took only a few shells exploding to turn these intractable peasants into sober soldiers, patient, warlike, capable of any sacrifice." These men were not downcast either, as indicated by their actions in the evening. Russell noted that:

> In the middle of my bastion a fire was lit, around which was grouped at random and wherever they found themselves, officers and soldiers; the seats of honor were always saved for the former, consisting for the most part of upside-down wheelbarrows, water kegs, old crates. Night fell, flasks were passed about, pipes lit, tongues wagged; and the hotter the day's fighting had been, the more lively the discussions, each telling of his prowess, true or false. It was like the conversation of every bivouac in the world from the siege of Troy, of classic memory, to that of Sebastopol.[75]

While these exchanges took place, the Piedmontese captured an advance post, Monte Pelago, and used this position to lay a heavy artillery fire upon Russell and his command. He instructed his men to build a traverse, but the completed fortification proved to be short-lived. The next day their position, Bastion No. 8, fell.

Across the bay a decisive battle raged, one that would seal the fate of the beleaguered forces at Ancona. The Piedmontese kept up an unrelenting artillery barrage on the fortifications which defended the entrance to the harbor. During the battle a battery occupied by the Papal forces took a direct hit, probably in its magazine. According to Russell:

> A tremendous explosion occurred, and an immense jet of flame, accompanied by a thousand pieces of stone and bronze, hurtled skyward, then fell on all sides like a deadly rainstorm. The falling debris obliterated the heavy pontoons that held the chain across the entrance to the harbor, leaving a gap of 500 meters open to the enemy . . . it was our death knell.[76]

With this blow, the defense of Ancona collapsed.[77]

After only eighteen days, the Papal War of 1860 had ended. Overall, the Pope's army received reasonable treatment from the victors, who were mindful that the eyes of the Catholic world were upon them.[78] Indeed, Russell asserted that the enemy soldiers, "Seemed to show us more respect than the population of the town [Ancona]," which they were leaving. Just as the prisoners of war arrived on the outskirts, "and at the moment that the last man passed through the gates of this unfortunate city," Russell judged "the moment to be right" to raise his "voice in a loud hurrah of farewell. 'Hurrah for the Pope!' and every voice repeated the shout at the top of their lungs; the walls, the city, the harbor, the ocean itself reverberated with the sound." Somewhat shocked, the Piedmontese guards "looked at one another in puzzlement trying to figure out what this bizarre noise was all

---

73. The above information was based upon ibid., 167-169.
74. Ibid., 173-177 provided the basis for the description of life during the siege of Ancona.
75. Ibid., 177-183.
76. Ibid., 184-185.
77. Trevelyan, *Garibaldi*, 225.
78. Ibid, 225.

about...." Then, one of their non-commissioned officers commented, "in a knowing way: 'Bah! Let them do it, they are Irish.' "[79]

Two days after this last hurrah, the Irish enlisted men were separated from their officers. The latter sailed on the ship *Conte di Cavour*, while the rank and file traveled overland. Their common destination was the city of Genoa. During the "long and monotonous crossing" the ship ran aground on a sand bar. Efforts to free the keel failed at first, which annoyed Lamoriciére. Russell wished to make a good impression, since Lamoriciére had instructed him to help correct the situation. Hoping to succeed where the Italians had failed, Russell asked Daniel Keily, who had served on a British man-of-war, to assist the ship's captain. Keily agreed, and some time later, the vessel was freed.[80]

Once they had overcome this obstacle, the remainder of the voyage went by without further incident. The Irish enlisted men, meanwhile, had a long and difficult march across the Italian peninsula and were subjected to indignities along the way. Making from twenty to thirty miles a day, the pace was particularly difficult for the wounded. Many fell by the wayside, unable to continue. After they recovered, they had to find their own way home, some wandering aimlessly over the countryside, penniless, awaiting passage back to Ireland. Some never made it home at all, dying in scattered places throughout northern Italy, or as far away as Paris.[81]

Those who survived also suffered once they arrived in Genoa. Russell recounted:

> ... it was my poor Irish, crowded in that great cistern of bricks on the outskirts of the city, without extra clothing to cover their exhausted bodies than the miserable shreds of a uniform that had gone through all the rigors of the campaign, having nothing to eat but stale macaroni and water, served meagerly at noon in a common pot by a filthy prison guard.[82]

Russell's efforts to obtain better rations for his men supposedly ran up against British opposition. Eventually, he managed to secure his own freedom, then went on to Rome where he joined the Papal authorities in negotiations to bring about the release of the other prisoners. Success followed and "some thirty junior officers" joined him in Rome, some of them being "destined to serve as the nucleus of a new corps...."[83]

Myles Keogh was one of those officers. With the defeat of the Papal forces at Ancona, the Battalion of St. Patrick perforce was disbanded. However, Papal officials decided to form the Company of St. Patrick to serve in the reorganized, albeit greatly reduced, Papal Army, which would be garrisoned in the one remaining Papal State, the Vatican. The formation of this unit acknowledged the service of the Irish to their Pontiff and kept alive the name of the old outfit.

Of the thirty-five or thirty-six officers with previous service, thirteen either joined or tried to join this new company—more than were needed, so a waiting list had to be made up. Those selected were the men who had gained the best reputation during the 1860 campaign. Myles Keogh was one of those retained as a second lieutenant, and so was his friend Joseph O'Keeffe. Dan Keily became a lieutenant, while Russell donned the epaulets of a captain which made him, initially at least, the unit's ranking officer. Some of the Irish enlisted men joined the Company, but not nearly in the same proportion as the officers. In fact, the outfit never numbered more than forty-six during the entire period of its existence. The short-lived company, founded on November 8, 1860, was disbanded on September 30, 1862, by which time it had dwindled to only twenty-two men. Upon the dissolution of the Company of St. Patrick, some of its members joined the Papal Zouaves.[84]

Before this, however, Keogh spent time in the neighborhood of Rome and in the Vatican itself. Life was somewhat slow-paced, with little prospect of any action since the French still provided an umbrella-force in the area. Perhaps Keogh learned more of parades than of arms during these days, parades in which he carried his sword in slow ceremonial marches from San Angelo to St. Peter's. Myles also may have mounted the Janiculum, a hill in Rome on the right bank of the Tiber opposite

79. Russell, *Dix Annees*, 193-197.
80. Ibid., 195-197.
81. Berkeley, *The Irish Battalion*, 218-220. According to the New York City *Irish American* (January 5, 1861), 1. The traders of Limerick, specifically a Mr. Carrick, promoted a movement in the Parish of St. Mary's to bring some of the men home. See also Hennessy, *The Wild Geese*, 142.
82. Russell, *Dix Annees*, 197-198.
83. Ibid., 202.
84. Berkeley, *The Irish Battalion*, Appendix D.

85. Hayes-McCoy, *Captain Myles Walter Keogh*, 5.

86. Regio Archivio di Stato, Rome, Busta 1861, foglio no. 40, Ministero delle Armi Pontificie, September 30, 1861 (copy from the collection of Colonel Jim Kehoe).

87. Berkeley, *The Irish Battalion*, 3; Trevelyan, *Garibaldi*, 204.

88. Harold Earl Hammond, ed. *Diary of A Union Lady, 1861-1865* (New York, NY: Funk and Wagnalls Company, 1962), 239.

89. "Pope Pius IX In Rome; Expulsion of Protestant Worship from Rome," *Harpers Weekly* (February 9, 1867), 84.

90. February 23, 1867, National Library Microfilm.

91. Myles confessed to Tom, "it is three years & a half since I heard mass except for one celebrated in a tent. . . . " June 1, 1869, National Library Microfilm. Elizabeth Custer also claimed that in the Seventh Cavalry there was a captain who had served the Pope and who "was a Romanist, but not an ultra one. . . . " On occasion, he would remark, " 'Why, I have so many notices of excommunication I feel strange if I waken and don't find one waiting for me every morning now.' "

Elizabeth Custer, *Following the Guidon* (Norman, OK: University of Oklahoma Press, 1966), 150-151. It is impossible to tell whether Mrs. Custer's story was true or just added color to her narrative.

---

the Seven Hills, to look down across the river at the former glories of Imperial Rome.[85] Even with site-seeing and other opportunities, Keogh undoubtedly must have become bored, homesick, and anxious about his career and future at this time.

In these days he found himself among the officers and men posted at Angani, south of Rome, along with Keily, Second Lieutenants William F. Stafford and James D'Arcy, Surgeon P. O'Flynn, and Chaplain Edward MacLoughlin. The whole contingent consisted of only these officers and thirty-five enlisted men, plus six in the hospital.[86]

While still serving near Rome, however, Keogh experienced disillusionment with the "narrow minded advisers of the Pope." Evidently, several of the inhabitants of the remaining Papal territory had come to resent the "inferior priests" who tended to the daily governmental affairs that appointed or elected lay persons performed in non-clerical societies. But the Pope, in the exercise of his temporal powers, employed clergymen to manage such affairs. Clergy served as legislators and administrators. With the power vested in these clerics, accountable only to the *curia* and not to the people, certain temptations, corruptive influences, and other abuses of power came to the fore. In consequence, the inhabitants of the States of the Church, incited by the unification movement, had come to resent their priestly officials.[87]

Myles and other Irishmen, mostly devout Catholics, could not help but see the results of these practices and were appalled by the conduct of some of the priests, having observed in Ireland dedicated clergymen performing only spiritual duties. After coming to America, Keily gave a grim account of the condition of the priests in Italy and said he feared to bring his Irish soldiers, whose faith was so pure and fervent, into the towns lest they witness the ill conduct and loose lives of the local clergy, who mostly kept coffee houses and engaged in other personal pursuits.[88]

Keogh was similarly scornful. He, too, denounced the conduct of the Roman clergy, a denunciation verging on anger. These feelings continued long after he had left Italy, as indicated in a February 23, 1867 letter to his brother Tom. What triggered this outburst was the Pope's prohibition against American Protestants being allowed to hold religious services in Rome. The United States had a resident minister there and he attempted to use the American legation's chapel for this purpose, but the Papal authorities banned him from doing so. For this reason, and because of a certain perceived friendliness to the Southern cause on the part of the Vatican, Myles was not pleased with the Holy See.[89]

Keogh launched into his critique:

> By way of speaking of Catholicism, it grieved most Catholics in this Country exceedingly to hear of the action of the Roman Govt't. in turning out reformed religionists from Rome. Rest assured, dear Tom, that the time is past for such proceedings and it can only impair the Church by showing to the World that intolerance in religious matters, now only heard of in Savage and barbarous Countries, is flourishing and extending under the rule of the Head of the Catholic Church. Times are too much ahead for such things . . . .

He concluded, " . . . *ignorant*, narrow minded Italian Churchmen" whom he knew to be "scoundrels" that had "scandalized" him by "their licentious conduct, and manners and habits," while he had served in Italy, were contrary to everything he had been taught about the proper role of clergy. He had turned to what he thought was an American view and adopted the attitude of his new home, which meant that "all religions are in the same boat, and be you Catholic or Protestant, you are judged only by your merits as a man . . . . "[90] Later, he would describe himself as a lapsed Catholic, a condition which may have grown out of his feelings about the Roman clergy to some extent.[91]

Just as Keogh and his comrades came to view their lot in the Papal service as being less than ideal, the American Civil War erupted. With the fall of Fort Sumter on April 12, 1861, President Abraham Lincoln called for 75,000 militia to fight for the North. Soon, both the Union and Confederacy were in need of trained and educated officers and each dispatched agents to Europe

Myles would leave his brother Thomas, sister Marian (standing next to Tom's left), and other family members to go off to a military career. Many of Myles' surviving letters were written to Tom, who remained in Ireland. *From a photograph by Lafayette of Dublin, courtesy of Gary Keogh.*

to sign up volunteers. Competition in this endeavor was strong, but the Union attracted more recruits, particularly among the Irish who had emigrated in greater numbers to the Northern states during the antebellum era. Still, the Confederacy made considerable efforts to gain support, sending Bishop Patrick Lynch and Father John Bannon to Ireland for example, to speak on behalf of their cause.[92]

The Union responded in a similar manner by enlisting the aid of such prominent clergymen as Archbishop John Hughes and Archbishop John Baptist Purcell, long time associates and advisors to William H. Seward, Governor of New York and eventually secretary of state under Lincoln. These men traveled to Ireland and Italy where they recruited veterans of the Papal War of 1860 for the Union.[93]

Seward came to be a driving force in such efforts, being convinced of the need to commission foreign officers "of military education and experience" into the service of the United States. Not only would they provide leaders for the North but also their "honorable employment" by the Union would deny their talents to Confederacy.[94] Lincoln even attempted to recruit Giuseppe Garibaldi to fight under the stars and stripes.[95] The Catholic clerics, however, set their sights on the Irish, such as Coppinger.[96]

Likewise, Archbishops Hughes and Purcell directed their attentions towards Keogh, Keily, and O'Keeffe, trying to entice them to America to fight for the Union. For instance, Myles met Archbishop Purcell in Rome according to a letter written by Richard J. Kehoe in 1863.[97] Moreover, Archbishop Hughes effectively endorsed the three men in his March 2, 1862 letter to Secretary of State William Seward. He also championed Keogh and Keily in another letter to Secretary of War Edwin Stanton.[98] It seems that Keily played an important role by encouraging his comrades to seek their fortunes in the American military.

Not long after meeting these Union delegates, Keogh, Keily, and O'Keeffe decided to resign their commissions in the Company of St. Patrick. These were adventurous

HEARTH & HOME

92. Hayes-McCoy, *Captain Myles Walter Keogh*, 8.

93. See John Rose Green Hassard, *Life of Archbishop John (Joseph) Hughes* (New York, NY: D. Appleton & Co., 1866), 448-490 and John H. Lamott, *History of the Archdiocese of Cincinnati, 1821-1921* (New York, NY: Fredrick Pustet Company, Inc., 1921), passim.

94. William H. Seward to Secretary of War Simon Cameron, December 6, 1861 as cited in Emory Upton, *The Military Policy of the United States* (Washington, D.C.: Government Printing Office, 1912), 242.

95. "Giuseppe Garibaldi," *The New Encyclopedia Britannica*, Vol, 5, 123.

96. Coppinger joined the United States Army based upon the recommendation of Archbishop Hughes according to "General Coppinger Dead," Washington *Post* (November 5, 1909), 2.

97. Richard J. Kehoe to "My dear friend" [possibly Tom Keogh], September 4, 1863, National Library Microfilm. Purcell visited Europe in 1862 and may have been in Rome at the same time as Hughes, who arrived early in February 1862. Francis Forman, Cincinnati Historical Society, to John S. Manion, October 27, 1968. See also Hassard, *Life of Archbishop John Hughes*, 472-479 for additional exchanges between Hughes and Seward.

98. In a March 1, 1862 letter from Rome which Archbishop Hughes sent to Secretary of State Seward he mentions, "Three young Irish gentlemen—Keilly [sic], Keough [sic] & Joseph O'Keeffe, who have served with honor & distinction in the Papal Army, have called upon me having made up their minds to enter the regular Army of the U.S. should they be fortunate enough to be accepted." Hughes asked that Seward recommend them to the Secretary of War. William Henry Seward Papers, Auburn Community College, Auburn, New York. Another source noted that Keogh and his companions had letters of recommendation to both Seward and Stanton. "Brevet Lieutenant Colonel Myles W. Keogh," *The Army and Navy Journal* (September 2, 1876), 58. This piece was undoubtedly written by one of the Andrew J. Alexander or his wife Eveline (Martin) Alexander from Ft. Brown, Texas where they were stationed at the time. The Alexanders met Keogh in the 1860s and developed a close tie

with him thereafter. For further details see Chapter 5 of this publication.

99. According to Berkeley, *The Irish Battalion*, Appendix D, Keogh resigned from Papal service on February 20, 1862, but did not leave Italy until around March 7.

100. Keogh asked his brother to subscribe to *The Illustrated London News* so that he could send it on to America where Myles could "see the Italian News." October 27, 1867, National Library Microfilm.

101. Myles told his sister Margaret that, "I have been offered a nice position in Italy again, but I declined it. I have determined that my wanderings are over & having seen you all again I will spend the balance of my life out here. . . ." September 30, 1867, National Library Microfilm. This offer came right after France temporarily withdrew its troops from Rome for the first time since 1850. Garibaldi made an attempt in France's absence to acquire the last of the Papal lands for Victor Emmanuel II, but the French responded by sending their troops back thus assuring that the Papal States remained under the control of the Roman Catholic Church until 1870 when all the Pope's temporal holdings were lost except for the Vatican.

102. Undated clipping, Gene Autry Western Heritage Museum Research Center, Myles Keogh Collection.

103. "Weekly Steamship Communication to New York," London *Times* (March 17, 1862), 3.

104. London *Times* (March 20, 1862), 11 and The New York *Times* (April 2, 1862), 8.

105. The year of Keogh's birth has been questioned. When he came to Frémont's staff he said had just turned 22. This was on April 12, 1862. Record Group 94, Adjutant General's Office, Letters received, Microfilm Roll 110, 1862, National Archives and Records Administration, Washington, D.C. Service File, National Archives indicates that he was 25 years old according to information he gave on June 11, 1866. This would have meant he was born in 1841. On October 25, 1866, however, he recorded the year of his birth as 1842. In 1869, he maintained on his citizenship papers that he was 27, which corresponds to a birthdate of 1842. At a Court Martial in December 1872 he gave a deposition

young men, bored with their routine in the Papal service and disillusioned by the conduct of the priests placed in charge of the Pope's temporal affairs, and they looked for new opportunities. The days of the Company of St. Patrick were numbered also. The Pope finally would disband the unit on September 30, 1862.[99]

Keogh must have had some inkling of this possibility as the dissolution of the outfit was alluded to in his audience with the Pope on or around March 7, 1862, after he had submitted his resignation. That day Keogh received benediction, a ceremony typically held when someone was leaving the Papal service. Afterwards, the Pope "expressed his love and affection for those whom he called his Irish children, told them that it was not necessary to have Irish soldiers in his service now, but that he knew that if ever he required their assistance" again that they would rally to his cause.[100]

Soon after this Keogh left Italy, although he retained an interest in the "Italian news" and even considered an offer to return for a position in 1867.[101] With Rome behind him, Keogh prepared for his journey to America. In short order, he and Keily found themselves in Liverpool, England, where they booked passage to the United States on the steamer *Kangaroo*. This was Monday March 17, 1862; St. Patrick's day. The two Irishmen took part in the local commemoration of their country's patron that day, a news clipping noting that:

> Father Nugent said they were united there that night to celebrate that festival, not only Irish, but English, French, and Spanish Catholics, and he saw also on the platform two men who fought nobly in the Pope's Brigade, one of whom he believed, gave up a very high position to become a defender of the Sovereign Pontiff (loud cheer).
>
> The gallant defenders of the Pope, at the request of Father Nugent, advanced to the front of the platform, and were enthusiastically cheered. One of them, Lieutenant Myles William [sic] Keogh addressed the meeting, and stated that he had only a few hours since arrived in Liverpool from Rome, and hearing that the festival was being celebrated, he hastened to be present (applause). Ten days before he had the pleasure of having an audience with the Pope . . . . Mr. Keogh then referred to the festival they were celebrating, and said that as long as they cherished the glorious reminiscences which belonged to their country, Ireland would never perish . . . .[102]

Keily and Keogh had booked passage through William Inman, the *Kangaroo*'s local agent, whose office was at No. 22 Water Street in Liverpool. An advertisement in the London *Times* that same day announced that the Liverpool, New York, and Philadelphia Steamship Company, sometimes known as the Inman Lines, intended to dispatch its steamships from Liverpool each Wednesday, calling at Queenstown, Ireland, the following day, with "passengers for Canada and the United States booked through on very advantageous terms." Cabin passage from Liverpool to New York cost fifteen, seventeen, or twenty-one guineas according to the accommodations, payable in gold. "Forward Passage," referring to lower class accommodations (steerage), was listed at six guineas, including provisions. Steerage passengers could pay in currency. In U.S. terms, a first class cabin cost $75 (round trip $100) and steerage passage went for $30.[103]

On Wednesday, March 19, the *Kangaroo* stood ready to sail. Keogh and Keily boarded the steamer that day, but O'Keeffe would leave the following week, aboard the *Etna*. The *Kangaroo*'s captain, Patrick McGuigan, swore to the ship's passenger list the day after the vessel docked in New York at 5 p.m. on April 1, after a thirteen day voyage. The document included eleven passengers occupying first class cabins, plus 178 who traveled main steerage.[104]

Keogh and Keily enjoyed the luxury of top-of-the-line cabins. Both men claimed British citizenship but expressed their intention to become citizens of the United States. Curiously, Myles' age was recorded as twenty-six when actually he celebrated his twenty-second birthday during the voyage.[105] Keily, born on September 6, 1829, was thirty-two at the time, but his age was put down as just twenty-eight. One gets the impression that these passenger lists were rather hastily and carelessly prepared, as evidenced by the many spelling errors and omissions of initials. Possibly, however, the two men wished to pass themselves off as being in their mid to late twenties, or their ages simply may have been estimated.[106]

Keogh and Keily did not waste any time in proceeding to Washington from New York. Once at the capital, they presented their letters of recommendation to Secretary of State Seward. Soon, both received commissions as captain. While in Washington, they stayed at the Metropolitan Hotel where they encountered their first American entrepreneur. Horace H. Day had invented a contrivance which he called a "poncho tent," one of many gadgets spawned during the Civil War by hopefuls looking to land a government contract. The article was a linen raincoat supposedly rendered waterproof by the application of India rubber. The attractive features were its low weight, a little over two pounds, and the fact that three soldiers could button their individual ponchos together to make a tent large enough to shelter them all. To promote this product, Day took written testimonials from several officers willing to confirm its usefulness. Consequently, he called upon Keogh and Keily at the Metropolitan and showed them his design, then asked them to furnish endorsements. Day sought out the two Irish veterans of the Italian War because of the romance and prestige associated with foreign combat, as evidenced by the Papal medals they wore on their chests. Keily acted as spokesman for the pair and proudly noted that he had earned the right to sign his correspondence with the title of "Chevalier de Pie IX and St. Gregory." He wrote:

> Having examined your India-Rubber Poncho Tent and tested its water proof qualities, I feel bound to say that it is the best Tent after that model I have ever seen.
> It is far superior to the Tent d'Abri, in use in the French Army, which I can say from more experience is all but worthless in heavy wet weather. Your Tent is more portable; and, being impervious to wet, must afford good shelter to the soldier in campaign.

Myles' comments, published just below Keily's, were as brief as could be. "I fully concur in the above" is all he set down on paper. Despite this brief statement, Day took out a two column advertisement in one of the Washington newspapers which described the merits of his poncho tent and displayed the various testimonials, the last two being those of Keily and Keogh.[107]

Having made their claim to consideration as military experts, Keogh and Keily received their first assignment soon after the confirmation of their commissions on April 9, 1862. While officially posted to John C. Frémont's staff, they both were seconded to the staff of General James Shields. Shields' division was operating in Virginia's Shenandoah Valley at the time, the command being in camp near Edinburg waiting for a bridge to be constructed over the Shenandoah when Keogh and Keily arrived. On April 13, Shields, still recovering from wounds sustained earlier, returned to his troops riding in a carriage. He received a thunderous applause as he reviewed the division.[108] Keogh and Keily probably took part in this review as Captain David H. Strother met with the "brace of Irish officers, attached to Shield's [sic] staff, and just returned from the Italian Wars," on April 15. Strother found them to be ". . . well-educated, gallant youths . . . ."[109]

It must have made Myles proud to have commanded such a favorable impression on that occasion. Indeed, everything looked promising. He was about to begin the greatest adventure of his life, as a Union officer in the Civil War.

that he was 29, or in other words that he was born in 1843. His Papal records provided the date March 25, 1840. Enrico P. Galcazzi to Most Rev. Mgr. Francis J. Spellman, January 17, 1939, Hugh Schick Collection, Burbank, California. This seems to be the actual date given the tradition of baptism for an infant at an early age. The "Baptismal Record" states that he was christened on March 29, 1840.

106. "Passenger Lists of Vessels Arriving at New York—1820-1897," Microcopy No. M-237, Roll 218 (March 27-May 5, 1862), List 259, 1 lines 3 and 4, Records of the Bureau of Customs, Record Group 36, National Archives and Records Administration, Washington, D.C.

107. "The Poncho Tent," Washington *National Intelligencer* (April 8, 1862), 1.

108. *New York Times*, April 13, 1862.

109. D.H. Strother, "Personal Recollections of the War by a Virginian," *Harper's Weekly* (December-May, 1866-1867), 430ff.

"Reconnaissance"

John Joseph Coppinger, 1834-1909

The most successful career enjoyed by any Irish veteran of Papal service was that of John J. Coppinger, who retired with the rank of major-general after forty-six years in the U.S. Army.

Coppinger was born at Middleton, County Cork, on October 11, 1834. He served five years in the British Army before joining the Papal forces, in which he received promotion to company commander in the Irish Battalion. During the Battle of Spoleto on September 17, 1860, Coppinger's men helped defend the gateway to the citadel of La Rocca against a storming party of Piedmontese troops spearheaded by the famous *Bersaglieri*. The citadel fell, but Coppinger's conspicuous gallantry won him both the *Ordine di San Gregorio* and the *Ordine di Piano*.

In September 1861, bored with his ceremonial duties at the Vatican, Coppinger took the opportunity of a leave of absence to seek a commission in the Union Army. With the assistance of Archbishop John Hughes of New York and Secretary of State William Seward, Coppinger received a commission as captain in the Fourteenth U.S. Infantry. A severe wound received at the Battle of Second Bull Run put the captain out of action for almost six months. Following service at Chancellorsville and Gettysburg, Coppinger was appointed to the staff of Brigadier General Romeyn Ayres, who commanded a brigade of regular army troops in the Army of the Potomac. From May 1864 to January 1865, Coppinger served on the staff of General Alfred Torbert, chief of cavalry in Sheridan's Army of the Shenandoah, and won brevets for gallantry at Trevilian Station and Cedar Creek.

John Joseph Coppinger (1834-1909) would become one of the highest ranking sons of Erin to don the U.S. Army uniform in the 19th century. After service with the Papacy, he would come to America and attain the rank of colonel in the Fifteenth New York Cavalry. In the post-Civil War era he obtained a regular army commission and is seen here as a lieutenant colonel in the Eighteenth Infantry Regiment. *Courtesy of Brian Pohanka.*

In the last months of the war Coppinger, now a colonel, commanded the Fifteenth New York Cavalry of Custer's division in the decisive Battles of Five Forks and Appomattox, where he again was wounded. "His ability as an officer is of the highest order," Custer wrote, "As a soldier I consider him a model."[1]

After being mustered out of volunteer service, Coppinger rejoined the Fourteenth on the Pacific coast. In 1866 he was transferred to the Twenty-Third Infantry, and won the brevet of colonel for his actions against hostile Indians. During 1872 Coppinger, then serving in California, endured a potentially disastrous scandal when a newspaper correspondent accused the dashing captain of seducing his wife. The journalist's charges appeared in a lengthy story on the front page of the San Francisco *Chronicle*, in which Coppinger was characterized as, "A gay Lothario in epaulettes . . . a roué and a bold, unprincipled adventurer . . . a serpent."[2] Coppinger denounced the charges as "infamous falsehoods,"[3] and demanded a court of inquiry. His request was refused, and in time the scandal was all but forgotten.

Coppinger's postwar climb up the ladder of promotion continued with commissions as major in the Tenth Infantry (1879), lieutenant-colonel, Eighteenth Infantry (1883), and colonel in command of the Twenty-Third Infantry (1891). In April 1895 he was promoted to brigadier-general in the regular army, and during the Spanish-American War he received the additional star of major-general of volunteers.

Despite his unquestioned soldierly skills, Coppinger's career received an additional boost from an important political source. In February 1883 the Irishman married Alice Blaine, daughter of the powerful Maine Senator James G. Blaine. The gray-haired colonel's marriage to a Washington belle 25 years younger than himself surprised the Blaine family and Washington society alike, though the wedding at the Blaine mansion on Dupont Circle was one of the most lavish in the city's history, and was attended by President Chester Arthur and his entire cabinet. Seven years later, Alice Blaine Coppinger died during a flu epidemic that earlier had claimed her talented brother Walker Blaine. She left her grief-stricken husband with two sons, aged four and six.

General Coppinger died at his home in Washington on November 4, 1909, and was buried at Arlington Cemetery under an imposing monument carved in the shape of a Celtic cross. All but forgotten today, Coppinger's eulogy might well be the same as a tribute he penned in 1894, honoring his old comrades Keogh, Keily, and O'Keeffe:

> They came directly from Italy, where they were lieutenants in the Pope's service. They went directly to the field in Virginia. They fought, they died—these gallant Irish gentlemen—dear old boys—God bless them."[4]

1. Recommendation in Coppinger's ACP File, National Archives.
2. San Francisco *Chronicle*, July 21, 1872, in Coppinger's ACP File, National Archives.
3. Letter, Coppinger to Assistant Adjutant General, Military Division of the Pacific, July 25, 1872, in Coppinger's ACP File, National Archives.
4. Coppinger's letter of March 15, 1894, in William H. Condon, *Life of Major-General James Shields* (Chicago: Blakely Printing Co., 1900), 265.

At left: An 1862 view of Keogh as a Union Army captain includes his *Ordine di San Gregorio* and *Pro Petri Sede* medals which were destroyed later in a fire. *Courtesy of National Archives.*

At right: Sometime in 1863, while serving on General John Buford's staff, Myles had this *carte de visite* made to show off his velvet collared uniform. *Courtesy of Glen Swanson.*

Chapter 4

"Unsurpassed in Dash:"
Keogh in the American Civil War

by Brian C. Pohanka

> ... here was the glorious reality of war; the bronzed faces, the worn uniforms; the well-tattered flags, the roll of the heavy guns ... while the long line of cavalry, their helmets and accoutrements shining in the morning sun, brought back one's boyish dreams of joust and tournament, and made the heart beat high with chivalrous enthusiasm.
>
> Charles Lever, *Charles O'Malley*

The three newly-minted captains, Myles Keogh, Daniel Keily, and Joseph O'Keeffe, must have been quite taken with their commanding officer. At fifty-two, Brigadier General James Shields was a spry and courteous man of medium height, whose open countenance and twinkling gray eyes exuded good cheer. A fellow Irishman, at sixteen Shields had left the mountains of County Tyrone and, after a brief stint as clerk on a merchant ship, had emigrated to America, where he carved out a career in Illinois as a successful lawyer and Democratic politician. Though largely self-educated, Shields' oratorical brilliance and social charm won him election to the Illinois legislature, and an appointment as state auditor and justice of the state Supreme Court. During his years in Illinois, Shields often encountered, and eventually feuded with, another politically ambitious lawyer named Abraham Lincoln. In 1842 Lincoln's sarcastic critique of Shields in the Springfield *Journal* led the Irishman to challenge the "rail-splitter" to a duel.

Given the choice of weapons, Lincoln picked broadswords. That farcical turn served to diffuse the crisis and, in time, the two became friends.[1] Shields served heroically as brigadier general of Volunteers in the Mexican War; at the Battle of Cerro Gordo he suffered a nearly fatal wound through the right lung.[2] Election to the U.S. Senate from Illinois, then Minnesota, confirmed Shields as one of the most prominent Irish-Americans of his time.

His supporters expected great things from James Shields, but in Virginia's Shenandoah Valley, in 1862, the General had his work cut out for him. Shields' force, 10,000 strong, had moved east of the Blue Ridge and was preparing to join General George McClellan's Army of the Potomac for a decisive advance on Richmond when a series of victories by the redoubtable Thomas J. "Stonewall" Jackson forced Shields' recall to the Valley. By the beginning of June, Jackson was retreating southward up the Valley, while Shields was at Front Royal, ready to coordinate his movements with the 15,000 troops of Major General John C. Frémont. Realizing that the combined Federal force would outnumber his army nearly two-to-one, Jackson concluded to engage and defeat Frémont before Shields arrived on the scene.[3]

General Shields' overconfidence played into Jackson's hands. In his haste to entrap the wily Stonewall, Shields dispersed his forces, sending a portion of Colonel Samuel

1. Condon, *Life of Major-General James Shields, Hero of Three Wars and Senator from Three States*, 44-48. Despite Condon's adulatory viewpoint, his study is the most detailed biography of Shields.

2. Ibid., 68-74. Shields was struck by a Mexican grapeshot that measured an inch and a third in diameter; the ball passed through his chest and exited near the spine. It was claimed that an enterprising surgeon saved the General's life by drawing a silk handkerchief through the wound on a ramrod.

MYLES KEOGH

3. James I. Robertson, Jr., *The Stonewall Brigade* (Baton Rouge, LA: Louisiana State University Press, 1963), 105.

4. *The War of the Rebellion: A Compilation of the Official Records of the Union and Confederate Armies*, Series I, Vol. XII, Pt. 3, (Washington, D.C.: Government Printing Office, 1885), 349. Referred to hereafter as *O.R.* with appropriate series, volume, part, and page.

5. Shields to Carroll, June 7, 1862, 2 a.m., O.R. Series I, Vol XII, Part 3, 352-353.

General James Shields, another Irishman, served the United States both in the Mexican War and the Civil War. In 1863, he resigned with the rank of brigadier general of Volunteers. *Courtesy of Library of Congress.*

S. Carroll's brigade on a twenty mile march to the village of Port Republic, which stood on a peninsula of land where the North and South Rivers met to form the South Fork of the Shenandoah. From there Shields expected Carroll to advance eighteen more miles to the town of Waynesboro, severing Jackson's line of retreat. On the morning of June 6, General Shields ordered the small detachment of cavalry he had on hand to ride ahead and join Carroll's force. Myles Keogh went with them, bearing an order from Shields that urged Carroll to strike the flank of Jackson's army.[4] At 2 a.m. the following morning, Shields sent Dan Keily galloping down the pike to Carroll with a dispatch that reflected the General's growing excitement. "You are within 30 miles of a broken, retreating enemy," it read, "You have only to throw yourself down on Waynesborough before him and your cavalry will capture them by the thousands." Keily had spent a sleepless night in the saddle carrying dispatches, but he must have been no less eager than his friend Keogh to be in the vanguard of the Union advance. Shields, who judged Keily "an able officer," designated the Captain as his "deputy" and instructed Colonel Carroll to "confer with him on all occasions."[5]

Accompanied by Captain Keily, Carroll arrived at Port Republic shortly after sunrise on June 8, 1862. With them were 150 troopers of the First Virginia (Union) Cavalry, and the four guns of Battery L, First Ohio Artillery. Keogh seems to have been elsewhere, perhaps hastening forward the four infantry regiments that comprised the bulk of Carroll's brigade. Carroll and Keily saw that most of Jackson's army was north of Port Republic facing Frémont's Federals. The Rebel supply wagons were strung out along the road in Jackson's rear, seemingly unsupported and separated from the main body by the town of Port Republic and the flood-swollen North and South Rivers. By seizing the bridge behind Jackson, Carroll not only would cut off the supply train, but also effectively trap Jackson between Frémont's and Shields' numerically superior forces.

Carroll's little detachment crossed the South River into Port Republic and headed for the strategic bridge. The Confederates were taken by surprise, and several of

Jackson's staff officers who had been quartered in the town were cut off and forced to surrender. Stonewall himself narrowly avoided capture as he spurred his horse across the bridge within feet of a startled Yankee artillery crew. Had Carroll fired the span at this point, his foray might well have gone down in history as one of the great exploits of the Civil War; but instead of burning the bridge, Carroll decided to hold it until his infantry arrived on the scene.

The Confederates quickly rallied from their surprise and turned the tables on their assailants. Two batteries began raining shot and shell on Carroll's command, stampeding the cavalry and two of the guns back across the bridge. A Federal cannon that had been deployed in the town was stranded when its panicked team galloped off with the limber chest. As a line of Rebel infantry came charging down on the bridge, efforts to save the gun hastily were abandoned. Another piece was left in the road when it became detached from its damaged limber. At this point, Carroll's foot soldiers appeared east of Port Republic, followed by Brigadier General Erastus B. Tyler's brigade and several batteries of artillery. But they were too late to be of assistance at the bridge.

What was undoubtedly the worst day of the war for Colonel Carroll was Dan Keily's finest hour. Yet a third gun and limber from the hapless Ohio battery was stuck to the hubs in a muddy field, all but two of the horses dead in their traces and accompanied by a single driver. Keily hastily dismounted and ran to the man's assistance, while another officer rounded up a group of infantrymen to come to their aid. Keily continued to labor at the gun as geysers of mud and jagged iron spumed up around him. Colonel Carroll later would pay tribute to Keily's "indomitable energy and courage."[6] He declared further, "I do not think I ever saw a more perfect piece of coolness & heroism."[7] It largely was due to Keily's efforts that the gun eventually was brought to safety. Keogh, who arrived in the last stages of the fight, no doubt was impressed equally by his old comrade's bravery.

So chastened were they by the reverse at the bridge, that for the rest of that day Carroll's and Tyler's Federal brigades stood by while Jackson fought Frémont's army to a standstill at Cross Keys, a mile and a half north of Port Republic. The next day, June 9, Stonewall crossed the rivers and struck back at his pursuers.

The Battle of Port Republic was Keogh's baptism by fire in the Civil War and, as General Tyler reported, both he and Keily "were in the hottest of the engagement, exposed to the enemy's fire from first to last."[8] Keily, who was sent forward to reconnoiter soon after sunrise, ran a gauntlet of musketry from the Confederate skirmishers to report that Jackson was advancing to the attack.[9] But if the Confederate commander expected an easy victory, he was soon deceived, for Carroll's and Tyler's men stood their ground against a series of poorly coordinated assaults. The vaunted Stonewall Brigade was brought to a standstill, and Confederate casualties mounted in the face of withering fire from three Union batteries deployed atop a strategic ridge that in peacetime had been used as a charcoal manufactory. Jackson realized that this "coaling" presented the key to the Federal position, and dispatched Brigadier General Richard Taylor's Louisiana brigade to flank and take the crucial high ground.

Just as it seemed that Carroll's and Tyler's outnumbered brigades would carry the day, Taylor's Louisianans came charging out of a thickly-wooded ravine and into the Yankee batteries at the coaling. The Confederates overran seven guns in a fierce hand-to-hand battle, only to see the prizes retaken by two Ohio regiments which rushed to the scene of the struggle. While galloping ahead of these counterattacking troops, Keily's horse took a fatal wound. At almost the same instant, a minie ball slammed into the left side of the Captain's face, fracturing his jaw, lacerating his mouth and tongue, and exiting through the right cheekbone.[10] Reeling in pain and shock, but still in the saddle, Keily guided his dying steed between the opposing lines of battle, exposed to what Colonel Carroll termed "a cross fire that a mounted man could hardly expect to live through."[11]

With most of the battery horses dead, it proved impossible to withdraw the Federal guns. A renewed Confed-

6. Colonel Carroll's Report, June 11, 1862, ibid., 699.

7. Carroll to Keily, December 19, 1862. National Archives, M650, Letters of Application and Recommendation, U.S. State Department.

8. General Tyler's Report, June 12, 1862, O.R., Series I., Vol. XII, Pt. 3, 697.

9. Carroll to Keily, December 19, 1862, op.cit.

10. Surgeon's Certificate of Examination in Keily's Appointment, Confirmation, Promotion File, National Archives.

11. Carroll to Keily, December 19, 1862, op.cit.

12. In a letter to his sister Ellen, dated October 2, 1864, Myles Keogh refers to this horse as "my old charger that had carried me through so many dangers since the battle of Port Republic when Keily was wounded." National Library Microfilm.

13. Nathan Kimball, "Fighting Jackson at Kernstown," *Battles and Leaders of the Civil War*, Vol. II, Pt. 1 (New York, NY: The Century Company, 1884), 313.

14. Washington *National Intelligencer*, (June 12, 1862).

15. General Shields to John Hughes, Archbishop of New York, August 31, 1862. National Archives, M650, Letters of Application and Recommendation, U.S. State Department.

16. Frank Moore, ed., *The Civil War in Song and Story* (New York, NY: P.F. Collier, 1889), 254.

17. 1st Lieutenant Walter Kempster, 10th New York Cavalry, "The Cavalry at Gettysburg," *The Gettysburg Papers*, Vol. I (Compiled by Ken Bandy and Florence Freeman, Dayton, OH: Press of Morningside Bookshop, 1978), 401.

18. Allan Nevins, ed., *A Diary of Battle, The Personal Journals of Colonel Charles S. Wainwright, 1861-1865* (New York, NY: Harcourt, Brace & World, Inc., 1962), 258.

19. George A. Agassiz, ed., *Meade's Headquarters 1863-1865, Letters of Colonel Theodore Lyman From the Wilderness to Appomattox* (Salem, NH: Ayer Company Publishers, Inc., Reprint of 1922 edition, 1987), 21. Lyman's letter to his wife was dated September 22, 1863. Photographs of Buford taken in the field in late 1862 confirm Lyman's description.

erate onslaught carried the coaling, and with it the battle. Tyler ordered the troops to fall back, Carroll covering the retreat as best he could. Both sides had lost roughly a thousand men in the clash at Port Republic, though the day unquestionably belonged to the South. Myles Keogh and his horse "Tom" had passed through the fight unscathed.[12] The Captain was sent ahead of the battered bluecoats to carry word of the defeat to General Shields. Colonel Nathan Kimball, commanding one of Shield's brigades, told how, "On the 9th, at sundown, Shields, now with me, received by the gallant Myles W. Keogh news from Tyler of his disaster."[13] Joseph O'Keeffe, who apparently had remained with Shields during the battle, must have been grieved to learn that Dan Keily had been carried from the field with an apparently mortal wound.

Keily would survive his terrible injury, and though his convalescence would be a long and painful one, he gained some comfort from the encomiums showered upon him. Keily "received praise from all who witnessed his conduct," as one Washington newspaper reported.[14] General Shields lauded his fellow Irishman's "coolest intrepidity," calling him "the noblest soldier on that field . . . a glory to his country and race."[15]

Any hopes that Shields had of renewing his efforts to bag Stonewall Jackson ended on June 11, when orders from Washington recalled his force to Front Royal. From there his army would move east of the Blue Ridge to Manassas Junction and Alexandria, safe within the defenses of the Union capital. Shields now was viewed as yet one more successful politician turned unsuccessful general, and his dispirited brigades were broken up and reassigned. Some regiments went to George McClellan's Army of the Potomac, then nearing the end of the inconclusive Peninsula Campaign, while others became part of the newly created Army of Virginia, commanded by Major General John Pope.

Full of fire and braggadocio, Pope had made his reputation in a series of minor victories in the War's western theater. The Lincoln administration seemed to view him as the perfect antidote to the slow-moving and uncooperative McClellan, and soon "Little Mac's" soldiers were being transferred from the Peninsula to join Pope's new command. One of Pope's first moves, and one of the few positive decisions he would make during his brief tenure in the limelight, was to appoint a Regular Army major named John Buford to the command of a four-regiment brigade of cavalry. On July 31, 1862, Captains Keogh and O'Keeffe were assigned to Buford's staff.

Brigadier General John Buford, a thirty-six year-old native of Kentucky whose family was deeply divided by the War, graduated from West Point in 1848. He had battled Indians on the Western frontier with the Second U.S. Dragoons. When war broke out, he made a long trek overland from Fort Leavenworth, Kansas, to cast his lot with the North. It was said that Buford had rejected a general's commission in the Confederate army, crushing the letter of recommendation in his hand and saying, "I'll live and die under the flag of the Union."[16] He threw himself into the business of organizing his new command with tireless energy and professionalism.

Buford "was a man of few words," one trooper recalled, "but was a tremendous worker."[17] Artillery Colonel Charles S. Wainwright described Buford as, "Never looking after his own comfort, untiring on the march and in the supervision of his command, quiet and unassuming in his manners."[18] A Federal staff officer named Theodore Lyman later would pen a marvelously depictive impression of *the* cavalry General.

> Figurez-vous a compactly built man of middle height, with a tawny moustache and a little, triangular eye, whose expression is determined, not to say sinister. His ancient corduroys are tucked into a pair of ordinary cowhide boots, and his blue blouse is ornamented with holes; from one pocket thereof peeps a huge pipe, while the other is fat with a tobacco pouch. Notwithstanding this get-up he is a very soldierly looking man. He is of a good-natured disposition, but is not to be trifled with.[19]

Those who knew Buford best realized that beneath his rather rough exterior was a kindly, warm-hearted man, quicker to praise than to blame, who took an almost fatherly interest in the careers of his young subordinates. Keogh's admiration grew for his new commanding officer.

Pope failed to use his cavalry to advantage in the campaign of August 1862, a series of engagements that culminated in yet another Union defeat on the old battlefield of Bull Run. The widely dispersed horsemen suffered greatly from the torrid summer heat in their largely fruitless effort to locate the advancing forces of Robert E. Lee's Army of Northern Virginia. Pope's poorly organized supply system further weakened both men and animals, and the blustering General showed an unfortunate propensity for accepting only the information he chose to believe. When Buford discovered a bold flanking move by General James Longstreet's Confederate corps, marching through Thoroughfare Gap in the Bull Run mountains to unite with Stonewall Jackson, Pope ignored the news. It was Longstreet's sweeping flank attack, on August 30, that put Pope's forces to flight in the Second Battle of Manassas. One of the casualties was Keogh's fellow Papal veteran John J. Coppinger, who received a severe neck wound while leading a company of the Fourteenth U.S. Infantry.

Late in the day, as the demoralized Federal soldiers retreated from the field, Buford's units engaged in a spirited fight with a Confederate cavalry brigade during which the General took a slight wound in the leg. It was a classic melee of mounted men battling pistol to pistol and saber to saber, and both Keogh and O'Keeffe were in the thick of the action. In a gesture characteristic of the man, Buford brought the gallantry of his young Irish aides to the attention of the U. S. Army's adjutant general, Lorenzo Thomas. "These gentlemen accompanied me into Virginia," Buford wrote, "and took active parts in almost every engagement the army had. They are young, spirited and accomplished gentlemen, and with me have proven themselves to be dashing, gallant and daring soldiers, ready and anxious for service at all hours and under trying circumstances. Their services during the Virginia Campaign were very arduous and of great value to me."[20] During Pope's retreat to the defenses of Washington, a sharp engagement took place at Ox Hill, near the hamlet of Chantilly. Amidst a blinding thunderstorm, Union Major General Philip Kearny, a colorful one-armed swashbuckler, was shot dead when he mistakenly rode into Rebel lines. On September 2, Captain Keogh went as part of the detail that advanced under a flag of truce to recover Kearny's body from the Confederates.[21] Two days later Robert E. Lee launched his army across the Potomac in a full-scale invasion of the North that culminated in the Civil War's bloodiest day, the battle of Antietam.

On September 10, Major General George B. McClellan, who had been recalled to command in the face of Lee's threat, appointed John Buford chief of cavalry in the Army of the Potomac. During the Antietam Campaign Buford seems to have remained at Army Headquarters, while Brigadier General Alfred Pleasonton exercised field command of the mounted arm. Because of Buford's largely administrative position, Keogh and O'Keeffe were seconded to McClellan's staff. McClellan later said of Keogh, "He appeared to me a most gentlemanlike man, of soldierly appearance, and I was exceedingly glad to have him as an aide.[22] At this time Keogh first met two other staff officers who would play important roles in his future. Captain Andrew J. Alexander of the Third U.S. Cavalry was a broad-shouldered, powerfully built Kentuckian whose flowing blond beard gave him the air of a Norse warrior. He and Keogh became fast friends. The second officer, Keogh's elder by three months and one of McClellan's favorite aides, was Captain George Armstrong Custer.

The Battle of Antietam was a strategic victory for the North, but McClellan failed to follow up his success. Weeks passed before his bloodied army crossed the Potomac into Virginia in the wake of Lee's retreat. Not long after Keogh posed for a photograph with a group of fellow staff officers, McClellan was relieved of command and replaced by Major General Ambrose Burnside. Buford and his staff retained their positions at Army of the Potomac headquarters, and on December 13 witnessed the horrifying carnage of Burnside's failed attempt to drive Lee from an impregnable position at

CIVIL WAR YEARS

20. General Buford to Adjutant General Lorenzo Thomas, October 5, 1862. National Archives, Record Group 94, Letters Received by the Office of the Adjutant General.

21. William B. Styple, ed., *Letters From the Peninsula, The Civil War Letters of General Philip Kearny* (Kearny, NJ: Belle Grove Publishing Co., 1989) is the best modern study of this colorful Civil War commander, but makes no mention of Keogh's involvement in the recovery of Kearny's body, which was escorted through the lines by Lieutenant Colonel Walter Taylor of Robert E. Lee's staff. Neither earlier biographies of Kearny nor the *Official Records* refers to Keogh in this context. The only reference to Keogh's participation in this episode appears in Luce's *Keogh, Comanche and Custer*, a source that must be used with some caution. However, since Buford's cavalry was operating in the vicinity at that time, there is no reason to discount the story.

22. Hayes-McCoy, *Captain Myles Water Keogh*, 13. McClellan's opinion of Keogh was related in G.T. Curtis, *McClellan's Last Service to the Republic* (New York, NY: D. Appleton, 1880).

MYLES KEOGH

23. Letter of Keily to Secretary of State William Seward, April 14, 1863, Seward Papers, Auburn, New York.

24. Hammond, ed., *Diary of a Union Lady 1861-1865*, 238-239. Through an error in the diary transcription, Keily is referred to as "Reilley," though it is quite clear that the veteran of the "Papal Brigade" and "chief of General Shields' staff" could be no one else. "He is a most interesting, intelligent man," Mrs. Charles P. Daly wrote; "He was wounded and has lost a part of his right jaw." Keily's ACP File at the National Archives shows him to have been in New York on a leave of absence on the date in question, May 14, 1863.

Keogh tugs at Alexander's beard in this good-natured view of the two men who would become long-time friends as a result of their service in the Civil War. *Courtesy of George W. Martin.*

Fredericksburg. Torrential rains crippled the Union commander's next effort to engage Lee. The embittered army settled down for a long winter in their encampments north of the Rappahannock River at Falmouth.

While Keogh and O'Keeffe shared the misfortunes of the Army of the Potomac, their friend Dan Keily endured a frustrating existence in Washington, D.C., where he boarded at the Ebbitt House, a hotel whose chief clerk, Thomas Rossiter, was a distant relative of Keogh's. Keily's wound had taken months to heal, but worse was the fact that he was now a staff officer to a general without a command. Once it became clear that Shields would never again lead troops in battle, Keily made repeated efforts to gain a commission in the Regular Army. Both Shields and Brigadier General James S. Wadsworth, commander of the Washington defenses, wrote to President Lincoln and Secretary of War Stanton on Keily's behalf. Keily himself penned a poignant appeal to Secretary of State Seward. "An interval of nine months has elapsed," Keily complained, "and I have not had any recognition of my services, nor have I heard from the War Dept." Clearly, Keily's pride was hurt when he wrote:

> If I were to remain in my present anomalous position I would suffer in reputation and be all but repudiated by those who know me. I am overlooked & forgotten by the War Dept . . . I am now a citizen of this great Republic devoted to all its institutions and ready to preserve the glorious cause of the Union at the sacrifice of my life if necessary. I have freely offered it up before, and now as then I am most anxious to do the same.[23]

Keily must have found it difficult to maintain a positive attitude during his months of idleness. When he dined with a prominent New York Justice and his wife, he commented, "Were I not in the service of the United States I might criticize its actions."[24] But in May, 1863, Keily's luck seemed to take a turn for the better. Brigadier General Charles P. Stone—whose own career had been marred by the controversy surrounding his actions during one of the war's first engagements, the disastrous Union defeat at Ball's Bluff—received permission to attach Keily to his staff. Soon Stone and Keily were en route to Louisiana, where Stone would serve as chief of staff to Major General Nathaniel P. Banks during the siege of the Mississippi River stronghold of Port Hudson.

In the spring of 1863 yet another new commander took the field with the Army of the Potomac: the hard-drinking and ambitious Major General Joseph Hooker. "Fighting Joe" saw to it that John Buford was given an active field command, and when Keogh rode to battle in April 1863 it was with the Reserve Brigade, an organization that contained the majority of the Regular Army cavalry units serving in the East. At 8 o'clock in the morning of April 13, Buford's troopers trotted out of Falmouth with the rest of the Cavalry Corps, embarked on an ambitious raid led by Hooker's new chief of cavalry, Brigadier General George Stoneman.

Buford and Stoneman were friends, and on the surface

An engraving in *Harper's Weekly*, after Alfred R. Waud's original art work, depicted Abraham Lincoln's review of the cavalry of the Army of the Potomac. General John Buford rides at the head of the forces while Keogh and O'Keefe appear behind their commander with their Papal medals pinned to their chests. *Courtesy Library of Congress.*

there were many similarities between the two. Stoneman hailed from western New York, was a graduate of the U.S. Military Academy, and a veteran of frontier service. Nearly six feet four inches tall, he was a lanky, hard-swearing, grim-faced ex-dragoon, whose seamed and craggy features made him appear older than his forty years. His dour disposition and characteristic brusqueness stemmed, at least in part, from poor health; for years he suffered from dyspepsia and a chronic case of hemorrhoids.[25] A.J. Alexander, recently promoted to lieutenant colonel, had served under Stoneman earlier in the war, and now held the position of assistant adjutant general on Stoneman's staff.

Stoneman's Raid was designed to interpose his 10,000 horsemen between Lee's army and Richmond. Hooker expected Stoneman to sever Lee's line of supply by destroying the strategically vital Orange and Alexandria Railroad at the town of Gordonsville. Meanwhile, Hooker would bring Lee to battle and defeat him. Stoneman then would be in an ideal position to check Lee's retreating army, paving the way for a decisive Union victory. Hooker's directives to Stoneman included the

25. Stoneman's Obituary appeared in, *Annual Reunion of the Association of Graduates of the U.S. Military Academy*, June 10, 1895.

26. Hooker to Stoneman, April 12, 1863. O.R., Series I, Vol, XXV, pt. 1, 1066.
27. Ibid., Buford's Report, May 15, 1863, 290.
28. E. R. Hageman, ed., *Fighting Rebels and Redskins, Experiences in Army Life of Colonel George B. Sanford, 1861-1892* (Norman, OK: University of Oklahoma Press, 1969), 203.
29. Ibid.

While still with Stoneman, Keogh sat astride his horse for an ambrotype (which is reversed.) As seen here, his long legs suited him for cavalry service. *Courtesy of Dr. Elizabeth Atwood Lawrence.*

In this picture of George Stoneman (seated on the right) taken during the Peninsular Campaign in June 1862, is Keogh's comrade A. J. Alexander (on Stoneman's right.) The second lieutenant resting his arm on Alexander is E. V. Sumner, Jr. *Courtesy of Library of Congress.*

injunction, "Let your watchword be fight, and let all your orders be fight, fight, fight."²⁶

Neither nature nor fate was kind to General Stoneman. While the Rebels soundly thrashed Hooker's main army in the Battle of Chancellorsville, Stoneman's troopers slogged their way through torrential rain that turned roads to quagmires and streams to raging torrents. The men's rations became a sodden, inedible mess and, since campfires were forbidden lest they reveal the raiders' location, the cavalrymen's soiled uniforms were rarely dry. The plight of the horses was even worse; dead and crippled animals marked the route of Stoneman's command.

Buford made the best of a bad situation, frequently sending his energetic staff officers in advance of the brigade to scout Rebel positions and determine the condition of roads and fords. On April 30 Buford's aide, Lieutenant Peter Penn-Gaskell, a member of a socially prominent Philadelphia family who had been detached to Buford from the First New Jersey Cavalry, engaged some Confederate pickets at Raccoon Ford on the Rapidan River. On May 2, Keogh accompanied British-born Lieutenant Leicester Walker's Company C, Fifth U.S. Cavalry, in a foray that snared a fifteen wagon supply train at Thompson's Cross Roads. Fifteen black teamsters and sixty mules fell into Federal hands; the former slaves chose the opportunity to escape to freedom, while the mules went to men whose horses had given out.²⁷

With his plans falling to pieces around him, on May 5, Stoneman ordered Buford to take the strongest horses from his command and move towards Gordonsville, hopefully throwing the enemy off the scent of the main body which would attempt to rejoin Hooker's command. "Buford was the man of all others to be entrusted with such an undertaking,"²⁸ one officer later wrote. For the next three days and nights, Buford's exhausted column remained on the move. A formidable body of Confederate infantry occupied Gordonsville, so Buford contented himself with destroying the railroad and supply depot at nearby Trevilian's Station.

On May 7, Buford learned that Hooker's defeated army had withdrawn across the Rappahannock and, though the river was in flood, Buford managed to effect a crossing at Kelly's Ford. By this time the troopers' fatigue was so great that whole regiments fell asleep in the saddles of their emaciated, sore-backed horses.²⁹

Buford's enterprise provided one of the few bright

moments in an otherwise dismal campaign, and elevated him to the command of a cavalry division. Buford, in turn, lauded the performance of Keogh, O'Keeffe, and the other members of his staff. The seven officers had been "severely worked," the General reported, but "rendered valuable service to me. Untiring and zealous, they have relieved me of much anxiety, and have prompted good feeling through the brigade."[30]

George Stoneman's fortunes plummeted in the wake of the failed raid. While absent in Washington on sick leave, Brigadier General Alfred Pleasonton took over for Stoneman as commander of the Cavalry Corps. Although far from brilliant on the battlefield, Pleasonton was nonetheless a good organizer, and he saw to it that the jaded men and mounts were brought back to their former level of efficiency. As May gave way to June, the opposing armies confronted one another across the Rappahannock River, on terrain that was becoming familiar territory to Keogh and his comrades.

On the afternoon and evening of June 8, 1863, Buford's division took position north and east of Beverly's Ford, ready to cross the Rappahannock at dawn as one arm of a pincer movement that Pleasonton hoped would ensnare Confederate General James Ewell Brown Stuart's horsemen, camped near the hamlet of Brandy Station. At 4 a.m. Buford's leading brigade splashed across the river and thundered down a narrow road, scattering the Rebel outposts in their path. The Battle of Brandy Station, the largest cavalry engagement of the Civil War, had begun.

Keogh was in the thick of the action that day, as were two of General Pleasonton's staff, Captain George Custer and Lieutenant George Yates, both of whom would die with Keogh at the Battle of the Little Big Horn. Keogh's friend, Alexander had retained his position as assistant adjutant general under Pleasonton, and also took part in the fighting. Though the Confederates had been taken by surprise, Jeb Stuart quickly recovered from the shock. Soon a grand melee raged over the rolling hills north of the Orange and Alexandria Railroad. As Buford attempted to fight his way to the other arm of the pincer movement—Brigadier General David McMurtie Gregg's division—he encountered fierce Confederate resistance. Major Charles J. Whiting's Reserve Brigade swung to the right and clashed with troopers commanded by General W. H. F. "Rooney" Lee, Robert E. Lee's twenty-six year-old son. Buford reported that, when Whiting's Regulars ran low on ammunition, "Out flew the sabres and most handsomely were they used."[31]

Buford dispatched Joseph O'Keeffe to Whiting's brigade and, in one charge by the Second U.S. Cavalry,

CIVIL WAR YEARS

30. Buford's Report, O.R., Series I, Vol. XXV, Pt. 1, 1090.

31. Buford's Report, June 13, 1863, General Joseph Hooker Papers, Huntington Library, San Marino, California. This portion of the fight at Brandy Station most likely occurred on the Yew Ridge, North of Fleetwood Hill.

Captain Keogh stands next to John Buford (seated) and fellow members of Buford's staff, (left to right) Lieutenant Peter Penn-Gaskell, Captain Craig W. Wadsworth, and Lieutenant Albert P. Morrow. *Courtesy of Library of Congress.*

32. Buford's Report, Huntington Library, op.cit.

33. Kempster, "The Cavalry at Gettysburg," *The Gettysburg Papers*, Vol. I, 400.

34. William L. Heermance, 6th New York Cavalry, "The Cavalry at Gettysburg," *The Gettysburg Papers*, Vol. I, 419.

35. *O.R.*, Series I, Vol. XXVII, Pt. 1, 930. In addition to Keogh, Buford's Staff at Gettysburg consisted of Captains Charles E. Norris, Craig W. Wadsworth, and Theodore C. Bacon, and Lieutenants John Mix, Peter Penn-Gaskell, William Dean, Albert Payson Morrow, Malcomb H. Wing and George M. Gilchrist. Both Keogh and Norris later would be breveted for their service in the campaign. In 1866 Morrow would join Keogh in the Seventh Cavalry as Captain of Company E.

36. Letter of Theodore Lyman in Agassiz, *Meade's Headquarters*, 213.

37. Captain Stephen Minot Weld, July 8, 1863, in *War Diary and Letters of Stephen Minot Weld, 1861-1865* (Boston, MA: Massachusetts Historical Society, 1979), 240.

the young Irishman galloped boot to boot with Captain Wesley Merritt who, like Custer, soon would be elevated to the rank of general. In the hand-to-hand fight that ensued, Merritt crossed sabers with a Confederate officer thought to be Rooney Lee himself, while O'Keeffe was shot in the right foot, unhorsed, and captured. Another of Buford's aides, First Lieutenant John Mix, had his horse shot from under him. While Keogh came through the fight without a scratch, it was no less a reflection on his bravery. "I am under many obligations for their prompt and untiring exertions," Buford would say of his staff, "I often had to send them where the fire was hot, and when their horses were jaded, but there was no hesitation."[32] Though the Federal cavalry ultimately yielded the field to their opponents, the jaunty Yankees at last had shown that they were the equals of Jeb Stuart's vaunted cavaliers.

Shortly after the Battle of Brandy Station, Lee moved north, bound for yet another invasion of the North. As Pleasonton tried to penetrate Lee's cavalry screen, action flared in sharp engagements at Aldie, Middleburg, and Upperville. On June 27 Buford's division crossed the Potomac at Edward's Ferry, paralleling the route through Maryland taken by the Army of Northern Virginia. The following day Hooker was relieved of command of the Army of the Potomac by Major General George Gordon Meade, who sent Buford's veteran troopers across the Pennsylvania line toward a town called Gettysburg.

Buford arrived at Gettysburg on June 30, and soon sensed the presence of a more formidable threat than Confederate cavalry. When one of his brigade commanders said, "You are unduly excited, General, I'll agree to take care of all the Rebels," Buford barked, "No, you won't. They'll come early in the morning, with skirmishers three deep, and you'll have to fight like the devil to hold your own till supports arrive."[33]

July 1, 1863, was John Buford's day in history. His courageous holding action—dismounted Yankee troopers staving off a superior force of grayclad infantry—bought enough time for Meade to rush reinforcements to the field. For four critical hours Buford delayed A. P. Hill's corps north and west of Gettysburg. At 10 a.m. Major General John Reynolds arrived at Buford's command post on Seminary Ridge, riding in advance of the Federal I Corps. "What's the matter, John?" Reynolds asked. "The devil's to pay," Buford responded. When Reynolds said, "I hope you can hold on till my corps comes up," the laconic cavalryman replied, "I reckon I can."[34] Keogh and the other members of the General's hard-working staff shared in the achievements of that day, Buford stating that their "coolness and gallantry cannot be excelled in this army."[35] In retrospect, Buford's stand on the first day of the battle of Gettysburg came to be viewed as a watershed in military tactics, demonstrating that the increased firepower provided by breech-loading carbines enabled dismounted cavalry to function as effectively as infantry.

Buford's division played a secondary role on the second and third days of the battle of Gettysburg, but was again in the vanguard during the pursuit of Lee's defeated army. From July 6-10 a series of spirited cavalry clashes took place between Hagerstown, Maryland, and Williamsport on the Potomac. On July 14 Buford advanced to the river, capturing 500 prisoners and a cannon. But the rest of the Army of Northern Virginia already had made the crossing into Virginia, cutting loose their pontoon bridge just as the Yankee horsemen reached the river bank. Buford shared the general frustration of Lee's escape, and was in no mood to trifle when a well-known army sutler was found to have been functioning as a Confederate spy. Buford had the unfortunate man summarily tried and executed, and a sign affixed to his corpse that read, "This man to hang three days: he who cuts him down before shall hang the remaining time."[36] Most of Meade's army would march past the grisly corpse; "I passed the body of a spy hanging to a tree," one officer wrote, "He was stark naked and was a most disagreeable object, as he had been hanging there for two days."[37]

Keogh missed this aspect, however, since he was absent from the army during a portion of the campaign. He eventually did receive a brevet as a major in the Regular Army, nonetheless, "for gallant and meritorious service in the Battle of Gettysburg." In late June, two of Keogh's cousins came to America via Halifax, Nova Scotia, arriving in New York at the very time that the Battle of Gettysburg was at its height. From there they eventually traveled to Washington, where they were put up by their distant relative, Thomas Rossiter at the Ebbitt House. Daniel Keogh O'Sullivan and Richard Kehoe were happy-go-lucky youths who obviously hoped to follow their cousin's example, and attain commissions in the American military service. Always sensitive to the needs of his kinfolk, Keogh managed to wrangle a brief leave of absence, and traveled to Washington. He waited there for six days and, when O'Sullivan and Kehoe failed to appear, returned to his post with Buford. Soon thereafter, when in his words "the army was fighting every day," Keogh received news of their arrival at the capital and again applied for leave "in the face of the enemy." Buford justifiably was angry, and Keogh was "refused with blame for applying at that moment."[38]

In the meantime, Keogh accompanied Buford's command, which crossed the Potomac on July 18, and by the 26th was at Warrenton, Virginia, again covering the Union front just south of the Rappahannock River. On July 27 a young Harvard-educated officer named Stephen Minot Weld noted in his diary that he crossed the river at Rappahannock Station and visited Buford's headquarters. Over dinner Weld chatted with his friend Craig "Tic" Wadsworth—a Captain on Buford's staff and son of Federal General James S. Wadsworth—then rode down to Warrenton "with Captain Keough [sic]," his mare going lame on the way.[39]

Despite 100 degree temperatures, military activity escalated on August 1 as Buford advanced toward Confederate-occupied Culpeper. The Union horsemen engaged two Confederate cavalry brigades in a hard-fought action on portions of the old battlefield of Brandy Station. Buford held the advantage until Rebel infantry came onto the scene, at which point the Federals withdrew to the Rappahannock line. The most dramatic moment of the day came when Buford's Eighth New York Cavalry charged through a deadly hail of canister in an attempt to take a Confederate battery. Stephen Weld described this incident, in which Keogh almost certainly was involved:

> The cavalry staff officers were a lively set of boys. Craig Wadsworth and a lot of them sat down while there was a short halt before going into a fight, and began playing poker. In a few minutes the game was interrupted by the call to arms, and off they went into the fight, and were in the charge on the four guns. It was as near a capture as anything I ever saw.[40]

The weather on August 2 was torrid enough to threaten the lives of both man and beast. Buford told Pleasonton, "It is ruinous to horseflesh, it is so hot."[41] At midnight, on August 3, he gave vent to the strain he was under, writing to the chief of cavalry, "I am disgusted and worn out . . . . There is so much apathy and so little disposition to fight and co-operate that I wish to be relieved from the Army of the Potomac."[42] Buford stayed at his post, however, through more inconclusive skirmishing during the month of September. On October 11 a maneuver by Lee against the Federal right flank forced General Meade to withdraw his forces to the north bank of the Rappahannock. Buford fought his way back from a position on the Rapidan River, linking up with Brigadier General Judson Kilpatrick's cavalry division for yet another battle with Stuart's horsemen at Brandy Station. The flamboyant Custer, commanding one of Kilpatrick's brigades, distinguished himself in this affair, leading a saber charge while his band played "Yankee Doodle." The sparring between Lee and Meade resumed on October 11, but this time Lee proved more successful, causing the Federal commander to pull back across the Rappahannock to Warrenton, then still further to Manassas. Buford's tired horsemen had been given the task of escorting the Army's vast wagon train, and did not figure in the bloody clash at Bristoe Station, or the cavalry fight at Buckland. At the conclusion of the Bristoe campaign, Lee again withdrew across the Rappahannock and the two armies resumed their old positions.

During all this time, Keogh still grappled with the

CIVIL WAR YEARS

38. October 21, 1863, National Library Microfilm.

39. *War Diary and Letters of Stephen Minot Weld*, 250.

40. Ibid., 254.

41. Buford to Pleasanton, August 3, 1863, O.R., Series I, Vol. XXVII, Pt. III, 833.

42. Ibid., 835.

43. October 21, 1863, National Library Microfilm.
44. Theodore Lyman in Agassiz, *Meade's Headquarters*, 35.
45. Ibid., 40.
46. Theodore Lyman to Henry Lee Higginson, November 2, 1863. Bliss Perry, *Life and Letters of Henry Lee Higginson* (Boston, MA: The Atlantic Monthly Press, 1921), 215.
47. Sanford, *Fighting Rebels and Redskins*, 215.
48. Theodore Lyman in Agassiz, *Meade's Headquarters*, 50.

Daniel J. Keily arrived in the United States with Keogh fresh from Italy. Keily earned the rank of brevet brigadier general as seen in this *carte de visite*. Medals from the Papal War adorn Keily's chest in the picture of the adventuresome Irishman when he was a captain in the Union Army.
Courtesy of Library of Congress.

obligation of having to find places for his ne'er-do-well cousins, Dan O'Sullivan and Dick Kehoe. The two managed to get down to the army by themselves, and Keogh convinced General Merritt to take O'Sullivan on his staff as an unpaid aide-de-camp. Dan Keily, now a colonel, was in the process of recruiting a cavalry regiment in occupied Louisiana, and Keogh wrote to his old friend asking if there might be a place for O'Sullivan in the new outfit. Kehoe, who was a rather sickly youth, was less fortunate, having no choice but to enlist as a private in the First Connecticut Heavy Artillery. Myles took pains to keep his brother Tom posted on the outcome of this affair, as the matter caused some strain between the two. In a rather self-pitying tone, the Captain advised his elder brother, "I have too few real friends in this world to sacrifice any to a perhaps mistaken conception of the facts as they really are."[43]

Though no more battles were fought, Buford and his officers still had their share of duties to perform. Meade's aide, Theodore Lyman, wrote his wife on October 22, "General Buford came in to-day, cold and tired and wet," but concluded, "The General takes his hardships good-naturedly."[44] Ten days later Lyman again encountered Buford, who commented, "He thought he could just 'boolge' across the river and scare the Rebels to death."[45]

The General's feisty disposition counted for a large part of his popularity with Keogh and the other young cavaliers in the division. While eschewing the gold braid and plumes of the more colorful cavalry leaders, Buford still managed to make war a dashing affair. Lyman commented that Buford was the "prime favorite" of the "cavalry bucks."[46] Another officer wrote, "He had the respect and esteem of every man in the army, and the cavalry loved him as a father."[47]

But the hard campaigning of the last few months had taken its toll on even as veteran a campaigner as Buford. On November 19 Colonel Lyman escorted a group of British observers to Buford's headquarters outside of Culpeper. "We find the Cavalry Chief afflicted with rheumatism," Lyman wrote, "which he bore with his usual philosophy."[48] In fact, Buford's illness was far more serious. Early in December, he was diagnosed as having a severe case of typhoid fever.

Keogh accompanied his ailing commander on sick leave to Washington, where General Stoneman put his rented home at their disposal. There, Buford's condition worsened, his weakened constitution unable to shake off the deadly fever. By December 16, it was clear that Buford was dying. Only then would Secretary of War Stanton, who was inherently distrustful of any officer with Southern antecedents, permit Buford's promotion to the rank of major general. As the end neared, Buford lapsed into delirium, alternately scolding and apologizing to his black servant, who sat weeping by the General's bedside. Stoneman, Keogh, and Alexander numbered among other old comrades who gathered at the bedside. When his major general's commission arrived, Buford had a few lucid moments, whispering, "Too late . . . Now I wish that I could live."[49] Shaken and distraught, Keogh helped his dying chief to sign the necessary paperwork, then co-signed it as a witness. Buford's last intelligible words were, "Put guards on all the roads, and don't let the men run back to the rear."[50] The General died as Keogh held him in his arms.[51]

Buford's death was a great personal loss for Keogh. "Poor Myles," Dan O'Sullivan wrote, "If the General lived Myles always had a sincere friend."[52] Fortunately, the Captain's depression at least was relieved partially when he learned that Joseph O'Keeffe had won his release from Rebeldom in a prisoner exchange. Keogh traveled to Annapolis to meet his friend, who seemed well enough, though still lame from the foot wound he had received at Brandy Station. Following their reunion, Keogh returned to the army at Culpeper to see to the welfare of his horses.

It must have seemed a rather grim encampment without Buford, and was probably one reason why Keogh accepted General Stoneman's offer of a position on his staff. Following his stint under Hooker, Stoneman had held an administrative position as chief of the Cavalry Bureau in Washington. The War Department granted his request for active duty on January 28 when he was sent west to take charge of the XXIII Corps at Knoxville, Tennessee. Keogh accompanied Stoneman as one of his aides-de-camp.

As it was, Stoneman commanded the corps for little more than two months. On April 9, 1864, he was appointed commander of the cavalry attached to Major General John Schofield's Army of the Ohio, with headquarters at Mossy Creek, Tennessee. Coincidental with Stoneman's transfer, Myles Keogh received his promotion to the rank of major in the Volunteer service, to date from April 7.

The Federal soldiers who campaigned in the Civil War's western theater liked to think of themselves as a far more rugged breed than the eastern volunteers. It is not surprising that the rough and ready midwesterners of Stoneman's new command looked askance at the General's dapper Irish aide-de-camp, fresh from the spit and polished ranks of the Army of the Potomac. Years later, Captain Theodore Allen, whose Company D, Seventh Ohio Cavalry served as escort at Stoneman's headquarters, recalled that his first impressions of Keogh were far from favorable.

> We did not like the style of Captain Miles [sic] Keogh; there was altogether too much style. He was as handsome a young man as I ever saw . . . He rode a horse like a Centaur. He had a fresh Irish complexion like the pink side of a ripe peach—more like the complexion of a sixteen year old girl than of a cavalry soldier. His uniform was spotless, and fitted him like the skin of a sausage; if there had been any more of the man, or any less of the uniform, it would have been a misfit . . . at all events we did not care much for Captain Keogh, and particularly did not like his style. We gave him the 'cold shoulder' and as he passed us snide remarks were passed, such as 'I wonder if his mother cuts his hair?' 'What laundry do you think he patronizes?', etc., and nobody permitted him to drink from their canteen.[53]

Fortunately, Keogh had little time to worry about his image. The western armies, under the overall command of Major General William Tecumseh Sherman, readied themselves for the great campaign against Atlanta. Stoneman and Keogh traveled to Lexington, Kentucky, where good horseflesh was abundant and a number of new cavalry units were being organized and drilled for service with Stoneman's command. Brigadier General Samuel D. Sturgis, who later would be Keogh's commanding officer in the Seventh Cavalry, assisted in the process. On April 29 Stoneman and Keogh left Kentucky at the head of 2,000 troopers, bound for Knoxville and Chattanooga, where Sherman expected them to arrive by May 5.[54]

Stoneman's three brigades—3,810 troopers—crossed the Tennessee River as part of Sherman's massive offensive, which incorporated three armies totalling nearly 100,000 men. As Sherman battled Confederate General Joseph E. Johnston south across Georgia, it fell to Stoneman's cavalry to screen the left flank, Schofield's Army of the Ohio. For most of the campaign, Stoneman would be scrimmaging with Confederate cavalry led by General Joseph Wheeler, one of the South's most formidable horse soldiers. The first serious fighting for Stoneman came in mid-May near Resaca. There, Major Keogh redeemed himself in the eyes of Captain Allen's hardbitten Ohioans.

Dismounted Rebel cavalrymen posted on a wooded knoll repulsed several attempts to force them from the position when Stoneman ordered Keogh to organize another assault on the hill. "A battalion of four companies (nearly 300 men) were placed at his disposal," Captain Allen recalled. "In column of companies he started at a brisk trot, and getting under fire raised himself in his stirrups, and with cap in hand, turned to the battalion and cried out, 'Hip, hip, hurrah boys! Here we go,' and breaking into a gallop, the battalion with Keogh well in the lead, charged on the enemy capturing all whose fleetness of horse did not permit them to escape." His dandyism forgiven, "Keogh ever after was a most welcome guest at every campfire, and every canteen in the regiment was freely proffered to him."[55]

It was Sherman's intention to live off the land. His orders to Stoneman, "to pick up whatever of provisions and plunder you can" reflected this ruthless philosophy.[56] The Yankee horsemen fulfilled their directives, cutting

49. Sanford, *Fighting Rebels and Redskins*, 215 and Moore, *The Civil War in Song and Story*, 254.

50. Moore, *The Civil War in Song and Story*, 254.

51. Richard Kehoe to Tom Keogh, January 1, 1864, National Library Microfilm. "He was greatly put about," Dick Kehoe wrote of Myles, "He attended B. till the last *died in his arms.*"

52. Daniel K. O'Sullivan to Tom Keogh, Natchez, Mississippi, January 27, 1864, National Library Microfilm. Dan recently had obtained a commission as first lieutenant in the Second Louisiana Cavalry, a unit being organized by Dan Keily, who would be its colonel. Interestingly, another officer in Keily's unit was Major Peter Penn-Gaskell, who had served on Buford's staff with Keogh.

53. Allen, "Reminiscences of a Volunteer," 227.

54. Sherman to Stoneman, April 28, 1864, O.R., Series I, Vol. XXXII, Pt. 3, 522.

55. Allen, "Reminiscences of a Volunteer," 227.

56. Sherman to Stoneman, May 13, 1864, O.R., Series I, Vol. XXXVIII, Pt. 4, 170.

57. Stoneman to Schofield, May 22, 1864, ibid., p. 287.
58. Stoneman to Quartermaster Lieutenant R. H. Humphrey, June 3, 1864, ibid., p. 399.
59. Keogh to his sister Ellen, October 2, 1864, National Library Microfilm.
60. Stoneman to Sherman, July 26, 1864, O.R., Series I, Volume XXVIII, Pt. 5, 264.
61. Ibid., 265.

Confederate railroads and destroying supply trains of arms and ammunition, but it presented rough work in a countryside a good deal less than fertile. Stoneman reported to Schofield that his horses "were nearly played out."[57] He went on, "My men and horses are entirely without anything to eat."[58] The campaign was a constant round of scouting and skirmishing, in which Keogh played a distinguished part. Later, he would be breveted for his gallantry in a fight at Dallas, Georgia.

On the Fourth of July, Keogh was invited to a picnic at the headquarters of Major General Frank Blair, commander of XVII Corps, whose cousin and adjutant general was none other than Keogh's old chum Alexander. A call to arms interrupted the festivities, and Keogh galloped into action on his favorite horse, "Tom." In a letter to his sister Ellen, Keogh told how the horse saved his life that day. "I suddenly rode into a heavy outlying picket of the Enemy," Keogh wrote, "Tom saw them as they rose up to deliver their fire & jumped sideways over a rail fence into the wood skirting the road [and] carried me safely out of danger."[59]

By the end of July, Sherman's forces had closed in on the defenses of Atlanta. As part of his strategy aimed at tightening the noose around the city, Sherman instigated a three-pronged cavalry operation that included Stoneman's command. Stoneman was to swing east of Atlanta, cutting the Georgia Railroad, then turn west, destroying the Macon & Western Railroad south of the city. But soon another element entered into the plan. Every Union soldier knew that thousands of their comrades languished in prisoner of war camps at Macon and Andersonville. The prison at Macon, in which Federal officers were confined, was an unpleasant place; but Andersonville, where 30,000 enlisted men were crowded into a vast pen, represented a place of almost unbelievable horror. On July 26, Stoneman proposed that his raid be expanded to include the freeing of the prisoners at Macon, as well as those at Andersonville, fifty miles to the southwest. "I would like to try it," Stoneman wrote, "and am willing to run any risks."[60] Sherman agreed, stating, "If you can bring back to the army any or all those prisoners of war it will be an achievement that will entitle you and the men of your command to the love and admiration of the whole country."[61]

On July 27, Stoneman moved out with three brigades and a section of Indiana artillery, some 2100 men all told. The first part of the raid went according to plan; the troopers destroyed the Georgia Railroad at Decatur, then turned south, burning more tracks, supplies and rolling stock east of Macon. But on July 30, Stoneman's plan began to go awry when his tired soldiers met unexpectedly heavy resistance from Georgia Home Guards and Militia in the defenses of Macon. After lobbing a few shells into the city from his two 3-inch ordnance guns, Stoneman decided to head south, crossing the Ocmulgee River below Macon. This move barely had gotten underway when Stoneman's scouts reported the arrival of a large Confederate cavalry force in Macon. Fearing that they would block him at the river, the General turned his men around and headed north, thus retracing his steps. At dark his weary troopers halted near the town of Clinton, little realizing that they were going directly into the arms of General Alfred Iverson's Confederate division.

Stoneman's men got little rest, as intermittent skirmishing continued until dawn. The Union column scarcely had started when it ran head-on into Iverson's force. The Rebels, well dug in, had barricaded the road leading north with felled trees and fence rails. Desperate to break through, Stoneman and his staff rode to the front and led a charge on the enemy position. The attack foundered, and discipline began to fall apart in the face of Confederate musketry and artillery fire. At this point, Myles Keogh spurred "Tom" along the embattled line and organized another assault, leading the charge in person. The Philadelphia *Inquirer* later would tell of how Keogh:

> Dashed in front, trying to rally the men, and having partially succeeded, dashed right upon the enemy; but he was soon deserted, except by some of the officers. This small Spartan band swept down upon the enemy, and for a moment checked their onward course; but

many a saddle being emptied, the few survivors had to return, among whom was the gallant Major, whose reckless bravery all who have returned praise."[62]

Sensing the collapse in Yankee morale, the Southerners began to close in on Stoneman's crumbling units. Confusion intensified when hundreds of runaway slaves or "contrabands" who had followed Stoneman's raiders came stampeding through the broken ranks. Realizing that the enemy surrounded him, at 4 p.m., Stoneman called his regimental commanders together and ordered those who wished to save themselves to make the attempt; he would cover their retreat. "The general was much broken down at the thought of surrender," one of his staff recalled, "he seemed to have but little regard for his own personal safety."[63] The better part of two brigades managed to cut their way out of the trap, including four officers of Stoneman's staff. Keogh chose to remain with his general, who made his stand with the Fifth and Sixth Indiana Cavalry and the two pieces of artillery.

Lieutenant W. W. Angel of the Fifth Indiana supervised the fire of his dismounted troopers from behind a rail fence when he saw Stoneman and Keogh directing the fire of the Union artillery. At that moment, a Confederate shell passed right through Stoneman's horse, just behind the General's leg. "The horse sank down," Angel remembered, "and the General got off and said: 'My poor Beauregard is killed.'"[64] Stoneman, exhausted, barely managed to remount a broken-down stray, then ordered a retreat to the next ridgeline. There, near a country parsonage called Sunshine Church, he made the decision to surrender. One of the last casualties of the fight was Myles Keogh's horse Tom. "The poor fellow," Keogh wrote, "I shall never have a horse like him again."[65] A flag of truce was dispatched toward the Confederate lines, and soon the Rebels were swarming about Stoneman, Keogh, and their 500 comrades in misfortune.

On the night of August 1, the thirty captured officers were marched into Macon to the very prison they had hoped to liberate. A week and a half later, they went by rail to Charleston, South Carolina to be confined in the large city jail. The prison, wrote one officer, "was a nice looking building outside, but a hell hole inside."[66] The heat was terrible and rations poor, consisting of handfuls of flour, rice, stringy beef, and molasses. At times, two or three days passed with no rations at all. To make matters worse, Charleston was under siege from Union ground and naval forces, and shells exploded in dangerous proximity to the prison. Fortunately, Stoneman and Keogh were able partially to alleviate their plight by purchasing additional food with money they had concealed in their clothing. As Keogh put it, "It cost us about 8 dollars each a day to keep from starving."[67]

The situation took a turn for the better on September 25 when Confederate General John Bell Hood agreed to release Stoneman and Keogh. The two were exchanged on the 27th, and by October 2 they enjoyed a welcome dinner at General Sherman's headquarters in Atlanta, which had fallen to the Union a week earlier. Keogh hastened to write his sister that he was safe, saying, "I thank God my dear Ellen I was thought enough of by Genl Sherman to be specially exchanged. I should I believe have died in a very short time and as it is I am almost broken down." Though his health had suffered, Keogh was pleased by the praise he received for his gallantry at Sunshine Church, commenting, "My prospects of promotion to a high position are greater than my most sanguine expectations." [68]

As he recuperated from his ordeal, Keogh briefly entertained the notion of transferring back to the eastern theater of operations, specifically Major General Philip H. Sheridan's Army of the Shenandoah. Joseph O'Keeffe was now a captain on Sheridan's staff, and had won the plaudits of his commander for accompanying Sheridan on the famous ride that turned the tide of battle at Cedar Creek. In a letter to Keogh's brother Tom, O'Keeffe said that Sheridan was anxious to have Myles on his staff, "And I am sure he would like General Sheridan very much."[69] Stoneman was more than willing to further his aide's ambitions, and recommended Keogh for promotion to the lieutenant-colonelcy of the Third

62. Philadelphia *Inquirer* (August 16, 1864), 8.

63. Report of Major Haviland Tompkins, Stoneman's provost marshal, August 12, 1864, O.R., Series I, Vol. XXXVIII, Pt. 2, 920.

64. Lieutenant W. W. Angel, 5th Indiana Cavalry, "Stoneman's Surrender," Washington *National Tribune*, (April 3, 1902). The horse was said to have been a pre-war gift to Stoneman from Pierre Gustave Toutant Beauregard, in 1864 a Confederate General officer.

65. Keogh to Ellen, October 2, 1864, National Library Microfilm. Of course, in time Keogh would own a far more famous horse—"Comanche."

66. Diary of Lieutenant James D. Cope, 116th Pennsylvania, in W. Springer Menge and J. August Shimrak, eds., *The Civil War Notebook of Daniel Chisholm* (New York, NY: Orion Books, 1989), 192.

67. Keogh to his sister Ellen, October 2, 1864, National Library Microfilm.

68. Ibid. Hard as it was, Stoneman's and Keogh's imprisonment was luxurious in comparison with the plight of the captured enlisted men, who were sent to the notorious stockade at Andersonville. On August 14, an exchanged prisoner smuggled a message from Stoneman to Union authorities in which the General described the "terrible mortality" occurring at Andersonville. "Thousands are without pants or coats," he wrote, "and hundreds without even a pair of drawers to cover their nakedness." O.R., Series II, Vol. VII, 616.

69. Joseph O'Keeffe to Tom Keogh, August 30, 1864, National Library Microfilm. Prior to his friend's exchange, O'Keeffe had written to his uncle, the Bishop of Cork, asking him to intercede with the Bishop of Charleston on Keogh's behalf. The other officer who accompanied Phil Sheridan on his famous ride to Cedar Creek was Major George "Sandy" Forsyth, later distinguished at the battle of Beecher's Island in the Indian Wars.

In late 1864 Keogh joined an unidentified group as one of thousands of people to be photographed atop Lookout Mountain in Tennessee. *Courtesy of Dr. Elizabeth Atwood Lawrence.*

New Jersey Cavalry, a unit that formed a part of George Custer's division in Sheridan's army. In enumerating Keogh's qualifications, Stoneman noted "his well-known coolness, gallantry and dash, his strict integrity, his devotion to his profession . . . His universal popularity with all officers and men, and his soldierly bearing."[70] There is evidence that Custer expected Keogh to receive the appointment, for in a letter to his wife Libbie, the General described the impending assignment to his division of "an officer from the Army of the West, now on General Stoneman's staff, who prior to the war served in European armies in the late Italian War."[71]

It is interesting to speculate what Keogh's career might have been had he joined Custer for the final drive on Richmond but, as it was, he chose to remain with Stoneman, who in mid November was given yet another opportunity to lead a cavalry raid. With the sanction of his superiors, Generals John Schofield and George Thomas, Stoneman began assembling a new force drawn from loyal Kentuckians and Tennesseeans. While Stoneman conferred with General Thomas at Nashville, Keogh, now the senior officer on Stoneman's staff, busied himself at Lexington, preparing troopers and horses for battle.

On December 10, Stoneman led two brigades totalling 5700 cavalrymen out of the Union base at Knoxville, Tennessee. His goal was southwestern Virginia, from where Lee's Confederate army drew a large part of its meager supplies. From the outset, it was clear that Stoneman's luck had turned. From Bristol, on the Tennessee/Virginia border, into the Old Dominion and on to Abingdon and Wytheville, Stoneman's Yankees scattered every force sent to meet them. On December 17, a Confederate lead mine and surrounding industrial complex was totally destroyed. At Saltville Keogh led one of Stoneman's brigades in a charge that dispersed a contingent of Virginia Home Guards, and the town's large salt works were put to the torch. By December 29, the cavalry was back at Knoxville, having taken 879 prisoners, 19 cannons, and 25,000 shells. Stoneman was pleased to report "the total destruction, as far as in the power of man to accomplish [of] all the foundries, mills, factories, storehouses, wagon and ambulance trains, turnpike bridges, &c. that we could find."[72]

Keogh spent an enjoyable winter in his quarters at Knoxville. By now, the end was clearly in sight for the Southern Confederacy. Thomas had routed Hood's forces at Nashville, Sherman had marched from Atlanta to the sea, and Grant was tightening his stranglehold on Lee's army at Richmond and Petersburg. Everyone realized that the spring campaign would see the final actions of the war, and Stoneman asked for one more chance to conduct a raid.

As Stoneman's chief aide-de-camp, on March 20, 1865, Keogh again rode out of Knoxville with his commander and Brigadier General Alvan C. Gillem's division, three brigades strong. On March 27 they spent a frigid night on the slopes of the Smokey Mountains, and the next morning advanced on Boone, North Carolina.

The local Home Guards were holding their monthly muster in Boone that day, when at 10 a.m. Keogh and the Twelfth Kentucky Cavalry thundered into town, revolvers blazing. Taken completely by surprise, the Confederates offered little resistance. Bewildered militiamen ran through the village as bullets splintered the houses around them. Anyone who fought back was shot down; nine were killed, sixty-eight captured, and the few survivors fled into the mountains. General Gillem had burned to the ground the local jail and courthouse. He reported, "Much credit is due Major Keogh and the gallant officers and men of the Twelfth Kentucky Cavalry engaged in this affair."[73]

Stoneman's brigades were continuing their rampage through North Carolina and southwestern Virginia when they learned that Petersburg and Richmond had fallen to Grant. On April 12, three days after Lee surrendered at Appomattox, Stoneman confronted 3,000 Confederates drawn up in the defenses of Salisbury, North Carolina. They were a motley crew, old men and boys, Home Guards and even a unit of Northern men who had gone into the Southern ranks to escape the hardships of prison. Stoneman ordered his entire line to attack, and the horsemen swept everything before them. Keogh was accompanying the Eleventh Kentucky Cavalry and, as General Gillem reported, "gallantly led it during the charge."[74] Captain Robert Morrow, a loyal Tennessean serving on Stoneman's staff, was celebrating his twentieth birthday; his left knee was shattered by a Rebel bullet as he galloped with Keogh in the charge. Yet Union losses were slight, and their booty immense. In less than half an hour, 18 guns, 17 flags, and 1364 prisoners fell into Federal hands. Over the next two days, 15 miles of railroad tracks were burned, as were cotton and ordnance factories, 100,000 uniforms, and 160,000 pounds of bacon.

Confident that the last weeks had atoned for his earlier failures, Stoneman departed from Knoxville on April 19, leaving behind two brigades to mop up the last few Confederate diehards. Keogh accompanied the General, realizing that for both of them, as for the whole country, the war was finally over.

Keogh, who now sported the silver oakleaves of a brevet lieutenant colonel, was in Washington, D.C. during the grand review of the triumphant Federal armies on May 23 and 24, 1865.[75] But it was far from an enjoyable occasion for him; Joseph O'Keeffe lay dying in the District's Providence Hospital.

O'Keeffe's bravery in Sheridan's Valley Campaign had brought him a commission as a major in the Second New York Cavalry, which he led in the final campaign against the Army of Northern Virginia. On April 1, as Sheridan's dismounted troopers pinned down a third of Lee's army at Five Forks, O'Keeffe fell from this horse, his right knee shattered by a Rebel bullet. His regiment fell back, but four men ran to the Major's assistance. Two of them were killed carrying O'Keeffe to safety, and the Major struck two more times, in the left shoulder-blade and arm. O'Keeffe never had recovered fully from the wound he had received at Brandy Station and, while in the hospital at Washington, the Brandy Station wound reopened. The amputation of his right leg failed to halt the spread of infection and, on the evening of May 30, after O'Keeffe had lapsed into unconsciousness, the last

70. Stoneman to the Governor of New Jersey, November 14, 1864, Keogh Collection, Gene Autry Western Heritage Museum. Another copy of this letter is in Keogh's Service file at the National Archives. "I shall hate very much to part with him," Stoneman wrote. The Third New Jersey was outfitted in a variation of the hussar style favored by European light cavalry units; the gaudy uniform won the New Jerseymen the nickname "The Butterflies.".

71. Marguerite Merington, *The Custer Story* (New York, NY: Devin-Adair Company, 1950), 133.

72. Stoneman's Report, December 27, 1864, O.R., Series I, Vol. XLV, Pt. 1, 808.

73. Gillem's Report, April 25, 1865, ibid., Series I, Vol. XLIX, Pt. 1, 330-331.

74. Ibid., 333.

75. Service File, National Archives. Keogh was given ten days leave on May 17, 1865; Providence Hospital, General Orders 232, Paragraph 40. Earlier leave and subsequent extension have to date not been located, but as O'Keeffe was being cared for at this hospital the connection seems a logical one.

Young Joseph O'Keefe eventually joined Keogh and Keily in the Union service. He died on May 30, 1865 as a result of wounds received in the Battle of Five Forks, Virginia, on April 1 of that year. *Courtesy of Brian Pohanka.*

---

76. O'Keeffe's Obituary in the Cork *Examiner* (June 27, 1865). He had been breveted lieutenant colonel of Volunteers for "most distinguished gallantry" in the final campaign. "He died as an infant falls asleep," the paper reported, "Clothed in the uniform of his new grade, he was placed in his coffin, and generals were proud to bear his pall." It had been intended to bury O'Keeffe beside General Buford at West Point. However, at his sister's request, the body was sent to Montreal to be interred beside his mother, who had died during her son's imprisonment at Richmond.

rites were administered. The twenty-three year-old officer died quietly at noon the following day, as Keogh sat at his bedside.[76]

It was with a heavy heart that Keogh returned to Knoxville, where General Stoneman had begun the duties of Reconstruction as commanding officer of the Department of Tennessee. Keogh would be one of ten staff officers assigned to Stoneman, and was cheered to find that Alexander, now a brevet brigadier general, would also be there as Stoneman's Chief of Staff. Alexander and his charming wife Evy shared quarters with Keogh and another staff officer in an attractive little house called "Croquet Cottage." General Stoneman and his wife were frequent visitors, as were two of the Union's youngest and most successful general officers —James H. Wilson and Emory Upton. Keogh particularly was taken with the brilliant, intense Upton, who soon was to become engaged to Mrs. Alexander's sister, Emily Martin. It was a happy time, and like many soldiers before and since, Keogh was struck by the abrupt fashion in which war gave way to peace. "I was like in a dream," he wrote his brother Tom, "and completely taken up with war."[77]

Realizing that his commission as a volunteer aide-de-camp eventually was bound to expire, Keogh set about gathering recommendations that hopefully would ensure him a place in the peacetime Regular Army. He probably was not concerned to any great degree, for his distinguished record spoke for itself, and his superiors were most obliging.

"He garnered high praise from his superior officers," General Alvan Gillem wrote, "He is unsurpassed in dash . . . is highly educated & accomplished." General Jacob Cox testified that Keogh's "soldierly bearing and spirit were a model . . . I know of no officer of his grade who made [a] more enviable reputation, or who proved more conclusively that he was born a soldier." General Schofield stated simply, "He is one of the most gallant and efficient young cavalry officers I have ever known."[78] With recommendations like these Keogh virtually was guaranteed a place in the post-war army. "I have enough powerful friends who will always see me provided for," he wrote to Tom, "& I have great hopes as to what the future may bring forth."[79]

In a letter written on Christmas Eve 1865, Myles told his brother, "I have had plenty of trials and have them still . . . My dear Tom my great weakness is the love I have for the fair sex & pretty much all my troubles come or can be traced to that charming source." Marriage seems to have been on Keogh's mind, for he continued, "Talking about marrying I cannot do it I am to [sic] proud to marry & have my wife support herself . . . If I had an economical wife I might get on gloriously."[80]

In the letters he sent to his family in Ireland, Keogh always was careful to preserve his privacy, no more so than when a member of the "fair sex" was involved. Still it is quite clear that during the year and a half he spent in Tennessee, Keogh was affected deeply by a tragic romance.

One clue comes in a letter he wrote to Tom on August 6, 1866, while on court martial duty in Nashville. "I am very very lonely," Keogh confessed, "I have had some things to try me severely so much so that the future is a matter of little importance to me so long as you all are comfortable . . . I now have no one else to care for."[81] The cause for Keogh's melancholy came into sharper focus on October 27, 1866, when he wrote Tom from Washington, D.C. "Now that my hopes are dead for my future earthly happiness & the dear creature I dreamt of being happy with lies yonder in Oakhill Cemetery where I have just visited her cold vault—I wish to tell you that I will devote myself to helping you provide for my darling sisters."[82]

"I shall never marry," Keogh wrote in 1867, "It may have been grief that changed me but changed I am & I seem to have only an idea that is for the happiness & comfort & above all the aggrandizement of my family."[83] And a letter dated June 1, 1869 provides yet another insight, when Keogh remarked, "This month has never passed since I left home without something very unpleasant occurring to me . . ."[84]

The identity of Keogh's "dear creature" can be deduced

Keogh, in a major's uniform, poses with an unidentified comrade, probably Tennessean Robert Morrow of Stoneman's staff, who had been wounded in the foot at Salisbury, North Carolina, on April 12, 1865.
Courtesy of Dr. Elizabeth Atwood Lawrence.

from a pattern of circumstances beginning with the records of Oak Hill Cemetery, a beautifully landscaped Victorian necropolis that sprawls on a terraced hillside in Georgetown, D.C. The cemetery files reveal that on June 23, 1866, twenty-eight year-old Abby Grace Clary was interred in a plot owned by her father-in-law, Colonel and Brevet Brigadier General Robert Emmett Clary. The general was a West Point graduate who made a career as an army quartermaster, and who from 1864 to 1866 was Chief Quartermaster of the supply depot in Memphis, Tennessee.[85]

Abby was the widow of Robert Emmett Clary, Jr., who in 1861 had received a commission in the Second U.S. Cavalry. The twenty-six year-old had been born in Michigan, and when war broke out was assisting his father, then stationed at Fort Crittenden, Utah. Young Clary had risen to captain's rank in the Second, and commanded a squadron of the regiment in Buford's Reserve Brigade, during Stoneman's 1863 raid. A photograph of Captain Clary reveals that he bore a striking resemblance to Myles Keogh, whom he certainly would have known as an active member of Buford's staff. However, the resemblance between the two was purely superficial; for the military career of Robert Emmett Clary, Jr. ended in dismissal and disgrace.

In July 1862, then-Lieutenant Clary was on sick leave in Washington when he was observed by other officers to be "drinking intoxicating liquors and creating a great noise and disturbance" on Pennsylvania Avenue and in the bar of Willard's Hotel. When placed under arrest, he refused to report to at General Wadsworth's headquarters as ordered. Clary was found guilty of "disgraceful behavior," but was acquitted of the charge of drunkenness and defiance of orders, and thus avoided a dishonorable discharge.[86] On August 31, 1862 Confederate cavalry captured Clary with most of his company during Pope's retreat from Second Bull Run. Clary was exchanged three weeks later.

On the eve of the great cavalry fight at Brandy Station, Captain Clary was undergoing a field court martial for drinking with a local farmer, then, while in a drunken

77. October 24, 1865, National Library Microfilm.

78. Letters of recommendation in Service File, National Archives, and in the Keogh Collection of the Gene Autry Western Heritage Museum.

79. December 24, 1865, National Library Microfilm.

80. Ibid.

81. August 6, 1866, National Library Microfilm.

82. October 27, 1866, National Library Microfilm.

83. Undated Letter c. 1867, Fort Wallace, Kansas, National Library Microfilm.

84. June 1, 1869, National Library Microfilm.

85. Records of Oak Hill Cemetery, Georgetown, D.C.; ACP File of Robert Emmett Clary, National Archives. Born in Ashfield, Massachusetts in 1806, Clary graduated thirteenth in the West Point Class of 1828, and had served at posts in Michigan, Missouri, Wisconsin, South Carolina, Florida, New York, Kansas, Louisiana, California, Texas, and Utah. During the Civil War, he was attached to General Pope's Army of Virginia, and later at the Office of the Quartermaster General in Washington. Colonel Clary was chief quartermaster of the Army's Memphis Depot from August 1864 to July, 1866. He retired in 1869, and died in Washington, D.C. January 13, 1890, at the age of 83.

86. Record Group 153, Records of the Judge Advocate General, Record of Courts-Martial Proceedings, National Archives, Washington, D.C., File KK 102. Lieutenant Clary had fallen ill with typhoid fever at Yorktown, Virginia in May 1862 during the early stages of McClellan's Peninsular Campaign. He was on sick leave in Washington through the month of June.

MYLES KEOGH

87. Ibid., File MM 728. Clary had been under arrest since May 18, 1863, and would remain so until September 24, when General Pleasonton declared the court-martial proceedings inoperative and ordered him to rejoin his regiment. Clary spent the greater part of that time in Washington, D.C. prompting Adjutant General James A. Hardie to complain, "This officer has been here doing nothing for months."

88. Record Group 153, Records of the Judge Advocate General, Record of Courts-Martial Proceedings, National Archives, Washington, D.C., File LL 1367. On February 25, 1864, Clary requested a copy of the proceedings of the General Court Martial by which he was tried, apparently in an effort to have the verdict overturned. In this, he was unsuccessful. National Archives, Record Group 94, Letters Received, Office of the Adjutant General.

89. Mrs. Stone died February 10, 1864, and her husband subsequently remarried. Stone served as a general officer and chief of staff of the Army of the Khedive of Egypt from 1870-1883. Another intriguing connection between the Clary clan and Keogh is the fact that in 1871 Keogh's friend and fellow Papal veteran John J. Coppinger visited General Stone in Cairo while on leave of absence from his post with the Twenty-Third U.S. Infantry. Coppinger's ACP File, National Archives.

90. Archives, Memphis Public Library and Information Center. The Memphis Register of Deaths indicates that Abby G. Clary's attending physician was Lieutenant Colonel John Edward Summers, a nineteen-year Army veteran who had served for three years as Medical Inspector for the Memphis garrison. "Gastro fever" may have been appendicitis, a disease very little understood in the 19th-century, and usually fatal. Abby was buried in the same grave as her husband in the Clary plot at Oak Hill. Stoneman's presence in Memphis in the first half of 1866 in part was due to anti-Northern agitation that exploded into violence in the first week of May. Two whites and thirty-eight blacks were killed, and property damage totalled $63,000. National Archives, Letters Received, Department of the Cumberland and Military Division of Tennessee, Record Group 393, Part 1.

91. Myres, *Cavalry Wife*, 36.

condition, threatening to burn the man's house down. Moreover, while on picket duty along the Rappahannock, he had been intoxicated to the point where he was unable to function as squadron commander. Clary was spared a second day of the proceedings, and was allowed to join his unit in the Battle of Brandy Station. The charges against him later were invalidated on a technicality when it was found that the members of the court had not been properly sworn in.[87]

Clary's ultimate brush with military authority came in January, 1864, when he underwent a third court martial for being "in a disgraceful state of intoxication" the previous month during the funeral of an enlisted man at Culpeper. Clary claimed that his conduct was due to earlier bouts with typhoid fever and rheumatism, but that defense did not hold up, and on January 6 he was sentenced to be dismissed from the military service of the United States.[88]

When and where Robert Emmett Clary, Jr. married Abby is as yet unknown, as is her maiden name. But it is clear that she accompanied her troubled husband to Memphis, where they resided at her father-in-law's quarters, and where the younger Clary died, at age twenty-eight, on December 10, 1864. An additional fascinating piece of circumstantial evidence linking the Clarys to Myles Keogh is the fact that another of Colonel Clary's children, Louisa, was the wife of General Charles Stone, the officer on whose staff Dan Keily served during the siege of Port Hudson.[89]

Memphis was within General Stoneman's Department of Tennessee, and Keogh accompanied the General there in January, 1866. Keogh remained in Memphis until June 10, when he temporarily was assigned to court martial duty at Nashville. A week later, on June 17, Abby Grace Clary died suddenly of "gastrofever."[90] One easily can imagine the difficulties Keogh may have encountered in courting the widowed daughter-in-law of a high ranking army officer, only to have his persistence cheated by death.

Myles Keogh soon would have the opportunity of putting this troubled period of his life behind him. On May 4, 1866, he had received a commission as second lieutenant in the Fourth U.S. Cavalry, then stationed in Texas. It was an appointment that caused some concern for Evy Martin Alexander, who learned that the unit "is noted among cavalry regiments for hard drinking."[91] She need not have worried on that account, for Keogh never served with the Fourth Cavalry. The day after Keogh had stood beside the grave of his "dear creature," he was en route for Kansas, and a new assignment as captain of Company I, Seventh U.S. Cavalry.

Chapter 5

THE GIRL I LEFT BEHIND:
Keogh and the Martin Family

by Lenora A. Snedeker

> The hope of final victory
>   Within my bosom burning,
> Is mingling with sweet thoughts of thee
>   And of my fond returning.
> But should I ne'er return again,
>   Still worth thy love thou'lt find me;
> Dishonor's breath shall never stain
>   The name I'll leave behind me.
>   "The Girl I Left Behind"

Whenever students of cavalry warfare hear the song, "The Girl I Left Behind," romantic visions of lovely damsels waving tearful good-byes to handsome officers are conjured up. To those interested in the career of Myles Keogh, speculation has centered around his relationship with Cornelia Eliza Martin, an elder daughter of a large family, of Auburn, New York. Many people are convinced that Miss Martin was the girl that Brevet Lieutenant Colonel Keogh left behind when he met his destiny at the Little Big Horn. Since Myles had close ties with the Martin family, it seems logical to assume that if Keogh had a special lady, it would have been a Martin daughter of comparable age, namely Cornelia. An inspection of the Irish soldier's friendship with the Martins does provide clues to Keogh's feelings toward this intriguing woman.

At first glance, it would appear that Keogh's introduction into the Martin circle came through Secretary of State William Seward. It was due to Seward's influence that Myles received a commission in the United States Army. Indeed, Dan Keily had written to the Secretary prior to his arrival in the United States with Keogh.[1] Secretary Seward's home was in Auburn, and he was a close friend to the Martins. That Keogh was to later become a periodic visitor to the Martin estate, Willowbrook, was coincidental to his contact with Mr. Seward.

Actually, the Auburn connection for Keogh began when he met Andrew Alexander, who in pre-war days was about to embark upon a business career in St. Louis, Missouri. Had the war not ensued, Andrew never would have considered entering the military. However, when events pulled him into the maelstrom of conflict, he turned out to be a very adept soldier. Probably Keogh and Alexander first shook hands when they both were on the staff of General George McClellan. Thereafter, the two officers' paths must have crossed frequently since they served together as aides to General John Buford and later General George Stoneman. In the summer of 1864, an incident occurred during the campaign in Tennessee that was vividly recalled by General James Wilson:

> On the 4th of July, many officers of the various Corps, visited Blair's headquarters to enjoy their hospitality, and among others, Colonel Keogh, that gallant young Irishman, who had served with Alexander on Stoneman's staff, and after escaping all the perils of the

[1] G.A. Hayes-McCoy, *Captain Myles Walter Keogh*, 10.

2. James B. Wilson, *The Life and Services of Brevet Brigadier General Andrew Jonathan Alexander* (New York, NY: Privately Published, 1887), 52-53.

The Throop family's prominence began with Enos Thompson Throop.
Courtesy of George W. Martin.

Rebellion was massacred by the Sioux Indians, with Custer at the Little Big Horn... On the day in question, while the enjoyment was at the highest and the woods were resounding with patriotic songs, a tremendous fire of musketry and artillery broke out on the extreme right, and called the merry revelers at once to the more serious business of the day. All jumped to their horses "with hot haste," and hurried to their appropriate posts. The enemy had sallied out from his lines, and was making a fierce attack. Matters looked serious for awhile, but that was an army of veterans, every one of whom knew what to do in an emergency. A sharp and bloody combat took place, and the Confederates were repulsed with a heavy loss to both sides.[2]

Later in the month, Keogh rode with Stoneman on the ill-fated attempt to free prisoners at Andersonville. The Union troops were defeated near Macon, Georgia. Stoneman and Keogh became prisoners themselves and remained incarcerated for two months until an exchange was arranged on September 30. The experience so debilitated Keogh that he needed a period of time to recuperate. Whether it was for this reason, or other contingencies, Myles apparently did not attend the wedding of Andrew Alexander to Evelina Martin on November 3, 1864, at Sand Beach Church near Auburn. With the nuptial, Andrew became a son in the Martin family by marriage and Keogh, in later years, a son by affection.

Finding the warmth of an adopted family gave Keogh a sense of home since his letters often indicated a longing to be with the kin he left in Ireland. Having decided to remain in the United States after the Civil War, Keogh found it difficult to travel back across the Atlantic to see loved ones. Consequently, the Martins partially filled the void.

Also, his relationship with the Martins bespoke of the close knit ties of the United States Army during this period. Officers of the time often formed a special fraternity, given the small size of the American military in the three decades after the war. They would band together both professionally and socially, as would Keogh and Alexander, along with a third military man, Emory Upton.

Finally, the influence of the Martins through their various political and social connections must have appealed to Keogh, too. In his day, gaining a commission required more than a dashing war record. One needed support from prominent allies. Certainly, the Martins continued to provide Keogh with connections to important people. Their family history sheds light upon why this was the case.

The Throop (pronounced Troop) Martin family's prominence began with Enos Thompson Throop, who was born in Johnstown, New York, in 1784. The untimely death of Throop's father left his mother with the difficult task of rearing four children. Although Mrs. Throop remarried, her new husband had a modest income, so prospects for Enos did not look promising. Fortunately, a Johnstown attorney and his wife, Mr. and Mrs. George Metcalf, saw potential in the boy. When the Metcalfs moved to Albany, because Mr. Metcalf had been appointed district attorney for four counties in that region, the fourteen year old Enos went with them to begin his apprenticeship in law.

Enos was admitted to the bar in 1806 and eventually settled in Auburn. Besides his law practice Throop became active in politics as a Jeffersonian Democrat. In 1828, Martin Van Buren went to Auburn to persuade the young attorney to be his runningmate when Van Buren campaigned for the office of Governor of New York later in the year. The ticket won and Van Buren was sworn in on January 1, 1829, but resigned on March 12th to be secretary of state in Andrew Jackson's cabinet. Throop then served out Van Buren's term as governor and was elected to the post in his own right in 1830.

Prior to this time, while horseback riding near Auburn, he discovered the site that was to become known as Willowbrook. In 1817:

Riding one day on his return from some official duty, along the road bordering the western shore of Owasko Lake, he was attracted by the picturesque situation of a

It was fortuitous that Martin decided to buy Willowbrook, where Keogh often was a guest. he stayed at the Upper House, shown here. *Courtesy of George W. Martin.*

small farmhouse, which he learned on inquiry was owned and occupied by Charles VanTine, a pioneer in the settlement, who had arrived in what was then a wilderness, early in the century, and had built a log house which was the first erection on the lake shore. There were around the main building, several smaller structures appropriated to various uses; the whole forming a convenient farm establishment.

The clear waters of the beautiful lake sparkled in the sunshine, and seemed to the interested traveler who was fascinated by the scene, like 'a crystal in a setting of emerald'.[3]

Soon after taking possession of the farm, Throop invited his mother and other relatives to take up residence. Enos and his wife stayed there as often as professional and political commitments would allow. When the owner was in Auburn, Willowbrook, as it came to be called, was the gathering place for luminaries of the early 19th-Century who were visiting the area.

Despite the comfortable life at Willowbrook, personal tragedy was to strike Governor Throop often and hard. His three children died in infancy, and in 1834 his beloved wife Evelina passed away. Four years later President Martin Van Buren appointed his old friend Throop as chargé d' affaire to the Kingdom of the Two Sicilies. With the prospect of a prolonged stay in Naples, Governor Throop decided to sell Willowbrook to his nephew and protege, Enos Thompson Throop Martin.

Mr. Martin was the son of the Governor's sister Mehetibel. He was born in Johnstown in 1808. The Governor took an early interest in his nephew's upbring-

3. Cornelia Williams Martin, *The Old Home*, Vol. I (Auburn, NY: Privately Published, 1894), 11-12.

4. Lenora A. Snedeker, ed., "The Martin-Seward Correspondence," (unpublished MS materials), Mary Martin to William Seward, August 4, 1870. Hereafter cited as Snedeker, "The Martin-Seward Correspondence."

ing, so it was inevitable that the lad should enter the field of law. After becoming an attorney, young Martin was employed as his uncle's private secretary in 1829 and 1830, the closing years of the Governor's first term. Upon the Governor's reelection in 1830, Martin resigned his post and set out for New York City to establish a private practice.

The venture proved to be a success. Enos Thompson Throop Martin became a prominent attorney in the city and a frequent contributor to various New York publications such as *The Corsair*, *The Mirror*, and *The Knickerbocker Magazine*. His talent in the literary arena was so respected that the New York *Sun* offered him steady employment. Comparing the potential for making money of the two professions, Martin wryly declined.

On June 1, 1837, Martin married Cornelia Williams of Utica, New York. The new bride was attractive, intelligent, charming, and an heiress to a fortune established by her father John Williams, a Utica merchant. The couple began housekeeping in New York City at 63 Clinton Place, where their daughters Mary and Cornelia, known as Nelly, were delivered. It was fortuitous that Martin had decided to purchase Willowbrook from his uncle. In 1840, the same year that Nelly was born, John Williams suffered what in modern terminology probably would be diagnosed as a stroke. For the next three years, the Martins, for all practical purposes, resided in Utica, caring for the invalid to the neglect of the law practice in New York. When Mr. Williams died in 1843, the Martins had to decide whether to resume their former life in Gotham, or plan their future around their home near Auburn. They chose to remain in upstate New York.

Once the decision was made, more farms were bought that surrounded the Owasco Lake property. In 1850 additions were built on to the original farmhouse and outbuildings were constructed. For several years the Martins spent the summers at Willowbrook and winters in Utica. When it was deemed that the house could provide year-round comfort, the Martins moved in permanently.

The additions to the main structure were certainly needed. The Martins were to have eleven children, ten of whom would live to adulthood. One daughter, Harriet, born in New York City, died in infancy. While domiciled in Utica, Mrs. Martin gave birth to Evelina (Evy), Throop, Emily, and Eliza (Lylie). The rest of the children, John, George, Edward, and Violet, entered this world at Willowbrook. As the children were growing up, it was an active, happy, and loving household.

The younger generation of Martins that Keogh came to know were made up of a variety of personalities. The oldest daughter Mary, affectionately called Molly, was born in 1838. In her early years, she was tutored at home by an Englishwoman, Miss Fleming, and then was sent to Miss Haines's boarding school in New York. While there, she was a piano pupil of Richard Hofmann, and in later years Mary was often called upon at Willowbrook to play the Civil War and sentimental songs of the era. An early inclination toward lung disease that was to plague some other members of the family was a continual drain on her physical energy. In the mid 1860s Mrs. Martin took Mary to Nassau in the Bahamas for a rest cure that caused the disease to go into remission but never really cured it. A particular favorite of William Seward's, Mary was invited to be part of his entourage when he made his world tour in 1870. Her reply projects a poignant image of a free spirit imprisoned within an imperfect body:

> I think if I were quite my own mistress, I should say that I would go and with pleasure. It would be very charming to go with you. . . I have wished to travel all my days. I have had dreams that did not end in a milliner's shop in Paris but reached to the Eastern world and delighted to end in India and China. . . I thank you for your kind invitation but I must decline.[4]

Cornelia Eliza Martin, or Nelly, was born the same year as Keogh in 1840. She also benefitted from Miss Fleming's tutelage and followed her older sister to Miss Haines's school. Upon completion of her formal education, Nelly returned home to help superintend the daily activities of what had become a large estate. In 1857, Governor Throop built a home on the property closer to the lake that became known as the Lower House. The

The younger generation of Martins were made up of a variety of personalities including Emily (left) and Cornelia (right) who stand behind Lylie and Myles Keogh. *Courtesy of George W. Martin.*

---

original farmhouse with its many additions became, of course, the Upper House. Enos Thompson Throop Martin had continued the tradition established by his uncle of making Willowbrook a haven of hospitality. On August 31, 1866, one of the most festive post war picnics was held on the lawn of the Lower House. In light of what happened a decade later in Montana, it must have been an occasion that the family recalled with bitter-sweet fondness. The guest list, headed by President Andrew Johnson, included General Grant, Admiral Farragut, Secretary of State Seward, and General Custer. The scene was described in these words:

> The entrances to Willowbrook were decorated with evergreen garlands in honor of the visiting Presidential Party. When General Custer was called on to make a toast he proposed three cheers for the ladies of Auburn, remarking he had observed "Sweet Auburn" contained more than her proportion of females. He said he couldn't make a speech except on horseback, and would therefore follow the illustrious example of his chief and speak with silent eloquence.[5]

In 1843 Evelina Martin was the first of the children to be born in Utica. The usual format was followed in Evy's schooling, a governess at home and a period of attendance at boarding school. She, of all the daughters, seemed to have inherited her father's literary talent. In later years Evy would keep a journal of her travels as an army wife that has provided scholars with valuable information about 19th-Century life in the military from the woman's point of view.

Evelina not only had a keen mind but also an outgoing personality that was apparently irresistible to anyone fortunate enough to know her. The Martins were close friends of Francis Preston Blair, Sr., the editor of the Washington *Globe* and his wife Eliza Violet. Often the Blair children would visit Willowbrook and, in turn, the Martin children would be guests of the Blairs in Silver Spring, Maryland. For the older Martin girls this meant an entry into Washington society and an opportunity to be part of the social events in the exciting capital city.

It was through the Blair connection that Evy met her future husband Andrew Alexander. Andrew's sister had married a Blair, and the Alexanders were related to such prominent families as the Madisons, Prestons, and Biddles. Andrew was born in 1833 in Sherwood, Kentucky, the youngest son of Andrew J. Alexander and Mira Madison. He also received his early education from tutors and then went on to college in Danville, Ken-

5. John S. Manion, Jr., "The Life, Loves and Legends of Myles W. Keogh," text of a speech given before Little Big Horn Associates, Sept. 23, 1978, 50.

6. Wilson, *The Life and Services*, 6.
7. Sandra L. Myres, ed., *Cavalry Wife, The Diary of Eveline M. Alexander, 1866-* (College Station, TX: Texas A&M Press, 1977), 15-16.
8. Edward S. Martin, *Some Accounts of Family Stocks Involved in Life at Willowbrook* (n.p.: Privately Published, 1933), 87.
9. Ibid, 88.
10. Snedeker, "The Martin-Seward Correspondence," Cornelia Williams Martin to William H. Seward, April 4, 1868.

tucky. The adult Andrew stood over six feet with blue eyes, a tawny, full, beard, and blonde hair.⁶ It was probably not long after their initial meeting that Evy and Andrew realized they were suited for each other.

Alexander enlisted in the Union Army as a lieutenant in what was to become the Third Cavalry. He soon joined General George McClellan's staff and later served with distinction as an aide to other Northern commanders. Toward the end of hostilities, he was stationed with the Division of the Mississippi which saw action in Tennessee, Alabama, and Georgia. At the time of the surrender at Appomattox, Andrew held the brevet rank of colonel in the Regular Army, which eventually would be raised to brevet brigadier general. With the advent of peacetime, the Alexanders had to decide which current the flow of their lives should follow. After due consideration, they opted to remain with the military. As Evy explained it, "In our profession we are spared all the annoyances of insurance, taxes, & etc . . . and we have only one thing to take care of — to see that our expenses do not exceed our income. . . Andrew and I very often discuss the pros and cons of army life and we always come to the conclusion that take it all together it is a good place."⁷

In July of 1865, Alexander became inspector general and chief of staff to his former commander General George Stoneman, whose command post was in Tennessee. Andrew and Evy set up housekeeping at Croquet Cottage in Knoxville, sharing quarters with other officers, including Myles Keogh. For the next twenty-two years Andrew Alexander served his country, principally in the Southwest, his faithful wife at his side. They were to have five children, but only one, a son, would survive to adulthood.

During Keogh's visits to Willowbrook, he probably did not see much of the Martin's sons. Throop, the

Evy and Andrew realized they were suited for each other. *Courtesy of George W. Martin.*

eldest, was born in 1844. During the war he entered the United States Naval Academy that was then in Newport, Rhode Island, but he was not cut out for the military. He left the Academy and went on to Union College where he earned his degree in 1866.

Throop pursued a business career, but not always successfully. Often his ventures were doomed by ill-fortune, although a lack of hard-headedness may have contributed to his failures. His younger brother, Edward, fondly recalled:

> He was a person of indomitable cheerfulness, very amusing, not at all lazy, but somewhat over-sanguine, so that he was apt to spend money before he got it and not always with fortunate results. He was perhaps unduly interested in having a good time, which is a defect in a money-maker but not a mortal ailment in a human being. His capacity for enjoyment was very great and also for providing enjoyment for other people.⁸

Throop was destined to succumb to consumption, which would claim the lives of two of his sisters. He was only forty-one when he died, leaving behind a wife and two children. Even at the end, luck had passed him by.

John or Jack Williams Martin was six years younger than Throop and totally different from the other Martin siblings. He was a "natural sportsman" and enjoyed hunting, fishing, and shooting, almost to the exclusion of other activities.⁹ On the threshold of manhood, he announced to his parents that he wanted to go to West Point. Meeting opposition to a military career, Jack wrote Secretary of State Seward asking for the appointment. Seward, of course, believed that the young man's request was sanctioned by the elder Martins and arranged for Jack's entrance. The Secretary learned differently when he received a thank you note from Mrs. Martin, which could be subtitled, "A Mother's Lament." She wrote:

> The poor hen who has raised a brood of ducks may flutter her wings and show signs of maternal distress, but nevertheless the web footed animals will dive into the muddy pool, and the mother, who would fain have

gathered him under her wings, can only gaze after her fledglings.[10]

Perhaps finding the regimen of the Academy not to his liking, Jack resigned after a couple of years and went into business in Albany. The experience as a merchant convinced him that he belonged in the military after all. He obtained a commission in the Army and had a distinguished service career, retiring years later because of a heart condition. George Bliss Martin, born in 1852, completed his schooling in 1870 and started out his mercantile career in Albany. Throughout his life, he was involved with several ventures. For many years he was in the business departments of the *Mail and Express* and the *Sun*, New York City newspapers. When elderly, his health declined and he returned to Willowbrook.

Edward Sanford Martin, the youngest son, became the most illustrious of the younger generation. Born in 1856, he attended prep school at Phillips Academy in Andover, Massachusetts and then entered Harvard. While a student at the university, he was a founder of the *Harvard Lampoon*, a publication of satire still highly regarded in literary circles. He was a co-founder and first editor of the original *Life* magazine, a position he held for 45 years. Martin also wrote a column, "The Easy Chair," for *Harper's Monthly* from 1920-1935. The memoirs of his childhood published under the title *Willowbrook* provide a vivid panorama of the halcyon days on the shores of Owasco Lake. The French government made him a Chevalier of the Legion of Honor for his writings during World War I. Lloyd George, the British statesman, called Martin "the greatest editorial writer using the English language today."[11] Edward outlived his brothers and sisters, succumbing on June 13, 1939.

Of the three youngest Martin daughters, Keogh's interest would have focused on Emily because she married his close friend General Emory Upton. Emily Norwood Martin was born in 1846 and by the war's end had completed her education. In the autumn of 1865, she spent three weeks with the Alexanders at Croquet Cottage in Knoxville. If she did not meet Upton at that time, she probably heard his name mentioned often. Certainly, she became acquainted with Keogh during her stay.

Emily was a small, pretty, fragile girl whose health was of constant concern to the family. She, too, suffered from consumption, and this condition probably was responsible for her deep-seated religious convictions. Her romance with Emory Upton most likely began when he confessed to her that he had lost his faith, and Emily was determined to help him find it. Emily's diary charts the progress of their relationship.

On Saturday, July 21, 1866, General Upton arrived at Willowbrook for a visit. After dinner, he and Emily strolled and had a "lovely chat." On Sunday they sat together in church. Later in the day they walked by the lake. Monday, the couple went on a long horseback ride and again walked in the evening. Emily confessed to her diary, "I like him very much."[12] At the beginning of 1867, Emily spent seven weeks in Washington. "I saw him [Upton] constantly—and long ere I left Washington I found my heart was not in my own keeping—but had almost unconsciously been given to him in all its freshness of first love!"[13] In May they became engaged. However, a short time later, Emily broke the engagement, probably because Upton had backslid on his religious conversion. Whatever the problem, things were smoothed over and, on November 17, they once again were betrothed.

Emory Upton was born in 1839 on a farm near Batavia, New York, the tenth child and sixth son of Daniel and Electra Randall Upton. Early in his youth he became interested in military history, and although he attended Oberlin College in the winter of 1855-56, Upton really had his heart set on West Point. Securing an appointment to the Military Academy, he entered on July 1, 1856 and graduated eighth in his class in 1861. During the Civil War, Upton saw varied service with the artillery, infantry, and cavalry. He participated in a large

Keogh's interest would have focused on Emily because she married his comrade Emory Upton. *Courtesy of George W. Martin.*

THE MARTIN FAMILY

11. *Time* Magazine, obituary (June 26, 1939).
12. John S. Manion, Jr., ed., "The Diary of Mrs. Emily Norwood Martin Upton," (unpublished MS) entries July 21 and 23, 1866.

13. Ibid., Nov. 29, 1867.
14. Brian C. Pohanka, "Myles Keogh," *Military Images*, (September-October, 1986), 21.
15. Merlin E. Sumner, ed., *The Diary of Cyrus B. Comstock* (Dayton, OH: Morningstar House, Inc., 1977), 296.
16. Myres, *Cavalry Wife*, 111, 114.
17. Pohanka, "Myles Keogh," 21.
18. Ibid.

number of engagements in which his skill in tactics and his bravery earned him the rank of brevet major-general by war's end.

Upton's most lasting contribution came in the postwar years. After brief stints in Colorado and Tennessee, he was transferred to West Point as a member of the board of officers appointed to consider the system of infantry tactics which he had prepared. This system was adopted in 1867 and has been the greatest single influence on the United States military services since its implementation. In 1870 Upton became commandant of cadets at West Point where he remained for five years and was an instructor. His influence on the corps during that time period was immeasurable.

Following West Point, in 1875, he was assigned to professional duty on a trip around the world. For almost two years, he studied the armies of Europe and Asia. Upon his return he was stationed at Fort Monroe, Virginia, and then was put in command of the Fourth Artillery and the Presidio of San Francisco.

Emory Upton's military career was brilliant, but his personal life was tragic. He and Emily were wed in February, 1868; two years later she died of consumption. In 1881, possibly incurably ill himself and still grieving for his young bride, General Upton committed suicide. He was buried in Auburn almost eleven years to the day that his wife had passed away.

Fate was not much kinder to Eliza Williams Martin, Lylie to the family. Born in 1848, she was married in the autumn of 1868, the second nuptial to be celebrated at Willowbrook that year. Her bridegroom was Grenville Tremain, a college friend of young Throop Martin. The couple settled in Albany, and when Grenville died in 1878 at the age of thirty-five, Lylie was left with five children to raise.

The youngest daughter Violet Blair Martin was born in 1859. Violet followed in the footsteps of her older sisters, Evy and Emily, by marrying into the military. Her husband, General Wilber Elliott Wilder, participated in the Plains wars and was awarded the Medal of Honor. He was an officer who helped bring about the surrender of Geronimo.

When he moved into Croquet Cottage in 1865, Keogh met his first Martin in the person of Evy Alexander. Neither of them could have envisioned that in the years to come, the Irish soldier's life would become interwoven with that of the Owasco Lake family. After Keogh's death, Evy wrote, "How it was he had so wound himself around our hearts I never could comprehend."[14] Keogh's initial impression of the perky bride probably was favorable. When Cyrus Comstock, General Grant's chief engineer, was introduced to Mrs. Alexander two weeks after her marriage, he recorded in his diary, "Alexander and his wife Evy Martin arrived in the city [Washington] in the evening. Miss Evy is looking very pretty. Alexander is very fortunate to have such a wife."[15] Comstock was later to marry into the Blair family, thus strengthening his ties to the Alexanders.

The year in Knoxville was a happy time for all the inhabitants of Croquet Cottage, and Evy seems to have functioned as a surrogate mother for the single officers. In subsequent entries in her diary, she refers to them as "my boys."[16]

Possibly at this time Keogh needed some maternal advice. Shortly after the war, Myles wrote to his brother Tom, "My great weakness is the love I have for the fair sex, and pretty much all my trouble comes from or can be traced to that charming source."[17] The member of the "fair sex" that Keogh had his eye on while living at Croquet Cottage was apparently Abby Grace Clary, the widow of Captain Robert Emmett Clary, Jr. She was living in Memphis at the home of her father-in-law, who was the chief quartermaster of the Memphis depot. How far the courtship progressed is uncertain. When she died in June of the following year at the age of twenty-eight, the young Irishman's grief was profound. In October of 1866 when he visited her tomb in Washington, D.C., he wrote home, ". . . My dear brother now that my hopes are dead for my future earthly happiness & the dear creature I dreamt of being happy with lies yonder in Oak Hill Cemetery where I have just visited her cold vault. . . I wish to tell you that I will devote myself to helping you to provide for my darling sisters."[18]

One of the officers who visited Croquet Cottage was

General James Wilson. When Wilson's engagement was announced, Evy wrote to him, mentioning Myles's reaction, "Colonel Keogh is most earnest in his congratulations . . . —I think the news of your engagement made him a little melancholy—one does not like to see all their bachelor friends deserting them."[19]

It is probable that another visitor to Croquet Cottage was Nelly Martin. The Martin siblings frequently traveled to each other's homes, especially when one of them, like Evy, would find it difficult to return to Auburn. If that was the case, Nelly's introduction to Myles Keogh and the other dashing cavalrymen made an indelible impression. Years later, her youngest brother Edward would record, "Nelly had a lively interest in men of the Army and of the Navy and loved to have them at Willowbrook. . . ."[20]

Keogh made his first trip to the home at Willowbrook in October 1866. Cyrus Comstock wrote in his diary that he visited the estate in the middle of that month, and Keogh was there. In addition, a letter from Evy Alexander to her mother dated October 28, 1866, stated: "I am glad that you liked my dear friend Keogh. We are both very fond of him and it has been a great gratification that he has been to our home. From his letter to Andrew he seemed to be so happy there. I should be very glad indeed if he were in the same regiment [with us]." By the time Emily Martin married Upton in February 1868, Myles was close enough to the family circle to be asked to be a groomsman and to sail on the same ship for Europe as the honeymoon couple. None of these plans came to fruition because, shortly before the wedding, Keogh slipped on the ice in Boston and broke his leg. When he arrived at Willowbrook in March, it was to seek solace while his bones mended. In the decade following the Civil War, the Irish cavalryman made periodic visits to Willowbrook. Only a few of these visits are on record, unfortunately. Edward S. Martin reminisced about those times, "I see him now, sitting in the library by the glass door reading *Charles O'Malley* to a circle of girls sitting around and working on something. *Charles O'Malley, The Irish Dragoon!* It never had a fitter reader than Keogh."[21] Certainly, Myles became a great favorite with the family, and when he was not there in person, he kept in contact by mail.

For Keogh, a stay with the family must have been idyllic. Fishing in the lake or strolling around the spacious grounds were activities to enjoy. People constantly were dropping by and an impromptu picnic might be the order of the day. Although Myles was not in residence on the following occasion, Mrs. Martin's account is typical of the unexpected that could occur at anytime:

> Early in the morning of a very promising day in the month of July, 1867, Gen. Alexander and our son George arranged a fishing excursion, and finding a boat on the lake awaiting their coming, they stepped into it

It is probable that one of the visitors to Croquet Cottage was Nelly Martin. *Courtesy of George W. Martin.*

19. Ibid.
20. Martin, *Some Accounts*, 84.
21. Ibid., 83-84.

22. Martin, *The Old Home*, Vol.II, 37-40.
23. Martin, *Some Accounts*, 10.
24. Myres, *Cavalry Wife*, 48.

with their bait and fishing apparatus, and rowed to the old-time fishing ground, where the beautiful perch readily came to the hook and promptly rewarded the anglers' toil.

Gen. Alexander's beloved mother was visiting us, and as I went to her room to say 'good morning' to her, from the veranda at her door, I was attracted by the sudden appearance of two gentlemen who stepped from the carriage and walked toward the house. Our friendly stag-hound Maida, rushed to the gate to meet our visitors and was warmly caressed by the distinguished guest, who accompanied our friend, Secretary Seward . . . and going out to receive him [I] learned that his companion was the British minister, Sir Frederick Bruce. . . .

Mr. Seward and his companion were soon joined by a large company of ladies and gentlemen from Auburn. . . . After receiving them, we asked Mr. Seward if he and his friends would lunch with us. He consented to this proposition and ere long the whole party took a stroll through the grounds. As we left the house, Mary laughingly said to me, 'Mother, I will set the table, and you must pray for something to put on it' alluding to the state of the larder, which was not prepared for such an impromptu visit; however, we had scarcely reached the shore when our fishermen, with a remarkable draught of shining perch, swept round the point of the cove and we were aglow with satisfaction at this opportune providence.[22]

On cool, rainy days, a crackling fire in the grate invited a gathering to tell stories of by-gone days. Often the other houseguests were military men, also, and Keogh could relive with them exploits upon the field of battle. Or the Martins might recount tales of family tradition. A favorite anecdote for Myles must have been how the Throops came by their name. Since one of Keogh's uncles had been hanged by the British, he must have felt an affinity with the ancestor who had needed to flee. Edward Martin years later included the saga in his Willowbrook memoirs.

There is a story that the true name of the Throop family is Scroope, and it derives from Col. Adrian Scroope, who fought in the Parliamentary army, was Governor of Bristol Castle in 1649, served on the High Court of Justice that condemned King Charles I, and signed his death warrant. After the Restoration he was tried, condemned and executed in 1660. But William Throope, who turned up at Barnstable, Mass., in 1666 and married Mary Chapman, was believed in the Throop family to be the son of the regicide, who had changed his name for reasons of politics and safety.[23]

As the younger Martins left home through marriage or to seek their fortunes in the world, more responsibility fell on the shoulders of the two oldest daughters, Mary and Nelly. When Nelly was not in Auburn helping to superintend the daily activities of the large estate, she was away visiting family or friends. Sadly, Nelly is often judged by the eccentricities caused by deafness in her old age but, as a young woman, she projected an image of affection, dependability, and even humor. Evy made an entry in her diary in 1866 that provides some insight:

Crossed the creek, a broad shallow stream this morning . . . Andrew was wishing the other day Nelly was along. I thought of her today when we seemed within an ace of going over a dozen times and feared she would have found this a 'harder road to travel' than the one General Stoneman's white mule carried her over.[24]

Certainly it was to Nelly that the family turned in time of crisis. In October 1868, concern for Emily Martin Upton's health found Nelly in Key West, Florida, to remain there with her younger sister for five months. It was hoped that the climate would cure, or at least alleviate, Emily's suffering from consumption. She did seem to improve and for a few months lived with her husband while he was stationed in Atlanta. However, in June of 1869 Emily became seriously ill again and was taken home to Willowbrook. That November, Upton and Nelly escorted Emily to Nassau in the Bahamas. Emory stayed a month but had to return to duty in the states, leaving his wife to the capable care of Nelly. Toward the end of March, 1870, it became evident that Emily was dying. General Upton was not able to get there in time, so Nelly faced the end alone. For the ten nights before her sister expired, Nelly had only two or three hours sleep a night as she recalled:

> You would have been surprised to see how much fatigue I have been able to endure. I stayed with Emily every night for ten nights. I only got three hours sleep out of twenty-four, and the last forty-eight hours I only slept two. . . . I knew God would give me strength for as long as I needed it.[25]

There are other kinds of heroics besides those performed on the battlefield.

The death of Emily in 1870 was the beginning of a difficult decade for the Martins. In 1872 their dear friend William H. Seward died, and in 1874 Governor Throop passed away. The shock of what was to occur on a lonely field in Montana was yet to come. In the ten years that Keogh maintained his relationship with the Martins, Nelly had to be affected greatly. She was no doubt there to pamper him when he was in residence and was one of his correspondents when he was not. Shortly before leaving on the mission that culminated at the Little Big Horn, Myles wrote Nelly a final letter:

> We leave on Monday on an Indian expedition & if I ever return I will go on and see you all. I have requested to be packed up and shipped to Auburn in case I am killed, and I desire to be buried there. God bless you all, remember if I should die — you may believe that I loved you and every member of your family — it was a second home to me.[26]

The following year, when Keogh's body was shipped to Auburn, Nelly with other family members, was at the depot to receive the "precious box."[27] A few days later Nelly wrote to Keogh's sister in Ireland:

> I longed to have you by my side as we went to receive the precious boy — that we might weep together . . . but I am glad you were not here for it was too sorrowful a sight and opened the wound apart — and made the old sorrow wake and cry. My brother and sisters and myself went to the station to receive the body and placing it in one of our wagons instead of a hearse . . . we took him to the receiving vault where we have deposited it temporarily. We laid flowers upon it and left it reluctantly for we feel it contains the remains of our darling.[28]

And so, Myles Keogh, by his own choice, had been brought to his final home in Auburn. Ever since then, stories have persisted that a leading factor in the Colonel's request was his romantic attachment for Nelly. Generations of students have tried to find conclusive proof that there was an "understanding" between them. But, no matter what scholars believe about the relationship of Myles Keogh and Nelly Martin, one essential fact stands out. Keogh knew Nelly for a decade, and had he wished to marry her, the opportunity was there. The really intriguing question is, why he did not.

First of all, Keogh's attitude toward wedlock was ambivalent. In one letter he wrote to his brother, "I am too proud to marry and have my wife support herself [but] I fancy if I had an economical wife I might get by gloriously."[29] Yet in another letter home he stated, "I never propose to form any ties. I might often have married for money but I never gave it a moment's serious thought and never propose to."[30] However, there is a tinge of wistfulness when Keogh commented about Henry Nowlan's engagement: "I am living with Nowlan and I find he is engaged to be married . . . to a sweet girl. He seems to like being in love."[31] Nowlan was Myles's closest friend in the Seventh Cavalry.

Secondly, there is a hint that Keogh did not have the finesse to be a successful suitor. For example, in 1871, Keogh requested that his commanding officer, George Custer, send "a handsome collection of flowers" to a certain "Miss Hf." However, the young lady in question did not return Keogh's affections, finding him "monotonous and uninteresting."[32] Obviously, Keogh assumed a romantic relationship that was nonexistent. A less naive man would have known better.

Finally, there was an aura about Myles Keogh that brought out the maternal, rather than the romantic instinct in many of the women that he knew. Evy Alexander mothered him from the days at Croquet Cottage and, after his death, Nelly Martin in letters to his sister

THE MARTIN FAMILY

25. Unpublished letter from Cornelia Eliza Martin to her parents, April 3, 1870, provided by John S. Manion, Jr.
26. Pohanka, "Myles Walter Keogh (1840-1876)," 11.
27. Manion, "The Life, Loves, and Legends of Myles W. Keogh," 50.
28. Ibid.
29. Hayes-McCoy, *Captain Myles Walter Keogh*, 35n.
30. Pohanka, "Myles Walter Keogh," 22.
31. Lawrence, *His Very Silence Speaks*, 88.
32. Merington, *The Custer Story*, 236.

This picture of Nelly Martin was one the family received after Myles' death, having been taken after 1878. *Courtesy of Gary Keogh.*

33. Manion, "The Life, Loves, and Legends of Myles W. Keogh," 50.
34. Hayes-McCoy, *Myles Walter Keogh*, 33-34.
35. Lawrence, *His Very Silence Speaks*, 88.
36. Eveline Alexander to Nelly Martin, September 17, 1881 (Elizabeth Atwood Lawrence Collection, Westport Harbor, MA).

In the late 1870s, another photograph of Nelly accompanied one of her letters of condolence to Margaret Keogh. *Courtesy of Gene Autry Western Heritage Museum.*

referred to him as the "precious boy."[33] At the time of his broken leg he received such kind attention from a lady who was acting as his nurse, "the young wife of an army officer," that he jokingly wrote he was "very much inclined to elope with her."[34] He may have been referring to Evy Alexander. He also seemed to seek out older women who probably represented mother figures to him. From Fort Abraham Lincoln he wrote, "Mrs. Sturgis the wife of the Colonel of my Regiment is perfectly charming & I find myself going there every day."[35]

There are two elements in the Myles Keogh—Nelly Martin relationship that often are used to dismiss the possibility of a romance. The most obvious factor that comes to mind is religious differences. A closer examination indicates, however, that church affiliation was not an insurmountable barrier. Nelly belonged to the branch of the family that was High Episcopalian. There used to be a witty saying that Anglicans were Roman Catholics who had flunked Latin. Certainly either Myles or Nelly could have made an accommodation on the religious question and have been comfortable with the decision.

Nor can clash of personalities be relied upon to provide the answer. The younger Nelly was a far cry from the cantankerous and domineering old woman that she became. Myles, who had maintained strong ties to his family in Ireland, must have admired the manner in which Nelly faithfully and competently handled difficulties that arose in her own household. And surely, her popularity as a houseguest with family and friends attest to a congenial nature. Keogh himself wanted Nelly to remember that he had loved her.

The key to their relationship lies in the psyche of Myles Keogh, the Irish cavalier. Keogh was the ultimate romantic, a posture that often makes great warriors but terrible lovers. Like most romantics, Myles was enamored with the idea of being in love, but there is a huge gap between the ideal and the reality. He could bury his heart in the grave with Abby Grace Clary, or joke of running away with a married nurse, or write sentimental poetry to a shallow woman, but he seemed to avoid relationships where a real commitment would be required.

Being flirtatious and charming was part of his make-up; however, he knew intuitively that he always would be happier by the campfire than by the hearthfire. A woman as intelligent and sensible as Nelly Martin would have been aware that Myles's sojourns to civilization were only temporary. Eventually, the camaraderie of the army post drew him back to the company of his fellow officers. A prolonged, conventional lifestyle would have destroyed his soul.

The burial of Myles Keogh in 1877 did not end the sorrows for the Martin family. The following year, Lylie's young husband died. She eventually would return to Willowbrook. It also became obvious during this time that the Martins were no longer wealthy. Exorbitant taxes during the Civil War and the devaluation of the dollar in its aftermath took their toll on the family's coffers. The oldest daughter, Mary, established a canning business that became so successful, that they had on their payroll as many as fifty people, and their preserves were sold as far away as New York City. Nelly supplemented the income by selling cakes and pastries.

In March 1881, the news of Emory Upton's suicide stunned the Martins. Eleven years earlier, Emily had been buried on the property. Her body was exhumed, and she and Emory were interred at Fort Hill Cemetery in Auburn. In the autumn of 1881, after visiting the site where Myles had died, Evy made this observation about the deaths of those two gallant soldiers, Keogh and Upton:

> Sad as were my thoughts of our Keogh's death, I could not but think—Ah! Emory! Your fate was still more to be lamented.
> You would have envied the soldier who died sword in hand, as you contended not against flesh and blood, but against principalities, against powers, against the rulers of darkness of this world!
> Like our blessed Lord—he saved others, himself he could not save.[36]

In 1883, Enos Thompson Throop Martin died in his seventy-fifth year. In 1884, Mary succumbed to complications of the lung disease that had plagued her so long.

She was forty-six years old. Nelly took over the canning business, which was more lucrative than baked goods. Due mainly to the efforts of Mary and Nelly, Willowbrook remained in the family until 1951, when the costs of maintaining the estate became prohibitive. All the old buildings are gone, and a housing complex has been erected in their place. In 1885 Throop died at Saranac, New York, a tuberculosis treatment center. On July 3 of that year, Andrew Alexander was forced to retire from the military because of illnesses that developed during his service years. In May 1887, he died at the age of fifty-four. The only male Martin left on the estate was George, who could function physically but had divorced himself from reality. As the century was drawing to a close, it was appropriate that Cornelia Williams Martin, the matriarch, expired in 1899 at the age of eighty-one.

Seven of the ten Martin offspring survived into the 20th-Century. Jack, who had retired from the army because of a heart ailment, became a gentleman farmer in Avon, New York. He was fifty-three when he died in 1903. Lylie died at Willowbrook in 1909 at the age of sixty-one. The following year, Upton Alexander, who had lived on the estate with his mother Evy, expired at the age of thirty-five. He was unmarried. Violet, the youngest daughter, passed away in 1919. She was sixty. Evy lived until she was seventy-nine, succumbing in 1922. George existed in his dream-like state another three years dying in 1925 in his seventy-third year.

Fittingly, Nelly, who had contributed so much to keeping Willowbrook solvent, was the last of the old generation living on the estate to go. In 1927, at age eighty-seven, Nelly's trials were over. It was left to Edward, her only surviving sibling, to write the memoir that chronicled the lives, loves, and losses of this fascinating family.

But the story did not end with Nelly's death. Rumors had circulated in the Auburn area for years about Nelly and Myles, fueled by Nelly's annual visits to Keogh's grave on the anniversary of his death. It was a pilgrimage she would make faithfully for fifty years.

Then, in 1939, Edward S. Luce made their relationship part of a lasting lore:

> Their friendship caused Keogh to lose his heart. . . . Whether or not this deep friendship was prevented from culminating into anything deeper, we do not know. We do know Keogh never married. Neither did this young lady; and for 50 years after this Gary Owen entered his Valhalla, she remained true to his memory, later to be buried beside him.[37]

Nelly is not buried next to Myles, but nearby. Nor can it be said that Keogh had lost his heart, though he was deeply fond of her. Those who conjecture that Keogh was the twelfth Martin, an adopted son, come closest to the mark. He was regarded as a member of the family, not as a suitor for Nelly. Andrew Alexander stated it best, "A hero in battle, he was as tender as a woman to those he loved. . . Those who had the honor of his friendship will mourn his loss as long as they live."[38]

Ironically, the most hardened realist cannot resist thinking of Myles Keogh and Nelly Martin in tandem when listening to "The Girl I Left Behind." The legends that have predominated through the mists of time have bonded them together more closely than any earthly marriage ever could.

---

37. Luce, *Keogh, Comanche and Custer*, 23.
38. Pohanka, "Myles Keogh," 24.

"Reconnaissance"

Myles Keogh
A Graphological Perspective

by P.D. Gleason

Many years ago, the Los Angeles Corral of the Westerners published Carroll Friswold's book *Frontier Fighters And Their Autograph Signatures*.[1] This work contains handwriting specimens from a number of participants in the 1876 campaign—including Sitting Bull! One section was devoted to a brief sample penned by Myles Keogh on May 26, 1863, which stated simply:

"Myles W. Keogh Capt. & A.D.C.
   Staff of Brig Genl. Jn. Buford
     Comdg. Regular Cavalry Brigade
       Army of Potomac."

Following this entry was a detailed analysis by Chattanooga graphologist Thurmena Munns, who had this to say about Keogh:

> The writing, well-spaced and positioned on the paper shows cultivation and refinement with a clear and lucid mind, proper sympathy and angle accorded to the vertical strokes. Also, a large and generous writing; but, still, not one who would easily be imposed upon, though one who would make every possible allowance for the shortcomings of others. He was patient, gentle, idealistic and protective. One not easily influenced.
>
> There is a great deal of logic shown in the solidarity of the words, with fine reasoning powers, capability, keen intelligence, the executive mind, firmness, ardor and control. He was self-possessed, dynamic, dependable, completely reliable and not in any sense wasteful.
>
> His intuition was strong, which sharpened his perception, gave him tact and understanding of human nature, one who instinctively does and says the right thing at the right time. Such a person would "know" without knowing why he knows.
>
> The boldness of his writing reveals a brave, courageous nature, self-reliant, unafraid, liking finish in all that is done. There is independence in decision, strong likes and dislikes in the heavy writing, love of color and great depth of emotion. It would be my conclusion that he was of noble stature and greatly loved.

Quite a remarkable assessment from only four lines of penmanship!

Handwriting was first used as a means of determining character during the 11th-Century in China. Since then, scholars from around the world have been making contributions to graphological research. The method itself is primarily a technical procedure; the study lies in the way letters are formed and words written. Actual word content does not play a dominant role. Handwriting characteristics fall into well defined categories, each of which can be classified as a "positive" or "negative" trait. Once all characteristics have been identified, they are evaluated and interpreted.[2]

Since the original Munns' analysis was based upon a mere four lines of Keogh script, a lengthier handwriting specimen might offer additional insight into his character and personality. The Ayer Collection in Chicago provided a copy of Keogh's May 13, 1867, "it is a waste of horseflesh" letter to Lieutenant Myles Moylan, which was then studied using available graphology reference works as guidelines.[3]

Initial results were surprisingly similar to the evalua-

---

[1] Carroll Friswold, *Frontier Fighters And Their Autograph Signatures* (Los Angeles, CA: Westernlore Press, 1968).

[2] For further background on the subject see Robert Holder, *You Can Analyze Handwriting* (New York, NY: Signet, 1969) and Claude Santoy, *The ABC's of Handwriting Analysis* (New York, NY: Paragon House, 1989).

tion by Munns. As in that analysis, the "positive" Myles Keogh shines through—educated, intelligent, and possessing sound judgement. He was trustworthy, honest, well organized, resolute, and diplomatic; ideal qualities in an officer, especially at staff level. He also took boundless joy in living, and was capable of great warmth and consideration for those he favored.

There is also a strong mixture of ambitions and frustrations in Keogh's handwriting. He shows great pride in his profession, but equal disappointment at the inability to achieve his lofty career goals—advancement potential being what it was in the "peacetime" Army. Keogh was passionate about his pleasures, but Plains duty hardly could be considered a hedonist's delight. Sexual frustration shows in his writing; little wonder, considering the limited availability of female companionship in that particular environment. He undoubtedly would partake in any pleasant diversion that came his way, alcohol being a logical, and relatively abundant option. Although contemporary accounts indicate Keogh had a fondness for the bottle, no visible signs of alcoholism are apparent in this letter. Those written later in his life may tell another story.

Other "negative" characteristics are also present in his penmanship. A number of signs indicate he was an extremely vain, narcissistic individual, which seems to be borne out by virtually every known photograph of the man. Considering the frustrations he felt in other areas of his life, pride in his personal appearance may have been the one goal he consistently achieved throughout his life. How appropriate that his body would be one of those not mutilated after the Custer battle!

Keogh's writing also shows aggressive tendencies, which would serve him well in combat situations. But those same tendencies, combined with his bouts of uncontrollable rage, would produce rather unpleasant consequences for those unfortunate enough to be involved; even more so if Keogh had been drinking beforehand. One never would know when to expect the "good" or "bad" Keogh. He was indeed a complex man.

It seemed unusual these negative aspects of Keogh's character would be overlooked in the Munns' analysis, since many of the same handwriting characteristics also are present in the sample she examined. Another look at her findings produced an interesting discovery—many of these attributes are, in fact, mentioned, but in carefully chosen terms. The wide range of feelings Keogh must have experienced with his frustrated ambitions might well be described as "strong likes and dislikes" while "ardor" would aptly describe his passions. "Self-possessed" is a polite term to use for vanity; "great depth of emotion" would apply to anger as well as affection. Graphological interpretation can vary with individual perspective; the reader must be the final judge as to whether handwriting analysis is a useful historical research tool or not.

History has chosen to remember Myles Keogh. Perhaps the portraits presented here will provide additional assistance in understanding this complicated, enigmatic individual. In 1867, he turned twenty-seven years-old; his life was already three-quarters finished. The Seventh Cavalry still was new, and death on a Montana hillside lay in waiting nine years beyond the horizon.

3. Myles W. Keogh to Myles Moylan, May 13, 1867 Ayer Collection, Accession 228/543, Newberry Library, Chicago, IL.

Three of Keogh's fellow officers, James Bell, Myles Moylan, and Henry J. Nowlan, sat for Leavenworth photographer E. E. Henry in the late 1860s. *Courtesy of Ethel Yates Gray.*

At left: In this *circa* 1870 photograph, Keogh wears the full dress uniform of a cavalry captain. His hat is a rather debonair interpretation of the official article. On his chest, he wears an assortment of his Papal medals—a full-sized Order of St. Gregory as well as a miniature of the same decoration, a miniature of his Medal of the Chair of St. Peter, and a Fifteenth Corps badge. *Courtesy of Dr. Elizabeth Atwood Lawrence.*

Keepsake
A recently discovered photo of Myles Walter Keogh

I wasn't particularly thinking about Myles Keogh as I went through the stack of photographs, and at first I didn't recognize him. An unrelated project had brought me to the Amon Carter Museum in Fort Worth, Texas, to look at prints made from unidentified glass plate negatives by Leavenworth, Kansas, photographer E.E. Henry. Suddenly, a somber-faced man stared back at me from beneath a large 7th U.S. Cavalry insignia. Across the top was a backward handwritten inscription, which when held up to a nearby mirror read: "Col. Koch, Koch or Kough." Col. Keogh perhaps?

Next to George Armstrong Custer himself, probably no 7th Cavalry officer has been written about and admired more than Captain Myles Walter Keogh. Often photographed, his handsome face is well known to students of the Little Big Horn. While this image looked different from any I'd seen of him, it quickly became evident that this was, indeed, a previously unknown photograph of Myles Keogh.

Hair longer than usual, moustache more closely cropped, and without his characteristic "Imperial" goatee, he appears heavier here than in his other portraits. A few gray hairs are starting to show. This image was the work of photographer E.E. Henry, who had a gallery in Leavenworth, Kansas, from 1864 until past the turn of the century. Henry not only recorded life in the bustling Missouri River port, he photographed military personnel from nearby Fort Leavenworth, the army's gateway to the frontier. So it wasn't surprising that he had a taken a photograph of Myles Keogh; the question was when.

A vintage print of this image might contain some clue, but none is known to exist. All that survives is the glass plate negative, which is not dated. The portrait was shown to a number of experts, including all three editors of this book: John Langellier, Kurt Cox and Brian Pohanka. Among the others consulted were military uniforms specialist Douglas McChristian, collector Glen Swanson and E.E. Henry authority David Phillips.

The gray hair and heavier appearance initially led me to speculate that this might be a late photograph of Myles Keogh, perhaps even the last ever taken. For that to be the case, though, Keogh had to have been in Leavenworth during the final year of his life. By the mid-1870s, Keogh and the 7th Cavalry were stationed at Fort Abraham Lincoln near Bismarck, Dakota Territory, hundreds of miles from Kansas. Keogh traveled to Louisville, Kentucky, for medical treatment while on sick leave from August 26 to October 14, 1875. Could he have passed through Leavenworth? The records at Forts Leavenworth and Lincoln were checked, and the local newspapers for those two areas reviewed, but there was no evidence that he had.

We know that elements of the 7th Cavalry were at Fort Leavenworth in earlier years, and Keogh himself was at that post in April 1868 and again from March until June 1870. Was this photograph taken on one of those occasions? Keogh's attire is consistent with those dates. But what of the heavier appearance and the gray hair? In letters to his brother in Ireland in the late 1860s, Keogh had said he was "getting too fat" and had "plenty of grey hairs." And finally, though undated, the style and size of the glass plate negative itself match others taken by E.E. Henry in the 1869-70 period.

So the available evidence seems to point to an 1868 to 1870 date for this new-found portrait of Myles Keogh. Perhaps the E.E. Henry photo was taken at a time when Keogh was in poor health or drinking to excess (in fact his 1868 tour at Fort Leavenworth followed a lengthy recuperation from a fractured leg). Also, Henry's portrait is printed from the original negative, adding a sharpness and clarity that may highlight features that are softened in the more familiar vintage albumen prints.

Perhaps further research can establish an exact date for this photograph. For now though, it takes its place among the other Myles Keogh portraits in this book.

JAMES S. BRUST, M.D.
San Pedro, California
March 17, 1998

Issued as a keepsake by Upton & Sons, Publishers, El Segundo, California, upon the second printing of *Myles Keogh: The Life and Legend of an "Irish Dragoon" in the Seventh Cavalry*, 1998.

KEEPSAKE
MYLES WALTER KEOGH

Reproduced by permission of the Amon Carter Museum. Accession number P1978.122.1.241, Captain Myles Keogh, E.E. Henry photographer, 1868-1870, Collodion wet plate negative, Amon Carter Museum, Fort Worth Texas.

Chapter 6

To Garry Owen and Glory:
Keogh and the Seventh Cavalry, 1866-1876

by Kurt Hamilton Cox

> . . . All the bright aspirations of a soldier's glory, all my enthusiasm for the pomp and circumstance of glorious war, fell coldly upon my heart; and I looked upon the chivalry of a soldier's life as the empty pageant of a dream
>
> Charles Lever, *Charles O'Malley*

If the Civil War had seemed to Myles Keogh to be, "like in a dream", then the situation in which he found himself on November 21, 1866 must have awakened him to the stark reality of his new life on the American frontier. Some days earlier, the newly appointed captain had departed the headquarters of the recently organized Seventh Cavalry at Fort Riley, Kansas. In temporary command of Company I, Keogh had orders to take post at Fort Wallace. Captain Michael V. Sheridan, who commanded Company L, rode with Myles across the bleak Kansas plains on his way to an assignment at Fort Morgan, beyond Wallace in the Colorado Territory.

Having arrived in camp near Fletcher, Kansas, after a pleasant march from Ellsworth, Myles and his small detachment looked forward to a short rest and a resupply of forage and rations. What they found instead was but a limited quantity of supplies, with food and fodder of such poor quality as to jeopardize the continuance of the march. Captain Sheridan, brother of the famous Civil War general, informed George Custer, his friend and commander, of the situation. "Here the hay is *bad, very bad,*" Sheridan wrote. He stated further that the rations, which consisted of nothing but flour, were "absurd." "I am informed," Sheridan complained, "that it will be worse at Wallace."

In an addendum to Sheridan's letter, Keogh expressed a sense of indignant frustration which would come to characterize this period of his military service, "It is an outrage to supply nothing in the way of bread, for green soldiers, but flour when the proper arrangements for cooking the article are *not* found possible to be obtained."[1]

That Keogh would address his new commanding officer in such a familiar manner was not unusual since the two had known each other during the Civil War. In fact, Keogh asked Custer to write a letter of endorsement for him a year earlier so that his name might be placed "in its proper light" before the board of officers who were charged with reviewing the records of candidates for the few openings for commissions in the Regular Army that would be available after Appomattox. Earlier, Keogh even had considered transferring to one of Custer's cavalry units. Later he wrote to Custer, "that in '63 the officers of your regiment without exception asked me to allow them to address a petition to the Secty of War asking my appt. to their rgt. but I refused as Gen. Buford told me he could do better than that for me." As Buford

1. Michael Sheridan to George A. Custer, November 21, 1866 (Lawrence Frost Collection, Monroe, MI).

had died without fulfilling this promise, Keogh felt he had been "left in the lurch, except [for] a few miserable brevets—which I care d—d little about."[2]

Keogh's efforts were not without result, as ultimately he received an appointment as a second lieutenant in the Fourth Cavalry, although he never would serve in that unit. The prospect of serving at such a low rank must have disappointed Keogh as he could not "think of accepting a subordinate position" to his brevet rank of major of Volunteers.[3] It was with some relief that he informed his brother, Tom, of news that afforded him the "utmost gratification"—his appointment as a captain with the Seventh Cavalry instead:

> I have had unequalled promotion & now when all the great Volunteer Army is scattered to the winds, I am one among the few selected to be retained in the regular Army—A. J. Smith one of our most distinguished Maj Genls is my Colonel. Custer the cavalry Genl is Lt. Colonel. . . Alfred Gibbs another Cavalry Genl has been appt major. I am 4th Senior Captain. This is for one of my age almost unprecedented in the regular Army with probably the exception of Genl Custer & one or two other officers who are in higher grades.

Keogh ended his letter with a characteristic embellishment that owed more to *Charles O'Malley* than the reality at hand, "The Rgt is one of Light Dragoons."[4] If he held any expectations that his new career on the Plains would resemble the life of such a dashing cavalier as O'Malley, then Keogh's arrival at Wallace surely dispelled such notions. Here, the adversaries were the elements, the infrastructure and, to a lesser degree, the Native Americans of the area. At this remote post, the gallantry and chivalry of the late war counted for little. One "unsurpassed in dash," now had to rely on other strengths in order to effect command.

On November 30, Keogh took charge of his new post, and, as if a harbinger of things to come, spent his first few days there incapacitated by illness. Sheridan's earlier assessment that, " . . . it would be worse at Wallace," was close to the mark.[5] The fort was the westernmost outpost of a defense system set up to guard the Smokey Hill overland stage and mail route. Handsomely situated on high ground overlooking gradually rising prairie, fed by a small stream, and bounded by a range of magnificent bluffs, the garrison was not unattractive altogether in terms of locale. In favorable weather, life at Wallace could be almost pleasant. But now winter had arrived in earnest, making life there a test of wills.[6]

Heavy snows impeded the delivery of wood, which had to be brought in from twenty to thirty miles away. Captain Sheridan and Company L had departed, commandeering five of the fifteen wagons at Keogh's disposal as well as the post scout, William "Medicine Bill" Comstock.

His scout's absence was but one drawback. The troop's horses were unsheltered except for bare walls, awaiting a temporary roof for want of some nails. Keogh's men remained in tents during temperatures as low as six degrees below zero. One company building was not completed yet, another having been so badly erected by the previous cavalry unit that there was grave doubt as to whether it could support even the lightest roof. Stoves were in evidence, but not a single foot of stovepipe existed so that, even if wood could be had to heat the tents, there was no way to burn it safely.[7]

These were the conditions under which Myles and his company labored at Wallace during their first few weeks of duty. Already on duty there and sharing their hardships was Company E, Third Infantry under First Lieutenant Joseph Hale. He had commanded Wallace prior to Keogh's arrival and would again in the Captain's absence. There was also Company D, Thirty-Seventh Infantry with First Lieutenant D. Mortimer Lee at its head, while Assistant Surgeon Theophilus H. Turner was in charge of the hospital. The post sutler, Joseph M. Badger, rounded out the local society, the last two men boasting good backgrounds and higher education. For instance, Badger was the son of the Reverend Norman Badger, a professor of languages at Kenyon College. First Lieutenant Frederick H. Beecher, also related to a clergyman, served at Wallace as acting assistant quartermaster.[8]

---

2. Myles W. Keogh to George A. Custer, November 28, 1865, (Lawrence Frost Collection).

3. Ibid.

4. October 27, 1866, National Library Microfilm.

5. Myles W. Keogh to Lieutenant J.S. Hammer, December 4, 1866, Fort Wallace Microfilm (Fort Wallace Museum, Wallace, KS). Hereafter referred to as Fort Wallace Microfilm. Keogh may have been suffering from the same malady that he told his brother Tom about a few months earlier while in Nashville, Tennessee. August 6, 1866, National Library Microfilm.

6. Robert Utley, ed., *Life in Custer's Cavalry* (New Haven, CT and London: Yale University Press, 1977), 64.

7. Myles W. Keogh to Lieutenant J.S. Hammer, December 4, 1866; Myles W. Keogh to H.E. Noyes, December 20, 1866, Fort Wallace Microfilm.

8. Utley, *Life in Custer's Cavalry*, 64.

Beecher, the nephew of Henry Ward Beecher and Harriet Beecher Stowe, had pursued a military career despite having been wounded in the late war, first at Fredericksburg and again, almost mortally, at Gettysburg. Although he survived both injuries to see duty on the frontier, Beecher suffered severely from his wounds for the remainder of his life.[9] As the post's quartermaster, it was his responsibility to oversee all construction. Despite the obstacles imposed on him by the harsh winter, he made sure that building continued at pace. By the year's end, one barracks had been completed and the holidays commenced by moving men from the tents into "warm, comfortable and elegant quarters."[10]

The officers, however, remained in tents. In a letter to his mother, Beecher noted that, when the weather became disagreeable, the officers of the post would "hive together for mutual sympathy." He related:

> There are five of us: Capt. Keogh, a very gallant man, perfect gentleman and scholar; Lieut. Hale, whom I like very much and respect; Dr. Turner, generous and true; Lieut. Lee, the possessor of much wit. We discuss many questions, Capt. K. generally taking the truthful side, seriously, for he is a true-hearted Irishman; I taking the doubtful side for fun. Lieut. H. acts as first critic, poking up the party that flags; Lieut. L. as jester; the doctor as audience.[11]

As the cold effectively had curtailed the excursions of the local Indians, such get-togethers helped pass the time.

The lull in activity likewise allowed for other diversions. Keogh often hunted in small parties consisting of one or two other fellow officers. He found it "Glorious Sport," stalking antelope and black-tailed deer with his Spencer carbine, and became quite a good shot. "If I had not become 'froze' pretty thoroughly," Myles wrote, "I should enjoy this life."[12]

One of the officers Keogh hunted with was his old friend, Albert P. Morrow who, as captain of Company E commanded the post below Wallace. He had served with Keogh on General Buford's staff. "I liked him much," Keogh reported in one letter, "He was considered quite a handsome fellow and was a very gallant soldier—as we would say in the Green Isle—The Devil among the Women."[13]

But the new post provided few opportunities for rekindling old friendships as there were other things to attend to. Though the mercury continued to plunge, Keogh's troops kept up the building of barracks and storehouses. At least the "fearfully cold" conditions allowed the commander to put up seventy-five tons of ice in the newly constructed ice houses, thereby providing a blessing when the season changed to searing heat and high humidity. "It will be glorious in the hot summer weather," Myles wrote, while his comrade, Beecher, intended to favor his visiting friends, "with a good glass of ice water next summer."[14]

It was a great pleasure, too, for Keogh to have a troop with the talents of carpenters, shoemakers, and "every trade going." He felt his charge gave him a measure of independence. He also found time to learn more about the command of men. He placed an Irish schoolmaster as a clerk in the quartermaster department, and was surprised to discover that another Irishman in his command had served with him in Italy. But, for the most part, he felt that his countrymen were not as orderly as the American and German soldiers, and had to be humored about their drinking habits.[15]

Keogh tried to foster a paternal relationship between himself and his troops. He felt that if he were just and kind, then his men would adore him. One soldier recalled of this period:

> ... The names of most of the leading men of the 7th have left me. But a few can still be recalled. There was Captain Gillette of C Troop, a wild reckless officer who had little regard for God, Man or the Devil. Capt. Keho [sic] was just the opposite. he acted as chaplin [sic] and called all the men 'my boys'.[16]

Perhaps this paternalistic attitude accounted for Keogh's uncompromising disdain for those in his command who took "French leave"—the deserters.

Because of the harsh conditions of the frontier posts, desertion in the newly formed Seventh Cavalry was

9. Utley, *Life in Custer's Cavalry*, 249.
10. Anon., *Lt. Fred H. Beecher—A Memorial of* (Portland, OR: Stephen Berry, 1870), 25.
11. Ibid, 28.
12. February 27, 1867, National Library Microfilm.
13. December 24, 1865, National Library Microfilm.
14. February 27, 1867, National Library Microfilm; *Lt. Fred Beecher*, 25.
15. February 27, 1867, National Library Microfilm.
16. Pohanka, "Myles Walter Keogh (1840-1876)," 11.

exceptionally high, even by the standards found elsewhere in the West. In fact, the men at some posts spent most of their time not in engagements with Indians, but in pursuit of deserters.[17] Keogh balked at orders mitigating the punishment of those who went over the hill, "making it neither disgraceful nor carrying with it any severe punishment," and blamed these orders for inciting his own men to desert.[18]

With this attitude, it is little wonder that Company I proved quite adept at catching deserters, perhaps inspired by Keogh's offer of a $30.00 reward (more than three months salary for a private) for each man captured. Soon, the guard tent at Wallace held as many as twenty-five of these "men who as a class are desperate scoundrels," mostly from Forts Morgan and Lyon.[19]

That desertion was regarded by Keogh as a great evil is not hard to understand. Manpower was at a premium on the frontier and especially so at Wallace. Hampered by the withdrawal of the civilian teamsters to Fort Riley and the constant need to send detachments to the various outlying stations, every available soldier was needed to continue the construction efforts. Because of the many other duties that fell to his command, Keogh could not even find time to drill his men properly.[20]

As warm weather returned to Kansas, Myles knew he would need soldiers even more than he needed construction workers and tried to prepare accordingly. In a February letter to his brother Tom, Myles noted, "the Indians are commencing to give us a great deal of trouble. I should not be surprised if you hear of their attacks at this Post soon."[21] Indeed, with the arrival of spring the Indians who were, as Keogh put it, "aggrieved at our taking up this line of country," began their raids in earnest.[22]

Myles initiation to the realities of Indian warfare occured early in March of 1867. Myles and a small party, consisting of Lieutenants Beecher and Hale, set out for Pond Creek Station where a large body of warriors had been seen earlier. They discovered that four braves had visited that place on foot, "all well armed with bright new Remington revolvers, well capped and carrying also carbines." Keogh saw two Indians going around the bluff a quarter mile distant, and attempted to overtake them. On reaching their position, Myles found they had disappeared. Lamenting the lack of a scout, he confessed, "I greatly miss Comstock, as he would have been able to follow them up and find out their intentions."[23]

Three days later, on March 24th, the station above Pond Creek sustained an attack, the occupants being driven off or killed. On March 26, Company I and twenty men from the infantry went in pursuit of a party of Cheyenne, as it had been reported that they had attacked Goose Creek Station fifteen miles west of Wallace. Again, no contact was made.[24]

Reinforced by twenty-five recruits brought by Second Lieutenant James M. Bell, Keogh was anxious to lend his cooperation to the Hancock expedition being undertaken elsewhere in Kansas.[25] Myles believed that Fort Wallace could take care of itself without the cavalry and that he and Company I, with Comstock's assistance, "might be able to do good service by cutting in the rear of the Indians (Sioux) evidently making for the Republican."[26] Keogh, however, was ordered to stay at Wallace and keep his troop ready to join the expedition at a moment's notice, "the want of supplies alone prevented this being done."[27] For the time being, Myles would have to be content parcelling out his troops to the various stations.

Since his arrival at Wallace, Keogh had sought to carry out orders that provided for the protection of the stage stations along the Smokey Hill. Detachments of both infantry and cavalry were expected to rotate in thirty-day shifts between Wallace and the other posts.[28] This arrangement was inconvenient and often a detriment to the running of the main post as it took away labor from construction and left a skeleton force to guard the fort itself.

Now the stage company was pressuring Keogh to furnish more guards, guns and ammunition. Keogh felt that if he complied with these requirements he would be

---

17. Chandler, *Of Garry Owen in Glory*, 7.
18. *Fort Wallace Bugle*, (June 5-6, 1965), 3. The exact incident which caused Keogh's ire was the desertion of three of his men from Cheyenne Wells with five horses, a pack mule, plus forage and rations. Keogh started a detachment after them with Comstock as guide and happily reported their capture between Pueblo and Denver. Previously, he confidently had voiced that he had "no fears of desertion." Myles W. Keogh to H.E. Noyes, January 22, 1867, Fort Wallace Microfilm.
19. Myles W. Keogh to M. Moylan, April 28, 1867, Fort Wallace Microfilm.
20. February 27, 1867, National Library Microfilm.
21. Ibid. There was a rumor that Keogh heard intimating that the Seventh was to be concentrated at Pueblo, New Mexico for the purpose of fighting the Mormons, but the "great expectations of hard fighting" Myles had never came to pass.
22. Myles W. Keogh to H.E. Noyes, January 1, 1867, Fort Wallace Microfilm.
23. Myles W. Keogh to H.E. Noyes, March 22, 1867, Fort Wallace Microfilm. The emphasis on the arms carried by the Indians is interesting as they are carrying weapons then in issue to the cavalry.
24. Myles W. Keogh to H.E. Noyes, March 24, 1867, Fort Wallace Microfilm.
25. Myles W. Keogh to H.E. Noyes, April 4, 1867, Fort Wallace Microfilm.
26. Myles W. Keogh to Commanding Officer, Smokey Hill District, April 20, 1867, Fort Wallace Microfilm.
27. Blain Burkey, *Custer, Come At Once!* (Hays, KS: Thomas More Prep, 1976), 10.
28. Myles W. Keogh to Assistant Adjutant General, Fort Riley, KS, December 15, 1866, Fort Wallace Microfilm.

obligated to furnish every available man to guard the stations. On April 26, Keogh wrote to Custer expressing his frustrations:

> It is ridiculous to expect me to protect the different stations unless I close up this post and divide the Garrison between 'Willow Creek' and Monument stations [and] at all the intervening stations.[29]

Unknown to Keogh, the stage company was also pushing both Custer and General Hancock for protection. Custer, by order of General Hancock, sent directions to Keogh to, "Extend all possible and necessary protection to the overland route, extending along the Smokey Hill, and render the transit of passengers and mail by said route safe from the depredations of Indians. . . ."[30] This was to be accomplished by assigning five men and one non-commissioned officer to guard each of the numerous stations between Wallace and Grinell Springs. These men were to fire on any Indian who approached closer than 1000 yards, and, as if to emphasize this, Custer ordered regular target practice for Keogh's men and "to report when done."[31]

When Keogh received these instructions on April 28, he immediately ordered them to be implemented precisely as Custer had indicated, adding, "The N.C.O. is to be vigilant and look out for mischievous conduct on the part of the Indians . . . one man is always to be on the lookout."[32] However, Custer was now in receipt of Keogh's earlier letter in which the Irish officer complained of the demands placed upon his command. In response to what he considered direct criticism of his orders, Custer had acting assistant adjutant, Lieutenant Myles Moylan, relay his displeasure to Keogh in a letter on May 3. The message read in part:

> Were it not that the Bvt. Major General Commanding had unlimited confidence in your intentions based upon a long and gratifying acquaintance with your soldier like accomplishments, he would have deemed one portion of your communication of the 26 Ult. highly improper and disrespectful, that in which you characterized certain dispositions of troops made by himself as Commanding officer of the sub district as 'ridiculous'. While appreciating the difficulties under which you labor, the language above referred to is regarded as unjustifiable. . . .[33]

Upon receiving his commander's rebuke, Keogh understandably felt "very anxious and uncomfortable." In a carefully worded reply, he assured Custer that he was neither guilty nor capable of the "unsoldierly and unofficerlike offense" of which he was accused. For good measure Myles added:

> I would state (were it not considered by me presumptuous to express my opinion in the matter) that such dispositions are entirely satisfactory and will result in the complete protection and safety of the different stations so guarded.[34]

Much to Keogh's relief, Moylan replied on May 11 that his "explanation" was entirely satisfactory, thereby ending the matter.[35]

Custer's orders were at first somewhat effective in repelling the ever-increasing hostile attacks. On one occasion, twenty to thirty Indians "with mischievous intentions" attempted to set the station at Big Timbers on fire but were, Keogh noted, "awed by the presence of the guard." Nonetheless, the Indian attacks grew in frequency.[36] On May 1, they burned down Goose Creek Station and stole the stock. One week later, Chalk Bluff and Monument Stations were attacked, but damage was held to a minimum. Soon second attempts were made to burn Chalk Bluff and also the station at Big Timbers.[37]

Frustrated by the seeming impunity with which the Indians moved, and constrained by Custer's orders to hold himself "in readiness to move at a moments notice," Keogh asked his superior for orders regarding the disposition of the Indians. "I am not informed if I am to kill them on sight," Keogh wrote, adding, "If the Indians are not followed to their villages and killed, then it is useless to expect peace or rest on this route".[38] Custer responded in no uncertain terms:

SEVENTH CAVALRY, 1866-1876

29. Myles W. Keogh to M. Moylan, April 26, 1867, Fort Wallace Microfilm.

30. G.A. Custer to M.W. Keogh, April 25, 1867, Record Group 391, Entry 877, Letters Sent, Seventh U.S. Cavalry, National Archives, Washington, D.C. Hereafter referred to as Letters Sent, Seventh Cavalry.

31. Ibid.

32. Special Order No. 28, April 28, 1867, Fort Wallace Microfilm.

33. M. Moylan to Myles Keogh, May 3, 1867, Letters Sent, Seventh Cavalry.

34. Myles W. Keogh to M. Moylan, May 8, 1867, (Custer Battlefield National Monument Collection).

35. M. Moylan to Myles Keogh, May 11, 1867, Letters Sent, Seventh Cavalry.

36. Myles W. Keogh to M. Moylan, May 10, 1867 (Custer Battlefield National Monument Collection).

37. Myles W. Keogh to M. Moylan, May 12, 1867 (Custer Battlefield National Monument Collection).

38. Myles W. Keogh to M. Moylan, April 26, 1867 (Custer Battlefield National Monument Collection).

MYLES KEOGH

39. M. Moylan to Myles W. Keogh, May 3, 1867, Letters Sent, Seventh Cavalry.

40. Ibid.

41. Myles W. Keogh to M. Moylan, May 12, 1867 (Custer Battlefield National Monument Collection).

42. Myles W. Keogh to M. Moylan, May 13, 1867 (Ayers Collection, Newberry Library, Chicago, IL).

43. Myles W. Keogh to M. Moylan, May 29, 1867, Fort Wallace Microfilm.

44. Myles W. Keogh to M. Moylan, June 11, 1867, Fort Wallace Microfilm.

45. J. Hale to M. Moylan, June 18, 1867, Fort Wallace Microfilm; Brian Pohanka, "Service Record of Myles Walter Keogh, Compiled and Edited from Post and Regimental Returns," (unpublished MS) hereafter referred to as Pohanka, "Service Record." Lieutenant Charles G. Cox spent only a short time with Company I on his rise up the Regular Army ladder. Having been appointed a second lieutenant of infantry in February of 1867 through political influence, he transferred to the Seventh Cavalry that same May. He then joined the Tenth Cavalry in August as a captain. By November, Cox was detailed to General Hancock's staff, but then his swift rise ended as quickly as it began. He was cashiered in 1870 for drunkenness and misappropriation of public property. Utley, *Life in Custer's Cavalry*, 254.

46. Ibid., 63-64.

47. Ibid., 68-78.

You will without regard to age, sex or condition kill all Indians you may encounter, belonging to Sioux or Cheyennes, except [if] you are convinced they belong to certain bands of friendly (?) Indians, reported as being on the headwaters of the Republican . . . it is not proposed to burden your command with prisoners. . . .[39]

In regard to Keogh's desire to follow the Indians, Custer advised somewhat prophetically,

As to your pursuing Indians, while it is not strictly forbidden, in doing so, you must exercise the greatest precaution against stratagem and surprise, remembering, that it is the Indians 'Ruse De Guerre' to decoy small Garrisons away from their position of defense."[40]

Feeling free now to take up pursuit, Keogh and fifty men from Company I set out the morning of May 12, to track Indians who had attempted to burn nearby Pond Creek Station. "I have no doubt," Keogh told headquarters, "that from this post with his [Comstock's] assistance the Indians could be found within a days march." The reality was not so simple, however.[41]

Having tracked the Indians for some seven miles, the trail led Keogh into an open plain. The small column went first in the direction of Twin Buttes and then turned in a course heading to the Sandy where they lost the trail. Returning to Wallace, Keogh wrote to Moylan of his disappointment the next day, stating:

I have never before appreciated the difficulty of pursuing Indians and I have concluded that without knowing exactly where to surprise their camp, or having a guide who can track them at a run, it is a waste of horse flesh and time to endeavor to come up with them.[42]

So ended Myles' first venture against Indians.

Keogh's second foray had better results. On the night of May 26, Indians ran off the herd of contractors' cattle from Pond Creek Station. Taking two days forage and rations and accompanied by Lieutenant James M. Bell, Keogh and Company I trailed the raiders. Although they did not engage the enemy, Keogh's men were able to recover all the livestock except for five head, which had been slaughtered.[43]

The attacks continued. On June 11, Lieutenant Bell arrived on the stage from Big Timbers, having fought a pitched battle with twenty-five Indians for four miles. One private from the Third Infantry was killed and one private from Company I was wounded. The Indians now had crossed the Platte River in force and Keogh feared that the detachments stationed at the stage posts would be killed. In a hastily written communique to headquarters Keogh reported, "I expect to be attacked here but feel confident of being able to repel them."[44]

Keogh predicted correctly as, on June 26, the garrison at Wallace was attacked, resulting in the first large Indian battle in which the Seventh Cavalry would be engaged. This action attracted a great deal of attention in the press and earned the commander of the fight wide acclaim. Keogh, however, was nowhere near the scene of the engagement. Ten days earlier, General Hancock, on his inspection of the Smokey Hill route, arrived at Fort Wallace. Escorted by Sergeant William H. Dummel and some men from Company G, Seventh Cavalry, Hancock made camp outside Wallace where he was greeted by Keogh, Hale, Bell, and Beecher. Two days later, Hancock started for Denver with Keogh, Lieutenant Charles Cox, and thirty-nine men of Company I as escort, leaving Lieutenant Hale in charge of the post.[45]

On June 21, Indians appeared in force around Wallace and attempted to drive off the stock. Sergeant Dummel and three men of Company G, accompanied by Sergeant William Hamlin and eight men of Company I, charged the Indians. Dummel was killed and another soldier wounded, but the Indians were driven off.[46] Three days later, the engineering party of General Horatio G. Wright arrived, with Captain Albert Barnitz and the remainder of Company G, finding Wallace in a state of siege. Consequently, it was Barnitz who engaged the force of nearly 200 Indians on the 26th.

In the melee, a sergeant, a trumpeter, a corporal, and three privates were killed. Two corporals and six privates were wounded while Sergeant Hamlin, of Company I, was placed under arrest for urging men to retreat at an inopportune moment.[47] The sergeant killed was Frederick

Wyllyams of Company G, a graduate of Eton and a member of an English family of some prominence. Wyllyams gained dubious fame as the ghastly subject of photographer William A. Bell of General Wright's survey party. The oft printed picture of his mutilated corpse provided a topic for one of Keogh's letters home:

> I send you a copy of a photograph I had taken of one of my Sergeants that the Indians killed last year. The top of the head was cut off. There was a party of engineers surveying the Pacific R.R. and they had a photographist along so I had it taken. This man was less brutally used than many others owing to our charging up to recapture some prisoners the Indians were trying to get off.[48]

Keogh did not witness this sight, however, since he was at Lake Station in Colorado at the time of Wyllyams' death. On July 3, he and Company I returned to Wallace with the First Battalion of the Fifth Infantry, the foot soldiers going into camp a mile from the post.[49]

A few days later, on July 8, Barnitz and Company G departed for Fort Lyons with General Horatio Wright's surveying party leaving in their stead Company F of the Seventh, that unit having arrived at Wallace the previous day.[50] The commander of this new outfit would prove to be a true friend to Keogh, even unto death. Keogh would write, "I have a nice fellow with me, an Irishman and a Catholic." Myles went on to record that this man:

> Formerly belonged to the 41st Foot English Army, a graduate of Sandhurst & served in the Crimea; he sold out his lieutenancy & came out here. His father as paymaster in the English Army & he has two brothers there still. His name is Henry J. Nowlan. He is a 1st Lt. in my rgt. & commands a troop. He is quite a handsome fellow and exceedingly pleasant. He is about six years older than myself but I feel much older & I think I look it. . . . We are fast friends.[51]

Nowlan, in fact, had begun his military career as an ensign with the Forty-first on August 11, 1854, after attending the Royal Military College where he received his degree in mathematics, fortifications, and military surveying. He distinguished himself as a lieutenant at Sebastopol, receiving decorations for both the Crimea and the Turkish War. He later served in the West Indies, from where he left British service in May of 1862 through the sale of his commission, a not uncommon practice of the period. Traveling to the United States, he became a first lieutenant in the Fourteenth New York Volunteer Cavalry, and saw action in several Civil War engagements, including the Red River Campaign of 1863, the march to Alexandria, Port Hudson, and other operations in that vicinity before being captured in June of 1863. Nearly two years later, he escaped at Columbia, South Carolina, and accompanied General Sherman on his march to the sea in 1865.

He transferred to the Eighteenth New York Cavalry that June. Subsequently, he went to Texas where he was severely wounded near Yorktown while attempting to arrest a man suspected of murder. Recovering, Nowlan gained an appointment as a second lieutenant in the Seventh Cavalry to date from July 28, 1866, the day the regiment was organized. By December 3, 1866 he had advanced to first lieutenant.[52]

Nowlan and his Company were now at Wallace with Keogh. A few days after their arrival there, Companies A, D, E, H, K, and M rode in under Custer's command, having returned exhausted and suffering from the lackluster Hancock expedition. On July 15, Custer and his entourage departed Wallace for Fort Riley. The events which followed would result in a court martial for Custer.[53] While Custer dealt with his problems, the horses of the command, which had been broken down by hard field service, were improving and by August Myles could report that they as well as the pack train soon would be in perfect order. With headquarters "particularly anxious that the Indians who had given so much trouble in that vicinity should be severely punished," Myles set out for the Saline River, expecting to strike Indian villages there in conjunction with a battalion of the Eighteenth Kansas Cavalry.[54] Apparently, no one received punishment except the cavalrymen and their mounts, as Myles was back at Wallace by August 16, in

SEVENTH CAVALRY, 1866-1876

48. August 15, 1867, National Library Microfilm.

49. Utley, *Life in Custer's Cavalry*, 81.

50. Myles W. Keogh to T. B. Weir, July 7, 1867, Fort Wallace Microfilm.

51. October 27, 1867, National Library Microfilm. Nowlan was only three years older than Keogh.

52. Brian Pohanka to Jack Manion, April 14, 1980 (J.S. Manion Collection, Beverly Hills, FL).

53. Chandler, *Of Garry Owen in Glory*, 4-5.

54. J.F. Weston to Myles W. Keogh, August 12, 1867, Record Group 393, Entry 793, Letters Received, Department of Missouri, National Archives, Washington, D.C.

55. Myles W. Keogh to T. B. Weir, August 16, 1867, Fort Wallace Microfilm.

56. Ibid. The appraisal of the cholera situation conflicts with the more serious picture painted by Barnitz in Utley, *Life in Custer's Cavalry*, 85-86. For vaccination order see General Field Order No. 19, H.Q. Div. of the Upper Arkansas, May 26, 1867.

57. Mrs. F.C. Montgomery, "Fort Wallace and Its Relation to the Frontier," *Collections of the Kansas State Historical Society* (1928), 224.

58. October 27, 1867, National Library Microfilm.

59. Ibid.

60. February 27, 1867, National Library Microfilm.

61. September 30, 1867, National Library Microfilm.

62. Ibid.

63. November 30, 1867, National Library Microfilm. Keogh had anticipated his Brevet for by June, perhaps prompted by the brevets awarded to both Michael Sheridan and Fred Benteen to date from March 2, 1867.

time to turn over command of that post to the newly arrived Captain H.C. Bankhead of the Fifth Infantry.[55]

Bankhead had lost his wife to cholera, which had broken out in the Fifth Infantry camp a mile below Wallace. Myles noted, "For a few days it has been appalling," but there were, "no deaths at this Wallace Garrison," perhaps as a result of the vaccination program initiated there in May.[56]

Keogh and his company thus were spared and spent the summer and autumn engaged in the usual escort duty and mostly fruitless scouting. Strangely, Keogh never mentioned in his letters home the mundane hardships which he surely must have suffered with everyone else at his remote post. He neglected to refer to the outbreak of cholera or the grasshoppers that filled the heavens in late summer and were so numerous as to be "one inch thick on the ground."[57] He did, however, describe his routine duties as:

> ... Up at daylight (always) to attend 'reveille', roll call-'Stable call' immediately after for one hour. Water call at 11 o.c. a.m.—Evening stables at 3 PM to 4 PM. 'Retreat' at sunset & tattoo at 8 o.c. p.m. When officer of the day I have to sit up all night & then make rounds twice after midnight & before reveille. I usually nod until 12 o.c. & then lie down in my toggins on my bed until it is time to go the rounds again. I am very happy.[58]

Soon, news followed that broke the routine somewhat. On October 21 and 28, 1867, at Medicine Lodge, Kansas, the Kiowas, Comanches, Cheyennes, and Apaches agreed to withdraw all opposition to the building of the railroad through Kansas. This treaty greatly reduced tensions along the Smokey Hill and relieved, in part, the strenuous duties of the cavalry. This happy circumstance coincided with the commencement of duck season. Consequently, Myles' attentions turned to hunting with his friend Nowlan.[59] Keogh's thoughts also went back to his family and home. For some time, he had planned to take a holiday in Ireland. In February, Myles indicated to Tom, "I have not yet given up the idea of paying you a visit," and that he would investigate the possibility of doing so "if I get through with the Indians safe."[60] Having completed his first year with the Seventh in relatively good order, Myles applied for a passport and made his intentions known to the family:

> I will most positively be back next year and have already made an engagement with some ladies to escort them as far as Paris via the French steamline to Havre. I will only delay a week in Paris and then go direct to you.

Myles concluded that if he waited much longer, "there may be too many obstacles in the way...."[61]

Being low on funds, he hoped to get some official duty to perform on his trip to Europe, "This will save me no end of expense and would make my visit of six months more agreeable to myself." In preparation for his trip Myles obtained duplicates of his Papal medals (which he lost in a fire), both large and in miniature.[62] But Myles expected to receive something even more valuable to him, and in November it finally came. Despite a lack of enthusiasm for such honors in his earlier writing, Keogh now proclaimed:

> I am happy to inform you that General Grant has obtained from the President for me two Brevets, one as Major for Gallantry at the Battle of Gettysburg and one as Lt. Colonel for Gallantry at the Battle of Resaca. So I am now a Colonel in the Regular Army and I feel that I have received a full reward. I should have disliked visiting Europe without this title and now having my order of St. Gregory and the position of Colonel in this army, I am but satisfied that I have carried out some at least of the rather visionary fancies we as boys indulged of long ago.

Yet there was a touch of melancholy in Keogh's achievement:

> I am still comparatively young but fail altogether in appreciating the position I have won at the high and happy standard I formerly fancied I should. You remember perhaps as vividly as I do, our parting at the R.R. Station in Carlow. Well I am no happier today that I was then and I feel that the strife is very much all the happiness.[63]

Perhaps his attitude could be traced to the sad news that Keily, his longtime friend, had fallen victim to yellow

Prior to the new uniform regulations in 1872, officers were allowed to indicate their brevet rank by wearing their appropriate insignia. In late 1867, having been brevetted a lieutenant-colonel in the regular army, Keogh was entitled to display that rank on his captain's uniform coat, as he does here. Also in evidence is his Medal of St. Gregory, this being the last time that photographs show him wearing any of his Papal decorations. *Courtesy of Custer Battlefield National Monument.*

fever in Louisiana. This loss, once more, reduced Keogh's circle of loved ones.

Since the latter part of the Civil War, Keogh's comrade had seemed plagued by a lack of good fortune. He received a number of uneventful military assignments and his career appeared to be doomed. He even faced a court martial at one point for inciting behavior "to the prejudice of good order and discipline" and for "conduct unbecoming an officer."[64] Keily managed to prove his innocence of both charges and for a while his star began to ascend once more. He even became a brevet brigadier general of Volunteers.

Unlike Keogh, however, after Appomattox, he failed to secure a spot in the Regular Army. Without other resources to fall back on, he headed south, seeking some advantage as many another Northerner had after the war. A short-lived partnership with merchants from New Orleans and the management of Oak Grove Plantation, in Pointe Coupée Parrish, came to an end when he died in October 1867. Keogh had hoped to bring the remains of his close companion to a final resting place in Washington, D.C., but it appears that such plans could not be carried out due to lack of funds.[65]

Such a sad state of affairs did not seem to dampen Keogh's spirit for the coming holidays, however, since he settled into new quarters with his friend Lieutenant Beecher. Their room was a favorite visiting place with "carpet, nice chairs, and a library that commands much attention."[66] For Christmas, Keogh provided two antelope for his troop's dinner and gave his soldiers a taste of some "Scotch brew, much to the satisfaction of the Irish in it."[67]

About this time, Myles learned of another opportunity to go home. His friend, General Emory Upton, was to be married in March and then would proceed to Europe the following week. Upton had chosen Keogh as his first groomsman and had offered to get him seven months leave for the trip. But unless he could secure $1,000, Myles could not afford the jaunt abroad. Even the journey to New York, where the marriage was to be held, would cost considerable money, but Myles felt he could not refuse.[68] In order to accommodate the General, Myles obtained a thirty-day leave of absence and left for New York on February 3, 1868. But he would be prevented from completing his travels. On February 14,

SEVENTH CAVALRY, 1866-1876

64. Daniel Keily, ACP File, National Archives, Washington, D.C. and Liber to Seward, October 9, 1865, Letters of Application and Recommendation, Microfilm 650, U.S. State Department, National Archives, Washington, D.C.; November 30, 1867, National Library Microfilm.

65. Mrs. John L. Morrison to Brian C. Pohanka, July 21, 1975. Searches among the records of all cemeteries in the Washington, D.C. area failed to locate Keily's grave.

66. *Lt. Fred Beecher*, 37. Beecher also added that he hoped the arrival of several ladies at the garrison with their husbands "will break for the better upon our old bachelor habits."

67. December 26, 1867, National Library Microfilm.

68. Ibid.

he accidentally fell on the icy sidewalks of Boston, breaking his leg.

Keogh was examined at the Medical Directors office in Boston, the physicians finding that he had sustained a transverse fracture of the right tibia an inch and a half above the external malleolus. He also ruptured the ligaments of the ankle joint.[69] Now incapacitated, Myles spent his time recuperating, first at Newport, Rhode Island, in the home of a former associate from his days on Buford's staff, Clement Biddle Barclay, and then at Willowbrook.[70] Myles' friends tried their best to make the time pass quickly as he was suffering "not only bodily but mental pain, the latter caused by his disappointment in being prevented from fulfilling his purpose of crossing the water and visiting his family."[71] In a letter from Willowbrook, Myles reiterated that he "had determined to go" to Europe, but this seems unlikely as there is no record of his applying for or receiving permission to travel abroad nor, with a thirty-day leave, much time to do so. But it may be that Myles did "so wish to surprise" his family.[72]

Myles' situation was not all pain and unpleasantness, however, since he reported that he was "charmingly situated" and had the "kindest attention" and a fair nurse to care for him — the young wife of an officer with whom he was "very much inclined to elope."[73] The bones of his leg mended nicely but with the ligaments of the ankle joint still torn, Myles' foot lunged around "in a most ridiculous manner."

Feeling that his recovery was close at hand, his thoughts turned toward his return to duty, "As the men who like me very much are getting discontented at my long stay away." The coming summer promised to be a busy one with the Indians, and Myles hoped that Sheridan, now in overall command of the department where the Seventh was posted, would rush things along.[74] Perhaps Myles' anticipation was heightened by his expectation of having command of the regiment in the absence of Colonel A. J. Smith, Lieutenant Colonel George Custer, and Major Alfred Gibbs. If so, he must have been disappointed because Major Joel H. Elliott received the command.[75]

Having traveled from New York to Leavenworth, Myles received his third twenty-day extension of leave and was quartered there with Michael Sheridan. Not until May 2, 1868, did he rejoin his company at Wallace and even then he was sick in quarters.[76]

With the Medicine Lodge Treaties of the previous fall and the more recent treaties at Fort Laramie with the Sioux, Brule, Oglala, Arapaho, and other northern tribes, the spring and early summer in Kansas were uncommonly free of hostile activity. As the summer wore on, reports of depredations increased to such an extent that an expedition was mounted to meet the threat of a renewed Indian offensive.[77] This force was placed under the personal supervision of General Alfred Sully, Commander of the District of Upper Arkansas.[78]

With his new mount, Comanche, Keogh traveled with Company I to its most recent station, Camp Alfred Gibbs, near Ellis Station, and returned to duty on June 17, 1868.[79] But his stay with Company I would be cut short as, the next day, he was ordered to Fort Harker for duty as acting assistant inspector general, District of the Upper Arkansas.[80] Whether Keogh sought this position because of the injury sustained to his leg or whether the job was given to him on the merit of his previous staff duty during the late war is uncertain. Captain Albert Barnitz summed up the situation quite well:

> Brevt. Lt. Col. Keogh is ordered to Fort Harker, as Acting Assistant Inspector General on General Sully's staff — not a very high position by the way, as it is properly that of a First Lieutenant — and takes $10 a month from his pay, (the allowance for commanding a company,) — but it is a very easy position, and I suppose even if not a very complimentary one, ought nevertheless to be accepted with gratitude.[81]

For his part, Myles seemed pleased with his new position. He indicated:

> The duties of my office are not onerous and needing only energy and a clear head with a facile mode of giving expression to ones observations on paper. My position enables me to live at great deal of comfort and enjoy liberty of going when and where I please at government expense.[82]

---

69. Record Group 94, Records of the Adjutant General's Office, Letters Sent, Seventh Cavalry Medical Cards and Union Staff File, February 18, 1868, National Archives, Washington, D.C. Hereafter referred to as Seventh Cavalry Medical Cards. While it is not certain exactly how Keogh broke his leg, newspaper accounts of the day cite numerous examples of individuals suffering from that injury on account of ice-slicked sidewalks.

70. Slidell to Tom Keogh, February 26, 1868, National Library Microfilm.

71. Ibid.

72. March 27, 1868, National Library Microfilm.

73. March 29, 1868, National Library Microfilm.

74. March 27, 1868, National Library Microfilm.

75. March 29, 1868, National Library Microfilm. As it seems inconceivable that Keogh would forget the existence of Major Elliot, it may be that Myles' hopes for command was more of a boast than an actual expectation.

76. Pohanka, "Service Record;" March 27, 1868, National Library Microfilm. Keogh stated that he would stay at Fort Leavenworth on furlough with Sheridan, presumably meaning Michael and not Phil.

77. Montgomery, "Fort Wallace . . . ," 225.

78. Chandler, *Of Garry Owen in Glory*, 9-10.

79. Ibid., 28. While Keogh was still on leave, Company I departed for Camp Alfred Gibbs on June 15. It is assumed he traveled with his men and supposedly he purchased Comanche at Ellis Station before he left on June 10. Luce, *Keogh, Comanche and Custer*, 86. In an alternate account, Edward Godfrey related that Keogh obtained Comanche during a skirmish with Indians in which Keogh's horse was killed under him. Keogh called for another mount which Lieutenant Charles Brewster (then in command of Company I, since Keogh was still on detached duty with Sully) supplied by dismounting one of his sergeants. That horse was Comanche. Brown, *Comanche*, 40. Elsewhere, Godfrey recollected that Keogh "chose this horse from a field mount" in September of 1868, the very time that Keogh could have been in the field. Edward Godfrey, *General George A. Custer and the Battle of the Little Big Horn* (New York, NY: The Century Com-

One of Keogh's first duties was the inspection of the posts and forts in Colorado and on the borders of New Mexico. Traveling mostly by stagecoach and horseback, Myles' three week odyssey included a marathon fifty mile trek from Fort Lyon to Fort Reynolds in one day. He did not experience any discomfort on the journey and ate "a hearty supper on arrival."[83] Shortly after his return from this outing, Keogh learned of the death of "Medicine Bill" Comstock. The ambush of Comstock and another scout at an Indian camp precipitated hostilities.[84] There was no doubt now about the necessity of a campaign and, on the eve of the Indian war, Keogh wrote to Captain Frederick Benteen, "This looks like business."[85]

On September 7, after being equipped and supplied, eight companies of the Seventh Cavalry, A, B, C, D, E, F, G, and I, along with three companies of the Third Infantry, joined by General Alfred Sully and his staff, crossed the Arkansas River and proceeded to march south toward the Cimarron River. For the duration of the expedition, the Indians kept up a sparse but harassing fire. From September 8-13, Sully's command was beset by the Indians in running skirmishes. The most determined fighting occurred on the 13th, indicating the proximity of the Indian villages, but Sully considered the sandy terrain unsuitable for the pack train and turned back the command northward. It was during these unproductive skirmishes that Comanche is said to have been wounded for the first time by an arrow.[86]

On September 17, as Keogh started back to Fort Dodge with Sully, Lieutenant Frederick Beecher met his fate on a small island in the Arickaree Fork of the Republican River. The battle that ensued there would be known thereafter by his name, a small testament to that brave individual and even smaller comfort for Myles at the loss of yet one more friend. It no doubt gave Keogh pause to think about the fragility of life in the West.[87]

The summer campaign had proven inconclusive. The depredations committed by the Indians continued unabated, generating an incentive in the military authorities to produce results. A winter campaign was decided upon with General Sully again in overall command, but Generals Sherman, Sully, and Sheridan resolved that this expedition would not commence without Custer.[88] Returning from his suspension at their request, Custer joined the command on Bluff Creek around October 6.[89]

The command, with Keogh in attendance, moved on through October and early November toward its new base camp and arrived at the appropriately named "Camp Supply" on November 19. Much excitement accompanied the final preparations for the campaign as anticipations of battle grew. Thirty days rations and forage were loaded into the supply wagons, indicating departure time was near. Orders were given directing the cavalry to move at daylight on November 23.[90]

Keogh would not be among those setting out on campaign that morning as, a few days earlier, General Sully had been ordered to return to his headquarters at Fort Harker. General Sheridan evidently had higher respect for Custer's abilities in regard to Indian fighting and found Sully's presence on the campaign to be superfluous.

It is not known what Keogh's thoughts were on the morning of the 23rd for, as the band played "The Girl I Left Behind Me," he and the rest of Sully's staff headed northward while Custer and the Seventh turned southward for the Washita and everlasting fame. Whether Myles was disappointed at being deprived of a soldier's chance for glory or merely was relieved at being spared the rigors of a winter campaign, only he knew. It is certain, however, that Keogh shared in neither the success of the campaign nor the hardships and deprivations that the rest of the regiment endured.

Although Myles was relieved from duty as acting assistant inspector general on January 2, 1868, there is an indication that he was not anxious to rejoin his regiment. It seems Keogh was willing to leave the Seventh Cavalry if he could be provided with a permanent assignment as an assistant inspector general.[91]

Lieutenant Colonel Nelson H. Davis, then assistant inspector general and Keogh's immediate superior, wrote a letter on Myles' behalf to the Inspector General, U.S. Army in Washington, D.C. In this letter, Davis testified to Keogh's "gallantry and efficiency as an officer," adding that Myles was "also a gentleman of intelligence, education and good character."

pany, 1921), 37. If Godfrey is to be taken at face value, this means that Comanche was acquired as a remount, wounded (see Note 86 below), then ultimately chosen as Keogh's personal horse all within the period of a few days in September, 1868; all of which is possible. When Keogh left Fort Wallace, he was under orders to take with him the company washer woman, Mrs. Annie Curran, and to transport her as far as the train went to Hays City. See Granville Lewis to Miles Keogh, June 6, 1868. Fort Wallace Microfilm.

80. Pohanka, "Service Record;" *Army and Navy Journal* (June 27, 1868), 715.

81. Utley, *Life in Custer's Cavalry*, 159.

82. August 15, 1868, National Library Microfilm.

83. Ibid.

84. Montgomery, "Fort Wallace," 226.

85. Myles W. Keogh to Frederick W. Benteen, August 31, 1868, Record Group 393, Entry 807, Letters Sent, District of Upper Arkansas (August-November, 1868) National Archives, Washington, D.C.

86. Chandler, *Of Garry Owen in Glory*, 10-11, 26-27; Luce, *Keogh, Comanche and Custer*, 27. Luce maintained that Comanche received his first wound on September 13, in a skirmish with Comanches on Bluff Creek, Kansas. Godfrey recalled that Comanche was wounded while Keogh rode him in "engagements with Comanche Indians on the Cimarron River or at Beaver Fork," which would be within this same time-frame. Godfrey, *General George A. Custer*, 37. Another Godfrey account implies that it was a bullet that wounded Keogh's mount. "Keogh was with the Advance Guard of pickets when his horse was wounded and when he came to camp was surprised when told his horse had been shot; he remarked that he heard the whir of the bullet and that the horse had jumped but he thought the 'whirr' had only startled the horse." Edward S. Godfrey papers, vol. IV, manuscript collection, Library of Congress, Washington DC.

87. Montgomery, "Fort Wallace," 228-233.

88. Chandler, *Of Garry Owen in Glory*, 12.

89. Ibid.

90. Ibid., 14.

91. Nelson H. Davis to Inspector General, U.S. Army, January 24, 1869 (Myles Keogh Collection, Gene Autry Western Heritage Museum).

92. August 13, 1868, National Library Microfilm.

93. Myles W. Keogh to Assistant Surgeon Henry Lippincott, July 12, 1869, Record Group 391, Entry 878, Seventh Cavalry Medical Department Record Book, Letters Sent. Hereafter referred to as Seventh Cavalry Medical Department. In this reference Keogh recalled the injury as occurring at Camp Supply, Indian Territory in January of 1869. But, as he did not leave Fort Dodge, Kansas for Camp Supply until February 18, 1869, he must have been in error.

94. Chandler, *Of Garry Owen in Glory*, 29.

95. "Descriptive Lists & Personnel Records- Individuals in the 7th Cavalry 'F-L'" (Custer Battlefield National Monument Collection).

96. Seventh Cavalry Medical Cards, April 30, 1869.

97. May 9, 1869, National Library Microfilm.

98. February 27, 1867, National Library Microfilm. In a letter to his sister, Margarette, Myles again made reference to an Indian woman, saying: "I sit for my picture [with] an Indian squaw." March 29, 1868, National Library Microfilm. No such picture is known.

99. Pohanka, "Service Record." More of what transpired during this ten days of service is recalled in a letter home which stated, "Yesterday, however, four troops of the Rgt were ordered after Indians & I also have been out on a twenty miles ride scouting with thirty men of my troop. I saw nothing however." June 1, 1869, National Library Microfilm. The scout Keogh mentioned was to investigate an Indian attack six miles southwest of Fort Hays, Kansas. Custer personally took Company I in the direction of the Indians but found nothing. Burkey, *Custer, Come at Once!*, 76.

100. Brian Pohanka, "Lt. Wallingford's Courts Martial," *Research Review* (September, 1977), 9.

Davis implied that Keogh sought service as an acting assistant inspector general because of "a severe injury from which he has not entirely recovered." This contradicts, however, Keogh's own report to his brother in August of the previous year. "I have recovered almost entirely from the ill effects of breaking my leg," Myles stated, " it is perfectly straight and eventually will be as straight as the other one. . . ."[92] In any case, Keogh did not receive the appointment.

While Company I and the rest of the regiment remained in the field, Myles continued to perform duty on detached service. On February 17, he arrived at Fort Dodge with twenty-nine recruits. The next day, Keogh departed for Camp Supply. At this base, he managed to injure himself again, this time severely spraining his left knee.[93]

In the meantime, the Seventh Cavalry finally had caught up with Myles, marching into Camp Supply on March 28. The next day, the exhausted and starving command started for Fort Dodge on a march that would see the loss of 276 horses.[94] Keogh, however, was not in attendance, having been found by Acting Assistant Surgeon John J. Marston to be "unfit for duty and unable to travel by reason of a severe strain of knee-joint."[95]

In April, Keogh departed Camp Supply with a pack train and twenty-five wagons bound for Fort Hays. Lieutenant Nowlan, who also had been on detached service at Camp Supply as regimental commissary of subsistence, accompanied Myles on this trip. The pair arrived at Hays on April 21 and rejoined their regiment, although Keogh would not return to active duty until May 29 on account of his sprained knee.[96]

Myles evidently enjoyed his free time, finding Hays to be a "delightful spot." The fine band and the numerous ladies present made things "very gay," but Myles was inclined to feel melancholy. "I am very foolish to even feel blue," Keogh wrote to his brother, "but I do. I have a position envied by many not alone in the army but by society." In an obvious reference to the Washita battle Keogh wrote, "We have knocked the Indians up a cocked hat, yet they are still on the warpath." He went on to say, "We have about ninety squaws spared from our last fight. Some of them are very pretty. I have one that is quite intelligent. It is usual for officers to have two or three lounging around."[97]

This reference to the Indian squaws must be looked upon as being tongue-in-cheek. When Myles was based at Fort Wallace he had written to his brother on the same subject, and with a similar bent:

> I shall I expect be able to provide myself with a squaw, the necessary article to an officer's full equipment out on the plains. — By the way I have seen some of these squaws and as the Quaker said of the famous statues of females 'I don't hanker after em!'[98]

On May 29, Keogh went back to duty and assumed command of Company I for the first time since June of the previous year. This period of stewardship would be brief, however, as Myles was relieved of command on June 7 and assigned to a board of general court martial. During the entire year of 1869, Myles Keogh commanded his company for only ten days.[99]

On June 8, Keogh arrived at Fort Harker for the court martial of Lieutenant David Wallingford. The president of the court was Colonel Nelson A. Miles and Major Lewis Merrill served as judge advocate. Also on the board with Keogh were Captains William Thompson and George Yates, although the latter ultimately retired from the court because of his prejudice toward the accused.

The trial of Wallingford came about because of an incident that had occurred at Hays City on April 17 of that year. While the exact charge against Wallingford was "conduct unbecoming an officer and gentleman," the specifics involved publicly consorting with enlisted men and "notorious prostitutes and lewd women" and for permitting a gambler named Cole to wear his officer's cap and uniform jacket. Due to the absence of Judge Advocate Merrill, the trial was delayed for three weeks until June 30.[100] In the interim, Keogh was placed on another court martial, that of First Lieutenant Jacob Henry Shellabarger, of Company M. Shellabarger actually had two trials, the first emitting from accusations of being drunk while on duty as post adjutant at Fort Leavenworth. He was acquitted on this charge.

Shellabarger's second trial, also for drunkenness, resulted from his appearing intoxicated, and dancing with a member of the Fifth Infantry band, at an enlisted men's ball. The ball ended with the lieutenant involved in a "disturbance" for which he was arrested. Not content with this disgrace, Shellabarger appeared in court in a "drunken condition." The lieutenant was found guilty and was dismissed from the service.

Following his dismissal, Shellabarger used political influence in an attempt to force his reinstatement, as he felt he had been "framed" and that Major Merrill was out to get him. Although President Grant declined to reappoint him, Shellabarger continued trying in 1870, 1872, 1876, and again in 1878. In April of that year, he wrote to his cousin claiming that Keogh had attempted to help and advise him and that Keogh and Thompson had told him that Merrill had swayed the court against him.[101]

Wallingford, meanwhile, having gone back to trial on June 30, also was found guilty. His influence must have been greater than that of Shellabarger, however, as the verdict was overturned due to the protest of his friends in Kansas.

Wallingford would be court martialed a second time, this time at Fort Leavenworth in March 1870. Being found guilty on all counts, Wallingford was dismissed on May 18. When asked on this occasion about the lieutenant's reputation, Keogh responded that it was ". . . about as bad as a man could possibly have . . . in every sense of the word, from common report, as regards money matters, and as regards his conduct as an officer and a gentleman, in every possible way." Furthermore, Keogh testified, "His treatment of his wife has influenced me towards him more than any other act of his."[102]

On August 12, 1869, Myles returned from his court martial duty, having been granted a twenty-day leave on a surgeon's certificate of disability.[103] Apparently his sprained knee was not healing well, for in a letter dated the previous June, Myles wrote to his brother,

I presume I told you that I had again strained my left knee and I am sorry to say that although almost three months have elapsed yet I am by no means well and I fear that permanent weakness may ensue — yet not sufficient to disable me.

The injury was sufficient to get Keogh a four month extension of his leave with permission to visit Europe, however. Myles' dream of going home was to happen at last.[104]

In June Myles again had written of his desire for a trip home. "I have knocked about so long that I feel the want of even a monthly rest among my family," he wrote, but he had despaired of his chances of ever doing so. It was Myles' intention to be sent to Europe with dispatches for the foreign ministers, but he was informed that the government no longer sent messengers. Instead, it used sealed bags on the regular mail steamers. This news blocked a hope Myles had entertained for a long time of going home.[105]

Despite this, Keogh must have resolved to get back to Ireland at all costs. On August 27, he telegraphed the office of Adjutant General E. D. Townsend from the Metropolitan Hotel in New York City, "Please telegraph me if my leave is granted or if it has been sent me, my passage is engaged on the *City of Paris* tomorrow. Can I go?"[106]

Myles indeed must have been anxious to depart for a few hours later he sent a second telegraph asking authority to leave. That day, Keogh learned that he had received his extension with permission to visit Europe.[107] The next day, with his recently received United States citizenship papers in hand, Myles Keogh boarded the *City of Paris* and sailed for Ireland. The steamer arrived at Queenstown (modern day Cohb, on Cold Harbor), on September 6.[108]

On September 20, while at the home of Tom, in County Carlow, Myles wrote to the Adjutant General requesting a two month extension of his leave. He enclosed a surgeon's certificate from Thomas O'Meara of the University Medical School and Dr. Herring Cooper stating that he:

101. Record Group 153, Records of the Judge Advocate General, Records of Courts-Martial Proceedings, National Archives, Washington, D.C., File PP 417.

102. Pohanka, "Lt. Wallingsford's Courts Martial," 9.

103. Special Order No. 146, Headquarters, Department of the Missouri, August 12, 1869. According to Lippincott on July 12, 1869, Keogh suffered from "chronic enlargement and partial loss of the use of the left knee joint," and would not be able to resume his duties for at least four months. "Seventh Cavalry Medical Department." This injury placed Keogh in the hospital at Fort Harker on July 23, 1869. Pohanka, "Service Record." On July 30, 1869 Lippincott repeated his previous assessment and added, "I have no doubt that care and rest will entirely remove all traces of the inflammation and its results."

104. June 1, 1869, National Library Microfilm.

105. Ibid.

106. Myles W. Keogh to E. D. Townsend, August 27, 1869, Record Group 94, Letters Sent, Adjutant General's Office, Files 180K (AGO) 1869 and 208K (AGO) 1869, National Archives, Washington, D.C. Hereafter referred to as "Files 180K/208K."

107. Myles W. Keogh to Robert Williams, August 27, 1869, ibid.

108. New York *Times* (August 29, 1869), 8 and (September 7, 1869), 8.

109. Myles W. Keogh to E. D. Townsend, September 20, 1869, "Files 180K/208K."

110. Ibid.

111. June 1, 1869, National Library Microfilm. An undated clipping in the Myles Keogh Collection, Gene Autry Western Heritage Museum reads "... A few days ago Col. Keogh visited this country [Ireland], having come home to Europe for the purpose of consulting Nelaton for an injury which he sustained by his horse falling during one of his encounters with the Indians in the far west." The Indian reference, of course, is apocryphal. See also "Dr. Auguste Nelaton," New York Times (September 22, 1873), 5 and (September 30, 1873), 1.

112. New York Times (February 21, 1870), 8 and New York Daily Tribune (February 21, 1870), 5; Myles W. Keogh to Tom Keogh, March 1870 (Elizabeth Lawrence Collection).

113. Lawrence, His Very Silence Speaks, 87.

Still labors under chronic inflammation of the knee joint, the result of an injury [and] that his heart's action is weaker than natural and his general health considerably deteriorated.[109]

The doctor further declared that Keogh was unfit for duty and would need two months in addition to the leave he had already been granted before he could resume his normal duties. Myles' request contained an additional inducement:

I would respectfully state that I shall visit most of the Camps of Instruction in France & I hope my time will be spent advantageously.[110]

Whether Keogh was touring military installations in France on the eve of the Franco-Prussian War is unknown. It was reported, however, that Myles had come to Europe to consult with the famous French surgeon, Dr. August Nelaton, about his injured knee. This might explain why he would volunteer to undertake the difficult and costly sojourn to France.

Dr. Nelaton, who resided in Paris, had gained acclaim for treating such luminaries as Garibaldi and Napoleon III, whose son he also had saved from a near fatal infection. To date, no information has been uncovered to indicate whether or not Myles was treated by Nelaton, or even if he ever arrived in France. But Keogh was granted the extension of his leave.

Nothing more is known of Myles' months in Ireland. One can only reflect on his thoughts in a letter to Tom written some months before his departure, and assume that his hopes had come to pass:

... Although I could write of things that are passing before me every day yet somehow I have a feeling that sometime in the future these scenes and incidents may more pleasurably & happily be related sitting all together by the same fire side. If this ever comes to pass part of what I have strived for will be accomplished & I will feel as if I had not lived altogether in vain when I have told to those dear ones at home the whole story of my life.[111]

On February 11, 1870, he concluded his stay and headed for the United States aboard the steamer *City of Brooklyn*.

Keogh in civilian garb. The faintest hint of a smile can be detected in this early 1870s era image taken by photographer E. Klauber. *Courtesy of Custer Battlefield National Monument.*

Arriving in New York on the 20th, Myles set out for Fort Leavenworth by way of Washington, D.C. and Indianapolis and reached his final destination in early March.[112]

The rest among his family that he had so longed for must have changed Myles' outlook tremendously. Without a hint of the depression that had pervaded his earlier letters he confessed "[I] have not felt so well for years both in spirit and health and in every way...." This trip caused him to state, "I feel like a new man."[113]

Now rested, Leavenworth must have seemed a natural progression from the familiarity of home and hearth, as it was the center of much socializing among the officer class. Keogh dined often with the Custers and visited the Sturgis residence almost daily. Horsemanship was a popular sport among those at Leavenworth. Keogh often obliged roommate Henry Nowlan with a riding mount out of his troop for the use of his friend's fiancé.[114]

On one occasion, a hurdle race was organized for the officers of the Seventh, causing much excitement among the local townspeople. The contestants were to be Custer, Keogh, Cooke, Bell, McDougall, Nowlan, and Abell, all of the Seventh Cavalry. Captain Chambers McKibbin represented the Fifteenth Infantry and Captain David H. Buel, the local Ordnance Corps officer, likewise participated. With over 2000 persons in attendance, the grand event began with all contestants taking the first hurdle together. However, as Keogh went over the second hurdle, his horse's forefeet struck the top of the obstacle and threw both horse and rider to the ground. Having been struck in the face and side by his fallen mount, it appeared that Keogh had sustained a serious injury. Custer, upon seeing Myles' predicament, pulled out of the race to lend his assistance. A newspaper of the day reported, "This painful accident to the gallant soldier and courteous gentleman, marred considerably the pleasure of the occasion and excited much sympathy in his behalf from all present."[115] Though Keogh had been knocked unconscious, he escaped without any fracture, dislocation, or internal injury, suffering only a laceration and a wounded ego. "He was soon himself," Elizabeth Custer recalled years later, "regretting with all his heart that he had proved a 'spoil sport'."[116]

As a result of his accident, Keogh went into the post hospital at Leavenworth the next day. Even though his wounds were not all that severe, he did not return to the command of his troop until the first week of June, taking another leave from July 24 to August 5.[117] Company I, by that time, had departed Fort Leavenworth for its new post farther west in Kansas, Fort Hays. In due course, Keogh joined his unit. Throughout that summer, Keogh and Company I performed the usual scouting and escort duty in the vicinity of the Saline River. Nothing of much import occurred during this time, save an incident that took place in early June on a mission between Forts Hays and Harker. On that occasion, Keogh's mount, Comanche, reportedly received a flesh wound in the right foreleg during a skirmish with Indians.[118]

In late October, another event took place which sheds some light on Keogh's evident popularity with his men. On the 21st, eleven mules were stolen from Keogh's camp. The following day, seven of the mules were found and one of the thieves was captured. Keogh, in accordance with General Order No. 28 of 1870, immediately offered a reward for the recapture of the remaining mules —the substantial sum of $200.00 per animal.

Using information obtained from the captured thief, Keogh and his company pursued the rustlers. They arrested them, shooting one in the process. According to the U.S. Marshall, Sergeant Clinton Andrews of Company I apprehended George A. Baldwin, who subsequently was sentenced to the penitentiary in Kansas for his crime. Keogh credited Sergeant Andrews with the arrest of the thief plus the recapture of seven mules. Two privates, also from Company I (Samuel Martin and Christie Armstrong) likewise received acknowledgement for the recapture of the remaining four mules. Their captain then recommended the three men for the prescribed cash reward.

However, as the seven mules accorded to Sergeant Andrews were recaptured *prior* to the offer of a reward, he clearly was not entitled to the $1,400 payment he was scheduled to receive. Quartermaster General Montgomery Meigs was disgusted at the entire matter. "I doubt the propriety, even the legality of payment of these rewards to soldiers," Meigs wrote. "I suggest," he continued, "that this large reward if interpreted as claimed offers inducements to men to procure or incite robberies with the purpose of betraying and capturing the robber and stolen animals."

The matter finally came before Secretary of War William Belknap who decided, ironically, that that payment would be made only for the four animals recaptured after the reward was offered, and that this would be given to Sergeant Andrews! Apparently, Privates Martin and Armstrong went into winter quarters on October 24 at Fort Hays a great deal less well off than they thought they should be.[119]

While his men spent their days at the fort, Myles began 1871 by taking a thirty-day leave of absence begin-

SEVENTH CAVALRY, 1866-1876

114. Ibid., 88.

115. Minnie Dubbs Millbrook, "Fort Leavenworth Races," *Research Review* (December, 1978), 19.

116. Pohanka, "Myles Walter Keogh (1840-1876)," 10.

117. April 30, 1870, Seventh Cavalry Medical Cards; Pohanka, "Service Record."

118. Luce, *Keogh, Comanche and Custer*, 44.

119. Record Group 393, Pt. 1, Department of Missouri Letters Received (1870) Myles Keogh to Department Headquarters, May 16, 1870, National Archives, Washington, D.C. Record Group 94, Adjutant General's Office, Letters Received, Through General Pope with endorsements from Quartermaster General Meigs and Secretary of War Belknap, January 12, 1871.

MYLES KEOGH

120. Chandler, *Of Garry Owen in Glory*, 35.
121. Ibid.
122. Merington, *The Custer Story*, 236-237. Lieutenant Charles Brewster had warned Custer earlier that Keogh was not friendly toward him, although this was years before. Charles Brewster to George A. Custer, September 7, 1867 (Lawrence Frost Collection, Monroe, MI).
123. Merington, *The Custer Story*, 236.

Looking dapper in his suit and bowler hat, Keogh effects the image of an urbane gentleman. In his gloved left hand, he cradles a bamboo swagger, a custom associated with British officers of the period. The swagger stick sometimes supplanted the saber, when not worn, to indicate a mounted officer's status.
Author Fred Dustin related an account that Keogh carried a cane surmounted by a silver dog's head.
Courtesy of Gene Autry Western Heritage Museum.

ning February 20. Nothing is certain of what he did during this time, save his appearance in New York. It has been conjectured that he returned to Ireland, but thirty days seems too short a period to go to the expense of a trans-Atlantic trip that would itself consume two weeks. It is certain, however, that Keogh reported for duty on March 26 at his new station of Baghdad, Kentucky. By this time, the Seventh Cavalry had been sent to the Department of the South to assist United States marshals in the arrest of violators of the Internal Revenue laws.[120] Also as part of its service, the Seventh was to protect the government's policies of Reconstruction against the attacks of the recently organized Ku Klux Klan.[121]

Keogh's service during this period proved uneventful, marked only by frequent trips to Louisville for detached service on boards of general court martial—and perhaps for other, more personal reasons. Newly promoted First Lieutenant James Calhoun wrote to his brother-in-law, George Custer, in April of 1871, "Col. K went to Louisville yesterday as he was lonesome. Letters from a certain party in New York do not content him much. This for yourself."[122]

The "certain party" Calhoun speaks of was a "Miss Hf" whom Keogh had met while on leave in New York. Apparently the Custer clique found Keogh's attention toward this woman amusing, as she most certainly did not reciprocate in his affection. In what Custer termed a "characteristic letter," Keogh wrote to his superior thanking him for calling on the object of his affections, "since she must feel lonely since I left." Myles wanted Custer to send her a "collection of flowers" but Custer chafed at the cost of such a request—not less than $25. Custer told his wife:

> It would be just like K's suspicious nature to suppose that I prompt Miss Hf to write the sharp letters she does . . . for she wrote him finally that his complaints were monotonous and uninteresting. So sensitive a man I wonder he can endure it. One of his letters to her that she showed me was full of poetry and very touching.[123]

Keogh also requested Custer to order for him some $50 sleeve buttons to be given to Lieutenant W. W. Cooke as payment on a bet. Added to the flowers, this brought the amount of Keogh's request in excess of $75. Custer would order the sleeve buttons, but he would send them C.O.D. "You know," he stated to Libbie, "I bear not the slightest animosity toward him, though I think he treated me unfairly. I do think him rather absurd, but would rather have him stationed near us than many others."[124]

The exact nature of Keogh's relationship to Custer and others has been a subject of much speculation. From this letter, it is obvious that Myles misinterpreted his relationship with Miss Hf, seeing an intimacy that did not exist and assuming a reciprocation of affection when none was forthcoming. The same could be said for Keogh's relationship with Custer. Keogh also unflinchingly sought financial favors, which is either the behavior of a cad or of one who saw his relationship in an almost familial light. Custer, on the other hand, looked upon Keogh only as a subordinate. That Custer continued to respect his abilities despite feeling that Keogh was "absurd," might be attributed to Custer's admiration of Myles' obvious professionalism as a fellow soldier. That Keogh expected Custer and others to view him exactly as he viewed them undoubtedly often left the captain disappointed. It is this basic misunderstanding of personal interaction that may account for his characteristic melancholic attitude on certain occasions.

In September 1871, Company I left Baghdad for its new station at Shelbyville, Kentucky. The duties of the cavalry remained the same however, assisting the government authorities in the arrest of illicit moonshiners and members of the KKK. Keogh spent his time as before, shuttling between his post and Louisville.[125]

In February, he received a twenty-one-day leave of absence on a surgeon's certificate of disability. He explained the nature of this illness in a request for a thirty day extension of leave dated March 18, 1872 at Taylor Barracks, Louisville, "I am suffering from extensive ulceration of the throat affecting the hearing and speech which has existed for several months past."[126]

It was perhaps during this period that Keogh made the acquaintance of Doctor John Arvid Ouchterlony, a physician of prominence in Louisville who, until 1868, had been in charge of the government dispensary there and, it is assumed, had continued his military associations. Keogh's detail to various court martial boards in that time possibly also brought the two men into contact.

Ouchterlony, a fellow Catholic, was an interesting man. He came to the United States from his native Sweden, where his father had been a cavalry officer. After his arrival in America during the 1850s, he studied medicine at the University of the City of New York. Later, he served as a surgeon in the Union Army then, when peace came, he moved to Louisville where he married the daughter of a prominent judge. Soon thereafter, he helped establish the Louisville Medical College, in which he became a professor of materia medica, therapeutics, and clinical medicine. He obtained a national reputation as a dedicated researcher, an inspiring lecturer, and an author on numerous medical topics. His knowledge extended beyond science into art and literature. Ouchterlony's home on Fourth Street, complete with its own chapel, must have been a comfortable haven for guests such as Keogh, who incidently spent his last leave there.[127] Keogh even mentioned the doctor in his will, assigning that gentleman the responsibilities of transmitting certain private papers to an individual he did not name. Presumably, this was a woman, although the exact nature of the relationship remains one more mystery about Keogh's life.[128]

The days in Louisville were numbered, though, as Company I stayed at Shelbyville only until December 30 when the unit departed by rail for its new posting at Lebanon, Kentucky. Shortly after their arrival at this garrison, Keogh and his troop did have at least one adventure—a skirmish with moonshiners in January that left Comanche with a flesh wound in the right shoulder.[129]

Though first ordered to proceed to Texas, the Seventh Cavalry was now to be sent, at General Sheridan's request, to the Department of Dakota. On March 1, Company I left Lebanon by train for Taylor Barracks in

---

124. Ibid.
125. Chandler, *Of Garry Owen in Glory*, 38.
126. Myles W. Keogh to Assistant Adjutant General, Department of the South, March 13, 1872, Record Group 393, Entry 4116, Part 1, Letters Received 1868-1883, Department of the South, National Archives, Washington, D.C.
127. J. Stoddard Johnston, *Memorial History of Louisville* (Louisville, KY: n.p., 1896), 627-628; Louisville Courier-Journal (October 6, 1905).
128. Ouchterlony's Will, Jefferson County, Kentucky, Will Book No. 27, 23.
129. Luce, *Keogh, Comanche and Custer*, 45.

130. Seventh Cavalry Medical Cards, March 6, 1873.

131. Chandler, *Of Garry Owen in Glory*, 38.

132. Harold P. Reeze, "Custer's Insurance Policy," *Real West Magazine* (December, 1970), 52.

133. Marcus A. Reno to O.D. Greene, November 6, 1873, Record Group 393, Military Department of the Missouri, Letters Received No. 3194 (1873), National Archives, Washington, D.C.

In 1872, a new uniform came into being. For cavalry officers this consisted of a double-breasted dark blue wool coat, shoulder knots, and a plumed helmet, worn by Keogh in this early 1870s view. *Courtesy of Gene Autry Western Heritage Museum.*

Louisville. On March 6, Keogh was admitted to the post hospital with catarrh, returning to duty March 13.[130] The day prior to Myles return, General Terry, in command of the Department of Dakota, requested two cavalry companies to accompany the Northern Boundary Survey on the US-Canadian line. Companies D and I were selected for this service, and after reaching Sioux City, Iowa, were separated from the regiment and travelled by rail to Fort Snelling, Minnesota.[131] While at Snelling, Keogh purchased a $10,000 life insurance policy. This started a trend among the officers of the Seventh, and the fortunate salesman, I.F.A. Studdart, was soon to add Lieutenant Colonel Custer, Captain Yates, and Lieutenants Calhoun, Crittenden, and Porter to his list of insured.[132]

Three troops, Companies D and I of the Seventh Cavalry and Company K of the Twentieth Infantry, formed the escort for the survey. The cavalry contingent, under the command of Major Marcus Reno, left Fort Snelling on the Saint Paul and Pacific Railroad on June 5, arriving at Breckenridge, Minnesota, the same day. From there, the squadron marched to Fort Pembina, Dakota Territory, passing through Fort Abercrombie on its way. Arriving at Pembina on June 22, 1872, the troops enjoyed a brief rest, as it was determined the cavalry should reach a primary depot at Turtle Mountain by July 10. That being accomplished, Reno ordered Keogh and Company I to escort the supply train and cattle herd to a second depot which would become the base of operations. This permanent depot was designated Camp Terry.

Though the cavalry escort had as its intended purpose the protection of the survey party from attack, there were, in fact, few Indians encountered and those not in the least hostile. "The detachments were so numerous that they were necessarily removed from the supervision (daily) of the officers," Reno reported, "and they were used virtually as assistants by the parties for which they were escorts." After an extended march, the troops would be sent out as flag bearers, stationing themselves at the heads of ravines and crests of hills. The horses, being seldom released from the saddle, had little opportunity for proper grazing and this had a deleterious effect on the stock.[133]

All was not hardship, however, as there was plenty of time for hunting and socializing. Captain Thomas Weir and Lieutenant W.S. Edgerly, of D Company, frequently joined Reno, Keogh, and Lieutenants Bell and Andrew Nave for dinner and evening strolls among the various camps. The cavalry encampment in particular seemed quite a popular spot, and much rustic entertaining was done by the Seventh's officers. Despite the occasional snow and rain and mosquito attacks, the duty was quite idyllic. One civilian member of the survey party, J. E. Bangs, wrote in his journal for September 16: "Walked over to Cavalry Camp in afternoon, saw Reno and Keogh —all rest out hunting and Minking."[134]

On October 13, the boundary commission's work was suspended for the year. All parties returned to Camp Terry. The march back commenced the next day via Fort Stevenson, then on to Fort Totten, where the command arrived on October 22 to take up winter quarters. During the march, the weather had turned very cold with snow falling. Three horses of the detachment died en route, casting a bitter denouement on what had been an uncommonly pleasant exercise.[135]

The rest of that winter, Company I remained at Fort Totten. On November 1, Myles received a thirty-day leave of absence, returning to duty December 13. Once on duty again, Keogh settled in to the daily routine of a frontier fort. Henry Allen Bailey, a recent recruit to Company I, wrote home to his family in late 1873 and early 1874 of his new life at Fort Totten, indicating:

> We have got a fine lot of officers. My captain's name is M. W. Keogh. He is a nice man. He says I am the best blacksmith he ever had in his company.
>
> I get a good deal of money doing little jobs for the officers, and think I can have quite a pile when my time is out.[136]

Keogh's generosity with his troops had not waned since the "mule reward" affair, as evidenced by Bailey's letter of January 1874 ". . . I ironed off a sleigh for the captain last week, and he gave me $10. I am going to have a ride in it with the First Sergeant. . . ."[137]

To assume, however, that all of Myles' charges at Totten were as pleasant as Private Bailey would be in error, as Company I had its share of scoundrels as well. For example, Corporal Samuel Frederick Staples had deserted his wife of three years and infant daughter to enlist in the cavalry in 1872. Likewise, Private Thomas P. Downing abandoned his wife who, at the time, was sixth months pregnant when he enlisted in 1873.

Downing, an Irishman born in Adare, County Limerick, had lied about his age upon enlistment. He was, in fact, sixteen years old and not twenty-one as he had stated. In a letter home, Downing responded to his father's threat to expose his real age in order to get him out of the army. "Come, now," Downing wrote, "the Govt. doesn't care if I am seventeen or thirty so long as I can perform a soldier's duty." The young Irish soldier added that it was pointless to threaten to tell Keogh about his "escapades" as the Army did not care about his civilian past. "In fact," he continued, "some of the hardest cases that I ever came across are at present serving in this company. . . ."[138]

One of those hard cases was Private Edward C. Driscoll who assaulted First Sergeant Frank E. Varden on June 24, 1875, saying, "I will fix him the God damned son of a bitch." Private Adam Hetesimer showed similar affection for Sergeant Milton De Lacy, trying to hit him with an axe when the sergeant attempted to apprehend the private for being absent from stable duty.

Sergeants Varden and De Lacy were not beyond reproach either, as Varden had deserted in 1872 and only after the considerable efforts of his commanding officer was he reinstated.[139] De Lacy himself deserted in May 1877 and was never apprehended. It was suggested by another deserter from Company I, Charles Prior, that these non-commissioned officers were as brutal as their captain and that the troop reflected the character of its commander. It is doubtful, however, that brutality alone could inspire in the men of Company I the loyalty that they ultimately would show, as Baily, Staples, Downing, Driscoll, Hetesimer, and Varden would all die with Keogh at the Little Big Horn.

Early in 1874, Myles made his last trip to his homeland. On April 6, he was granted leave to attend to personal business in order to claim his inheritance of property at Clifden Castle, County Kilkenny. Having inherited the property from his Aunt Mary Blanchfield, Myles would, in turn, give his right and title to Clifden to his sister, Margaret.[140]

Myles sailed from New York on the *City of Richmond*,

---

134. "Journal of J.E. Bangs," *North Dakota Historical Society* (1913), 219-234. Bangs mentions an "Indian scare" on Friday, July 18 but nothing came of this incident. Apparently, the only Indians encounterd were two Wah Peton Sioux on July 25.

135. Marcus A. Reno to O.D. Greene, November 6, 1873, Letters Received 3194 (1863).

136. Henry Bailey Letters, October, 1873 (Custer Battlefield National Monument Microfilm Collection).

137. Ibid., January, 1874.

138. National Archives Pension Files, Myles W. Keogh.

139. John M. Carroll, *A Bit of Seventh Cavalry History With All Its Warts* (Bryan, TX: J.M. Carroll, 1987), 5. On March 7, 1872 Keogh requested that Pvt. Frank E. Varden be restored to duty without trial. When that request was not favorably considered, Myles asked for a reconsideration of the case of the late Sergeant of Troop I. See N.A. RG 393, Pt. 1 Entry 4115. Index, LR, Dept of the South.

140. Keogh was in Washington, D.C. until May 19, 1874, and left for New York the following day. See Pohanka, "Service Record."

MYLES KEOGH

141. *New York Times* (May 24, 1874), 12 and (September 28, 1874), 8.
142. Hart, *Irish Pedigrees*, 506-509.
143. Pohanka, "Service Record."
144. Seventh Cavalry Medical Cards, July 18, 1875.

At least one of Keogh's medals appears in a later photograph as seen in this O. S. Goff view of Emma and Nellie Wadsworth. The sisters wear the uniforms of W. W. Cooke and Tom Custer, as well as one of Keogh's St. Gregory medals in an effort to counter Tom Custer's two Medals of Honor. During an episode in which Keogh and other officers attempted to teach the young ladies to shoot firearms, the Irish soldier asked, "what will you girls ever do with yourselves?" *Courtesy of Chester E. Nelson, Jr. Collection.*

on Saturday, May 23. What transpired on his trip is not known as no account remains, but it may be assumed that his nearly three months at home passed with as much happiness as had his earlier trip in 1869. Keogh then steamed to New York aboard the *City of Chester* on September 27, having left Queenstown on September 18. After spending a month in the East, Keogh reported to duty on November 9 after an absence of seven months.[141]

Although back in uniform, Company I was not to see much more of its commander in 1875 than it had in 1874. This last full year of Keogh's life was marked by repeated illness and extended leaves of absence. For instance, on February 13, he was admitted to the post hospital at Fort Totten with acute diarrhea but returned to duty three days later. On the 26th of the same month, Keogh reported at Saint Paul, Minnesota, where he served on detached service until April 24th.[142]

Companies D and I had changed station to Fort Lincoln while he was away, and it was there that Keogh reported on May 25, then resumed his responsibilities as company commander on June 1. Only a month and a half passed before the surgeon again reported Keogh as sick in quarters, saying that he was, "Suffering from debility, the result of an attack of remittent fever, attended with extreme nervous prostration." The next day he was admitted to the post hospital with another case of acute diarrhea. He would not be back on duty until August 9.[143]

With Keogh's frequent illnesses and applications for leave of absence, it is little wonder that his superiors became annoyed. When Myles applied in August for a medical leave of absence, Custer stepped in and wrote to the Assistant Adjutant General on August 2:

> I recommend that no action be taken on application of Captain Keogh for sick leave until the action of a board of medical officials directed to examine him and report today is known. I do not believe that officer should receive the leave he has applied for.[144]

Custer wrote the same day to Post Surgeon C. C. Byrne telling him to make a "careful examination" of Keogh, "with a view of determining if that officer is fit for duty. . . ."[145] Surgeon Byrne's report followed the next day:

> In my opinion after a careful examination Captain Keogh is at this time able to perform light duty, viz: attend courts martial and roll calls. I am also of the opinion that his present progress towards convalescence continues. Captain Keogh will within ten days be able to perform guard and all ordinary garrison duty.[146]

Despite Custer's recommendation that Keogh's applica-

SEVENTH CAVALRY, 1866-1876

Taken during the same period as the scene on Custer's front porch (frontispiece), the "hunting party" lounged along the banks of the Little Heart River outside Ft. Lincoln. Keogh appears to the right of his commander, leaning on a chair. Although not evident here, Keogh was several inches taller than Custer. *Courtesy of Gene Autry Western Heritage Museum.*

145. George A. Custer to Assistant Adjutant General, August 2, 1875, Record Group 393, Post Correspondence, Fort Abraham Lincoln, National Archives, Washington, D.C.

146. George A. Custer to C.C. Byrne, August 2, 1875, ibid.

147. George A. Custer to Assistant Adjutant General, August 3, 1875, ibid.

148. Martin F. Schmidt to J. S. Manion, September 18, 1968 (J.S. Manion Collection, Beverly Hills, FL).

149. Pohanka, "Service Record.".

150. Myles W. Keogh to Assistant Adjutant General, April 30, 1876, Record Group 393, Department of Dakota, Letters Sent and Received, National Archives, Washington, D.C.

tion for leave be disapproved, he was granted a thirty-day ordinary leave beginning August 26. Keogh's address during this leave was listed as 215 Fourth Street, Louisville, Kentucky—the home and office of Dr. John Ouchterlony.[147]

Whether Keogh's medical condition during this period was serious or frivolous is a question of much speculation. Certainly Custer felt that Myles was taking advantage of his illness and the tone of Custer's letters suggests he felt Keogh was shirking his responsibilities as captain of Company I. Also, since the exact relationship between Keogh and the Kentucky physician may have been as much personal as professional it cannot be said for certain whether Myles' stay in Louisville was for reasons of health or for enjoyment. It is possible that both motives brought him there.

Regardless of why Keogh went to Kentucky, at the end of his leave he rejoined the Seventh, on October 14, 1875 and assumed command of his company. From that time, until the moment of his death, he remained with the regiment, reporting for duty every day.[148] That is not to say that he did not attempt to free himself from his post at Fort Lincoln. In fact, on April 30, 1876, a few days before departing on the campaign that would culminate in the Battle of the Little Big Horn, Myles addressed the Assistant Adjutant General of the Department of Dakota. Keogh requested that he be granted a thirty-day leave, with permission to reapply for an extension of fifteen days.[149] He asked that this take effect October 1, 1876, should active operations in the field be at an end.[150] Keogh, of course, would never make use of this furlough. Fate had intervened, and for the first time in his career, Myles Keogh would take part in a major campaign with the Seventh Cavalry.

Keogh would be a frequent visitor at the Louisville home of his friend, Dr. John Arvid Ouchterlony. *Courtesy University of Louisville.*

123

"Reconnaissance"

THE WARREN FAVOR AFFAIR

> Lieut. Hale has just returned with the bodies of Favor and Thompson. . . . They were shot full of bullets and arrows and were scalped.
>
> Myles Keogh, May 9, 1867

Timber was vital at Fort Wallace for building and fuel but in western Kansas, then as now, it was not easy to obtain. As quartermaster, Lieutenant Frederick Beecher let contracts to civilians who would provide the materials to the post. They could not use the standing timber on the military reservation, however, as this was government property. This meant that they had to haul their loads from far away or cut trees by contract or squatters right if they wished to use nearby sources.

This restriction caused problems with one of the contractors, Warren Favor. He and his wife, Nannie, occupied a five-room "dug out" about four miles west of the fort.[1] At first, the boundaries of the Wallace reservation had been ill-defined, and evidently did not embrace the Favor homestead. Ultimately, the government claim was expanded to include their plot. Keogh then ordered the Favors to vacate the premises and move elsewhere.[2]

Shortly after this, in May 1867, Indians burned Goose Creek Station, located several miles from the Favors' spread. Worried about moving in the midst of this violence, Favor sent word to Keogh asking that he and his wife be allowed "to remain until we could see some way we could get away safely."[3] At least at the dug out he had a sort of defensive position built up using the wood he had cut between January and March, 1867. This hollow square provided a temporary corral for Favor's mules and a breastwork which afforded more protection than exposure in open country as the Favors traveled to a new location.

This makeshift bastion began to disappear, however, since, beginning in mid-March, troops from the post came out in wagons and loaded wood for the fort from Favor's stockpile. Activity continued despite Favor's protests. After around sixty cords had been removed, he engaged the services of an attorney, Hiram J. Graham of Denver, to try and secure payment for the seized wood as well as to obtain money for deliveries made to the post under an earlier contract. Beecher would not allow payment for the seized wood since he claimed that it had been procured from the government domain, despite the fact that Keogh had allowed Favor to work at Big Timber on the reservation in late 1866.[4]

Keogh backed Beecher. The Favors had become convinced that the two officers were trying to drive them from their land "for fear we would be able to show their dishonesty and they would be reprimanded." The allu-

---

1. "The Indian War," *Rocky Mountain News* (June 10, 1867), 2; *U.S. Census*, 1870, Colorado, Arapaho County, Denver, 32.
2. United States Court of Claims in the Case of Nannie Spencer, Administratrix for Warren Favor, vs. the United States; General Jurisdiction Case No. 6330, Record Group 123, National Archives, Washington, D.C.
3. Ibid.
4. Jos. T. Hale to J.S. Hammer, December 7, 1866, Fort Wallace Museum Microfilm.

sion was to Favor having made a lower bid than the individual given the contract. The charges continued that "a certain officer [Keogh] of the United States was in collusion with other government contractors to supplant Favor...."[5]

When Warren Favor and his employee, John Thompson, were killed by Indians in "a running fight" in May 1867, the episode might well have ended there.[6] That was not the case. Just a few days after he reported the death of the two men, he sent another piece of correspondence to his superiors. The Captain indicated that Graham had approached him and "had the audacity to hint that I could share his profits" if Keogh was willing to provide a receipt for the seized wood.[7]

This fight to secure a settlement for the Favor estate went on to the Court of Claims in 1874, and even continued on to Congress later in the decade, where Keogh and Beecher were accused of "brutal treatment" and "persecution" which caused Favor to lose his life, and his family to suffer "untold horrors."[8] Unsuccessful in this pursuit, Nannie Favor did not give up. As late as February 16, 1892 she again approached the Court of Claims with a letter requesting compensation for $3570.[9] So far as can be determined, this settlement never was obtained.

5. *Petition of Harvey Spaulding*, H.R. 1037, "Bill of relief of Nannie Spencer," 45th Cong., 2nd Sess., Serial No. 1822, House Report No. 15, December 6, 1877.

6. Myles W. Keogh to George A. Custer, May 9, 1867, Fort Wallace Museum Microfilm.

7. Myles Keogh to Chief Quartermaster of the District of Upper Missouri, May 14, 1867, Fort Wallace Museum Microfilm, Wallace, Kansas. In a letter to headquarters, August 26, 1867 Keogh restated that Graham had tried "to bribe me to swindle the Government," and in a deposition made on December 10, 1872 in the office of John M. Harlan, attorney for the United States, Louisville, Kentucky he underscored that Graham wanted Keogh to arrange for vouchers to be made out for "a figure two or three times greater" than the wood actually delivered by Favor. Keogh went on to testify that Graham "told me that it was a way they had in Colorado and out West to fix things up agreeable to both parties...." United States Court of Claims in the Case of Nannie Spencer.

8. *Petition of Harvey Spencer*. This document also refers to, "The brutal Keogh."

9. In fact, Mrs. Favor, who later remarried and became Nannie Spencer, received $3570 in March of 1869, but she did so under protest as this was only for 102 cords of wood and not the larger amount claimed. Consequently, she gave Harvey Spaulding of Washington, D.C. power of attorney to pursue the matter in court. United States Court of Claims in the Case of Nannie Spencer.

"Reconnaissance"

WILLIAM AVERILL COMSTOCK, 1842-1868

> No Indian was half so superstitious as Will Comstock. He had his 'medicine' horse, 'medicine' field glasses, 'medicine' everything, in fact.[1]
>
> Theodore R. Davis, "A Summer on the Plains."

If ever a larger than life fictional character saw embodiment it was in the person of William Averill Comstock, better known as "Medicine Bill." Appropriately, Comstock was the grand nephew of author James Fenimore Cooper, whose fictional hero, Natty Bumppo, defined the character of the American frontiersman.

By all accounts a daring and capable man, "Medicine Bill" distinguished himself as a scout at the new post of Fort Wallace, first for the Second Cavalry and then continuously for the Seventh Cavalry. Myles Keogh had nothing but superlatives for him. "This man Comstock has been in Govt. employ for over 5 years," Keogh wrote in reply to an accusation against the scout, testifying, "If I am to judge of his character by what I have seen of him since last November, I should consider him an unusually intelligent, temperate and trustworthy man. . . ."[2]

Indeed, Comstock was well educated. The son of wealthy Michigan parents, "Will," as he also was known, defied the stereotype of the rough and vulgar westerner, although newspapers of the time did not hesitate to cast him in that light.[3]

In January 1867, Comstock's reputation had come to the attention of George Custer, who promptly requested his services at Fort Riley. Keogh wrote a letter of introduction for Comstock, calling the scout, "An excellent man [and] an eccentric genius and an ardent admirer of everything reckless and daring." With a hint of whimsy, Keogh added, "Comstock has never yet seen a R.R. train and his satisfaction I believe is improved by this accidental granting of his fondest wishes, Viz: seeing Custer and the R.R."[4]

While Comstock's reaction to meeting Custer is not recorded, his first experience with a train is. Writing in *Harper's New Monthly Magazine*, Theodore Davis recalled, "While on the Platte Comstock saw a locomotive for the first time. His surprise was inexpressible. 'Good Medicine! Good Medicine!' shouted Will. 'Look at the Tu-te!'"[5]

Comstock's high standing within the community at large is evidenced by an incident that occurred early in 1868. Apparently, "Medicine Bill" had entered into some arrangement with the wood contractor for Fort Wallace, a man named Wyatt. For unknown reasons, Wyatt and Comstock came to a disagreement. Some accounts say that Wyatt cheated the Indian guide, others that he merely angered Comstock with boasts of his days with Quantrill's raiders. Whatever the reason, when Wyatt got up to leave the post sutler's store, Comstock shot him several times in the back. Wyatt ran out of the store and dropped dead.

Comstock was arrested and taken to Hays City for trial. The nature of the crime and the surplus of witnesses seemed to insure a guilty verdict. But such a mundane

---

1. Theodore R. Davis, "A Summer on the Plains, *Harper's Monthly* (February, 1868).
2. M. W. Keogh to H. E. Noyes, March 22, 1867, Fort Wallace Microfilm.
3. Gray, "Will Comstock," 94.
4. M. W. Keogh to G. A. Custer, January 21, 1867, Lawrence Frost Collection.
5. Davis, "A Summer On the Plains."

outcome would not have been appropriate to such an epic character. Despite the evidence, Comstock was acquitted.

One version of the trial has Justice J. M. Joyce asking the main witness whether the shooting was done with "felonious intent." When the witness responded that he did not know Comstock's intentions but did see him shoot Wyatt dead, the Judge replied, "If the shooting was not done with felonious intent, and there is no proof that it was, the prisoner is discharged for want of said proof!"[6]

Another account has Comstock pleading guilty to the charge, whereupon Judge Joyce intones, "Ye are a damned fool for tellin' it. I discharge ye for want of ividence!" Whichever version is more correct, the high regard in which the scout was held is apparent.[7]

However, "Medicine Bill's" luck could not hold out forever. Comstock, accompanied by Abner "Sharp" Grover, was sent to the camp of Chief Turkey Leg to enlist his aid in an attempt to quell a recent outbreak of hostilities. While in the Cheyenne camp, news arrived of an engagement with the Seventh Cavalry, and the scouts were asked to leave. Accompanied by four warriors and three boys, Comstock and Grover were allowed to travel some distance from the camp before their escort turned on them, killing Comstock and leaving Grover for dead.[8] In suitably mysterious circumstances, Will Comstock's body was never found.

6. Gray, "Will Comstock," 95.
7. Montgomery, "Fort Wallace," 226.
8. Gray, "Will Comstock," 96.

"Reconnaissance"

A Matter Of Drink

by Kurt Hamilton Cox and John S. Manion

In 1911, David Burton Long, a former hospital steward at Fort Wallace, recalled an incident involving his commanding officer—Myles Keogh:

> Capt. Keogh was fine looking, a perfect soldier in appearance, but he would, as many other officers in the army did, get drunk and do many stunts that if told would make the American people blush at the acts of our nation's defenders. One night about 12 o'clock in his drunken condition he had 'Boots and Saddles' sounded, got his company out and made a cavalry charge over the prairie for an hour or two after an imaginary enemy and returned to quarters about 2 o'clock in the morning. The tramping of the horses and noise of the sabers and carbines as they passed my tent woke me up. I was sure it was the Indians that had made a raid on the post, but soon found out the cause of the disturbance and went back to bed.[1]

Long's blunt account is perhaps the first published record of a matter that has proved of great interest to students of Myles Keogh—his reputation as a drinker. To fellow Irishman and biographer, G. A. Hayes-McCoy, Keogh suffered at the hands of those who called his sobriety into question, "because of the popular belief that all Irishmen drink." Such a defense is not, borne out by contemporary evidence to the contrary however.[2]

Captain Albert Barnitz, in a letter to his wife, recalled the drinking habits of his associates, "Capt. Gillette and Major Beebe are confirmed inebriates and the same may be said of Col. Keogh—they are seldom sober."[3] Barnitz, though, recently had given up drink and rather self-righteously looked askance at those who continued to imbibe noting, "Almost all the old officers drink a great deal. . . . A man is not regarded as sociable who does not . . . have something for his friends to drink, and he has a very small chance of becoming popular with the drinking class unless he indulges a little himself. . . ."[4]

In a thinly disguised portrayal of Keogh, Elizabeth Custer recounted that an Irish officer who had been in the service of the Pope became so "hopelessly boozy" that his striker, Finnegan, "concluded that the safest place for the valuables and the family funds was in his own quarters." This "Irish Officer" had literally given himself up to be directed as his striker wished, even declaring that he had no further responsibility in life.[5]

Custer biographer F. F. Van de Water reiterated and amplified Mrs. Custer's account, calling Keogh a "swaggering bibulous soldier of fortune" and "a devil-may care Irishman with mustache and imperial and an unholy thirst which he could curb only by placing all his cash in the hands of Finnegan, his striker (or batman) and actual guardian."[6]

However, Mrs. Custer reveals that it was not uncommon for officers to "turn themselves over to their strikers." In one of her unpublished manuscripts, she wrote of a similar arrangement Lieutenant Thomas B. Weir had with his man Kellar who, "Took care of his (Weir's) money and bought everything for him. If he asked for

---

1. David Burton Long, "A Short Biographical Sketch of the Life of David Burton Long, Written by Himself" (Boulder, CO. unpublished MS, 1911), 12.
2. Hayes-McCoy, "Captain Myles Walter Keogh," 42.
3. Utley, *Life in Custer's Cavalry*, 203.
4. Ibid., 184-186.
5. Custer, *Following the Guidon*, 150-151.
6. Van de Water, *Glory Hunter*, 152, 297.

money, they (Kellar seems to have had a helper) gave him just enough and withheld enough to keep him in necessary funds. They both wept when he remained out fearing he was drunk. They grumbled about the Sutler's Store and followed his weaving steps unseen ready to watch that no fall or accident happened to him. . . ."[7]

Author Fred Dustin wrote in *The Custer Tragedy* of his acquaintance with two former Company I members, Charles Prior and Andrew Nichols. The two men told him that Keogh, "Was continually under the influence of liquor in a greater or less degree whenever it was obtainable." Prior related that once his friend Nichols had some difficulty with his sergeant, knocking him down after the sergeant had attempted to beat him. The partially intoxicated Keogh, after hearing of the incident, pursued Nichols, armed with a heavy cane having a silver dog's head for a handle, that he habitually carried. According to Dustin, Keogh was not at all hesitant in using this cane "on the heads of enlisted men who incurred his displeasure" and in this instance sought to use it on Nichols, demanding repeatedly, "What did you hit my sergeant for?" Prior and Nichols deserted shortly thereafter.[8]

That Myles Keogh knew the effects of drinking is certain. He prohibited the sale of liquor around Fort Wallace and complained to the acting assistant adjutant general when he feared that the master of nearby Pond Creek Station would start selling it. "This, I need not say," Keogh wrote, "will be a source of constant trouble to the officers at this post, as soldiers will, if they have an opportunity of procuring whiskey, and if so minded find parties to sell clothing to so as to furnish money, [and] buy that much prized article."[9]

Keogh's double standard relaxed around Christmas 1867, when he reported to his brother that he had "just received 10 gals of fine Scotch whiskey and Kelley is making us a brew in my sitting room." Keogh gave a taste of the "Scotch brew" to his men at their troop dinner, "Much to the satisfaction of the Irish in it."[10]

This Christmas dinner was quite a contrast to the one given a year earlier. Lieutenant Beecher reported at that time, "No liquors except water and coffee were served, for the Post, in part from principle, in a great measure from necessity, is temperate."[11]

A few weeks later, Beecher reported to his family, " . . . The officers of this post, have entirely discarded liquor of any kind, either for ourselves or men. . . ." How long it took Keogh to break this pact is unknown, but if David Burton Long is to be believed, he did so with a vengeance.

That Myles Keogh not only drank but also occasionally took it to excess is a certainty not even his fiercest apologists can deny. On the other hand, even his detractors must admit that Myles Keogh never openly allowed his drinking to impugn his reputation as a professional soldier. Whether Keogh's problem with alcohol effected his career in more subtle ways is still a matter open to conjecture.

7. Elizabeth B. Custer Microfilm, Custer Battlefield 4-3519 ff.
8. Dustin, *The Custer Tragedy*, 236.
9. Keogh to Noyes, March 4, 1867, Fort Wallace Microfilm.
10. December 26, 1867, National Library Microfilm.
11. *Fred Beecher Memorial*, 24.
12. Ibid., 25.

First Lieutenant John Carland appears on the right with fellow officers of Company B, Sixth United States Infantry, Captain Stephen Baker (center) and Second Lieutenant Charles Henry Ingalls. Carland, an attorney in civilian life, prepared Keogh's will before the Irishman's unit rode off to the Little Big Horn. *Courtesy of Ethel Yates Gray.*

Chapter 7

Into the Valley of Death:
The Historiography of Keogh's Role at the Little Big Horn

by John Phillip Langellier, Ph.D.

> ... the veil which conceals the future seems to be removed, and a glance, short and fleeting as the lightning flash, is permitted us into the gloomy valley before us.
>
> Charles Lever, *Charles O'Malley*

Not long after Keogh made his application for another leave, the Seventh Cavalry at last received its marching orders. Keogh and Company I prepared to set out with Custer's column as part of the right wing under Major Marcus Reno's direct authority.[1] The force left Fort Lincoln on May 17, making twelve miles that first day as they moved along the Little Heart River. Elizabeth Custer accompanied her husband to this point but would turn back as the unit moved further on the next morning. In so doing, she avoided the foul weather which set in thereafter. During the next four days, rain and hail impeded progress. The elements made the passage unpleasant for men and animals alike. At least the officers were able to enjoy some relief since scout Charley Reynolds kept their mess supplied with antelope and mountain sheep as a break from army rations.

By May 27, they had logged some 135 miles and now entered the badlands on the fringe of the Little Missouri River. At this point Reynolds found it difficult to locate a crossing. Custer went with Captain Thomas Weir's Company D to locate a trail. They were successful but it was a problem to cross here. Not until May 29 did they succeed in bringing the wagons across. That night, they set up camp, having made only thirty-one more miles during the previous forty-eight hours. From this base, Terry sent Custer out to look signs of hostiles. He took along Lieutenant Charles A. Varnum and twelve Ree scouts on this jaunt while most of the Seventh, including Keogh, remained with the main body.

By May 31 Custer had rejoined the regiment but he had no new information to share. That evening, the weather again took a turn for the worse. On June 1, rain turned into snow. Terry decided to keep the command in camp. The march would not resume until June 3. Over the next two days they plodded along for another twenty miles toward the Powder River. On June 6, Reynolds failed to discover a suitable route for the supply train. Again, Custer led the way. The force moved onward. In the meantime, Ree scouts went forward, linked up with the *Far West* near the mouth of the Powder, and retraced their steps back to Terry with mail and a dispatch from Captain James W. Powell. This latter document indicated that a party of some forty Indians had been spotted

1. Utley, *Cavalier in Buckskin*, 168.

MYLES KEOGH

2. Gray, *Centennial Campaign*, 110-124 covers the period of time discussed in this section in some detail. In providing a first-hand account of the column as it proceeded in May through June, Acting Assistant Surgeon James Madison DeWolf's letters and diary are most useful. See Edward S. Luce, ed., "The Diary and Letters of Dr. James M. DeWolf," *North Dakota History*, (April-July, 1958), 33-81.

3. General Terry's field diary is cited by Richard Upton, ed. and comp., *The Custer Adventure* (Fort Collins, CO: The Old Army Press, 1975), 13.

4. Upton, *The Custer Adventure*, 13.

5. Hays-McCoy, *Captain Myles Walter Keogh*, 41. One of the enlisted men with the column recalled that Reno wanted to push on and find Indians, but was persuaded to return to Terry with his report. Francis Johnson Kennedy, unpublished MS, no date, Dustin Collection, Custer Battlefield National Monument.

6. Upton, *The Custer Adventure*, 15.

7. Hays-McCoy, *Captain Myles Walter Keogh*, 42.

8. Frederick F. Van De Water, *Glory-Hunter: A Life of General Custer* (New York, NY: The Bobbs-Merrill Company, 1934), 152, 297, and 319.

9. Hays-McCoy, *Captain Myles Walter Keogh*, 42 and n129; Lawrence, *His Very Silence Speaks*, 89-90; Charles Kuhlman, *Legend into History: The Custer Mystery* (Harrisburg, PA: Stackpole Co., 1951), 28 and 216.

10. Lawrence, *His Very Silence Speaks*, 90. Also, according to a note from H. J. Nowlan to Miss M. Keogh in the Myles Keogh Collection of the Gene Autry Western Heritage Museum, the will went to St. Paul, in care of I. F. A. Studdart, for safe keeping. A press clipping from the *Army and Navy Journal* (August 5, 1876), in the scrapbook of Annie Gibson Roberts Yates, Captain Yates' wife, mentioned that Keogh supposedly stated "I don't know what may happen to me, and as I have not disposed of some things I have I want to make a will." He then asked that if anything happened to him that the sealed envelope containing his will should be opened and his papers sent to his sister in Ireland. Below this Mrs. Yates wrote "He also left his satchel full of private

near the Tongue River. That news prompted Terry to seek further intelligence.[2]

Terry then selected Company A (under Myles Moylan) and Keogh's Company I as his escort on a side scout toward the Yellowstone River. Setting out on June 8, at 12:30 p.m., the detached units rode for dozens of miles before linking up with the main column lower down on the Powder River.[3]

Next came another effort to find the enemy. Keogh controlled Companies B, C, and I on this foray while Yates had E, F, and L and Reno took overall charge of the expedition. On June 10, all six troops set out with a Gatling gun at 3:00 p.m., "to reconnoiter the valley of the Powder as far as the forks of the river, then cross to Mizpah Creek, to descend that creek near its mouth, thence to cross to Tongue River and descend to its mouth."[4] Reno exceeded this order and pushed on to the Rosebud before turning back with no direct contact. Nevertheless, he did see indications of a large movement leading westward.[5]

By June 20, Reno, Keogh, and the right wing had reunited with the remainder of Terry's force, which by now had encamped at the mouth of the Powder. The next day, Reno's report gave the General enough information to formulate a course of action. Calling together Custer and Gibbon, Terry "communicated to them the plan of operations which [he] had decided to adopt." It was that Colonel Gibbon's column should cross the Yellowstone near the mouth of the Little Big Horn, and thence up that stream, with the expectation that it would arrive at the last-named point by the 26th . . . ." In turn, Custer would, "Proceed up the Rosebud until he should ascertain the direction in which the trail discovered by Reno led; that if it led to the Little Big Horn it should not be followed . . . ."[6] Afterwards, Custer gathered his officers, gave them their instructions, and discontinued the dual wing formation under Benteen and Reno.

With the briefing over, the officers dispersed. Tom Custer and James Calhoun gathered with Keogh and several other officers in a round of singing.[7] According to one source, the comrades also gambled and perhaps drank, with Keogh "redeyed and impoverished" stumbling down the gangplank at the end of the evening.[8]

The validity of this statement is doubtful. It seems likely that Keogh actually spent his time in a more sober fashion after the songfest since he prepared his will with the help of Lieutenant J. A. Carland, a former attorney turned Sixth Infantryman.[9] Afterward, Keogh gave this document to Lieutenant Henry Nowlan in a sealed envelope and told his friend to send the paper to Ireland in the event he were killed. Although he previously had disposed of his property in Europe, Keogh did have a life insurance policy with New York Life Company which he had taken out in 1873. He was insured for $10,000. Nowlan was to receive $1000. After all Keogh's debts had been paid, the balance was to go to Keogh's sister Margaret, along with any of his personal effects. The only exception was a leather valise containing his papers which he had left with Mrs. Eliza Porter, the wife of Keogh's second in command, First Lieutenant James E. Porter. These were to be burned, however, unless Nowlan believed that certain ones should be retained, in which case they should be sent to the family.[10]

Regardless of what may have transpired the night before, on the morning of June 22 preparations to separate from Terry got underway. At noon, according to Lieutenant Edward S. Godfrey, of Company K, "The 'forward' was sounded, and each regiment marched out of camp in column of fours, each troop followed by its pack mules." Terry, Gibbon, and Custer stationed themselves nearby and reviewed the men as they went off to meet their date with destiny. The mules caused difficulties throughout the rest of the day but, beyond this, nothing of great note took place until a halt was called about 4:00 p.m., after only a twelve mile ride. Around sunset Custer ordered "officer's call" to be sounded. As his subordinates assembled, a serious mood prevailed, with little conversation being carried on, and that in undertones. Once everyone had gathered, Custer announced, "Until further orders, trumpet calls would not be sounded except in an emergency; the marches would begin at 5 a.m.

sharp; the troop commanders were all experienced officers, and knew well enough what to do, and when to do what was necessary for their troops...." Custer reserved only two elements to his direct control—when to move out and when to make camp, "He took particular pain to impress on his officers his reliance on their judgement, discretion, and loyalty." His whole approach differed from the "brusque and aggressive, or somewhat curt" manner in which he usually spoke. Additionally, he was candid and open which was not his style. In this, "He showed concessions and a reliance on others; there was an indefinable something that was *not* Custer."[11]

How Keogh perceived Custer's possible personality shift cannot be answered although, by one account, it must not have concerned him to any great degree. On June 23, Lieutenant Winfield S. Edgerly of Company D spent the evening with Keogh and Lieutenant James Porter. The men sang, talked into the night, and Keogh even told his comrade that he wanted to send a letter to St. Paul, where Mrs. Edgerly was at the time, in order to ask her to purchase some things for his bachelor quarters back at Fort Lincoln.[12]

The next evening, after the unit had traveled further on, Keogh continued in the same steady way, calling loudly to Benteen at the end of the day's march that he had saved "a snug nook with beautiful grass" for the older captain where he might bunk down. Benteen indicated, "The reply to this was characteristic of the Plains, something like 'Bully for you, Keogh, I'm your man!'" Once settled in and the "frugal repasts which went for dinner" had been consumed, Keogh and Porter joined Benteen with a few more officers. All listened to Lieutenant C. C. DeRudio as he spun his yarns. While Benteen wisely attempted to get some sleep, the others continued their sessions for a while.[13] Then, "About 10:00 that same night 'Boots and Saddles' was sounded, not by a bugle, as usual, but by a half smothered whisper . . . ."[14] Soon, Keogh joined his fellow officers by lantern light, where Custer told them that they would move in the dark since reports from the scouts indicated that the Indian encampment was nearby. Once daybreak came, the command would rest, while scouts would be sent out to find the exact location of the village. They would strike at dawn on June 26.[15]

Pulling out near midnight, Keogh and his Company I fell heir to escorting the mules, a duty which proved aggravating as packs worked loose and their cargos came off in the dark. DeRudio indicated that this situation infuriated Keogh, who cursed the packers and their mules, "turning the air blue with his oaths."[16] To speed things along, the impatient Irishman directed that any rigs which held up progress would be cut away so that the train could advance. Benteen recounted a conversation at the crossing of Mud Creek in which Keogh stated that they could go back after sunrise and pick up the aban-

First Lieutenant James Porter was second in command of Company I. He died along with Keogh and the other men of this troop. *Courtesy of Custer Battlefield National Monument.*

THE VALLEY OF DEATH

papers with Mrs. Porter (wife of his lieutenant) to be burned." Gray Family Collection. In terms of insurance, Keogh had taken out his policy with New York Life (Policy No. 98-830, which he kept in his "small field desk" at Fort Lincoln), for $10,000, several years before the Little Big Horn. Other Seventh Cavalry officers had policies with the same company, including Custer, Calhoun, Crittenden, and Porter, all supposedly for $5,000. *Army and Navy Journal* (July 15, 1876). According to another source, Yates and Crittenden were insured for twice that amount while Keogh only carried $5000. Hardorff, "Captain Keogh's Insurance Policy," 17-19. Keogh himself mentioned $10,000 in the will made out on June 22, 1876, while probate papers copied by Luce also reflected this figure. The will indicated that Nowlan would receive $1000 and that either Nowlan or Porter would take care of the "personal effects . . . and such" as were deemed "valuable as mementoes to my family." These were to be sent to Margaret. The document went on to require that all the papers "be burned except such as Lt. Nowlan may select to send to my sister—A small Russian leather Valise with cover now at [Fort] Lincoln, will be turned over to Dr. Octerbury [sic] of Louisville, to be given by him to the party he knows of." Copy of Will Made By E. S. Luce, Custer Battlefield National Monument.

11. Captain E. S. Godfrey, "Custer's Last Battle," *Century* Magazine (January, 1892), 358-384.

12. Portions of Edgerly's letter of July 4, 1876 appears in E.C. Bailly, "Echoes from Custer's Last Fight," *Military Affairs* (1953), 170-173.

13. Benteen's recollections of this sequence of events appeared in Brininstool, *Troopers With Custer*, 71-72. Benteen also related an unusual dream he had later about Keogh. He wrote his wife that in this dream Keogh insisted "upon undressing in the room in which you were. I had to give him a 'dressing' to cure him of the fancy." Connell, *Son of the Morning Star: Custer and the Little Bighorn*, 291. In part, this incident led Connell to conclude that Keogh was, "Without doubt . . . created for the astonishment and delight of ladies; every picture of him projects a Mephistophelian sexuality."

14. Francis M. Gibson unpublished MS, Elizabeth Custer Collection, Custer Battlefield National Monument Roll 6, Frame 6201. Gibson,

who was a First Lieutenant of Company H, also stated that Keogh had asked him to share some bean soup that night but "that supper was never served" since, when word came for the officers to report, "The untouched soup was emptied on the prairie and the simple mess outfit packed away never to be opened again by its owner."

15. Utley, *Cavalier in Buckskin*, 180-181.

16. Kenneth Hammer, ed., *Custer in '76: Walter Camp's Notes on the Custer Fight* (Provo, UT: Brigham Young Press, 1976), 83 quotes DeRudio on the pack train matter.

17. Benteen in Brininstool, *Troopers With Custer*, 72.

18. Richard G. Hardorff, "Packs, Packers, and Pack Details: Logistics and Custer's Pack Train," in Gregory J. W. Urwin and Roberta Fagan, ed., *Custer and His Times: Book Three* (Conway, AK: University of Arkansas and the Little Big Horn Associates, 1987), 231.

19. Godfrey, "Custer's Last Battle," noted that the command halted about 2:00 a.m. According to Lieutenant George D. Wallace, however, the troops made eight miles from 1:00 A.M. to daylight. Gray, *Centennial Campaign: The Sioux War of 1876*, 166. Regardless of the exact time, the pack train remained in the rear, and appeared later according to Hammer, *Custer in '76*, 83, and John M. Carroll, ed., *The Benteen-Goldin Letters on Custer and His Last Battle* (New York, NY: John Carroll, 1974), 180.

20. Edward S. Godfrey's interview in Hammer, *Custer in '76*, 74.

21. Godfrey, "Custer's Last Battle," stated, ". . . That the troops would take their places in the column of march in the order in which the reports of readiness were received." Benteen came first, not wanting to wait. After that, the assignments were made by seniority rather than by time of reporting.

22. Edgerly emphasizes this in his letter of July 4, 1876 (see Bailly, "Echoes from Custer's Last Fight," 172) which indicated that Custer seemed to be mending fences over past differences within the regiment. It would seem that there was some sort of rift between Custer and Keogh prior to this point. The cause and the extent are unknown, if indeed this was the case at all.

doned items.[17] The reasoning was sound but would have an unexpected impact as the day wore on.[18] In the meantime, by 2:00 a.m. on June 25, while the other units reached their bivouac, Keogh and the mules continued to struggle and did not catch up until some time later that morning.[19]

Reunited, all went about their various activities, "some breakfasted, most slept." The scouts continued to search for the enemy however. A small detachment under Sergeant William A. Curtiss of Company F also went back along the trail to find some lost items of issue. The troops discovered a small band of Indians who had found one of the discarded hard bread boxes from the mule train. The two sides exchanged fire, but the warriors fled without harm to either group. Word of this encounter reached Captain George Yates who conveyed the intelligence to Keogh. Keogh passed the information along to the regimental adjutant, Cooke, who then told Custer about the incident.[20] This bad news, coupled with the reports from the scouts that three parties of mounted braves had been spotted nearby, dashed Custer's hopes of launching a dawn attack on June 26.

At around noon, Custer called his officers together once again, this time along the banks of what became known as Reno Creek.[21] Here, he made assignments, strictly "by the book" (Upton's 1874 *Cavalry Tactics*), although at first the idea was to give marching orders based upon which captains' reported the readiness of their outfits first.[22] Custer actually created four battalions, with Reno, as the only other field grade officer, obtaining Companies A, G, and M. Benteen, as senior captain, received D, H, and K. The remaining six units (the old right wing contingent) would go to Keogh and Yates, due to their being the next senior officers, although it is not clear exactly how the assignments were made. At his inquiry, Reno implied that Companies I, C, and part of E, presumably all under Keogh, attacked the ford at the mouth of Medicine Tail Coulee, rather than being atop Nye-Cartwright Ridge as some students of the battle believe.[23] Since Sergeant James Bustard's horse was found dead on the village side of the ford, this seems

possible.[24] Later, one historian asserted that Keogh had I, L, and B (which was with the pack train as escort), while the most popular present-day theory contends that he commanded C, I, and L.[25] Yet in another source, *Custer's Luck*, Keogh had three companies and Yates two (C and E), although this seems illogical since it would have meant that Yates was not in command of his own troop.[26]

The battalion configuration remains only one of many unresolved mysteries. The lack of concrete evidence in a number of key areas lies at the heart of the matter. Had it not been for these many unknowns, neither Custer, Keogh, nor the Little Big Horn would have received the extensive attention of generations of scholars, enthusiasts, and arm-chair tacticians! The last fact known about Keogh's role on June 25 is that he accompanied Cooke and Reno early on until Reno's battalion reached the river, watered its horses, and made the crossing. After that, no one can say with certainty what his final dispositions were.

Nevertheless, numerous writers have presented differing and often heroic scenarios about his actions and those of his men. The first speculation came from the pen of Frederick Whittaker. In his 1876 edition of *A Complete Life of Gen. George A. Custer*, he maintained that Company L fell first under an onslaught from the Indian village. Keogh's men then dismounted and their horses ran off. Stranded, "Every man realized that it was his last fight, and was resolved to die game. Down they went, *slaughtered in position*, man after man, dropping in place, survivors contracting their line to close the gaps" until there were no more alive.[27]

Later, two military observers reached different conclusions. Upon his visit to the battlefield, Lieutenant John Gregory Bourke indicated:

> It looked to me as if Keogh must have attempted to make a stand on foot to enable Custer to get away because he and his company died in one compact mass, whereas from here on the graves are scattered in irregular clumps and at intervals about like those in a slaughter of buffaloes . . . .

A native of Rhode Island, Henry Bailey would die in far away Montana as the blacksmith of Company I. *Courtesy of Custer Battlefield National Monument.*

Evidently, Custer's men broke at the point where Lieutenant Crittenden was killed, stampeded on the knoll where brave Keogh turned to make his stand, and what few remained alive, ran like frightened deer for the river from the little bluff where Custer died.[28]

A Second Cavalry officer, Lieutenant Edward J. McClernand, offered the opinion that, "An appreciable interval of time must have elapsed between the order for Calhoun to fight on foot and the similar order given Keogh; if they had been dismounted by the same command the dead horses of the two troops would have been found closer together . . . ." McClernand did not think Keogh's men stampeded; rather he believed that once Custer, "had established himself, he ordered Keogh and what was left of his troop" to join him at Custer Hill.[29]

In 1889, Garrick Mallery joined the debate with his publication of "Picture Writing of the American Indian." This article took the perspective of Indian narratives, including that of the Sioux, Red Horse. That warrior recalled the Cheyenne had spoken to him of "an officer who rode a horse with four white feet." He wore a buckskin jacket and was killed later on during the battle. While the Plains Indians had "for a long time fought many brave men of different people," it was said that "this officer was the bravest man they had ever fought." The man "saved the lives of many soldiers by turning his horse and covering the retreat."[30] Red Horse did not know whether this was Custer or not, but three later authors made a case that the courageous figure was, in fact, Keogh.

The first to reach this conclusion was Will A. Logan, the son of Captain William Logan, an Irish-born officer who was with the Seventh Infantry under Gibbon. Supposedly, as a seventeen year-old, the younger Logan accompanied his father's unit as a civilian. He would arrive at the Greasy Grass in late June 1876 where he claimed to have seen the horror of the battlefield, including Custer's corpse which was "stripped naked, scalped, and with more arrows sticking in him than any other man [with] the possible exception of . . . Tom Custer." These "facts" were concealed, however, so as not to upset Mrs. Custer.

Conversely, Logan related that "On lower ground and some distance from Custer's position [was] another command of dead soldiers lying in a circle, grouped in squads." Supposedly, "Their commanding officer was a tall bald-headed Irishman, with long red sideburns. He was one of only two men that we found fully dressed and unscalped." The Indians had taken one of his side-burns "in lieu of a scalp," and had "started to strip him of his clothes" until they found that he wore "a fine gold chain necklace holding a cross of gold." Because they knew this was a religious symbol, they "abandoned their looting of the body . . . ."

Here, the self-proclaimed eyewitness had combined Keogh and Cooke into one individual, yet he went on at

23. Reno's entire testimony can be found in W. A. Graham, *The Official Record of a Court of Inquiry Convened at Chicago, Illinois, January 13, 1879, by the President of the United States Upon the Request of Major Marcus A. Reno. . . .* (Pacific Palisades, CA: W. A. Graham, 1951), 499-542. Hereafter referred to as "Court of Inquiry . . . Marcus A. Reno."

24. William G. Hardy, of Company A, told Walter Camp that he saw DeLacy's horse dead on the Indian side of the river down near the ford, which prompted Camp to speculate that the horse might have been captured and led across to the other side. Walter Camp Collection, Box 2, Folder 4, Special Collections Brigham Young University Library, Provo, Utah.

25. For example, Hays-McCoy, *Captain Myles Walter Keogh,* 44 believes that Keogh commanded B, I, and L. On the other hand, Richard G. Hardorff, *Markers, Artifacts and Indian Testimony: Preliminary Findings on the Custer Battle* (Short Hills, NJ: Don Horn Publications, 1985), 41, supports the contention of the assignments of C, I, and L to Keogh as does Utley, *Cavelier in Buckskin,* 182. Utley drew upon Hardorff for this segment of his book. Hardorff also pointed out that Lieutenant Myles Moylan thought that these were the troops assigned to Keogh's battalion based upon his testimony at the Reno Court (his testimony is in "Court of Inquiry . . . Marcus A. Reno," 183-211, and in an interview with Camp he speculated that Keogh had either Companies I, B, C, or L while Yates had F, E, C, or L. Box 6, Folder 5, Camp Collection, BYU. At the same inquiry and in a letter of July 4, 1876 to his wife, as well as in an August 18, 1881 article for the Leavenworth *Times,* Lieutenant Edgerly pointed out that Keogh, in fact, had a battalion under his control but none of these documents shed any light on which companies made up his contingent. Some have said that this was not the case at all, however, and that Custer actually kept direct command over the five companies that went with him. Reno's original report even stated: "I was ordered by Lieutenant W.W. Cooke, adjutant, to assume command of Companies M, A, and G; Captain Benteen of Companies H, D, and K; Custer retaining C, E, F, I, and L under his

immediate command, and Company B, Captain McDougall, in rear of the pack-train." *Annual Report of the Secretary of War*, Vol. I (Washington, D.C.: U.S. Government Printing Office, 1876), 32. It is interesting to note that W. A. Graham's *The Story of the Little Big Horn Custer's Last Fight* (New York, NY: Collier Books, 1962), 35 stated "Whether battalion assignment of these five companies [C, E, F, I, and L] was in fact made is immaterial, since Custer retained them all under his personal command."

26. Edgar Stewart, *Custer's Luck* (Norman, OK: University of Oklahoma Press, 1955), 321.

27. Frederick Whittaker, *A Complete Life of Gen. George A. Custer* (New York, NY: Sheldon & Co., 1876), 597-598.

28. John G. Bourke Diaries, Vol XXI, 65-66; 69-70, United States Military Academy, West Point Library.

29. For further details read E. J. McClernand, "With Indians and Buffalo in Montana," *Cavalry Journal* (January, 1927), 7-54.

30. Garrick Mallery, "Picture Writing of the American Indians" in J.W. Powell, *Tenth Annual Report of the Bureau of Ethnology, 1888-1889* (Washington, DC: U.S. Government Printing Office, 1889), passim.

31. Wallace David Coburn, *Battle of the Little Big Horn* (N.P.: Overland-OutWest Publications, 1936). This was republished in *Montana* (Summer, 1956), 28-41.

32. The acknowledgments in Luce, *Keogh, Comanche and Custer*, xiii, included a reference to Charles Kuhlman, who granted "permission to use and include his article 'A Dramatic Incident in the Custer Battle,'" as part of Luce's study, and which indeed served as the basis for Chapter 7, 49-63. All the above references from Luce were taken from this section. Kuhlman incorporated his earlier manuscript into *Legend Into History* (Harrisburg, PA: The Stackpole Co., 1951), 203-207. Not only did he cite Two Moons and Red Horse but also he included statements from Wooden Leg. Based upon these stories and an examination of the photograph taken around the original Keogh grave area in 1879 (thought to have been taken in 1877), he deduced that Keogh left Porter with Company I "and turned to the spot of the greatest immediate danger, the mo-

great length to recount the Indian descriptions he had heard years later about a "dauntless white Irish war chief" who with "his pitiful little force coolly battled on. Never for an instance showing signs of fear, they valiantly faced the menacing red death that each knew was inevitable." One by one they fell until "now—at last—the unconquerable white chieftain fought and bled . . . *alone.*"

Preparing for the end, the Indians observed this last survivor as he "busily engaged in gathering all the rifles and belts of his dead braves and depositing the articles within the triangle of dead horses." Awed by "this brazen defiance" some of the leaders spoke about letting the "white man go scot-free . . . arguing that his medicine was too strong and that they would lose too many valuable men and ponies." Others even contended that he "was too brave to die and had won his freedom by the masterly fight he had put up." Efforts to get the man to surrender only brought a deadly reply in bullets. After several more warriors fell from his accurate aim, the Indians attempted "a new strategy, creeping forward on hands, knees or bellies, in a quarter moon line, keeping up a steady fire. Slower and still slower came the shots from the white man . . . " as the men inched forward "and then it happened!" At some point "Every Indian was on his feet shrieking out his war yells and rushing forward . . . pow-pow-pow-pow-pow-pow . . . came six lightning pistol shots from the triangle and six red warriors died in the air."

The firing had halted and through the smoke came "the terrible, death-dealing white war chief." Holding an empty revolver in one hand and a saber in the other this one-man army lunged at the enemy killing "three more of the bolder braves." Finally, they overwhelmed him but, "His slayers claimed that they never touched his body for he was so brave that they wanted the signs to remain . . . to show others how this warrior of warriors had fought and died." Thus, the "*greatest* hero" of the Little Big Horn went down. He was "the last man —Captain Myles Keogh!"[31] Shortly after this provocative, highly imaginative story was released, Dr. Charles Kuhlman provided an account which he also allegedly based upon Indian oral tradition. His preliminary work and later book likewise contended that the valiant man spoken of by such participants as Red Horse, Two Moon, and Wooden Leg was Keogh.[32]

Perhaps inspired by these earlier tributes, most particularly that of Kulhman, Edward Luce carried on in the same vein. Indeed, he went to lengths to add credence to these earlier efforts. Luce's *Keogh, Comanche and Custer* dismissed the possibility that either George or Tom Custer was the fabled officer. He also indicated that neither Cooke nor Captain Thomas French could have been the man, although French maintained that he was the heroic figure in his own writings and even mentioned Red Horse in his claims to this honor.[33] Luce described what he thought was Keogh's role in the fight to underscore his contention that this was the noble officer from the Indian oral history.

According to Luce, Custer deployed Company I, along with Company F, in response to "a large number of warriors" who were "on the plain to the west and southwest" as well as those who "were coming up the deep ravine" to his northwest. These two companies went "on the spur of the ridge running from the hill northward. The remaining three troops were held in reserve a few yards to the east protected by the crest of the ridge west and south." Companies I and F formed a dismounted skirmish line in order to lay down fire. For about forty-five minutes they were the only troops actually engaged. In due course, Companies C and E went into action. Soon, the situation deteriorated. Custer recalled Companies I and F, ordering them to retreat along with Company L. Luce thought that, "Captain Keogh, as ranking officer, undoubtedly carried orders to join Benteen and the pack train several miles in the rear." He surmised that Keogh "probably also carried additional orders for Benteen . . . ."

These plans went astray as Company L was cut off, while Company F ran into an ambush. Since the latter unit had lost its officers, Keogh came to their aid. Luce penned a romantic reconstruction of what he imagined must have entered Keogh's mind at that moment:

> He looked from the fleeing troopers to the Indians and saw . . . something that aroused in his Irish heart both fury and compassion; saw a number of recruits on terrified horses with arrows dangling from their flanks and hind quarters, sidewinding or pivoting on their forefeet, and the exulting warriors almost upon them. It was too much for him. Barking out the order, 'Company, Halt!' he pulled his beloved Comanche sharply to the right-about and with 'spur of fire' went single-handed to the rescue, shouting to Lieutenant Porter as he passed him to 'stand fast.' As he came to the endangered men, he turned his horse to get at the offending arrows, pulling them out, taking the men in turn and sending them on their way.

This, to Luce's way of thinking, was "the most plausible conjecture" of what happened to Keogh and his group. Likewise, Luce believed that Keogh did not attempt to retreat but instead made every effort "to fight his way back to Custer." During this segment of the exchange, Keogh rode "back and forth between the two platoons of Company 'F'," commanding by "voice and example" which prompted the men to respond "splendidly to the leadership." For Luce, then, Red Horse's noble officer and the man in a "buckskin shirt . . . who rode up and down the line all the time shouting," as described by Two Moon in an interview with Hamlin Garland, could be none other than Keogh.[34]

Not everyone reached the same conclusions, however. For one, William A. Graham, another student of the battle, reacted adversely to Luce's interpretation. In correspondence, Graham told Luce the one portion of *Keogh, Comanche and Custer* that invited criticism was chapter seven, which covered the battle. Graham faulted Luce for using "Dr. Charles Kuhlman's highly—indeed wholly—imaginative and conjectural attempt at reconstruction of the fight, which, while interesting, is hardly consistent with the final statement of your preface that 'the author has written history, not manufactured it.'" Graham continued, "The most that can be said for Kuhlman's speculation, I think, is that the incidents conjured by his vivid imagination *might* have happened."[35] To take Kuhlman's descriptions as fact was, for Graham, the weakest link in Luce's argument.

No doubt, Graham would have expressed a similar opinion about information found in *Custer's Fall* by David Humphreys Miller. Again, the author based his evidence on supposed personal interviews with Indian survivors. He recounted that, while the bodies were being stripped after the firing had ceased, the following event occurred:

> Among the bravest of the soldiers was a big man with a stubby black beard and long mustaches which curled up at the ends. Several Cheyennes . . . had ridden him down toward the end of the fight. He had acted much as the leader of the soldiers might have been expected to act, although the white metal bars he wore had little meaning to the Indians—they assumed the captain's insignia was some sort of personal medicine. His body lay among those part way down the slope, near the barricade of dead horses.
> Amazingly he seemed to come to life right before their eyes. He propped himself up on one elbow and looked around him as though he had just arrived from another world. Looking about with wild expression on his face, almost like that of a madman, he gripped a pistol in his right hand.
> A courageous Sioux warrior ran forward, grabbed the revolver out of the man's grasp, then turned it on him and shot him through the head. The Cheyennes mustered up enough courage after that to strike and stab him until they were all sure he was dead. He was the last man of Custer's command to be killed on the ridge. This brave man may well have been Captain Myles Keogh, gallant Irish soldier of fortune, former papal guardsman and Civil War hero.[36]

Once more, not only is Keogh the "bravest" of the white soldiers but also he is the last to fall! Additionally, the assignment of command to Keogh as the next senior

mentarily shattered Troop 'F' in the leadership of which he was to distinguish himself as the 'bravest man the Sioux ever fought.'" Kuhlman postulated that, "Captain Keogh remained with Troop 'F' to the end. He went down under a rush of stampeding horses near the last surviving members of the troop."

33. In a letter, Captain French stated that, as the troops were falling back, he made a stand "and tried to fight the battle alone." He then referred to Red Horse who must have thought that French was "a spirit from the bad place" since the war chief saw no less than "eighteen of his men" die at French's hands. Thomas H. French to Mrs. Augusta Cooke, June 16, 1880, Hagner Collection, New York Public Library.

34. Hamlin Garland, "General Custer's Last Fight as Seen by Two Moon," *McClure's* (September, 1898), 443-448.

35. Letter from W. A. Graham to E. S. Luce, January 4, 1940, Hugh Shick Collection, Burbank, California.

36. Miller, *Custer's Fall*, 116-117.

37. John Stands in Timber and Margo Liberty, *Cheyenne Memories* (New Haven: Yale University Press, 1967) and J. C. Ryan, ed. and comp., *Custer Fell First: The Adventures of John C. Lockwood* (San Antonio, TX: Naylor, 1966) also represent the view that Custer was struck early in the fight. In theory, if this were so, Keogh, as second senior officer would have assumed command.

38. Lawrence A. Frost, *The Custer Album: A Pictorial Biography of General George A. Custer* (Seattle, WA: Superior Publishing Company, 1964), 156-157.

officer after Custer was in keeping with Miller's theory that Yellow Hair was an early casualty of the battle.[37]

Some years later, Lawrence Frost, while not entering directly into discussion about Keogh's last moments did follow Kulhman's interpretation of certain troop movements. Frost contended that Custer sent Keogh's Company I, along with F and L, " . . . toward Calhoun Hill, hoping that they would continue on and make contact with the troops on Weir Point, and return with them" to his holding position. According to Frost, "As these companies rode eastward they had gone but a few hundred yards when they were ambushed by Sioux under Crazy Horse and Cheyennes under Two Moon. . . . " The encounter increasingly became heated. Frost thought that as the units with Keogh "retreated to the east they ran into the concealed warriors under Gall. It was all over in a short period of time, and then the warriors returned to Custer's small band." After a brief encounter, the few defenders at Custer Hill also were silenced.[38]

An article by Robert Ege expanded on Keogh's place in this final phase. Ege argued that Company I took a "defensive position on the ridge" and at its "upper end" became "completely surrounded by hostiles. . . . " Remaining here for an hour and a half, Custer finally sent word to Keogh that he was to ride "to the general's command post." Leaving Lieutenant Porter in charge, "Keogh hastened southward along the lower east side of the ridge, riding 'Comanche.' " Once Keogh had reached Custer, the two spotted Benteen's guidons through field glasses. This prompted Custer to make "the only defined movement of his troops after assuming the position on the ridge. It was also a maneuver that caused the leading role in the Battle of the Little Big Horn to revert from Custer to Captain Myles Keogh."

Ege believed that Keogh, with his battalion (Companies I, L, and F—a configuration that would not have been possible if Yates also had a battalion), spread out on a "lengthy dismounted skirmish line." This would provide "a protective corridor to screen the oncoming Benteen and his column from a possible Indian flanking attack." Ege proposed that it was while carrying out this mission:

Keogh, through courageous action and great deeds, gained the lasting respect of those who fought against him. The Irish captain's attempt to place his troops south along the ridge drew a strong counter-action from the Sioux. Some of his platoons were separated, then cut to pieces by smashing volleys from Indians concealed in the ravines, yet Keogh rode back and forth along the rise in a futile effort to reunite a dwindling command. He was constantly exposed to a withering enemy barrage, but he fought back with an abandon that both amazed and scattered the advancing warriors. This 'wildman' didn't hide behind dead horses. He rode a very alive horse directly at them. He was possessed of 'strong medicine.'

Myles Keogh fought with a precise fury that was completely foreign to the Indians. He single-handedly covered a segment of a soundly beaten Troop 'F' in their attempt to return to the main body of their company. Alone, he rode directly into—and over—some of the braves who were trying to isolate them.

Keogh was fully aware of the order sent to Benteen. That order stressed 'be quick.' We can easily imagine the thoughts that fleetingly passed through the brave Irishman's mind. 'How in the hell long would it take the sorely needed men and supplies to get here? . . . They were a scant three miles away nearly an hour ago. . . . There was little opposition in between them. . . .'

Some of the epithets shouted at the Indians in Keogh's 'blue brogue' were undoubtedly shared by Benteen.

Indians were rapidly rendering Keogh's position impossible. They had infiltrated his line of advance. Every clump of sagebrush, and every clod of dirt bigger than a man's hat, concealed an armed warrior. (These were able hostiles who had followed the leads of Sioux Chief Gall and the great Cheyenne, Two Moon. They had crept up unobserved through cuts and gullies from the northeast. Others from the southwest, probably followers of the fierce Cheyenne, Lame White Man, who had wreaked such havoc on troops 'C' and 'E' an hour ago, were now taking a toll of the men along the ridge.)

Suddenly it occurred to Keogh . . . as it must have to Custer . . . *the reinforcements weren't coming!* It was a bitter pill to swallow before dying, especially for the valiant Keogh. . . .

The field was bedlam now. Horses were bolting and

unsaddled troopers were being hacked to bits. The Indians were spurred on by the confusion in the shattered formations.

Through a momentary clearing in the overhanging pall of dust and smoke, Keogh glanced back to see Custer and those behind him, firing from behind downed horses. He, too, was undergoing a brutal onslaught. Keogh's position was untenable. 'Comanche' was down and the loose horse a trooper had helped him mount was getting groggy.

The Irishman was well past the point of no return. Amid screaming horses, smoke, and the swirling gray dust, Keogh recalled the Crow and Arikara scouts who had accompanied the command. Only that morning—it seemed like a week ago—all had chanted their death songs. Even 'old Guts,' Charley Reynolds, had emptied his war sack.

As in the case of George Armstrong Custer, there was no Indian who could claim a personal victory over Keogh. He fell in the heat of battle making a heroic—but hopeless—attempt to reform a platoon of soldiers being butchered by the sheer force of countless warriors.[39]

While exciting reading, Ege's analysis drew upon a number of unsubstantiated suppositions.

Unlike Ege, Richard Hardorff attempted to establish Keogh's battle role through more analytical means.[40] In *Markers, Artifacts and Indian Testimony*, he stated:

> On arrival at Calhoun Ridge, Custer must have called a hurried conference with the other officers. Most scholars concluded that a defensive strategy was developed during this consultation, and that Troops I and L were assigned to cover the withdrawal of the balance of the troops. However, such theories ignore Custer's personality which excluded the possibility of withdrawal and defeat. Custer's philosophy accepted victory as being synonymous with attack. It should be clearly understood that Custer had delayed action as long as possible until forced to take the initiative. Further delay would only impair his chances of success, and after vacating Nye-Cartwright Ridge the first opportunity for a bold front came near Calhoun Ridge. He most aggressively pursued this, probably with the second battalion commanded by Captain Myles Keogh.
>
> . . . Sergeant Daniel Kanipe stated that C Troop was assigned to Captain Keogh's battalion, and since Keogh was the senior captain he would have naturally commanded three troops, a belief also held by Lieutenant Myles Moylan. We may assume that in addition to I and C Troops, the third unit assigned to Keogh was L, because the bodies of both Captain Keogh and Lieutenant Calhoun were found with their respective commands, farthest away from Custer Hill. . . .
>
> To initiate his offensive, Custer ordered Captain Keogh's battalion to take possession of Calhoun Ridge, the western terminus controlling the river and Deep Coulee. The purpose of this move was to find another river crossing, and since the river bottom near Medicine Tail Coulee was blocked by constantly arriving warriors, it became imperative to find a crossing further down. However, Captain Keogh's command had attempted to gain control of Deep Ravine, the southern branch of which borders Calhoun Ridge on the north. Several troopers were slain near the head of this branch, which passage leads to a natural ford across the river.
>
> Evidence to support this theory comes in part from the Indian accounts which state that when Custer descended from the high eastern ridge his troops moved as if to reach the river lower down. The western position of the slain bodies also refutes the premise that Custer was acting defensively. Moreover, the bluff top at the extreme western end of Calhoun Ridge contained a quantity of expended military casings, denoting a position held by Captain Keogh's battalion. . . . However, this same location also contained a quantity of shells from various other weapons, which suggests that the position was overrun by Indians, some of the soldiers having been shot down and the balance driven back towards the 'Last Stand' area.

Hardorff continued by indicating that it seemed "quite plausible" that "a squad of Captain Keogh's troopers might have been stationed on the bluff to clear the opposition from Deep Ravine and to gain a passage to the river below." He further postulated "that C Troop originally occupied the western end of Calhoun Ridge, while Troops I and L were stationed farther east near Calhoun Hill." The last two units felt increasing pressure as Custer moved on with Yates' troops after realizing that this was a

39. Robert J. Ege, "Legend Was a Man Named Keogh," *Montana* (Spring, 1966), 27-39.
40. Hardorff, *Markers, Artifacts and Indian Testimony*, 40-43, 46-48, 52, and 64.

41. Hardorff took this statement from George B. Grinnell, *The Fighting Cheyennes* (Norman, OK: University of Oklahoma Press, 1956), 351.

42. As stated above, this photograph was taken in 1879, not 1877. The whole "cherry bush" theory was one dreamt up by Kuhlman. No such bushes were there during the battle in 1876.

43. The above excerpts were taken from Connell, *Son of the Morning Star*, 292-293.

44. Ibid., 293.

fight for survival requiring "a better defensive position." Consequently, Keogh's and Calhoun's forces blazed on alone. It appeared to Hardorff that Company I protected the horses for both troops from its position "lower down on the flank. . . ." According to a Cheyenne account they were all on foot, having lost their horses. They attempted to work their way toward the gray horse troop (Company E), although about half were without carbines, but continued to use their revolvers in close fighting "almost hand to hand—as they went up the hill."[41] Those of Keogh's battalion who retained their horses "galloped as fast as they could toward Custer Hill. . . ." During this intense combat, the two sides fought each other at no more than a hundred yards apart. In the chaos the retreat toward Custer "resembled a buffalo stampede. . . ."

Finally, Hardorff nominated Mitch Bouyer as the buckskin clad white man of great bravery who Two Moon mentioned, rather than Keogh, as Kuhlman and others had hypothesized. Also, Keogh seems to have been on horseback "while attempting to cover the retreat of his command." This was Hardorff's explanation of why Comanche was not captured since he would have been with the horse holders if Keogh had been on foot. Furthermore, "The fact that Keogh's body was found in the rear of the column suggests he might have been acting as a file closer." He would have drawn considerable "enemy fire which again gives reason for the many wounds inflicted upon his mount."

If Hardorff provided one of the more analytical treatments of Keogh's possible role in the final fight, Evan Connell's description in his *Son of the Morning Star* represented the distillation of most of what had been said about the man in the past. He wrote:

> The spot where Keogh fell has been deduced from an 1877 photograph of a marker left by the burial party. The sergeants of his company lay near him, not far from a cluster of wild cherry bushes, and some historians theorize that a volley delivered by several Indians hiding in these bushes might have killed all of them at once.[42]

Keogh and his horse Comanche probably were crippled by a single bullet. The reason for thinking so is that a bullet passed through Comanche, emerging at about the spot where a rider's knee would have been, and Keogh's left knee was shattered. Such a reconstruction is fragile, but there is also testimony of a Sioux named Little Soldier who watched a bluecoat—thought to have been Keogh—kneeling and shooting from between the legs of a horse. This bluecoat died with the reins still clutched in one hand, a fact which may have prevented Indians from taking the horse. Little Soldier thought the wounded animal would recover, and he needed a horse, but he refused to touch one whose reins were held by a dead man.[43]

Connell concluded that Keogh deserved to be known as "one of the Seventh's most redoubtable fighters." The "one wasichu of enormous courage" spoken of by some Indian participants "quite possibly [was] the aggressive, rude, alcoholic, and somewhat melancholy soldier from rural Carlow."[44]

In these two short paragraphs, Connell summed up the numerous suppositions which had evolved over the years to become the story of Keogh's role at the "last stand". What had emerged over the generations was a tradition of the hard-fighting, fearless professional, capable of strong leadership by unflinching example. Keogh was second only to his commander in the crucial part he played that day, if the interpretation of many past historians is correct.

Whether this portrait is accurate or not remains one of the many unanswered questions from that fateful battle, although archeological efforts ultimately may shed more light on the matter. Regardless of future possibilities, Myles Keogh has come to embody the legend which has grown up around the Little Big Horn. He occupies a lofty place in the cast of characters of this tragic drama alongside the likes of Custer, Crazy Horse, Sitting Bull, Benteen, and Reno. Thus, his niche in history seems assured for as long as the uncertain events along the Greasy Grass hold a fascination for generations to come.

Red Horse recalled one man with Custer's column was the bravest he had ever seen in a fight. A few later writers would conclude that this was Keogh. *Courtesy of Glen Swanson.*

As the warriors made their final rush, triumphant shouts proclaimed that all the soldiers had been killed. A crowd of old men and young boys who had watched the battle from a safe distance, now rushed their ponies among the bodies. But not all the soldiers had expired. One wounded officer—a captain—still lived, though in a dazed condition. He raised himself upon an elbow, glaring wildly at the Indians, who shrank from him, believing him returned from the spirit world. A Sioux warrior wrested the revolver from his nerveless hand and shot him through the head. Thus died the last of Custer's battalion, his identity unknown.

        Wooden Leg

We gave directions immediately for every Indian to take his horse and arms; for the women and children to mount their horses and get out of the way, and for the young men to go and meet the troops.

Among the latter was an officer who rode a horse with four white feet. The Indians have fought a great many tribes of people, and very brave ones, too, but they all say that this man was the bravest man they had ever met.

I don't know whether this man was Gen. Custer or not; some say he was. I saw this man in the fight several times, but did not see his body. It is said he was killed by a Santee, who still holds his horse. This officer wore a large-brimmed hat and a buckskin coat. He alone saved his command a number of times by turning on his horse in the rear in the retreat. In speaking of him, the Indians call him "The man who rode the horse with four white feet". There were two men of this description, looking very much alike, both having long yellowish hair.

        Red Horse

Then the Sioux rode up the ridge on all sides, riding very fast. The Cheyennes went up the left way. Then the shooting was quick, quick. Pop—pop—pop very fast. Some of the soldiers were down on their knees, some standing. Officers all in front. The smoke was like a great cloud, and everywhere the Sioux went the dust rose like smoke. We circled all round them—swirling like water round a stone. We shoot, we ride fast, we shoot again. Soldiers drop, and horses fall on them. Soldiers in line drop, but one man rides up and down the line—all the time shouting. He rode a sorrel horse with white face and white fore-legs. I don't know who he was. He was a brave man.

        Two Moon

Two Moon told of a brave white man who rode up and down the line shouting to his comrades. Could this have been Keogh? *Courtesy of Glen Swanson.*

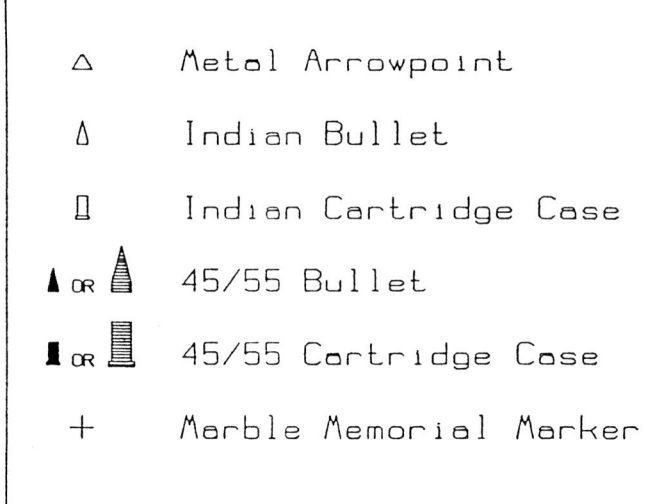

Definitions of symbols used in figures 1-1 through 1-6.

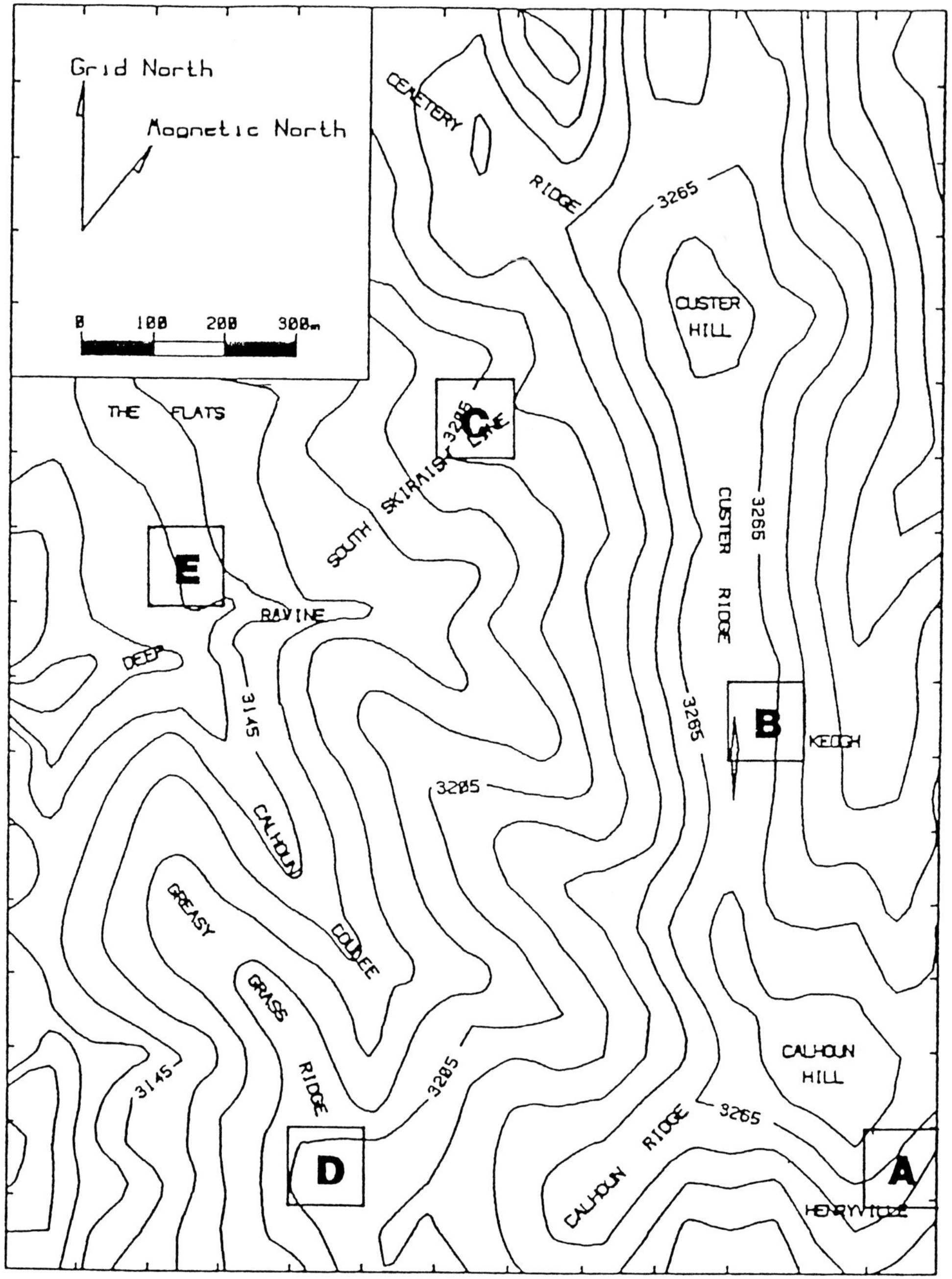

Figure 1-1. The location of 100 m square grid units resurveyed using 2 m interval metal detector sweeps during inventory evaluation phase provides an overview of the general locations and features of the Little Big Horn fight.

Chapter 8

THE KEOGH EPISODE:
Archaeology and the Historical Record

by Richard A. Fox, Jr., Ph.D.

> There are few sadder things in life than the day after a battle.
>
> Charles Lever, *Charles O'Malley*

Archaeology helps to overcome the deficiencies in and limitations of the historical record. While details of the Custer battle presented here are subject to revision, the overall conclusions cannot be disputed. The Custer battalion suffered from the effects of tactical disintegration of enormous magnitude. Once tactical stability was lost the command offered little effective resistance. Archaeology bears this out and provides the means by which the historical record can be properly interpreted.

Before examining the Custer battle as related to the Keogh episode, introductory remarks are necessary. There is no doubt the battle commenced in the Medicine Tail Coulee area (Figure 1-1) and progressed northward. Though the early stages of the fight have been steeped in controversy for years, three facts now seem incontestable. First, the five companies of the Seventh Cavalry which eventually perished in the Custer battle operated as a battalion consisting of two wings. Second, the battalion wings were separated during the early skirmishing while in Medicine Tail Coulee. Third, and finally, the battalion reunited, if only briefly, at or near the Calhoun Hill vicinity, thus setting the stage for the battle's celebrated climax.[1]

The 1874 tactics prescribed wing composition on the basis of company commander seniority.[2] The five companies that entered the Custer battle consisted of Companies C, E, F, I, and L. Their respective commanders, with dates of rank and seniority were Captain Tom Custer (December 2, 1875, third in rank), First Lieutenant A.E. Smith (December 5, 1868, fourth in rank), Captain Yates (August 19, 1867, second in rank), Captain Keogh (July 28, 1866, first in rank) and First Lieutenant Calhoun (January 9, 1871, fifth or last in rank). According to prescription, therefore, the battalion wings should have consisted of Companies I, C, and L in the right wing, with Keogh commanding, and F and E as the left wing, commanded by Yates.[3]

The left wing, then, consisting of companies F and E, very likely approached the mouth of Medicine Tail Coulee, eventually making its way up Deep Coulee to the Calhoun Hill area (Figure 1-1). The right wing (Companies I, C, and L) remained on the ridges to the east, finally converging with the left wing at Calhoun Hill (Figure 1-1). The left wing apparently moved up Deep Coulee in battle lines, according to the Cheyenne Brave Wolf, an observation confirmed by Two Moon who described the movement of dismounted soldiers in two "wings," no doubt sets of companies.[4] The right wing proceeded in "two lines."[5] Apparently both wings

*The text, notes, and illustrations for this chapter were taken from the forthcoming publication, *Discerning History Through Archaeology: The Custer Battle*, by Richard A. Fox. Published by the University of Oklahoma Press.

1. Statement of Lone Bear, (unpublished MS, January 1909, Camp Collection, Custer Battlefield National Monument). Hereafter referred to as "Lone Bear Statement."
2. This is based on Emory Upton, *Cavalry Tactics, United States Army* (New York, NY: D. Appleton and Company, 1874).
3. Hammer, *Custer in '76*, passim.
4. Grinnell, *The Fighting Cheyennes*, 352 cites Brave Wolf; Hardorff, Markers, *Artifacts and Indian Testimony*, 42 gives Two Moon's version.
5. This was according to Stands in Timber as recorded by M. B. Moore, "It Was a Day of Bravery: Eyewitness Accounts of the Custer Fight." (unpublished MS, 1987).

MYLES KEOGH

6. R. H. Nichols, ed., "Reno Court of Inquiry" (unpublished MS, 1983), 36 and 74.

7. Ibid., 18 and 520.

8. Miller, *Legend into History*, 35.

9. Hardorff, *Markers, Artifacts and Indian Testimony*, 49.

10. Graham, *The Custer Myth*, 103.

11. This was according to Gale as found in Usher L. Burdick, ed., *David F. Barry's Indian Notes on the Custer Battle* (Baltimore, MD: Wirth Brothers, 1949), 25.

12. M. I. McCreight, *Firewater and the Forked Tongues: A Sioux Chief Interprets U. S. History* (Pasadena, CA: Trails End Publishing Co., 1947), 113.

13. Statement of Two Eagles (unpublished MS, 1908) Camp Collection, Custer Battlefield National Monument. Hereafter referred to as "Two Eagles statement."

14. Stanley Vestal, "The Man Who Killed Custer," *American Heritage* (February, 1957), 7.

15. McCreight, *Firewater and Forked Tongues*, 113.

16. J. K. Dixon, *The Vanishing Race* (Glorieta, NM: The Rio Grande Press, 1973), 176.

---

attained Calhoun Hill in good tactical order. This provides the setting in which Keogh's contingent can be examined in the light of archaeological and historical data.

Historically, the Keogh episode is highlighted by total disintegration, and this complements the archaeological record nicely. But unlike Calhoun's force, which gave way under pressure, the transition from tactical stability to disintegration at the Keogh sector was induced primarily by fear and panic, panic which spread from the Calhoun sector to the Keogh sector when it came under heavy attack.

The Keogh episode ended with right wing soldiers in complete disorder. Several Reno officers viewed the Keogh sector in the aftermath of the fight. Lieutenant Wallace thought, on the basis of body positions, that the retreating men were running in file and fighting at intervals, but not in skirmish order.[6] Second Lieutenant Edward Maguire, like Lieutenant Edgerly, thought he saw "some sort of a skirmish line."[7] Despite hedging slightly, these men, guided by emotions and military training, saw tactical stability which did not exist.

Indian testimonies are replete with reference to the skirmishing on Calhoun Hill—the role of Company L. And now, with the help of archaeology, their references to Company C can be understood. But Company I remains virtually invisible in the historical record until the moment of the Indian attack. Documentary accounts suggesting that Company I was deployed in a battle line of any form are wholly absent. And there are no evidences of such found in archaeological traces. These observations are revealing; they strongly indicate that Company I held intact in the rear beyond Calhoun Hill (north of Company L which manned the skirmish line). Company C doubtless accompanied I, serving in a reserve role as well. Only as threats increased did the wing commander commit Company C, sending it from reserve into the Calhoun Coulee action. Prior to this, the wing had been deployed exactly in the formation prescribed by tactics.

This posture—L on the skirmish line with two companies, C and I, in reserve—should not be unexpected. The wing experienced subdued, desultory fighting for some time prior to disintegration. Under these situations reserve unit tactics could be utilized effectively. And the presence of Company I as a reserve unit can be expected for it was commanded by Captain Keogh, the senior wing officer. The right wing reserve companies held in the rear, perhaps, as tactics specified, no more than 300 yards distant from the active skirmishers on Calhoun Hill. Following the excursion by Company C into Calhoun Coulee, disintegration evidently struck so quickly that Company I, as archaeology shows, could not mobilize with any effect.

Indeed, one of the two left wing companies, also was held in reserve before the onslaught brought on by the failure of Company C. At this moment, the left wing operated around Custer Hill and it eventually received the few survivors of the right wing disintegration. Paralleling L of the right wing, Company E of the left is highly visible in the historical record; Company F, like I in the right wing, is not. The reason was that Companies E and L actively engaged in skirmishing, while I and L, holding in reserve, did not. Warriors in their testimonies naturally emphasized the action to the neglect of those units not engaged. Despite this, there are a few clues referring to the right wing reserve unit, including one of White Bull's accounts.

After departing the Calhoun area, and before the breakdown of command and control there, White Bull noticed " . . . soldiers [that] were divided into two bunches."[8] Red Feather reported a similar configuration "on one side of the hill," noting that Crazy Horse, a Sioux leader, drew some fire when he "rode between the two parties."[9] Company L occupied the Calhoun hilltop, thus the two "parties" on the hillside (more properly the east side of Custer Ridge) possibly constituted Companies C and I. The two parties or "bunches", on the other hand, might have been Companies C and I in one group and Company L in the other. The former option seems likely though, for Two Moon saw three "branches" of the right wing, each "with a little ways between them."[10]

These soldiers, Two Moon observed, all dismounted and some soldiers led the horses over the hill. Company L's horseholders and the right wing reserve doubtless were those that led the mounts away.

Infiltration from the north (the right wing rear) started some time after Indians began moving up Calhoun Coulee (west of the right wing). Gall told D. F. Barry that Crazy Horse and Crow King feared the soldiers would move north and attack the Indian encampment. They were right, although the attack never materialized. These two warriors, and others, proceeded northerly down the Little Big Horn valley to prevent this. Crow King, however, left Crazy Horse, most likely at Medicine Tail Coulee, and crept into Calhoun Coulee on the west side of the right wing. The Crazy Horse contingent proceeded further down the valley, crossed the river and went over Custer Ridge to its east side.[11] According to Flying Hawk, he and Crazy Horse "followed up the gulch to a place in the rear of the soldiers that were making the stand on the [Calhoun] hill."[12] Crazy Horse had infiltrated the rear of the right wing. The warriors eventually got very close to the soldiers. Two Eagles, apparently among or near them, said they infiltrated the draws just below the crown of Custer Ridge.[13]

White Bull informed Vestal, in an unabashed attempt to denigrate the role of Crazy Horse, that he led the daring rides between soldiers.[14] Whatever the case, following these personal deeds of bravery, the Indians attacked. Flying Hawk's account suggests that Crazy Horse (and others) fired at soldiers on Calhoun Hill, whereupon they "broke and ran as fast as their horses could go to some soldiers that were further along the ridge toward Custer" (Custer Hill).[15] Flying Hawk's account leaves the impression that Crazy Horse's attack was wholly responsible for entropy during the Calhoun episode. More likely this attack took advantage of Lame White Man's success west of Custer Ridge. In fact, Runs the Enemy mentioned an attack against bunched up soldiers on Calhoun Hill after the Lame White Man charge.[16]

Lame White Man's foray spurred attackers other than

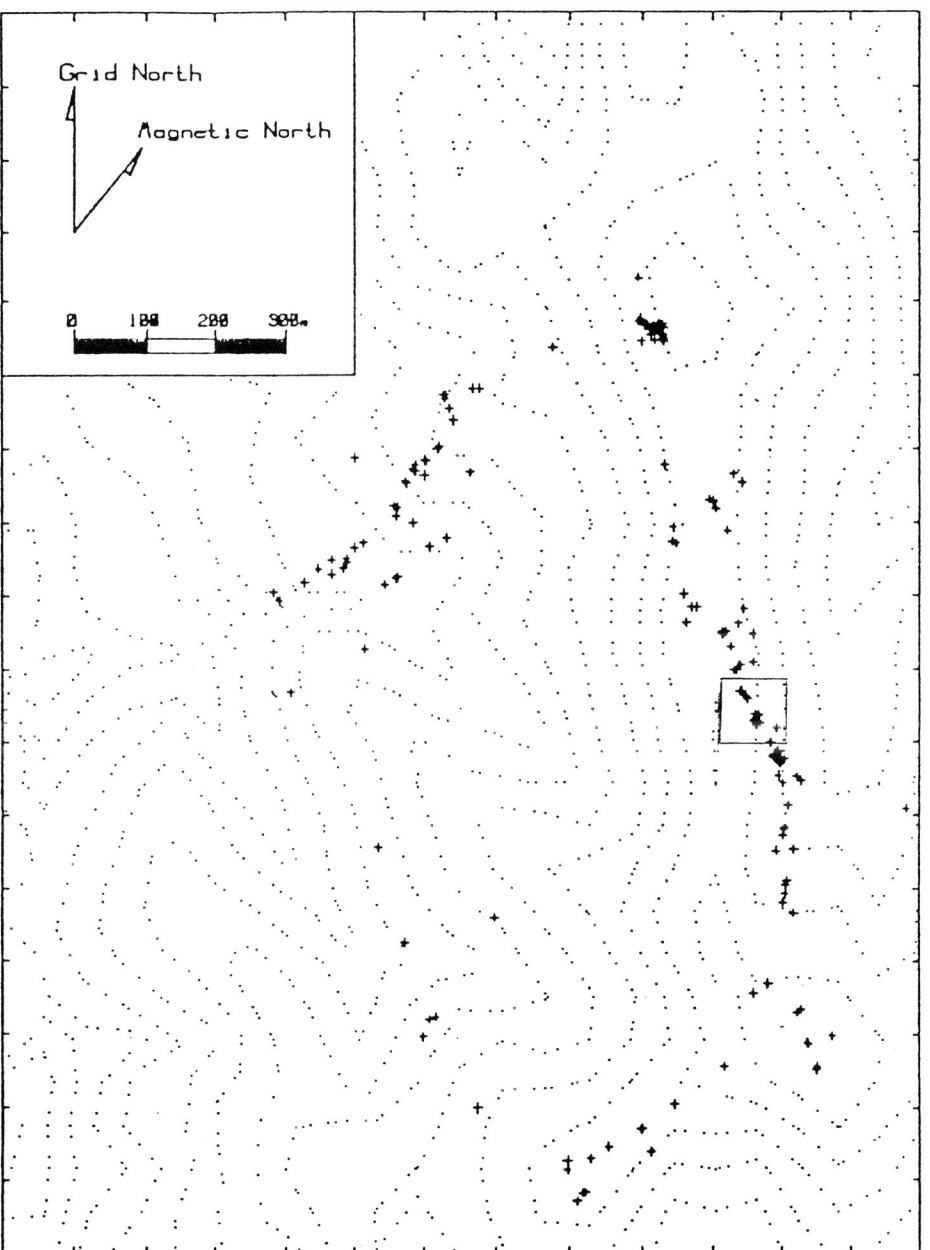

Figure 1-2. Placement of marble markers on the Custer battlefield corrected for pairing errors. The area within the box represents the spot where Keogh's marker is placed along with a number of men who fell around him.

17. Stanley Vestal Notes (White Bull Interviews), Campbell Collections, Box 105, Notebook 24. Western History Collections, University of Oklahoma, 59 and ibid., Notebook 23, 140-147.

18. Dixon, *The Vanishing Race*, 176.

19. T. B. Marquis, *Wooden Leg: A Warrior Who Fought Custer* (Lincoln, NE: University of Nebraska Press, 1931), 232-233.

20. Dixon, *The Vanishing Race*, 182 and L. Tillett, *Wind on the Buffalo Grass* (New York, NY: Thomas Y. Cromwell Company, 1976), 103.

21. Hammer, *Custer in '76*, 207.

22. Hardorff, *Markers, Artifacts and Indian Testimony*, 48.

23. Ibid., 48.

24. T. B. Marquis, *Custer on the Little Bighorn* (Lodi, CA: Marquis Custer Publications, 1967), 39 (quoting Bighead).

25. Tillett, *Wind on the Buffalo Grass*, 103; Dixon, *The Vanishing Race*, 181.

26. Kenneth Hammer, "Camp Manuscript, Transcripts of Articles and Field Notes of Walter M. Camp (unpublished MS, No D., Lilly Library, University of Indiana, Bloomington), 632.

27. Marquis, *Custer on the Little Bighorn*, 39 and Grinnell, *The Fighting Cheyennes*, 351.

28. Hardorff, *Markers, Artifacts and Indian Testimony*, 48.

29. He Dog in Hammer, *Custer in '76*, 207.

30. Ibid., 201.

31. "Two Eagles Statement."

32. Hammer, *Custer in '76*, 199.

33. Miller, *Custer's Fall*, 35.

34. See Foolish Elk and Turtle Rib in Hammer, *Custer in '76*, 199 and 201, as well as Flying Hawk in McCreight, *Firewater and Forked Tongues*, 113.

35. Tillett, *Wind on the Buffalo Grass*, 103; Dixon, *The Vanishing Race*, 182.

36. Hammer, *Custer in '76*, 201.

37. This was according to Wooden Leg as cited by Marquis, *Wooden Leg*, 232.

38. Based on White Cow Bull in David Humphreys Miller, "Echoes of the Little Bighorn," *American Heritage* (June, 1971), 34.

Crazy Horse. In the confusion wrought by Company C as it clambered from harm, Gall and those who rode with him, some of whom breached Calhoun Hill via the Henryville position, almost certainly pounced. Gall's role is obscured hereafter. But White Bull's is not, and his party evidently joined the attack as well. In testimony transcribed and sketched by Vestal, White Bull briefly described the effects of the massive assault.[17] The White Bull party "charged [the] first company", whereupon "the [first] bunch run [sic] to the second bunch and the second run to the third . . . ." Right wing survivors had spilled from Calhoun Hill (first bunch), through the Keogh sector (second bunch) toward Custer Hill (third). Once again seized with immodesty, White Bull claimed the attack materialized only after he started out. But the credit, as best can be determined, must go to Lame White Man, the spearhead of an assault which ultimately included contingents with Gall, Crazy Horse, Yellow Nose, Contrary Belly, White Bull, Comes in Sight, Two Moon, Runs the Enemy, Crow King, and probably other notables unknown to us.

Like Flying Hawk and White Bull, Runs the Enemy also described panicky flight into the Keogh sector.[18] The flight doubtless proceeded toward Company I. From his position further east, Wooden Leg found a "band" of soldiers on the east side of Custer Ridge (Keogh sector).[19] He fired into this group from a distance, intimating that many others near his position did the same. Two Moon evidently found himself among these. Later in the Keogh episode he helped kill a "troop" of soldiers.[20] Evidently Two Moon assaulted Company I, though its positioning in the Keogh sector is not recognizable archaeologically. As stated, the absence of material evidence for Captain Keogh's troop suggests the attack came at a time when Company I functioned as a reserve rather than a fighting unit.

Apparently Crazy Horse and his "followers," spurred by the confusion of Company I under attack and soldiers fleeing from Calhoun Hill, charged at this time. He Dog told Camp the charge "split up soldiers into two bunches." Several Oglalas concurred, noting that the rush on the soldiers "cut the line in two bunches."[21] The "line", of course, reflected little more than a line of men in flight rather than any type of effective tactical deployment. Several Oglalas concurred, noting that the rush of the soldiers "cut the line in two."[22] The charge apparently carried some Indians over the crest to the west side of Custer Ridge where other Sioux had congregated.[23] These Indians, recently involved in the Lame White Man attack and now following the panicky soldiers (as indicated archaeologically by Indian pathways), had moved along Custer Ridge on its west side.[24] Two Moon was one of these; he eventually joined Indians east of Custer Ridge.[25] Lame White Man was there too, for friends found his body on the western ridge slope just below the crest and opposite the Keogh sector. Indeed, Red Bird made it clear Lame White Man chased soldiers involved in the Calhoun episode into the Keogh sector.[26]

Company I, as a reserve unit ill-prepared for a sudden deterioration, quickly fell into disarray as the Calhoun panic spread and emboldened Indians pressed the attack. One result was the loss of horses. The Cheyennes described this loss in general terms.[27] Several Oglala Sioux suggested that here and there a horse would break loose, but it seems that recollection amounted to an understatement.[28] Many steeds scurried away. Some mounts stampeded toward the river.[29] More critically, not every beleaguered soldier lost his horse; some retained them and the Indians described the disparity between mounted and dismounted troopers.

Turtle Rib recalled a running fight with soldiers on foot, these men fighting coolly compared to the mounted men.[30] The latter, he thought, seemed to be "stampeded." Two Eagles said it was a moving fight from Calhoun Hill to Custer Hill with "most of the soldiers dismounted" (i.e., they had lost their horses).[31] Foolish Elk also saw "men on foot . . . shooting as they passed along, but the men on horses rode away . . . as fast as they could go."[32] But not all dismounted soldiers acted in a composed manner. Some, according to White Bull, "ran like scared rabbits," while others mounted their horses after a bugle sounded.[33] The bugle reference seems to indicate that officers properly responded to the Keogh sector attacks, though with little success.

Apparently most mounted soldiers rode to the north in an attempt to reach Custer Hill.[34] Two Moon, and obviously other warriors (as indicated by Indian pathways), kept advancing as the soldiers fled northward.[35] Turtle Rib, though, saw some soldiers riding in the opposite direction.[36] These men possibly were the four who, according to Indians, tried unsuccessfully to escape to the south.[37] Soldiers afoot, many also trying to gain Custer Hill, were left to fend for themselves. And most in the Keogh sector probably were dismounted.[38] Sufficient confusion developed so that Indians shot soldiers from behind.[39] Red Horse mentioned hand-to-hand fighting but did not elaborate.[40] Grinnell, interpreting Cheyenne accounts of the close-in fighting, stated that half the soldiers fought with pistols, not carbines.[41] Sioux and Cheyenne warriors led Miller to believe that the dismounted troopers, unlike those with horses, were unable to join in the breakthrough to Custer Hill.[42] Brave Wolf saw it the other way around but, given the proliferation of marble markers at the Keogh and Calhoun sectors, it is apparent that only a few made it to Custer Hill.[43]

As for the fighting, Lone Bear said it was the hardest during the Keogh episode.[44] His reference, however, is the only one of its nature encountered in the primary sources to date. Flying Hawk suggested that Company I tried to make a stand and "fired some shots."[45] Two Eagles indicated it was a "slight stand."[46] These passages bespoke of rather desultory firing, and this is reflected in the archaeological record. Lone Bear's account is not. Also, Company I was not deployed in an effective fighting formation. After this "stand," according to Flying Hawk, the soldiers "made another stand" before they fled to Custer Hill.[47] This next stand must have occurred after the charge which separated the soldiers into two bunches.[48] Runs the Enemy referred to the results of the attack.

On this retreat the soldiers now broke the line and divided, some of them going down the eastern slope of the hill [ridge], and some of them going down to the river. The others came back [fell back] to where the final stand was made [Custer Hill], but they were few in number then.[49]

There are corroborating accounts of soldiers going toward the river. Two Eagles said that eight to twelve men made a "dash" over to the west side of Custer Ridge, though he did not think they were trying to "run away."[50] In the strict sense Two Eagles was correct. Like those who fled to Custer Hill, these men too tried to reach safety with the left wing. White Bull also noticed this over-the-ridge movement. Once troopers from Companies C and L, those still alive, had joined their comrades in the Keogh sector, "some" did not continue to "run straight." Rather than fleeing to Custer Hill, these men ran "toward the river [and they] were all killed."[51]

Concurrent with flight over Custer Ridge, Runs the Enemy described the movements of the two bunches of soldiers.[52] The two groups were apparently sufficiently close together for White Cow Bull to fire into both without changing his position.[53] One group made for Custer Hill, the other went down the eastern ridge slope. Marble markers clustered around the Keogh memorial stone likely represent the latter group (Figure 1-2). Much has been made of this cluster of markers. A number of eyewitnesses saw the bodies at this cluster and concluded that Captain Keogh attempted to rally his men.[54] Others suggest the Keogh group was attempting to reach their horses, though these probably were lost early in the episode.[55] The circumstances surrounding behavior during the break up of tactical unity and flight, however, present an alternative explanation.

The distribution of the dead immediately surrounding Captain Keogh has been described variously as a "pile of men," or "all in a bunch", troops "piled in a heap", and "one compact mass."[56] While the bodies were separated for interment, the clustered markers today generally reflect these descriptions. Shock, sudden confusion, and perhaps a lack or loss of leadership pervaded the Keogh sector as loss of cohesiveness set in. Given a disordered

ARCHAEOLOGY AND HISTORY

39. Red Feather in Hardorff, *Markers, Artifacts and Indian Testimony*, 49.
40. Graham, *The Custer Myth*, 62.
41. Grinnell, *The Fighting Cheyennes*, 351.
42. Miller, *Custer's Fall*, 143.
43. Runs the Enemy in Dixon, *The Vanishing Race*, 176.
44. "Lone Bear Statement."
45. McCreight, *Firewater and Forked Tongues*, 113.
46. "Two Eagles Statement."
47. McCreight, *Firewater and Forked Tongues*, 113.
48. He Dog in Hammer, *Custer in '76*, 207; Hardorff, *Markers, Artifacts and Indian Testimony*, 48.
49. Dixon, *The Vanishing Race*, 176.
50. "Two Eagles Statement."
51. Vestal, (White Bull Interview), op cit., 139.
52. Hammer, *Custer in '76*, 207; Hardorff, *Markers, Artifacts and Indian Testimony*, 48.
53. Miller, "Echoes of the Little Bighorn," 34.
54. Graham, *The Custer Myth*, 89.
55. Bighead in Marquis, *Custer on the Little Bighorn*, 39; Moore, "It Was a Day of Bravery," 48.
56. Kanipe in Hammer, *Custer in '76*, 95; Graham, *The Custer Myth*, 88 and 99; Bourke in Hardorff, *Markers, Artifacts and Indian Testimony*, 50.

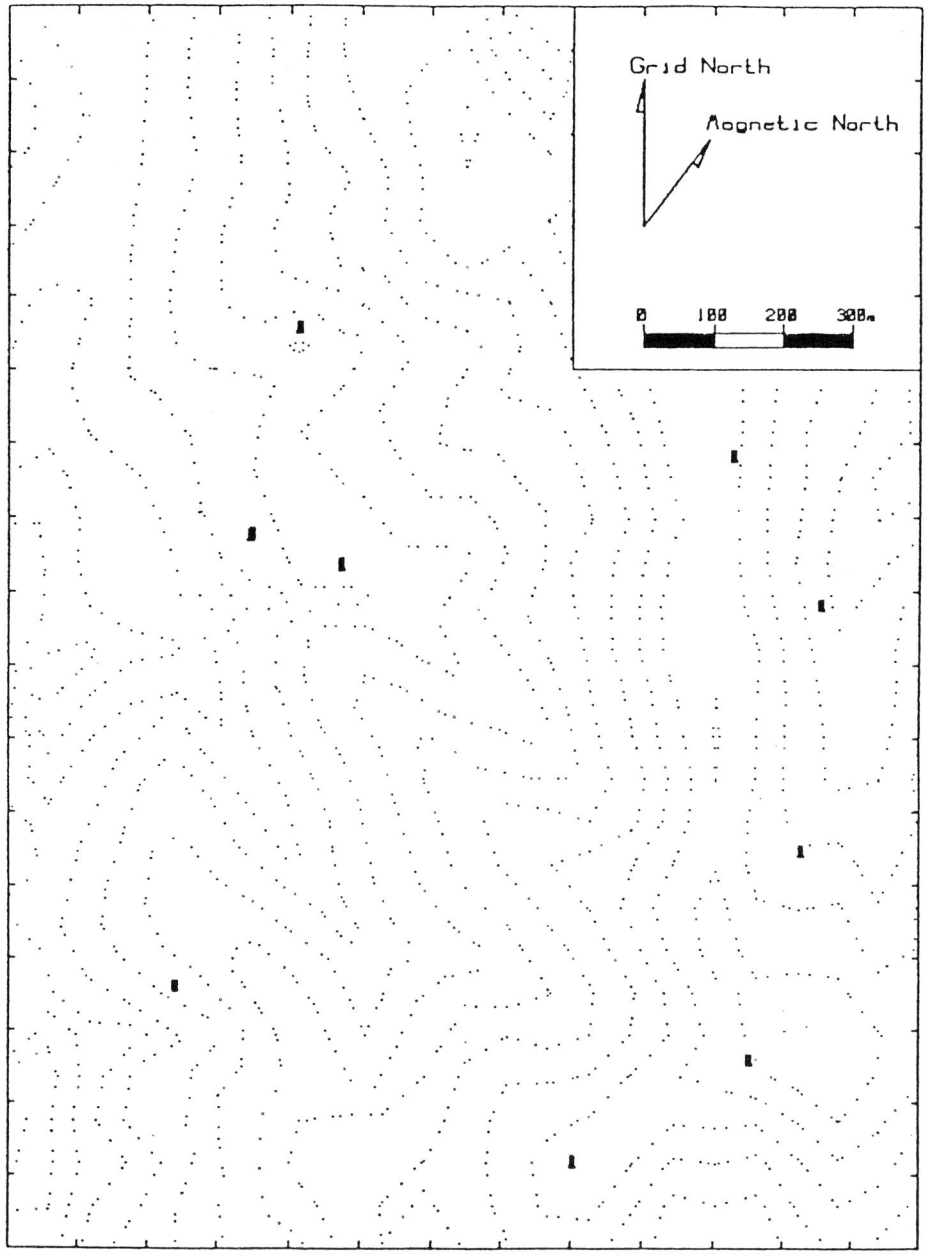

Figure 1-3 represents the distribution of Colt .45 cartridge cases in the Custer battlefield study area.

environment, bunching behavior is the most likely explanation for the clustering. Indeed, the marker distributions throughout the Keogh sector do not convey any semblance of tactical order. Instead, they better fit Miller's description of the struggle, taken from Sioux and Cheyenne eyewitness testimony, of "little knots of soldiers" surrounded by Indians.[57] Miller visited the site with his Indian informants, and their testimony may have been influenced indirectly by the marker patterning. But in 1877, before the markers were placed, Lieutenant Bourke viewed the actual graves, noting they, " . . . are scattered in irregular clumps and at intervals about like those in a slaughter of buffaloes . . . . "[58] Runs the Enemy remembered that right wing flight resembled a buffalo stampede, and Bourke saw the end result. There can be little doubt that what is seen today in the Keogh sector markers resulted from panic and fear, not from a determined exploitation of tactical alternatives.

The presence of soldiers in the Keogh sector from the three right wing companies complements archaeological and other historical evidences of flight from the Calhoun sectors. Their presence is also consistent with confusion arising from disintegration. Stable units do not mix together. In the Keogh sector, at least one Company L trooper (Private C. Graham) could be identified, and an observer identified First Sergeant Edwin Bobo (Company C) near the body of Captain Keogh.[59]

Age and stature estimates calculated from skeletal remains at one Keogh sector marker (#200) fit the profiles of six right wing soldiers (four from C and two from L) and only 3 from the left.[60] Two of the possible left wing candidates were identified elsewhere, leaving only a single individual who fits the age and stature estimates.[61] But it is not likely the remains represent this person. Contemporary observers did not identify any left wing troopers in the Keogh sector — they recognized only C, I, and L soldiers. Among those in the Keogh cluster were two sergeants from Company I (Varden and Bustard, although another account places Bustard in the village).[62] Trumpeter Patton and Corporal Wild, both from Company I, were also in the cluster.[63]

Company I's first sergeant, Frank Varden, also fell in the cluster which was found around Keogh's body. *Courtesy of Custer Battlefield National Monument.*

Edwin Bobo was first sergeant of Company C, yet his body was found near Keogh after the battle. *Courtesy of Custer Battlefield National Monument.*

57. Miller, *Custer's Fall*, 140.
58. Hardorff, *Markers, Artifacts and Indian Testimony*, 50.
59. Kanipe in Hammer, *Custer in '76*, 95. See Nowlan's map in Nicholas, "Reno Court of Inquiry," 737.
60. D. D. Scott, R. A. Fox, M. A. Connor, and D. Harmon, *Archaeological Perspectives on the Battle of the Little Bighorn* (Norman, OK: University of Oklahoma Press, 1989). 83.
61. Hammer, *Custer in '76*, 120, 137, 139, 146, 248; Hammer, "Camp Manuscript," 107; Statement of F. Berwald, Camp Collection, Brigham Young University, Box 6, Folder 12; Frances Taunton, *Custer's Field: a Scene of Sickening, Ghastly Horror* (London: The Johnson-Taunton Military Press, 1986), 20-21.
62. Nichols, "Reno Court of Inquiry," 520; Hammer, "Camp Manuscript," 672.
63. Hammer, *Custer in '76*, 58 and 130; Taunton, *Custer's Field*, 35; W. R. Hurt and W. E. Lass, *Frontier Photographer: Stanley J. Marrow's Dakota Years* (Lincoln, NE: University of Nebraska Press, 1956), Figure 90.

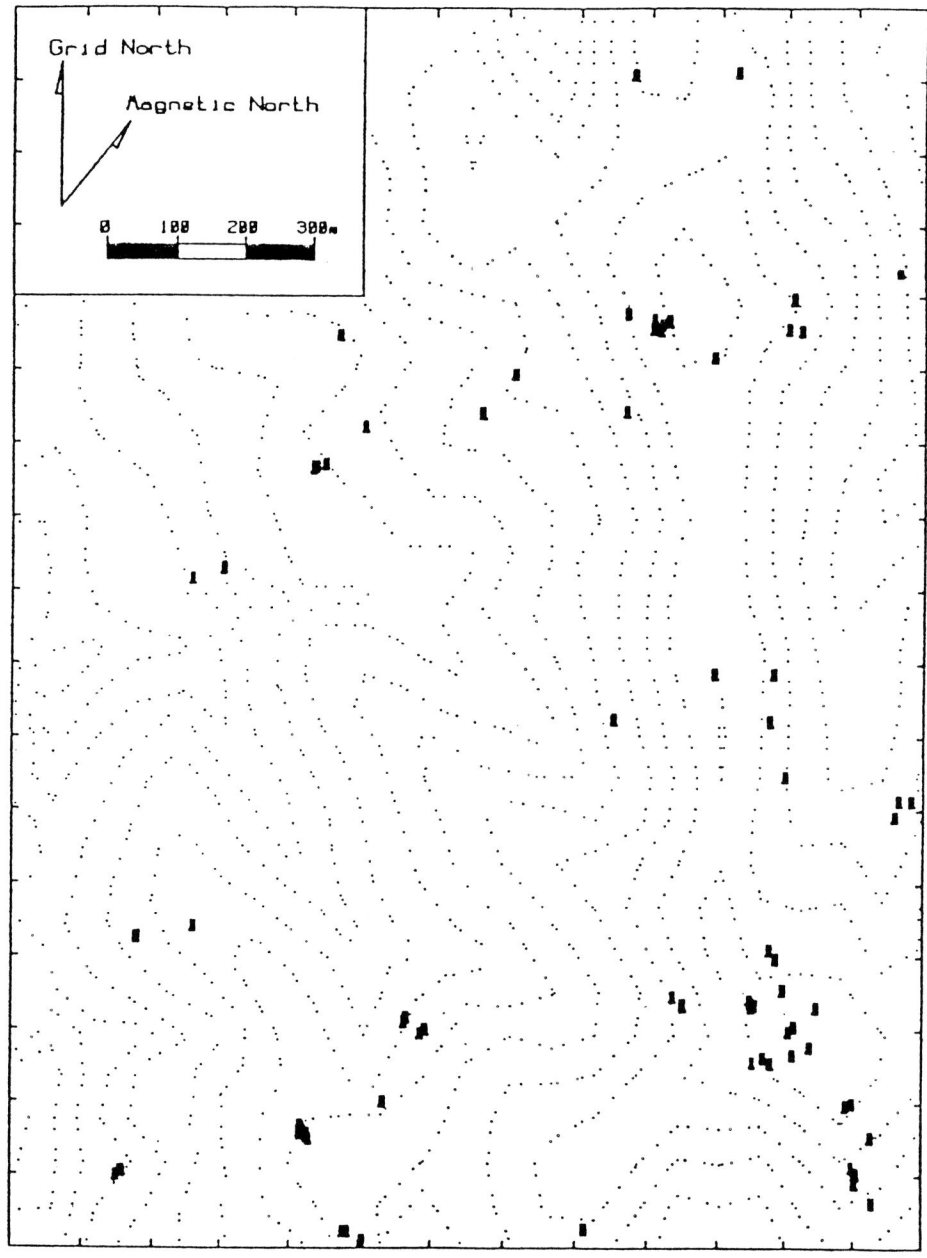

Figure 1-4 depicts the distribution of .45/.55 cartridge cases in the Custer battlefield study area.

Like marker patterning, the archaeological record concerning the role of firearms in the Keogh episode is consistent with choas and retreat. Physical evidence for firearm use by either adversary is poor. Possibly artifact collecting by relic hunters among the Keogh sector markers has impaired the archaeological record. But historical evidence, which is consistent with archaeological conclusions, suggests that there never was much to collect. Hardorff made the same observation, though he thought the lack of evidence for firearm use did not detract from the belief that the troopers fought intensely.[64]

Red Feather noted that the Indian charge was stimulated by the impression that the soldiers' guns were empty.[65] Red Horse described hand-to-hand fighting during the Keogh episode.[66]

These developments help explain the paucity of archaeological evidence for the use of Springfield carbines. The carbine had a limited effectiveness in close-in fighting. It is a single-shot weapon requiring deliberate and repeated loading for optimum operation. Therefore it is likely that many soldiers, when closely confronted, abandoned this weapon. This behavior probably prompted Sitting Bull's and Red Horse's observations that the soldiers could not fire quickly enough, and many in panic simply threw down their arms.[67] Indeed, in one incident, a Keogh sector soldier, confronted face-to-face with White Bull, fired and then threw his carbine at White Bull's head.[68]

Gall remembered: "the soldiers threw their guns aside and fought with little guns."[69] He erroneously assumed their ammunition supply had dwindled. Grinnell's Indian informants also implied that soldiers used the Colt revolver.[70] According to Dewey Beard, an Indian warrior, "some" troopers fired their pistols at close range.[71] But the poverty of Colt casings at the Keogh sector suggests pistol use was minimal. The fighting ended before there was time enough to reload, or soldiers found too little time to discharge all six rounds.[72] In a scene where fleeing soldiers, acting as if drunk, were shot from behind and jerked bodily from their horses, resistance must have been sporadic and, as might be expected during panicky flight, individualistic.[73] In fact, Two Eagles, when asked if the troopers were running or fighting, said most of them were killed while "moving."[74] He might as well have said "while fleeing."

Other accounts suggest substantial numbers of Indians fought armed with clubs, knives, and hatchets, handy for counting coup on live enemies.[75] The Indian testimonies are replete with descriptions of coup honors. In the close-in fighting many of the soldiers were probably dispatched with these weapons rather than firearms. This would help explain the relatively few Indian cartridge cases and bullets found in the Keogh sector (compared to the Calhoun Hill vicinity).

Foolish Elk watched the Keogh episode from east of Custer Ridge and saw that the "men made no stand" as they went toward Custer Hill.[76] Turtle Rib called it a "running fight."[77] Clearly the weight of archaeological evidence, and confirmatory historical accounts, indicate that the Keogh episode simply represented a continuation of tactical break up which began during the Calhoun episode. The entire right wing had crumbled. Historical data to the contrary, myths of group coherence no longer can be entertained. In the Keogh episode, developments are entirely consistent with expectations derived from disintegration models of men in combat.[78] Men fled through the Keogh sector to Custer Hill, to the denouement. Yet the flight was to units which remained tactically stable for the moment. These units were involved in the Cemetery Ridge segment of the battle.

Consequently, flight from the Calhoun sector to the Keogh sector links the two episodes and establishes a south to north flow during the erosion of combat effectiveness. This flow also is evident in individual Indian pathways, which indicate that Indians involved in the Calhoun Hill episode likewise fought at the Keogh sector. As the soldiers fled Calhoun Hill, the Indians followed. The Keogh sector, however, is characterized by the virtual absence of evidence for intense fighting on the part of the troopers. This is astounding considering that marker placements at the sector suggest that as

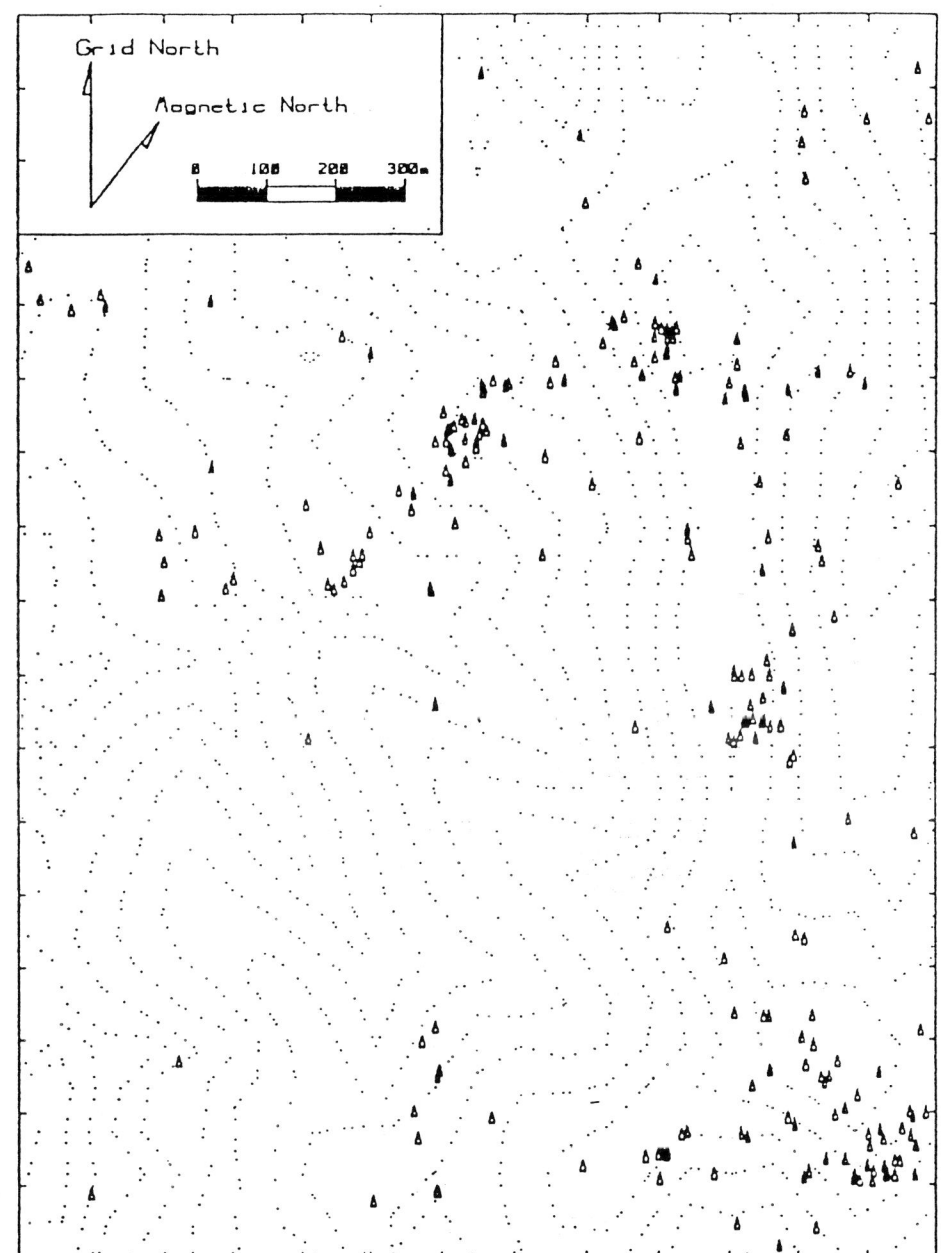

Figure 1-5 provides data on the distribution of Indian bullets (all calibers) in the Custer battlefield study area.

64. Hardorff, *Markers, Artifacts and Indian Testimony*, 65.
65. Ibid., 49.
66. Graham, *The Custer Myth*, 62.
67. Tillett, *Wind on the Buffalo Grass*, 70.
68. Miller, "Echoes of the Little Bighorn," 36.
69. Graham, *The Custer Myth*, 91.
70. Grinnell, *The Fighting Cheyennes*, 351.
71. Tillett, *Wind on the Buffalo Grass*, 94.
72. Stands in Timber and Liberty, *Cheyenne Memories*, 201.
73. "Statement of Hollow Horn Bear," (unpublished MS, June 1909, Camp Collection, Custer Battlefield National Monument), Red Feather in Hardorff, *Markers, Artifacts and Indian Testimony*, 49; Miller, *Custer's Fall*, 142; Miller, "Echoes of the Little Bighorn," 36.
74. "Statement of Two Eagles."
75. Gall in Tillett, *Wind on the Buffalo Grass*, 75; Dewey Beard in Miller, "Echoes of the Little Bighorn," 38; Stands in Timber and Liberty, *Cheyenne Memories*, 201.
76. Hammer, *Custer in '76*, 199.
77. Ibid., 201.
78. Red Bird in Hammer, "Camp Manuscript," 630.
79. For more on the topic of combat psychology consult: A. du Picq, *Battle Studies* (Harrisburg, PA: The Military Service Publishing Company, 1946); G. Dyer, *War* (New York: Crown Publishers, 1985); R.A. Gabriel, *No More Heroes: Madness and Psychiatry in War* (New York, NY: Hill and Wang, 1987); Sam C. Sarkesian, *Combat Effectiveness: Cohesion, Stress and the Volunteer Military* (Beverly Hills, CA: Sage Publications, 1980).

many as seventy soldiers died during the episode. Colt 45 cartridge cases number only three (Figure 1-3), and there are only four 45/55 cases at the sector. Figure 1-4 illustrates the few 45/55 cases with respect to the Keogh sector markers. The Indian bullets in Figure 1-5 tend to confirm the sector as a cavalry position.

The northerly flight of soldiers from Calhoun Hill implies that the Keogh sector was, by virtue of its apparent safety, relatively stable at the time of disintegration. Despite the many deaths at the Keogh sector, however, there is no concrete evidence for tactical deployments. On the basis of archaeology, then, the best explanation for the extant data is that flight from Calhoun Hill continued through the Keogh sector. Flight can account for the relatively few government cartridge cases in the sector. And, in fact, the markers are distributed from Calhoun Hill nearly to Custer Hill. Indian pathways indicate that Indians followed the fleeing soldiers, firing at them as they proceeded north.

Figure 1-6 illustrates, on the basis of Indian cartridge cases, the known Indian positions at the Keogh sector. The evidence for Indian firing at the sector is not great, particularly in light of the many deaths which occurred. Indeed, the scarcity of Indian cases at the Keogh sector is curious given the fact that firearms were used extensively at Calhoun Hill and its environs. This noticeable archaeological transition suggests that many Indians abandoned the firearm in favor of close-in fighting during the soldiers' flight.

In sum, the Keogh episode seems permeated with the behavioral characteristics of disintegration generated at Calhoun Hill. Certainly there is no evidence for sustained, tactical resistance on the part of the soldiers. And the paucity of bullets and cartridge cases, plus the many dead, is consistent with such behavior. Inference suggests that close-in fighting developed as the northerly flight continued. The soldiers' flight, which claimed many victims, was toward the left wing near Custer Hill.

Thus, the transition from tactical stability to instability at Calhoun Hill signaled the beginning of the end of the Custer battle. Bunching behavior and flight, exhibited archaeologically, evidently resulted when troops stationed at Calhoun Coulee and Calhoun Ridge failed to stem the attack at Greasy Grass Ridge. Archaeological evidence at these two sectors suggests brief fighting, though a number of soldiers died. This failure caused the original skirmish line at Calhoun Hill to redeploy into positions designed to meet the threat posed by Indians to the west. The change in skirmish positions suggests that the original skirmish line faced little serious threat as the Indian attack from Greasy Grass Ridge mounted. The redeployment, however, allowed Indians from the south to seize the advantage and move closer to Calhoun Hill. Much of the Indian firing at Henryville probably occurred at this time. The second skirmish line, now faced with attacks at the front (from Greasy Grass Ridge) and the left flank (from Henryville), began to waver. It is at this point that discipline among the command eroded and bunching began to occur.

The exodus which began at Calhoun Hill continued through the Keogh sector northerly toward Custer Hill. Troops possibly were stationed at the Keogh sector. If so, they seemingly engaged in little or no fighting prior to disintegration setting in since evidences of tactical deployments are lacking there. This is consistent with the observations of few serious threats prior to disintegration at Calhoun Hill. The action of Keogh and his command seemed, therefore, to be of short duration as the panic from Calhoun's group spread and overwhelming waves of Indians attacked and destroyed this second body of troopers.[79]

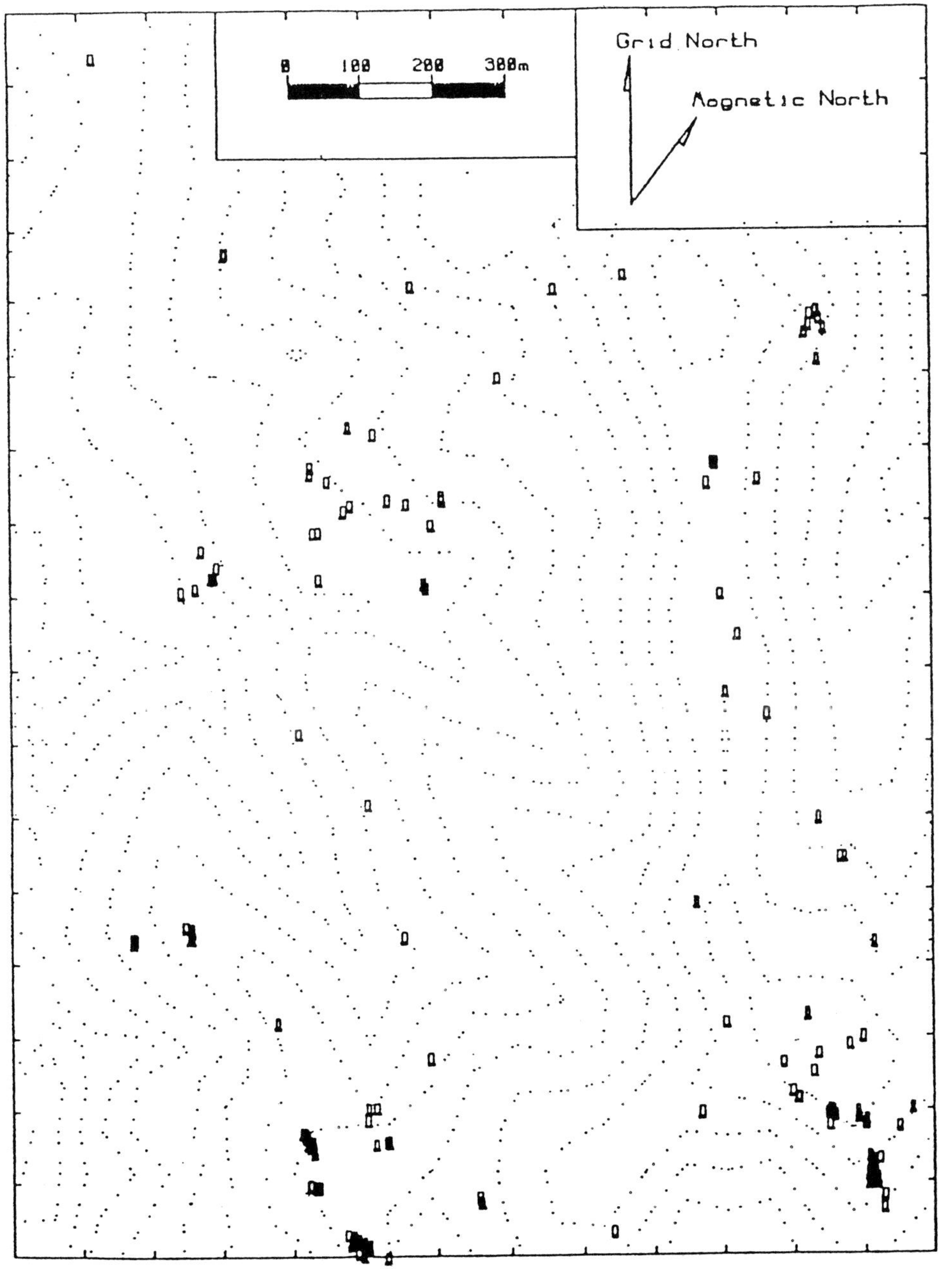

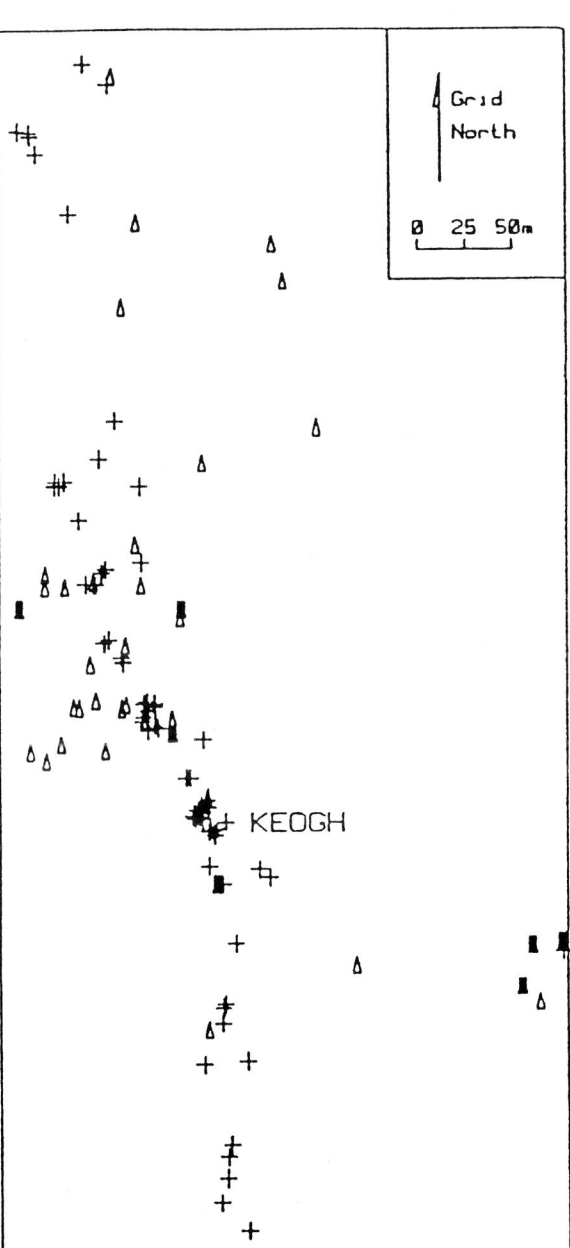

Figure 1-6 depicts the distribution of Indian cartridge cases (all calibers) in the Custer battlefield study area.

Figure 1-7. Enlargement of the Keogh sector depicting .45/.55 cartridge cases, Indian bullets, and marker locations.

Keogh's Company I guidon was one of many items recovered subsequent to the battle. According to Anson Mills, Keogh's gauntlets were found wrapped inside of the guidon when it was recovered after the Battle of Slim Buttes, on September 9, 1876. *Courtesy of Custer Battlefield National Monument.*

Chapter 9

Taps:
Keogh's Burial and Memorials

by Francis B. Taunton

> And Irish Nora's eyes are dim
> For a singer, dumb and gory;
> And English Mary mourns for him
> Who sang of 'Annie Laurie.'
>
> Bayard Taylor, "The Song of the Camp"

On June 28, 1876, the men of Custer's regiment who had survived the two-day engagement advanced over the field where more than 200 of their comrades lay mangled and lifeless. The companies involved in the burial formed a long skirmish line in order to locate and inter as many as possible of the troopers who had fallen with Custer. It was apparently the task of Company D to bury Myles Keogh and his men, for one of the officers of this company was to testify three years later: "Captain Keogh had evidently been wounded as we found that his leg had been broken...."[1]

Keogh's company was found in a "depression just north or below Crittenden (Calhoun) Hill and on the slope of the ridge that forms the defensive line furthest from the river...."[2] According to the same account, Company I had apparently attempted to "rally by company" and were killed in a bunch. To some extent this would seem to be borne out by Theodore Goldin who was to write in 1931: " 'I' troop lay in a slight depression and looked as though it had ben formed IN A HOLLOW SQUARE with KEOGH and one or two others in the center...." Edgerly, however, disagreed. He had written in 1881 that Keogh's company had "evidently been falling back towards the knoll [Custer Hill] . . . fighting as they retreated." Wallace, however, testified in 1879 that Keogh's men had been killed "running in file" but did not think this indicated skirmish order. Nevertheless, it seems clear that a "pile of men" was discovered around Keogh and that these included First Sergeant Frank Varden and Sergeant James Bustard, a compatriot of Keogh. Across Keogh's breast lay Trumpeter John W. Patton. Nearby was Corporal John Wild, who may have served as guidon bearer, and surrounding these were a dozen or so other enlisted men including First Sergeant Edwin Bobo of Company C.[3]

Many of those killed were mutilated terribly but in Keogh's case such mutilation appears to have been stopped when a Catholic medallion was discovered. It may have been an *Agnus Dei*, or the *Medaglia Pro Petri Sede* presented to Keogh and others by Pope Pius IX after the Papal War of 1860. This medallion was found around Keogh's neck and apparently secured by the senior captain of the regiment, Frederick Benteen of Company H.[4] Later on, numerous other "relics" related to Keogh would be recovered.[5]

The burial of the men of Custer's battalion was a hurried affair. The urgent need to transport the wounded

---

Portions of this chapter were based upon an article written by the author which appeared in the English Westerns Society *Brand Book* in April, 1965 and has been reprinted here with permission of the English Westerners Society.

1. "Court of Inquiry . . . Marcus A. Reno," 456.

2. Edward S. Godfrey to E. S. Paxson, January 16, 1896. The greater part of this letter has been reproduced in Graham, *The Custer Myth*, 345-346. See also ibid., 89.

3. Ibid., 219; Theodore Goldin to Albert W. Johnson, July 27, 1931; Leavenworth *Times* (August 18, 1881); "Court of Inquiry . . . Marcus A. Reno," 71-72; Hammer, *Custer in '76*, 58, 95, 121, and 130. John S. Gray, "Captain Clifford's Newspaper Dispatches," Chicago Westerner's *Brand Book* (January, 1971), 81-83 and 88; George Schneider, ed., *The Freeman Journal: The Infantry in the Sioux War of 1876* (San Rafael, CA: Presidio Press, 1977), 58-59; Both Freeman and Clifford served with Gibbon. Hammer, *Custer in '76*, 102 and Stewart, *Custer's Luck*, 469. One of the men from Company I claimed they could recognize Wild and Patton because they were the tallest and shortest men in the troop respectively. Francis Johnson Kennedy (Fred Dustin Collection, Custer Battlefield National Monument), 5. This was not actually the case since a review of Carroll, *They Rode With Custer*, passim, indicated that there were men with the outfit that were taller or of equal size to Wild and individuals who were shorter than Patton.

4. According to Trumpeter John Martin (Giovani Martini), an Italian presumably raised as a Roman Catholic, Keogh "had a gold chain and Agnus Dei Catholic emblem on his neck which the Indians had not taken and Benteen secured this." Hammer, *Custer in '76*, 102. Mrs. Elizabeth Custer mentioned that "A Catholic officer" in the Seventh Cavalry "often wore an *Agnus Dei*...." Custer, *Following the Guidon*, 68. Supposedly, Keogh was known and respected by the Indians, thus they did not mutilate him for this reason and because of "a silver charm, the *Agnus Dei*," which he wore. Julia B. McGillycuddy, *McGillycuddy Agent: Dr. Valentine J. McGillycuddy* (Stanford, CA: Stanford University Press, 1941), 87. The informant for this supposedly was Crazy Horse. Captain Henry Freeman of the Seventh Infantry indicated that the *Agnus Dei* was worn by Keogh. Schneider, *The Freeman Journal*, 58-59. Another Seventh Infantry officer on the scene after the battle, Captain Clifford, repeated this. Gray, "Captain Clifford's Story," 82-83. Conversely, one of Keogh's men thought that his captain had a gold crucifix hanging around his neck. Francis Johnson Kennedy (Fred Dustin Collection, Custer Battlefield National Monument), 5. Of later historians, Fred Dustin assumed the *Agnus Dei* was what Keogh wore on that day and which the Indians "either overlooked or purposely left...." Fred Dustin, *The Custer Tragedy*, 185. Kuhlman, *Legend into History*, 207 and Miller, *Custer's Fall: The Indian Side of the Story*, 173 concurred. A more recent writer also related that Keogh may have been spared from mutilation "perhaps because of a Catholic medal (possibly an Agnes [sic] Dei) he wore on a chain about his neck." Pohanka, "Myles Walter Keogh," 11. Taking a different stand, Luce contended that Keogh carried a leather case around his neck which held his "Medaglia di Pro Petri Sede" from Pius IX attached by a cord. The pouch and its contents were never recovered. According to Luce, because they thought this was "powerful medicine," the Indians did not desecrate Keogh's body. Luce, *Keogh, Comanche, and Custer*, 62. Connell, *The Son of the Morning Star*, 290-291 essentially accepts Luce's interpretation, although the author mentioned the *Agnus Dei* and a cross hanging from a gold chain as two of the other common references. An 1876 press clipping provided by Ross Kehoe, of Clifden, Kilkeeny, now in the Myles

In 1879, Captain George Kaiser Sanderson led a detail to the Custer battlefield to rebury the fallen troopers and place markers at the site of death for those officers who had been reinterred elsewhere. This included Keogh. *Courtesy of Coffrin's Old West Gallery, Miles City, Montana.*

to a hospital more than 700 miles away took precedence over the proper interment of the dead. In the majority of instances, earth was scooped over the naked corpses with knives, spoons, and axes. In the case of the officers, a numbered stake was driven into the head of each grave and this tallied with the numbers appearing on the map of the battlefield prepared by Lieutenant Edward G. Maquire, General Terry's acting chief of engineers, in order to facilitate discovery and recognition when the time came to remove the bodies to the East.[6]

Myles Keogh had no next-of-kin in the United States, though a brother and sister subsequently emigrated there from Ireland. He had been on very friendly terms with the Martin family of Willowbrook, three miles outside the town of Auburn, New York, however. The family immediately made inquiries as to the possibility of his body being brought out of the Yellowstone country. Eveline Martin had known Keogh both before and after her marriage to Colonel Andrew J. Alexander, and late in July she wrote to the General of the Army, William T. Sherman, asking for his assistance. He replied:

> I will send your letter with an endorsement to General Sheridan who will doubtless forward it to General Terry who will in due time cause the bodies of all of the officers who fell with Custer to be removed to the Yellowstone and may be to Fort Abe Lincoln whence they can be sent to their Friends-I'm afraid that Uncle Sam will not pay the expenses further than Lincoln but of that hereafter. Now my understanding is that all the bodies were carefully buried near where they fell by the men of General Terry's command . . . and I do not think that he will be able to do much more in the way of removing the dead till he and Crook have punished Sitting Bull for the past, during which I fear many other noble fellows must go down and be buried in that desolate region of Earth . . . .[7]

Mrs. Alexander subsequently communicated with Myles Keogh's sister, Margaret, who was living at Clifden, County Kilkenny, Ireland. After expressing her sympathy, and reminiscing on her friendship with Myles, wrote: "I trust we shall be able to carry out his desire & lay him to rest by the side of my dear little children— one of whom knew and loved 'Uncle Keogh,' & was dearly loved by him."[8]

There is thus no mystery as to why he was buried in Auburn, yet Henry J. Nowlan, one of his closest friends, suggested to Margaret Keogh in July that her brother be buried at the Roman Catholic Cemetery at Louisville, Kentucky, "Where he will be near many of his dearest friends."[9] But the Martin family knew what Myles wanted. He had asked to buried at Auburn. That was where he would find his last resting place.

On May 26, 1877, Lieutenant-Colonel Michael V. Sheridan boarded the army supply boat *Fletcher* at Fort Abraham Lincoln. From there he set out up-river to the site of Post No. 1 at the mouth of Tongue River. When completed, this post would be named in honor of the memory of Myles Keogh. Here he met Captain Nowlan who, with Myles' former company, had been ordered to accompany him on his mission. Commanding Nowlan to march Company I overland to the site of Post No. 2 (later to be named Fort Custer), Sheridan continued by boat to meet him at the confluence of the Big and Little Big Horn Rivers, where the fort was being built. On June 29, they were united and three days later, with a detachment from Company I and some Crow scouts, the two officers were camping across the river from the field of Custer's battle, on the ground which only the year before had been the scene of a vast encampment of Plains Indians. Myles Keogh was to be returned to civilization, together with the other officers who had fallen the year before.

The task of exhumation soon was accomplished and, by the evening of Independence Day, the remains of the officers had been placed in pine boxes and transported to Fort Custer to be guarded in the only building constructed. Five days later they were placed on board the *Fletcher*, arriving at Bismarck and Fort Lincoln on July 12.[10]

Two days passed before Colonel Sheridan arrived back in Chicago. On July 16, he corresponded with Eveline Martin's sister, Nelly:

BURIALS & MEMORIALS

Keogh Collection of the Gene Autry Western Heritage Museum titled "Sioux respect for an Irish soldier" subscribed to the belief that Keogh always wore a scapular, and this was what was left on the body after the battle. Hayes-McCoy, *Captain Myles Walter Keogh*, note 15 voiced the same opinion and goes on further to state that the Papal medals "have not been traced." This is not the case, however, since they are still in the hands of Keogh's family, and thus seem not to have been with Keogh at the battle.

5. Anson Mills stated that he recovered Company I's guidon at Slim Buttes, a pair of gauntlets belonging to Keogh, and much other material from Custer's command. Anson Mills, *My Story* (Washington, DC: Press of Byron S. Adams, 1921), 430-431. A sergeant likewise "remembered finding . . . a locket, a picture of Captain Keogh, two gold-mounted ivory-handled revolvers, and a Spencer sporting rifle," in the same village. Jerome A. Greene, *Slim Buttes, 1876, An Episode of the Great Sioux War* (Norman, OK: University of Oklahoma Press, 1982), 72-73. Keogh had used a Spencer sporting model for hunting during his days in Kansas. This may have been the weapon he carried at the battle. McDougall mentioned that Keogh's watch and a photograph of McDougall's sister were recovered at the same time. Hammer, *Custer in '76*, 70. James Willert, ed., *Bourke's Diary, from Journals of lst Lt. John Gregory Bourke, June 27- Sept. 15, 1876* (La Mirada, CA: James Willert, Publisher, 1986), 220 also stated that the guidon and one of the gauntlets came from the village. The revolver's recovery is noted in Connell, *Son of the Morning Star: Custer and the Little Big Horn*, 291. It is unclear whether the piece actually was retrieved, however, as a refugee Sioux in Canada supposedly had the piece and would "keep it until the friends of the dead owner would redeem it." *Army and Navy Journal* (November 3, 1877), 196. Supposedly, the picture of McDougall's sister also was found. Nowlan obtained the Pontifical Zouave photograph from a Sioux Indian about a year after the battle. Luce, *Keogh, Custer, and Comanche*, 63n. Nowlan had this copied in a larger size and gave the copy to the family. This picture is now in the collections of the Gene Autry Western Heritage Museum as are Keogh's 1872 pattern dress helmet, saber belt, shoulder knots, and certain other items.

As indicated in this *circa* 1890 view taken by Christian Barthelmess, a new marker was erected for Keogh at the battlefield later in the 19th century. *Courtesy of Casey Barthelmess Family, Miles City, Montana.*

Lastly, Joe Bush, a "little yellow bull Dog" which "came out of the fight" had been with Company I as an unofficial mascot of sorts. John Burkman (Elizabeth Custer Collection, Custer Battlefield National Monument).

6. Report of Lieutenant Colonel M. V. Sheridan, July 20, 1877, in Graham, *The Custer Myth*, 375.

7. Information originally provided to the author through the courtesy of Ross Kehoe, now the Myles Keogh's Collection, Gene Autry Western Heritage Museum.

8. Ibid.

9. Ibid.

10. Graham, *The Custer Myth*, 361-378.

11. Courtesy of Ross Kehoe, now Myles Keogh Collection, Gene Autry Western Heritage Museum.

I found your letter here on my return to Chicago. Col. Keogh's remains were recovered & are now at Fort Lincoln in charge of Lieut. Nave to whom I was directed to give them by Captain Nowlan. I have sent to Lincoln a metallic case to receive them & Lt. Nave will send them to Willowbrook as soon as he can for Nowlan informed me that he had written him to do so.

We had no difficulty whatever in identifying poor Keogh's remains, and they were carefully exhumed, so you will have the satisfaction of knowing all that is left of him on earth will be entombed in accordance with his request-at Willowbrook.[11]

Apparently Nelly Martin asked for details of when the casket would arrive at Auburn, for, on July 20, Sheridan wrote:

Headquarters Military Division of the Missouri
My dear Miss Martin,

Your letter arrived this morning. I have written Lieut. Nave directing him to inform you by telegraph when Keogh's remains would leave Lincoln. I will telegraph Dr. Octerlay [sic] when they start if I am here but I am afraid I may be absent, so I would suggest that you telegraph him also, as Nave will telegraph you.

I regret very much that I will not be able to be present at poor Keogh's funeral, for he was one of my truest friends, but I have been directed to go to West Point with the remains of General Custer and therefore cannot go to Willowbrook.

Yours Truly,
M. V. Sheridan[12]

At midnight on Wednesday August 15, Keogh's body arrived by rail at Auburn and the Martin family went down to meet the train. Placing the casket in a wagon they took it to the receiving vault at the Fort Hill Cemetery. A few days later, Nelly Martin sent a letter to Margaret Keogh: "There has been so much delay in receiving this precious boy that we have decided to postpone the funeral until October in order to enable Gen. Alexander and Captain Nowlan to be present and other members of the family who are now necessarily away." There was more, much more, in her letter, but the language of commiseration and sorrow needs no portrayal here.[13]

On October 25, Myles Keogh was buried in the family plot of his friends. The City of Auburn went into mourning that day. The flags at the state armory, and on other public buildings, hung at half-mast. The procession assembled outside the St. James Hotel, the dark blue uniforms of the military pall-bearers mingling with the black of the family mourners. Thirteen officers were there, including three generals. As a captain in the Regular Army, Myles was entitled to a full company escort and all the somber grandeur of a military funeral.

At 2 p.m. the pall-bearers started forward through the city streets, followed by the civic band and a company escort of the Twenty-Ninth Volunteer Regiment, under the command of Lieutenant Robert P. Judge, Company G. Then came the hearse, draped in the scarlet, blue and white of the national colors, and behind were carriages taking the Martin family and other mourners to the cemetery. And as they jolted along, the dull echo of the minute guns could be heard thundering from nearby Port Seward.

At the receiving vault, the casket wrapped in the "Stars and Stripes" was placed in the hearse. Then up to the Enos Throop Martin lot marched the procession. Under the shadow of the tall trees thrusting upward into

Two monuments would serve as memorials to Keogh at his Fort Hill Cemetery grave in New York—one ornate, with military symbols, and a plain Christian cross, added a few years later at its base. *Courtesy of Lenora Snedeker.*

BURIALS & MEMORIALS

12. Keogh Collection, Gene Autry Western Heritage Museum.
13. Ibid.

the autumn sky, the small group of mourners gathered around the open grave. Although a Catholic, Keogh was buried with an Episcopalian ceremony and those present listened as the Reverend Dr. Brainard read the service. The band played a dirge and three volleys crashed out in final salute to the memory of a gallant soldier. The Auburn *Morning Herald* closed its account as follows: "The obsequies were most solemn and imposing and in every way befitting the rank and noble record of the fallen brave in whose honor they were held."[14]

A year passed. In December 1878, Nelly Martin wrote to Keogh's sister; the monument had been completed.[15] At its rear was the record of service of the late Irishman and on the front was carved the following inscription:

BVT.LT. COL. MYLES KEOGH
CAPT. 7TH CAVALRY, U.S.A.
BORN AT
ORCHARD, COUNTY CARLOW, IRELAND

MARCH 25 1840
KILLED IN ACTION WITH SIOUX INDIANS
JUNE 25 1876
SLEEP SOLDIER!
STILL IN HONORED REST
YOUR TRUTH AND VALOR WEARING
THE BRAVEST ARE THE TENDEREST
THE LOVING ARE THE DARING

Over time, this "beautiful marble monument" suffered from "years of weather erosion and acid rain." By 1989, in the interest of preserving the marker, Brian Pohanka of Alexandria, Virginia and Lenora Snedeker of Oxford, New York made arrangements with Berg Memorials of Auburn to clean the headstone.[16]

In the 1970s, Pohanka also had endeavored to have the placement of Keogh's original grave properly recognized. At some point following the removal of the body to New York, and the erection, in 1890, of marble headstones to mark the original gravesites of Custer's men, Keogh's marble marker at the Custer Battlefield was moved sixty-feet from where the Irish officer fell amidst a group of eighteen other soldiers. Using early maps of the grave locations prepared by Walter Camp and others, as well as employing the 1879 Stanley J. Morrow and the ca. 1895 Christian Barthelmess photographs of the first grave sites, Pohanka then "matched up" the evidence with the supposed position. Neil Mangum, then serving as the Custer Battlefield's historian, cleared a small area away from where the Keogh monument had once stood. He located a brick foundation at the exact spot that the other data indicated. Consequently, the marker was relocated to the correct location. During the 1985 archeological survey, wood and nails, possibly from the original wooden marker which stood at the locale in the late 1870s, were discovered.

Although Myles' mortal remains stayed in his adopted country, he is not forgotten by the land of his birth. A memorial to the fallen Seventh Cavalryman exists at St. Joseph's Church in Tinryland, County Carlow. There, a stained glass window is found which depicts the Holy Family. The inscription reads:

> Erected to the memory of Thomas Keogh, Park, died 14 August, 1897; his wife, Alice, died 21 April, 1875 and his brother, Bvt. Lt. Col. Myles W. Keogh, Captain, 7th Cavalry U.S.A., killed in action 25 June, 1876.[16]

14. Keogh Collection, Gene Autry Western Heritage Museum; Luce, *Keogh, Comanche and Custer*, 118-119.

15. Courtesy of Ross Kehoe, now Myles Keogh Collection, Gene Autry Western Heritage Museum. Generals Alexander and Upton also are buried in the Throop Martin lot. Letter to the author from Fort Hill Cemetery Association, February 15, 1964. Francis Taunton, *Custer's Field: Scene of Sickening Ghastly Horror* (London: Johnson-Taunton Military Press, 1986), passim. For additional information on general aspects of the reburials from the battle read Richard G. Hardorff, *The Custer Battle Casualties: Burials, Exhumations, and Reinterments* (El Segundo, CA: Upton and Sons, Publishers, 1989).

16. "Keough [sic] monument gets cleaning," Auburn *Citizen* (August 11, 1989), B1 and B2.

17. John Monahan, "This Carlowman Fell During General Custer's Last Stand," *The Irish Digest* (January, 1964), 37.

The Song of the Camp
By
Bayard Taylor

"Give us a song!" the soldiers cried,
   The outer trenches guarding,
When the heated guns of the camps allied
   Grew weary of bombarding.

The dark Redan, in silent scoff,
   Lay, grim and threatening, under;
And the tawny mound of the Malakoff
   No longer belched its thunder.

There was a pause. A guardsman said,
   "We storm the forts to-morrow;
Sing while we may, another day
   Will bring enough of sorrow."

They lay along the battery's side,
   Below the smoking cannon:
Brave hearts, from Severn and from Clyde.
   And from the banks of Shannon.

They sang of love, and not of fame;
   Forgot was Britain's glory:
Each heart recalled a different name,
   But all sang "Annie Lawrie."

Voice after voice caught up the song,
   Until its tender passion
Rose like an anthem, rich and strong,—
   Their battle-eve confession.

Dear girl, her name he dared not speak,
   But, as the song grew louder,
Something upon the soldier's cheek
   Washed off the stains of powder.

Beyond the darkening ocean burned
   The bloody sunset's embers,
While the Crimean valleys learned
   How English love remembers.

And once again a fire of hell
   Rained on the Russian quarters,
With scream of shot, and burst of shell,
   And bellowing of the mortars!

And Irish Nora's eyes are dim
   For a singer, dumb and gory;
And English Mary mourns for him
   Who sang of "Annie Lawrie."

Sleep, soldiers! still in honored rest
   Your truth and valor wearing:
The bravest are the tenderest,—
   The loving are the daring.

"Reconnaissance"

Captain Keogh's Medals

Much confusion has resulted from the various accounts about what Myles Keogh had on around his neck at the Little Big Horn. As candidates authors have mentioned an *Agnus Dei,* a scapular, or one of the decorations awarded to Keogh for his Papal military duty.

Beginning with the first option, the *Agnus Dei,* this religious symbol may be traced back possibly as early as the 5th-century, A.D. It seems that the remnants of the pascal candle used in connection with Roman Catholic Easter services were distributed to the faithful in early times. Later, clean wax mixed with chrism was prepared into a disc which was sometimes oval and, in other cases, round in shape. These measured about six inches in diameter and bore the figure of a lamb as well as a banner or cross in many instances. Images of saints, or the coat of arms and the name of the pope "are also commonly impressed on the reverse." During "the Wednesday of Easter week these discs are brought to the Pope, who dips them in a vessel of water mixed with chrism and balsam, adding various consecratory prayers." The following Saturday, the Pope gives these to each bishop and cardinal present at Mass.[1]

A second possibility, the scapular, dates back to parts of the habit worn by monks in the Middle Ages. By the 13th-century "devout lay people, living in the world but desiring some corporate form of religious life," were permitted to wear "Third Order Scapulars." These were generally little more than large, plain pieces of the cloth of the type used to make the monks' habits. "One of these was worn on the chest and the other on the back," while strings or tapes connected these swatches over the wearer's shoulders. A few centuries passed when an abbreviated version, called the "Small Scapular," came into existence. With the passage of time, the use of this form spread to even more of the laity. In certain instances they were miniatures (averaging less than two inches) of the Third Order style, or they could be "of a single piece that was hung around the neck by a string." In addition, they frequently carried an embroidered picture of the Virgin Mary, or of a saint.[2] One source contends that the type Keogh had was the so-called "brown scapular" associated with the Carmelite Order.[3]

Of the military medals associated with Keogh, the *Pro Petri Sede* (For the Chair of Peter), receives the most attention in the various secondary sources. A December 8, 1860 decree authorized this award which carried with it a year's seniority for those who remained in the Papal forces. It was given to individuals who had fought in the 1860 war and was somewhat analogous to the U.S. Army's Good Conduct Medal.[4] Light gold in color and circular in shape, the planchet is not much larger than a silver dollar. The obverse side carries the Latin words: *Pro Petri Sede—Pio IX—P.M.—A. XV,* the latter being the abbreviation for *Pius IX Pontifex Maximus, Ano XV*

---

1. "Agnus Dei," *The Catholic Encyclopedia* (New York, NY: Robert Appleton Co., 1907) Vol. I, 220.

2. "Scapular," *The New Catholic Encyclopedia* (New York, NY: McGraw-Hill Book Co., 1967) Vol. XII, 1114-1115.

3. Louis Kaczmarek, *The Wonders She Performs* (Manassas, VA: Trinity Communications, n.d.), 102. The author used as his source *Chroniques du Carmel* (July, 1892), 70.

4. Berkeley, *Irish Battalion,* Appendix D.

(Pope Pius IX, [issued] in the fifteenth year of his pontificate). The reverse side displays the inscription *Victoria Qvae Vincit Mvndvm Eides Nostra* (Our faith which conquers the world [is] our Victory). A floral bow-shaped beam provides a means for the ribbon to be attached. The upside down cross symbolizes St. Peter, who according to tradition was crucified in this manner. The snake swallowing its own tail represents the power of evil which is being subdued by Christianity.

The other award which Keogh brought with him from Rome was the St. Gregory, given to only six of Keogh's comrades, but later distributed to others, including Myles.[5] One of the best descriptions of the medal recorded:

> In 1831, some years before he restored the Order of the Spur, Pope Gregory XVI instituted an Order bearing his name, but called after the canonised Pope of the seventh century. The Order of St. Gregory the Great was and is still bestowed for deeds of military bravery and for actions of great men, hence it is divided into two classes, one for the soldiers and one for civilians. These are sub-divided into sections of varying importance, the distinguishing marks being the methods of wearing the ribbons, crosses, and plaques of the Order. The principal decoration is a Maltese gold cross of eight points set with a red enamel. In the centre, within a circle of blue enamel, is the head of St. Gregory with the traditional dove of gold, and round the image is the inscription in gold letters: "Sanctus Gregorius Magnus." [St. Gregory the Great] Pope Gregory issued strict regulations regarding the wearing of badges of this Order, and forbade them to be set in jewels or brilliants without permission. The ribbons are red with an orange border. The Grand Chancellor of the Order is the Cardinal Secretary of State, and the list of the English speaking members is conspicuous by the large number of Irish names that appear therein.[6]

The reverse bears the words: *Pro Petri et Principe* (For Peter and Prince) inscribed in the center. Around the edge is found *Gregorious XVI P.M. Anno I* to indicate that this was for Gregory XVI, the Supreme Pontiff during year one of his reign.

Keogh lost both of these originals in a fire on the night of January 10, 1865 while staying at the Galt House in Louisville, Kentucky. Two years later, he replaced them through Dexter Bradford of New York who sent a full-sized set and miniatures to Keogh from Paris.[7] This fact, and other evidence, such as several photographs which depicted Keogh sporting the medals, indicated just how much the decorations meant to him.[8] Despite this, they were not of a nature to wear on a campaign, and probably would have been left behind at Fort Lincoln for safekeeping. Since the family retains them, the statement made by Luce and some others that Keogh had at least one of them with him on June 25, 1876 does not seem accurate.

5. Berkeley, *Irish Battalion*, Appendix D; Pancani, "Last Crusade," 3;

6. Undated clipping, Keogh Collection, Gene Autry Western Heritage Museum.

7. September 30, 1867 and March 22, 1875, National Library Microfilm. Keogh also lost important papers to the flames.

8. After receiving his brevet as a lieutenant-colonel Keogh told Tom that he was ready to visit Europe, something he "should have disliked" doing without his new "title" and his "Order of Chavelier di Gregorio."

Philip Carey (with folded arms) would play Keogh in Walt Disney's *Tonka*. *Courtesy of Vincent Heier.*

Chapter 10

The Legend Continues:
A Checklist of Keogh in Fiction, Poetry, and Film

by Rev. Vincent Heier

> Keogh's reputation rests
> Upon which view to take.
> Some make him seem ascetic.
> Some claim he was a rake.
> Whatever were his foibles,
> Keogh was skilled in war.
> In the War Between The States,
> Was noted on that score.
>
> F. A. Lydic, *Comanche! Oh Comanche!*

The "soldier of fortune" commanding "Wild I" was a "sharp-eyed, swarthy-skinned man," with a "big black mustache and a little pointy underlip beard," and "merry Irish eyes." "A victim of a raging thirst," he "must have had something going for him that day." This composite description as found in various works of fiction can only be of one man, Myles Keogh, and the day in question is none other than June 25, 1876.

History often remembers Keogh as the rider of the horse, Comanche, alleged "sole survivor" of the "Last Stand." That circumstance has led to much speculation of his background, especially as found in Edward Luce's seriously flawed *Keogh, Comanche and Custer*. In this pivotal 1939 work, Keogh emerges as one of the most recognizable figures in the tragic story of the Little Big Horn. Thus, while not holding center stage like Custer, Reno, or Benteen, Keogh's colorful persona can stand on its own as a secondary character whose "walk-on" role has fueled the imaginations of novelists and poets in very interesting ways.

In the earliest fictional accounts of the fight along the Greasy Grass, the target audience was generally the younger reader. Here, the obvious focus of attention was George Armstrong Custer. Myles Keogh was not defined as a character at all. Not until 1898 did Elbridge Brooks' novel, *Master of the Strong Hearts*, even refer to Keogh, and, in this instance, only as related to his horse. This interesting passage ran:

> . . . The ghost of the troop-horse came within the lines, and stood trembling before the bivouac fire. 'It's one of ours!' cried Captain McDougall, who stood by. 'Stir up that fire, Jack, won't you? Let's see if we know it.'
>
> The flare shot up, and in its light the newcomer stood revealed. Bleeding from severe wounds, weak and weary, and with a desire for pity and comfort that was deeply pathetic shining in his eyes, the scarred but beautiful sorrel laid its head against the captain's shoulder as if to claim protection.
>
> Jack sprang forward.
> 'Why! it's Comanche!' he said.
> 'You're right, Jack. By Jove! it is,' cried the captain, flinging his arms about the neck of the sorrel. 'Poor Myles Keogh! It's his Comanche. And I believe, boys,

MYLES KEOGH

1. Eldridge S. Brooks, *Master of the Strong Hearts: A Story of Custer's Last Rally* (New York, NY: E. P. Dutton and Co., 1931), 296.
2. Ralph Bonehill, *With Custer in the Black Hills* (New York, NY: Grossett and Dunlap Pubs., 1902), 238.
3. Edwin L. Sabin, *On the Plains With Custer* (Philadelphia, PA: J. B. Lippincott Co., 1913), 45.
4. Cyrus Townsend Brady, *Britton of the Seventh* (New York, NY: A. L. Burt Co., 1914), 347.
5. *Ibid*, 352-353.

he's the only living thing we shall ever see from our side of that battlefield. Let's give him a rousing welcome, boys. Come! three for Comanche!'

And about the bivouac fire the cheers of welcome rang out so lustily that, from all the camp, came officers and men anxious to know the cause and to join again in a salvo of welcome to the noble charger Comanche, sole survivor of the fight, gallant Captain Keogh's splendid Kentucky sorrel.¹

Just a few years later, Ralph Bonehill's novel, *With Custer in the Black Hills*, went on to reflect the apparent valor of Keogh and his men:

A mile further on was another ridge, and here Captain Keogh's company was placed, and here they, too, died to a man, fighting bravely to the last. Why did they not retreat? It was impossible, and besides, they had been ordered to stand, and stand they did, until the very last officer or private perished.²

In 1913, Keogh once more received passing notice in Edwin Sabin's *On the Plains with Custer*, being described as one, "Who served the Pope as well as in the Army of the Potomac."³ It was in 1914, however, that Cyrus Townsend Brady gave him a larger part in *Britton of the Seventh*, one of a growing number of adult-focused works which began to appear during this period. The novelist described Keogh and his unit holding "the right of the line:"

'Keogh' said the General, 'the Indians, who are in great force, are running. If we can keep them on the jump we can afford to sacrifice half the horses in the command.' The Irishman responded, 'General' . . . , saluting and looking back at the lean, bronze faces of his veterans, their eyes snapping, their cheeks flushing, 'we will do all that men and horses can do.'⁴

The column then moved on, as the Indians began their charge. Keogh senses imminent disaster, while Custer dispassionately deploys the command:

The soldiers stared at them [the Indians] in astonishment. 'My God!' said Keogh, 'there must be a thousand of them!'

'Here they come!' exclaimed the adjutant.

Sure enough. Bending low over their ponies, they were racing across the plateau apparently intending to extend on the right flank of the column, I Troop's left as it faced them. What those Indians could be doing there, what it meant, was not evident to anyone at first, and there was no time for speculation or discussion. An emergency had developed, a crisis which had to be met. A counter-charge was impossible against such a force.

Instantly Custer cried to Keogh, 'Dismount and deploy!' Then he nodded to the men of his staff. 'Halt the other troops. Let them take position on this ridge. Stop Calhoun on Keogh's left. Dismount the men. Move the horses to the rear. Prepare to repel the attack.'

A half a dozen men of the staff raced away to the other troops and as they reached the successive units, the column halted, the men leaped from their saddles, the horses were told off in fours and given to a horseholder and moved to the rear of the high ridge.

So well disciplined were the troops that the movements were effected and the orders obeyed in less time than it takes to tell them.

'Hold your fire, Keogh,' said Custer, 'until it will tell.'

Then he turned and rode along the line, calling words of soldierly encouragement to each troop as he passed.⁵

At this point, Keogh's character is beginning to emerge not merely as another officer, but as a soldier whose valor and abilities can be compared to those of Custer himself. This transformation came to pass at just about the same time the popular image of Custer was to be challenged forever by the work of Frederick Van De Water. In 1933, Van De Water published his novel on the Little Big Horn, *Thunder Shield*. When introducing the officers of the newly formed Seventh Cavalry, the author describes a curious scene in the sutler's store:

Through the clatter of amusement-hungry voices, came measured, discordant moanings from across the parade-ground where the newly organized band practiced . . . . When Captain Miles [sic] Keogh bowed stiffly and wished the company a careful good night, Avery, watching the uncertain tread of his departure, muttered to his neighbor:

'It will be well if, he doesn't run into the Old Man.'

Captain Benteen, a war-time colonel of cavalry, rumpled the shock of white above his hard ruddy face and followed Keogh from the room with truculent eyes.

'Miles [sic] is safe,' he said grimly. 'Custer has queer spells of blindness. Now if I were as drunk as he—....⁶

Keogh's only other appearance in the book is when:

Tom Custer, Calhoun and Keogh, red-eyed and rueful, crept ashore at sunrise from the Far West where they played poker with Grant Marsh and Captain Crowell of the Sixth Infantry. Crowell won a thousand dollars in I.O.U.'s and later destroyed them.⁷

Van de Water would incorporate this later passage verbatim into his subsequent 1934 anti-Custer biography, *Glory-Hunter*.⁸ Thus, like Custer, Keogh fares no better at the hands of this author.

Some interesting descriptions of Keogh appear in certain later "classic" examples of adult-oriented Custer fiction. This is especially the case in Ernest Haycox's 1943 masterpiece, *Bugles in the Afternoon*. The obvious reference to Luce's book and particularly the erroneous connection of Keogh, DeRudio, and Nowlan appears in a depiction which portrayed Keogh as:

... sharp-eyed, swarthy-skinned man with a pointed black imperial and indigo black mustache. It was Hines who described Keogh to Shafter. 'There's three soldiers of fortune in this outfit. Nowlan and DeRudio and Keogh have served in Europe. Nowlan is a fine one and DeRudio is all right when he don't get excited and start talkin' Eyetalian at us. This Keogh, now, is the hardest of the lot, a martinet when he's sober and one that will throw the back of his hand at a trooper when he feels like it.⁹

Luce seemed to have inspired other writers in addition to Haycox, as did Van De Water, since Fairfax Downey, in his 1948 novel *The Seventh's Staghound*, incorporated information from both these authors. Downey attributed Keogh as the source for the Seventh Cavalry's "Garry Owen" and mentioned his drinking problems, as seen in this telling depiction:

That march, its lively six-eight tempo ideal for cavalry, had been suggested by Captain Myles Keogh, one of the company commanders. Keogh, once a Papal Zouave and a veteran of hard fighting in Africa and our own war, had learned it in his native Ireland from his father, member of a Royal Irish Lancer regiment. On pay days the Lancers consorted at Owen's Garden, a tavern for which their song was named, to roar out its chorus over foaming tankards of ale. It was ironical that the Seventh's march, originally a drinking song, should have been introduced by Myles Keogh, himself the victim of a raging thirst. That officer drank up his pay as fast as it was doled out to him by his striker, to whom he has handed it over, since he could not trust himself not to spend every cent of it on whiskey. Change the words of Garryowen here and there, and it was just as appropriate for the Seventh's wild pay day sprees as for the Lancer's.¹⁰

Later in the story, as the Seventh attempts to rescue a white girl captured by the Indians, Custer confronts the chief, ordering that he be taken to the lodge where she is held:

Captain Keogh ran after them, making a protest.
'Sir,' he begged, 'let me take a squad into that lodge first and clear the place out. Might be an ambush.'
Keogh knew Indian trickery.... Keogh had seen more than a few skirmishes when attacking warriors had broken and galloped off in retreat when their chief fell. Likely enough this chief figured that the loss of their leader would have the same effect on the soldiers....
But Custer, brave to the point of rashness, ignored the precaution of his company commander.

Within fifteen minutes, as he emerges from the council lodge, Custer orders Keogh to take over. A flabbergasted Keogh complies, "knowing better than to oppose Old Curley twice."¹¹

Another noted attempt to fictionalize Custer came in Will Henry's (Henry Allen Wilson's) 1950 work, *No Survivors*. As the battle progresses, the main character makes his way to Company I's position, just in time to see Keogh's fall:

As I ran hunched and dodging to Keogh's position, I constantly had to leap the prostrate, frequently still struggling bodies of downed horses and troopers. Nobody

6. Frederic F. Van de Water, *Thunder Shield* (Indianapolis, IN: Bobbs-Merrill Co., 1933), 237-238.

7. *Ibid*, 340.

8. Frederic F. Van de Water, *Glory-Hunter: A Life of General Custer* (Indianapolis, IN: Bobbs-Merrill Co., 1934). This significant revisionist biography marked a turning point in Custer literature. Brian Dippie in his, *Custer's Last Stand: The Anatomy of an American Myth* (Missoula, MT: University of Montana Press, 1976), 69, has stated, "The success and immediate influence of *Glory-Hunter* has obscured the fact that Van de Water was not primarily a historian, but a novelist, and a popular one at that. Much of the impact of his biography can be traced to his skillful treatment of Custer's life as a story with a made-to-order plotline, a strong cast of characters and the single dominant theme expressed in the book's title."

9. Ernest Haycox, *Bugles in the Afternoon* (New York, NY: Grossett and Dunlap Pubs., 1943), 214-215.

10. Fairfax Downey, *The Seventh's Staghound* (New York, NY: Dodd, Mead and Co., 1948), 70-71

11. *Ibid*, 99-101.

12. Will Henry, *No Survivors* (New York, NY: Random House, 1950), 295.
13. Hoffman Birney, *The Dice of God* (New York, NY: Henry Holt and Co., 1956), 316.
14. *Ibid*, 342-343.
15. *Ibid*, 344.
16. Kenneth Shiflet, *The Convenient Coward* (Harrisburg, PA: Stackpole Co., 1961), 114.
17. *Ibid*, 209-210.
18. Thomas Berger, *Little Big Man* (New York, NY: Dial Press, 1964), 354.

was attending the wounded. Nobody could. Every hand that could hold a gun was holding, and every finger that could press a trigger, was pressing—hard.

'Keogh! Get your command back at once. Pull them in. Get those men on the other side of the gully back over here at once. Pull them in. Pull them in!'

'Who in God's name are you?' gasped Keogh, getting shot out of his saddle the minute he spoke, a Sioux slug low through both lungs. I pulled him back of a dead horse and flopped on my belly beside him as I answered.

'Runner, from Reno. He and Benteen are coming. But so are a thousand Sioux. Right up that gully in your center. I could see them pouring into the lower end of it from up there where I just came from. If you don't get those men out of there right—' But Captain Myles Keogh wasn't listening to me. He wasn't listening to anybody. He was bleeding to death.[12]

If "names are changed to protect the innocent," or guilty, such is the case with Hoffman Birney's 1956 work, *The Dice of God* which would be the basis for the movie *The Glory Guys*. Here the Custer character is named General Tuthill and the fictionalized hero named Demas. In a touching scene, the hero receives a religious medal from an Irish trooper, Mike McKeown:

'You're not a Cath'lic, Demas, and it'll mean nothing to you; but wear it for luck and because Mike McKeown asked you to. I've never had it off my neck since it was hung there by a cardinal of the Church after the Holy Father himself had blessed it. It carries the image or the picture or whatever you'd call it of Saint Sebastian, Patron saint of soldiers. He died a martyr—shot to death with arrows. The heathen you'll be fightin' will be usin' arrows, too. Will you wear it, Demas?' 'I will, Mike, and thank you.'[13]

Mike McKeown easily can be seen as an indirect figure for Keogh since one of the many stories of Keogh was his wearing of a religious medal supposedly given to him by the Pope. In the final chapter of the novel, the author gives the names of the company commanders and Company I is under a Captain Chase. In the battle, he ably sizes up the desperate situation, realizing "instantly that it would be suicidal for his thirty-six men to charge five or six hundred Indians, and he shouted the command to fight on foot."[14] Birney went on to describe Company I's demise:

One moment there had been twenty-six or -seven men and their officers, Captain Chase and Lieutenant Berthold, who stood bravely against the charge—then there were perhaps ten scattered troopers who smashed at the yelling Indians with their clubbed rifles. Chase was ridden down by a Sioux on a claybank pony, then brained by a second rider.[15]

Even unmentioned, Keogh emerges as a true hero in the "Last Stand".

Another interesting novel, *The Convenient Coward*, from 1961, deals with one more controversial character in the Little Big Horn story, Marcus Reno. On the steamer *Far West*, Tom Custer, Calhoun, and Keogh are playing cards when Keogh invites Reno to join their game. The ominous feelings of what is to happen even makes Keogh reflect:

They played one or two hands and Myles Keogh finished his drink, throwing out a card with his other hand. 'Wild Eye's ready,' he laughed, referring to his company. The ends of his long mustache moved with his unusually red lips, or which only looked unusually red against the dark beard and mustache.

They finished the round and Keogh eyed his glass seriously.

'I'm going to have Garland make out a will for me,' he said, closing slender fingers that could have been a musician's around the glass.[16]

Later in the battle, Keogh is "riding his lines on the claybank" as the Indians move closer:

Myles Keogh looked down at his own two companies. The Uncpapas and Minneconjous and Blackfeet were shooting and moving up toward them. He looked back toward the other end of the ridge.

'All right, me bucko. It's a go for you,' he said. 'Don't stop for anything, not even for one of your men if he's hit. These Reds are a fair plague around us and only a 'swift ride and a ruthless heart will get you through.'

Porter saluted and trotted back along the line and got

his men mounted. They waved to Keogh as they started down the back slopes of the hogback ridge. McIlhargey watched them until they disappeared below the crest of the ridge.[17]

Again the obvious bravery of Keogh is noted by the novelist's pen and, once more, Van De Water's influence is in evidence.

Next, *Little Big Man*, Thomas Berger's biting 1964 satire on the myths of the Old West, provided a familiar description of Keogh. In a conversation with the novel's narrator, Jack Crabbe, a certain Sergeant Botts claimed that Benteen and Keogh were the only two officers he had any use for, although, "In the case of the latter, Botts never cared for the Catholic religion, he let on, and in addition Keogh was something of a drunk, although he was naturally brave rather than drinking to get his courage up as Major Reno."[18] Crabbe himself described Keogh as a man with a "big black mustache and pointy underlip beard . . . ." According to Crabbe, "Keogh was an Irishman that had served in the personal guard of the Pope in Rome before coming to the U.S.A." Needing a piece of writing paper, Crabbe spoke to Keogh who replied to the request:

> 'Ah sure . . . go and tell Finnegan to give you a sheet from my writing case.'
>
> Finnegan was his striker, who according to Botts kept all of Keogh's money when he was at Fort Lincoln, lest the Captain drink himself to death on it. 'Finnegan's more like his guardian than striker,' Botts said.
>
> I thanked him and started away, when Keogh put an odd question.
>
> 'Would you be writing your will?' he says.
>
> 'How'd you know that?'
>
> He gave a merry laugh, which was odd considering what he had said then: 'I made my own last night. But that was after Tom Custer and Calhoun took me at poker, so I don't have much to leave behind.'
>
> 'Why then did you make it?' I asked humorously . . . .
>
> 'For the sheer hell of it,' says Captain Keogh, and his eyes was bright even in the dusk.[19]

This exchange, which again drew upon Van De Water as well as Frederick Whittaker, continued to paint Keogh as "the devil-may-care type . . . ."[20] Crabbe also recounted that, "The Sioux later claimed that a whole platoon down on Keogh's and Calhoun's front committed suicide; I never saw such and I don't believe it happened."[21]

Another popular work which related accounts concerning Keogh was Mari Sandoz' 1966 *The Battle of the Little Big Horn*. While supposedly written as history, the style, content, and lack of documentation actually places this book into the category of an historical novel.[22] She, too, relates the account of Tom Custer, Calhoun, and Keogh passing time at poker on the *Far West*. Her "Irish soldier of fortune" appears infrequently throughout the rest of the book until the description of the final engagement. Here she states, "Custer had the soldiers of fortune: the swaggering Irishman, Miles [sic] Keogh, apparently from the French Foreign Legion and the Papal Guard; Cooke of the 'Queen's Own' of Canada; and the cripple-armed Smith of the Gray Horse Troop."[23] This reference is more fancy than fact since Keogh was not in the Foreign Legion while DeRudio and Nowlan were the other individuals in the Seventh who may have qualified as soldiers of fortune, not Cooke or Smith.[24] In describing the field after the battle, Sandoz once more launches off into a flight of make-believe:

> . . . the Custer brother-in-law, Calhoun and Custer's favorite, Keogh, both lay dead on the far rise. Keogh, who had come out from the Foreign Legion and the Papal Guard to a ridge in Sioux country, lost one of his side whiskers there, stripped off as an unusual scalp.[25]

Sandoz' last detail confused Keogh with Cooke.[26]

While Sandoz' text was well known, Lewis Patten's *Red Sabbath* remains relatively obscure. Nonetheless, the novel has an interesting twist in that Keogh is not mentioned, but his headgear is, as indicated by the story's hero:

> I glanced around. We were backing out of the ravine, with a momentary advantage because we were higher than the Sioux attacking us. Down in the bottom of the

THE LEGEND CONTINUES

19. Berger, *Little Big Man*, 360-361.
20. Van de Water, *Glory Hunter*, 152.
21. Berger, *Little Big Man*, 387.
22. Mari Sandoz, *The Battle of the Little Bighorn* (Philadelphia, PA: J. B. Lippincott Co., 1966). In Helen's Stanfer's biography, *Mari Sandoz: Story Catcher of the Plains* (Lincoln, NE: University of Nebraska Press, 1982), 260-261, the author states that *The Battle of the Little Bighorn*, Sandoz' last major work, was well-received, "Prepublication comments by readers asked to evaluate the book were jubilant; 'it read like a dream,' with the readability and suspense of a novel," and yet, "some critics objected to what they saw as an undue emphasis on scanty evidence and to her use of fictional techniques such as invented dialogue."
23. Sandoz, *Little Bighorn*, 106.
24. Luce, *Keogh, Comanche and Custer*, 35 mentioned that Keogh, Nowlan, and DeRudio were identified as the Seventh's soldiers of fortune.
25. Sandoz, *Little Bighorn*, 125.
26. The obvious reference is to Lieutenant William Cooke, not Keogh. In Thomas B. Marquis', *A Warrior Who Fought Custer* (Minneapolis, MN: Midwest Co., 1931), 240, the author related Wooden Leg's account as follows:

> I took one scalp. As I went walking and leading my horse among the dead I observed one face that interested me. The dead man had a long beard growing from both sides of his face and extending several inches below the chin. He had also a full mustache. All of the beard hair was of light color, as I recall it. . . I think the dead man may have been thirty or more years old. 'Here is a new kind of scalp,' I said to a companion. I skinned one side of the face and half of the chin, so as to keep the long beard and get on the part removed.

Marquis identifies this soldier as Lieutenant Cook [sic]. This is corroborated in testimony given by Luther Hare and Charles DeRudio during interviews with Walter Camp. See Hammer, *Custer in '76*, 68 and 87. Glaring errors such as these reflect the faulty research Sandoz employed throughout this book.

27. Lewis B. Patten, *The Red Sabbath* (Garden City, NY: Doubleday and Co., 1968), 98.
28. Steven Utley and Howard Waldrop, "Custer's Last Jump," in Terry Carr, ed., *Universe 6* (Garden City, NY: Doubleday and Co., 1976), 49.
29. *Ibid*, 60.
30. *Ibid*, 63.
31. *Ibid*, 69.
32. *Ibid*, 73.
33. *Ibid*, 75.
34. Douglas C. Jones, *The Court-Martial of George Armstrong Custer* (New York, NY: Charles Scribner's Sons, 1976), 278.
35. Charles K. Mills, *A Mighty Afternoon: A Novel of the Battle of the Little Big Horn* (Garden City, NY: Doubleday and Co., 1980), 8-9.

> ravine, among the milling horde of Indian bucks, I caught a glimpse of a light-colored campaign hat that I instantly recognized. It had belonged to Captain Keogh, the wild Irishman, the soldier of fortune who had once been a Papal zouave.
>
> I reached out and touched Lieutenant Payne's arm. I pointed at the Indian wearing the hat.
>
> Payne glanced at him, then back at me. His teeth were white as he yelled, 'Keogh could have lost his hat! Reno lost his and so did Weir!'[27]

This would be an ominous sign of the disaster which had befallen Custer and his command.

One of the more imaginative approaches to Little Big Horn literature, a short story entitled "Custer's Last Jump," was written as if taken from a series of actual documents pieced together in order to offer an "alternative time-stream in which George Armstrong Custer lost his final battle to the Plains Indians' Air Force-six fighter planes expertly piloted by such warriors as Crazy Horse and Black Man's Hand."[28]

The premise is that aviation had been discovered before the Civil War, and that the battle was a conflict waged in the air. Major John S. Moseby of the Confederate Air Force forms his raiders, and trains Crazy Horse to fly an airplane. The warrior becomes an able pilot who then fights against the Union. The story moves on the Custer's own Civil War experience as a military aviator. He becomes acquainted with Benteen who "would remain commander of the 505th (Balloon Infantry) until his capture at the Battle of Montgomery in 1866. While he was a prisoner of war, his command was given to another, later to figure in the Western Campaign, Lieutenant Colonel Myles W. Keogh."[29] After the war, "Lieutenant Colonel Keogh, acting commander of the 505th for the last twenty-one months, but who had never been on jump status, was appointed by Custer as commander of K Company, 7th Cavalry."[30] By 1876, the Seventh Cavalry, "under Keogh and Major Marcus Reno," set out on a campaign against Crazy Horse and Sitting Bull. Custer, aboard his airship, *Benjamin Franklin*, one of eight crafts in the 505th Balloon Infantry, is overhead while below "his horse soldiers rode behind the very capable Captain (Brevet Lieutenant Colonel) Myles Keogh."[31] Custer planned to have Keogh strike the enemy from the south, Reno to the east, with himself and the 505th coming from the north.[32] The battle raged as the Indians in their airplanes outmaneuvered the airships. Keogh's fate, as well as Custer's, was sealed as related in detail:

> The hundred-odd parachute infantrymen who made good their escape from the airship were scattered over three square miles. The ravines and gullies cutting up the hills around the village quickly filled with mounted Indians who rode through unimpeded by the random fire of disorganized balloon infantrymen. They swept them up, on the way to Keogh. Keogh, unaware of the number of Indians and the rout of Reno's command, got as far as the north bank of the river before he was ground to pieces between two masses of hostiles. Of Keogh's command, less than a dozen escaped the slaughter. The actual battle lasted about thirty minutes. . . .
>
> Some of the men were not found for another two days, Terry and his men scoured the ravines and valleys. Custer himself was about four miles from the site of Keogh's annihilation: the Boy General appears to have been hit by a piece of exploding rocket shrapnel and may have been dead before he reached the ground. His body escaped the mutilation that befell most of Keogh's command, possibly because of his distance from camp.[33]

While this intriguing story obviously manipulates history, it remains significant by elevating Keogh to a central figure in the drama.

By way of contrast, another "what-if" tale, *The Court Martial of George Armstrong Custer*, by Douglas Jones, speaks little of Keogh. Instead, the book proposes that Yellow Hair alone survived the Little Big Horn. He returns only to face charges. Now mad, he breaks down before Libbie, seeing . . . Myles Keogh on the battle ridge, that's it, dear Myles, face the east, face them as they come from the draw and volley them."[34]

Charles Mills' *A Mighty Afternoon* gives more play to the character, "Myles Keough." For him, the "soldier of fortune" of "Wild I" Company was a "tall, slender, curly-haired thirty-four-year-old with dark snapping eyes, a Vandyke beard, and clipped mustache."[35] In the early chapters of the book, Myles is usually in conversation with fellow officers, including Benteen and Godfrey. In one telling exchange, he seems to sense the disaster that awaits the command:

> Benteen and Keough skylarked-that is, drank coffee, outset by Keough's former opponent in the Italian Civil War, DeRudio, and later by the roly-poly commander of B Company, Captain Tom McDougall. Flat-faced Captain French of M Company joined them briefly for a discussion of tactics.
>
> 'All this lines and angles stuff is nonsense to me,' he declared in his gin-husky voice, his black eyes glittering in the light of the small coffee-pot fire. 'Ask me, there's too many Napoleons around once the shooting starts. When I was in the 10th During the war, it seemed we had more people running outside the formation telling us to keep dressed right than were actually in the ranks doing the job.'
>
> 'You can't complain about that in the 7th,' Keough observed.
>
> French nodded. 'GAC's a man after my own heart. None of your senseless orders. Just "Follow me, men."'
>
> Benteen spoke up. 'I always find it better to give suggestions rather than orders. After all, most grown men don't have to be told how to fight.'
>
> 'Exactly,' French said, a little unclearly. 'There's only one rule in fighting—That's the old rule of Donnybrook Fair: "If you see a head, hit it"—simple.'
>
> DeRudio was a little dubious. 'East would help to know where we go and why.'
>
> 'What's wrong with: "There's the enemy"?' French demanded.
>
> 'It seems to me I've heard that expression before,' McDougall put in.
>
> 'Balaclava,' Keough supplied, 'the Charge of the Light Brigade.'
>
> 'Well, we don't have to worry about charging cannon where we're going,' Benteen decided. 'It'll be mostly trot, trot, trot, and once in a while shoot at a feather sticking up behind a rock.'
>
> 'These Indians are poor shots,' French declared.
>
> 'Don't you believe it,' Benteen told him.[36]

Later, at the battle, Keough receives orders to command both his own Company I and Calhoun's Company L, and move north to the ridge while Custer leads the other three companies to the ford. At the ford, Custer is shot. The command attempts to regroup, with devastating results. Mills then depicts Keough's unflinching bravery under fire:

> Myles Keough was forced to halt a second time. Jim Calhoun's company was deployed and their bay horses suddenly bolted east toward the broken ground behind the ridge. Indians scattered as Keough [sic] galloped back and along the ridge accompanied by Sergeant Varden and Trumpeter Patton. The three men saw the reason for the stampede at once.
>
> L Company's horse holders looked like porcupines as they lay lifeless on the reverse slope of the hill Calhoun was trying to hold. The big impassive blond brother-in-law of Custer was hatless. He was bent over one-eyed J. J. Crittenden, who crouched awkwardly, an Indian arrow stuck in his back. Crittenden was trying to stand and Calhoun was holding him down. Calhoun looked up as Keough and party jolted to a halt beside him.
>
> 'Our ammunition's gone,' he said coolly.
>
> Keough turned to Patton.
>
> 'Sound Recall,' he told the trumpeter as he surveyed his own company under Lieutenant Porter making slow but steady progress north—away from Calhoun.
>
> 'Go on,' Calhoun told the Irishman calmly. 'We'll buy some time for you.'
>
> Keough's eyes flashed. 'We'll stick together,' he said incisively.[37]

Refusing to abandon his comrades to make good the escape of his own men, Keough's and Company I's final moments are vividly presented:

> Captain Myles Keough saw the sudden mass move and stopped his own I Company on its way to help L Company.
>
> 'This way!' he called, pointing. I Company turned as one and began to jog forward. The led horses and their holders were unable to keep up. To their right, the east, Indians swarmed up out of the hollows and charged. They drove in between I Company and its lead horses east toward the badlands.
>
> Keough halted I Company.
>
> 'Form a hollow square!' lanky Sergeant Varden shouted above the din.

36. Mills, *A Mighty Afternoon*, 35.
37. Ibid, 115.

MYLES KEOGH

38. Mills, *A Mighty Afternoon*, 120-121.
39. *Ibid*, 178.
40. Jonathan Scofield, *The Frontier War* (New York, NY: Dell Publishing, 1981), 285.
41. George Macdonald Fraser, *Flashman and the Redskins* (New York, NY: Alfred A. Knopf, 1982), 349.
42. *Ibid*, 351.

Keough's mount stumbled and the Irishman howled in pain as an Indian bullet broke his leg and plowed on through into his horse's side.

Trumpeter Patton grabbed his company commander by the nape of the neck and held him half suspended in air until two troopers came to his assistance. It was the last thing he ever did. As he released Keough to the care of two privates, he pitched forward, a Sioux arrow in his back.

The Indians rode over I Company.[38]

After the engagement, Keough's body is found in the midst of his men:

Captain Weir, working a little ahead of Edgerly and on the east slope of the steep ridge, found I Company, he sent a galloper after Benteen.

When the senior captain appeared in response to the summons, Weir pointed at a cluster of white and partially blackened bodies, mutilated almost beyond recognition.

'Myles Keough,' he reported succinctly. 'You can tell by the medal around his neck. One of my boys recognized the trumpeter lying across him. Sergeant Varden's here too. And Bustard. Looks like they were ambushed in a group.'

Benteen was testy as he took the 'Pro Petri Sede' medal Weir had secured from Keough's mutilated body.[39]

Mills' writing bespeaks of fairly extensive research, not only in Luce, but of other historical sources too. Indeed, his depiction of Custer's early death follows Miller and similar narratives which reach that conclusion. Consequently, the Irish "soldier of fortune" again occupies a lead part in the battle while Custer is of somewhat secondary importance to the ultimate fate of his command.

Conversely, Jonathan Scofield's *The Frontier War*, published in 1981, mentioned Keogh only in passing, lumping him together with Cooke and Reno as Custer gives his orders subsequent to the attack on the village.[40] The next year, George MacDonald Fraser's *Flashman and the Redskins* found more space for Keogh. In this engaging fictional portrait, the seventh volume of the memoirs of Sir Henry Flashman, Keogh appears shortly after the main character arrives at Fort Lincoln. Flashman referred to Keogh as "a jolly black Irishman who had family connections with the British Army and that didn't suit Custer either."[41]

A social gathering at the home of the Custers provided another opportunity for the pair to be in contact with each other. Flashman remembered Keogh at the occasion:

There were charades and games every evening, and much singing round the piano—I can still see it so plain still; little Reed, who was Custer's nephew, turning the sheets for Libby [sic], and Terry with his eyes shut, rendering 'My Old Kentucky Home' and 'My love is like a red, red rose' in fine tenor, and Custer bright-eyed as he leaned on a chair, smiling fondly at Libby [sic], and her quick loving glance at him from the music, and Keogh quite overcome with sentiment and drink muttering 'Oh Jayzus, Ginneral, it's a darlin' gift of song, a darlin' gift,' and the young folk holding hands while the firelight flickered on the wooden walls and the buffalo head over the mantel.[42]

Departing from this sentimental scene, Flashman later would come to a very different setting, as he finds himself at the battle. During the clash he makes his way to Keogh's position. Here, he tumbles out of his saddle, and into Keogh's arms:

'Where's the General?' he yelled, and I could only shake my head and point dumbly towards the carnage behind me—but it wasn't visible, and I saw that somehow I'd ridden over the crest, on the far side of the river, and the crest itself was alive with Indians firing at us, rushing closer and firing again. Keogh yelled above the din:

'Sergeant Butler!' A ragged blue figure was beside him, gold chevrons smeared with blood and dust. 'Ride out!' See if you can find Major Reno! Tell him we're hemmed in and the General's dead!'

He shoved hard at Butler, who turned and slapped the neck of a bay horse that was lying among the troopers; it came up, whinnying, at his touch, and as Butler grabbed the reins he came face to face with me, and he must have seen me at Fort Lincoln, he said:

> 'Allo there Colonel! Long way from 'Orse Guards, ain't we, though?' Then he was up and away, head down, going hell for leather at the advancing Sioux, and thinks I, by God, it's that or nothing, and scrambled on my own beast as the red tide flooded in amongst us.[43]

Flashman thereby eludes death, but Keogh stays behind to perish with his command. Once more, he has outlasted his leader, and goes down fighting as a hero.

The commander of Company I continues to appear in more recent paperback novels, including E. J. Hunter's *White Squaw, Horn of Plenty*. Here, Keogh is mentioned as being placed in charge of one of the two battalions under Custer, the other being led by Captain Yates.[44] Still more recently, Jim Miller's *That Damn Single Shot* resurrects the misspelling of the name as "Keough", of "Wild I" Company.[45]

More recently, in *Broken Eagle*, by Chad Oliver, the main character, Singletary (a fictional Benteen), finds Keogh's body:

> There were only two corpses that did not seem to have been molested. One belonged to Myles Keogh. Myles still had his Italian Catholic Medal around his neck. He must have had something going for him that day, Singletary thought. Keogh's wounded horse, Comanche, was the only living creature left on the battlefield.
>
> The other unmutilated body was that of George Armstrong Custer.[46]

In this instance it seems Luce had triumphed in keeping Keogh, Comanche, and Custer together in death, even as in life.

Finally, through "time travel" Keogh, Custer, and the Seventh all can be brought back to life as in the 1990 novel, *Remember the Little Big Horn*. Although not a featured character in the story, the Irish Captain once again appears as an heroic figure during the last stand. The authors speak of his steadfastness in the face of death:

> Directly to the east, Myles Keogh still sat on his horse. He was trying to rally his rapidly shrinking command. He shouted orders, pointed at the enemy, and tried to establish fields of fire, but the command was disintegrating too quickly...
>
> 'Come boys,' yelled Keogh. 'Hold on. Make your shots count.'
>
> There was a sudden stinging at his knee. Pain flashed up his leg. For an instant he thought he was going to be sick. Instead, he clamped his teeth.
>
> Leaning forward, he forced his horse, Comanche to kneel. The animal followed Keogh's instructions and the officer slipped from the saddle. Wrapping the reins around his hand, he sat on the ground, still shouting at his men, trying to get them to fight harder.
>
> A second round caught him in the chest. He grunted and said quietly, 'Oh.' slowly he fell back, still holding onto the reins of his horse.[47]

Here again, Comanche and Keogh make their "last stand" in adult fiction together but what of books written for the juvenile audience?

Here too, Myles Keogh became a familiar figure, mirroring much of what had appeared in works for older readers. As indicated by Elizabeth Lawrence in *His Very Silence Speaks*, the youth-oriented writings, particularly about the horse Comanche, even became a source for some non-fiction accounts![48] Alice Gall and Fleming Crew's short story, "Comanche", is one such example. Here the horse is depicted as being "ridden by Captain Miles Keough [sic], whose favorite mount he was."[49]

Still, the classic case remains David Appel's sentimental *Comanche*. Told from the point of view of the horse, the novel incorporated not only most of the Comanche lore, but also almost all the Keogh legends. For example, Appel ascribes the introduction of "Garry Owen" to "...Myles Keogh, who had learned the song in his native Ireland and suggested that it be adopted by the Regiment."[50] As for Keogh himself, Comanche views his master as:

> ...a tall, broad-shouldered man with thickly curling black hair. His eyes were almost the exact color of his blue uniform and they were merry Irish eyes, touched with a smile. He had incredibly long lashes and heavy

43. Fraser, *Flashman*, 413.
44. E. J. Hunter, *White Squaw #8: Horn of Plenty* (New York, NY: Kensington Publishing Co., 1985), 184.
45. Jim Miller, *That Damn Single Shot* (New York, NY: Ballantine Books, 1988), 160.
46. Chad Oliver, *Broken Eagle* (New York, NY: Bantam Books, 1989), 279.
47. Kevin Randle and Robert Cornett, *Remember the Little Bighorn!* (New York, NY: Charter Books, 1990), 169.
48. Lawrence, *His Very Silence Speaks*, 229 states, "Because these books intended for young readers have in effect transcended their intended genre to find wide acceptance as general works in their field consulted by adults, they cannot be dismissed as worthy of only slight attention."
49. Alice Gall and Fleming Crew, "Comanche," from *Each in His Way* (Oxford: Oxford University Press, Inc., 1937) and reprinted in Perpetua, Synon, and Rankin, eds., *These Are Our Freedoms*, 174. This book was used as a reader in Catholic parochial schools. Alice Gall
50. David Appel, *Comanche: The Story of America's Most Heroic Horse* (Cleveland, OH: World Publishing Co., 1951), 21.

MYLES KEOGH

51. Appel, *Comanche*, 110.
52. Ibid., 112-113
53. Ibid., 130.
54. Ibid., 154.
55. Ibid., 148.
56. Ibid., 149.
57. Ibid., 150.
58. Hayes-McCoy states in his, *Myles Walter Keogh*, 35 that, "Although Keogh's troop was present at the Washita, he himself was not there. He accompanied the expedition to Camp Supply near the border of the Indian Territory (now the State of Oklahoma) but, still acting in his capacity of staff officer, returned with Sully to Fort Harker when Custer began his search for the winter villages."

brows, but, unlike the other men in the Regiment, he was smooth-shaven.[51]

Because of Keogh's love for Comanche the bond between the two grows beyond a mere horse and master relationship. In a conversation with a sergeant about his mount, Keogh makes this clear:

> 'That's right,' Keough said. 'I don't know why, but I've taken a liking to that horse. Lord knows he's as ugly as the Pooka.'
> 'Pooka, sir?'
> Then, as he often did for his own amusement, Keogh began to speak in his native dialect. 'Phwat's a Pooka?' It's not easy to describe. It's a horse but it isn't a horse atall, atall. No mortial horse 'ud behave like the Pooka nor throt so far without gettin' tired. Faith, I dunno, but since you've asked me, I'll say that the Pooka is the avil sperit in the shape of a horse. Owld Beelzebub hisself.'
> 'I see,' said the Sergeant, although I could tell from the expression on his weatherbeaten face that he had hardly understood a word the Lieutenant said. "Is the Lieutenant thinking of naming the horse Pooka?"
> 'No, Sergeant,' Keogh said, thoughtfully. 'No, because I don't think he has a mean streak in him. And I'm superstitious. I had a horse named Satan once, a big black gelding, and he was shot under me while I was with the Papal Guards in Italy. Like Jeithe I didn't leap off quickly enough and was pinned under the horse's body for some time. Not a pleasant experience during a battle.'
> 'No, sir,' Kincaid said. 'That was before the Lieutenant was given a commission by our government, wasn't it?'
> Keogh nodded. 'And before Appomattox, I had another horse killed under me. He was a strawberry roan named Red Devil. I was a major then, my brevet rank, as you know, and I had to take a horse from one of my men. I didn't like to do that, but the orders came to charge and I had to lead my troop against the Rebs.'
> 'The Lieutenant forgets, sir,' Kincaid said, smiling, 'that I was with him in that battle.'[52]

Later in the book, Comanche confesses; "I loved Myles Keogh, I worshiped him."[53] They served together in the Fourth Cavalry and later Keogh asks for transfer to the Seventh. Keogh soon begins to question Custer's leadership, as well as his favoritism, and admits: "I detest officers who put their personal desire for prestige above their regard for the safety of their men."[54] Still, his dedication to duty is obvious as is expressed in a moment of reflection with Comanche:

> 'While I was fighting with the Papal Zouaves, Lord Alfred Tennyson published a poem which my sister sent me. It is called "The Charge of the Light Brigade," and was based on a news dispatch describing the death charge of six hundred men in the Crimea, almost exactly fourteen years ago.'[55]

After relating the verses of the poem, Comanche observes that his master was, " . . . not a young man in his twenties as I had always thought. His face was unlined and his Irish eyes were young and gay, but now I could sense his maturity."[56] Keogh describes his father—the one who taught him "Garryowen"—as, "A member of the Royal Irish Lancers, he was, and on payday the Lancers would gather at a tavern, Owen's Garden, to change their money into ale as fast as they could."[57] The author also has Keogh participate in the 1868 attack on Black Kettle's village, though in actuality he was not present.[58]

One humorous aside by the horse is his observation that:

> . . . to Custer's disgust, whenever Keogh was forced on social occasions to converse with pompous southern gentlemen, he invariably spoke with a broad brogue. Because I alone could understand him when he spoke in various languages he had at his command, I alone realized that my Captain was the most educated officer in the Regiment.
> It was all I could do to keep from laughing when he pretended to be as illiterate as our young Irish trumpeter whom no one could understand unless he spoke through his cornet. I was not the only one who felt like laughing when Keogh lapsed into a brogue with a 'Bejabers, yer Honor.'

Captains Nowlan and DeRudio, former Papal Zouave

officers themselves, often could not suppress smiles. And handsome Captain Benteen of H Troop, although a southerner himself, made no attempt to disguise his amusement. In fact, Keogh's brogue often set him off in the local dialect, and from then on all attempts at dignified social discourse were abandoned.

By the end of our tour duty in the south, the officers and troopers were definitely divided into two groups; they were Benteen men or they were Custer men, and, as Keogh put it, 'niver the twain shall meet.' Needless to say, Keogh and his best friend, Henry Nowlan, were Benteen men.[59]

Here the Keogh, DeRudio, and Nowlan connection, as reported by Luce, appears once again. Comanche even becomes the "confidant" of his master as the horse reflects:

'During these walks, trot and canters, my Captain talked to me as though I were the American representative of his family in Ireland. After long periods of inaction, he would grow homesick and I often wondered why he did not give up his commission and return to his native land.

The answer was, I learned eventually, that the girl he adored died on the eve of their wedding. He stayed in Ireland only long enough to attend her funeral, then left never to return.

The other bachelor officers in the Regiment were always falling in love, and most of them were either married or engaged when we started off for the march to the Yellowstone. So Myles Keogh, by his very devotion to the memory of his "Colleen," was set apart from them, just as I had always been set apart from other horses. He seemed to know that he was my only friend and made up for it in every way that he could.'[60]

The story moves quickly to the Little Big Horn in which Comanche and his hero are brave to the end:

'My Captain did not dismount. If I could have talked I would have begged him to shoot me and use my body as a shield. I knew that within an hour we would all be dead—officers, troopers and horses, and I wanted to die first. I did not want to live one single second after my Captain's brave heart stopped beating.'[61]

As the fight raged, Comanche valiantly tried to protect "his Captain:"

'I felt the sting of a bullet as it pierced my side. At almost the same moment my Captain slid from the saddle and I saw that his leg was buckled under him. The same bullet had broken a bone of his before it went on to plow through my flank. Although bleeding badly, I got down on my knees as we had been trained to do, placing my body between him and the mad horde. He smiled at me to show that he understood.'[62]

Confronting the pair, was Comanche's old Indian nemesis, Yellow Bull, who had taken the horse from his first master, White Bull, only to mistreat him:

'Many of the officers had ceased firing their carbines, saving their bullets for just such Indians who dared to come within killing range. But, although my poor wounded Captain fired until the firing pin jammed, none of his shots touched Yellow Bull. He, like Yellow Hair, our chief, had been born lucky. He rode straight for us, firing steadily. One of his shots struck me on the flank and another crashed into my shoulder, but I scarcely felt them.

Nothing mattered now except that my Captain was no longer smiling. He was dead.'[63]

Avenging Keogh's death, Comanche then tramples the hated Indian. The horse is rescued later, comforted in the knowledge that, "my Captain had not been scalped or mutilated in any way."[64] While the book truly amplifies the Comanche legend, Keogh's role is assured as well. Appel's novel became the basis for Walt Disney's movie, *Tonka*, spawning two children's books based on the film and, a 1976 novelization of the screenplay by Kathleen Daly.[65]

Another well known children's work which has helped forge the Keogh legend is Quentin Reynold's *Custer's Last Stand*, published in 1951. Just before the battle, Custer gives Comanche to Keogh because he already had Dandy and Vic and "Keogh's favorite mount had hurt his leg and was hobbling around the stockade." When Keogh comments that Comanche is "the strongest horse I ever

THE LEGEND CONTINUES

59. Appel, *Comanche*, 165-166.
60. Ibid., 171.
61. Ibid., 215.
62. Ibid., 217.
63. Ibid., 217.
64. Ibid., 219.
65. *Walt Disney's Tonka* (New York, NY: Dell Publishing Co., 1958); Elizabeth Beecher, adapter, *Walt Disney's Tonka* (New York, NY: Golden Press, 1959); Kathleen N. Daly, *Tonka* (New York, NY: Pyramid Books, 1976).

66. Quinton Reynolds, *Custer's Last Stand* (New York, NY: Random House, 1951), 165.
67. Loring MacKaye, *The Great Scoop* (New York, NY: Thomas Nelson & Sons, 1956), 88.
68. *Ibid.*, 94.
69. Margaret Leighton, *Comanche of the Seventh* (New York, NY: Ariel Books, 1957), 43.

rode," Custer responds laughingly, "he might outlast all of us."66 And he did.

A slightly different approach to Little Big Horn fiction came in *The Great Scoop* by Loring MacKaye. Published in 1956, its hero, Jon Olson, is a young apprentice for the Bismarck *Tribune* during the exciting summer of 1876. He befriends a girl whose father is a sergeant in Company I. In meeting Keogh for the first time, the boy learns much about the Captain:

'And I'm Irish, and so is Lieutenant de Rudio [sic] and heaven only knows what else we are, except that we're all Americans and proud of it. What do you say, Olson?'

'That's right, sir,' answered Jon, firmly.

'So you're a newspaperman, eh? Pretty young for that, but we all start young, don't we? I wasn't much older than you when I left Ireland to fight for the French in North Africa and only a little older when I was fighting for the Pope in the Papal Zouaves. Then a lot of us came over to fight for the Union in the Civil War. That was a real shindig. But of course, you wouldn't know much about that.'67

Later, when Jon hears "Garry Owen," the girl explains to him that:

'Captain Keogh brought it over from Ireland. Daddy says it was the drinking song of the Fifth Royal Irish Lancers when Captain Keogh's father was an officer in the regiment.'68

Another significant contribution to the Comanche story is Margaret Leighton's *Comanche of the Seventh*. While not as sentimental as Appel's novel, the author definitely sees both the horse and his master in heroic terms. Keogh is described by Tom Custer this way:

'But I'll say this for our wild Irishman. He may not know how to hold on to his money, but he does know horseflesh. He can always seem to get everything there is from his mounts.'69

Then Leighton summarizes Keogh's background furthering the legends of past authors:

Myles Keogh had seen more of the world and of adventures at twenty-eight than most men twice his age. He was born in Ireland, son of an officer in the Fifth Royal Irish Lancers. His mother, a cultured woman who had been a belle in her youth, had hoped for a different career for her son. She had sent him to good schools and later to Dublin University.

After two years there he grew bored and restless. 'I know enough Latin to know that Myles means "soldier," and it's a soldier I will be.'

He scanned the world for excitement and learned that the French Army was fighting against wild Arab tribesmen in North Africa. Together with several friends he embarked for Algeria . . .

He might have stayed in Algeria indefinitely if a call had not come to him from another part of the world. Trouble had begun in Italy and the Pope sent out an appeal for Catholic youth to come to his aid. With four young comrades—Nowlan, DeRudio, O'Keefe and Coppinger—Keogh joined the papal forces and they were all commissioned in the Battalion of St. Patrick in the summer of 1860 . . . .

For his exceptional services and gallantry in action, Myles Keogh was awarded the medal, 'Pro Petri Sede,' by the Pope himself.

After only a few weeks of combat the papal army was defeated. Keogh and some of his comrades made their way to Rome after the surrender and were reorganized into a small force of papal guards, and in this Keogh, DeRudio and Nowlan were commissioned.

Their duties were to act as police about the Vatican and take part in ceremonies and receptions. Two years of this quiet life in Vatican City were enough, however, for the 'three musketeers.' 'There's a war begun in America, a war between the northern and southern states,' Keogh said. 'That's the place for us.'

Soldiers of fortune once again, they resigned their Vatican commissions and sailed for America to join the fighting. It was not difficult for officers with combat experience to find places in the hard-pressed Union Army. Within two months Keogh was mentioned in dispatches for 'prompt, officer-like behavior in the hottest of the fighting and exposed to enemy fire . . . .'

By the war's end, Keogh had fought in a hundred battles including Antietam and Gettysburg and emerged without a wound. He was mustered out of the voluntary service but promptly rejoined the regular army. On the western plains the army was fighting tribesmen as fierce and wild as the Arabs of Algeria, and where there was fighting, Myles Keogh must go.[70]

As related by Leighton, the adventures of Keogh and Comanche are lifted from other sources, including incidents from Mrs. Custer's books.[71] Obviously, the endurance of Comanche is unquestioned, as found in this interchange between Keogh and Custer:

> 'He's almost a match for my Dandy here. I wonder what the record is for the useful life of a cavalry horse? If I hadn't forsworn gambling I'd like to make a bet that my Dandy will outlast your Comanche.'
> 'Or I might almost bet that both of them will outlast the two of us,' Keogh suggested, with his easy laugh . . . .
> A small cloud had covered the brilliance of the sun and Keogh felt himself shiver with a sudden sense of cold. An old Irish superstition remembered from his childhood swept across his mind. 'Someone's just been walking over my grave,' he found himself thinking.[72]

While the author's sentiments are not very open to Indian sensitivities, Keogh is the only person who voices any feeling for their plight. He indicates:

> 'To tell the truth I don't blame the old savage [Sitting Bull] for preferring the free-roaming life of the wild Indian to begging and starving around the agencies. Faith, I'd choose the same myself if I were he.'[73]

This quotation is interesting as it is a paraphrase to Custer's own remark in *My Life on the Plains*.[74]

The final meeting with his old friend Lieutenant Nowlan reflects the sense of questioning that the regiment feels going into the campaign:

> Nowlan hesitated a moment. 'You're wearing your medal, aren't you, Myles?' he asked. 'Just in case—'
> Keogh nodded and touched the front of his buckskin blouse. 'Yes, it's here, right enough.' A shadow had crossed his face, but he shook his head as though to rid himself of it. 'With it—and the luck of the Irish—and the best horse in the world under me—I think my scalp's safe.'
> 'Well, God keep you, then,' Nowlan said, and the comrades of many years clasped hands.'[75]

The battle, as described by Leighton, draws mainly on Indian accounts to confirm the heroism of Keogh and Comanche:

> Years afterward the Sioux and Cheyennes told tales of a black-mustached captain in buckskins who rode his mount back and forth between two separated platoons of troopers, trying to draw them together. Time and again he saved men by turning his horse between them and the enemy.
> How he stayed alive so long, exposing himself so recklessly, was a wonder to them all. His mount was already bleeding from many wounds, but it responded gallantly to his every signal. Could the horse be bullet proof, like the one the Hunkpapa Sioux had in their camp, long ago? Could the silver medal that flashed at the man's bared throat be medicine strong enough to keep their arrows away? In the end horse and rider went down, swept under with the last few survivors by the charging wave of Gall's warriors.
> 'The bravest man we ever fought,' said Two Moon, the Cheyenne chief.[76]

Jeff Jeffries' 1959 children's novel, *Seventh Cavalry*, tells the story of farm boy Jim Peters who becomes a bugler in Keogh's Company I. The Captain even allows the young man to exercise his "wonder horse," Comanche.[77] Keogh's role throughout the book is as a mentor as well as the lad's commander. Keogh also is portrayed as loyal to his superior in turn:

> Of the officers attached to Fort Abraham Lincoln only Captain Keogh remained unchanged by the almost mutinous atmosphere that surrounded him in the officer's mess. He went about his duties with the same unsmiling countenance that was normal to him. He was never seen to show by as much a flicker of his eyelashes that he had private feelings or thoughts about the way the commander was driving his regiment.
> Captain Keogh was a soldier, through and through. It was his job to take orders and to give orders. He did just that, bottling up his thoughts and feelings with rigid self-discipline.[78]

THE LEGEND CONTINUES

70. Leighton, *Comanche*, 43-45.
71. Custer, *Following the Guidon*, 150.
72. Ibid., 110-111.
73. Ibid., 163.
74. George A. Custer, *My Life on the Plains, or Personal Experiences with Indians* (Norman, OK: University of Oklahoma Press, 1962), 22. Custer wrote: "If I were an Indian, I often think I would greatly prefer to cast my lot among those of my people who adhered to the free open plains rather than submit to the confined limits of a reservation, there to be the recipient of the blessed benefits of civilization, with its vices thrown in without stint or measure."
75. Leighton, *Comanche of the Seventh*, 177.
76. Ibid., 192-193.
77. Jeff Jefferies, *Seventh Cavalry* (London: Collins, 1959), 98.
78. Ibid., 131.

79. Jefferies, *Seventh Cavalry*, 186-187.
80. A. M. Anderson, *Grant March-Steamboat Captain* (New York, NY: Harper & Row, Publishers, 1959), 178.
81. Ibid., 203.
82. A.M. Anderson, *Comanche and His Captain* (New York, NY: Harper & Row, Publishers, 1965), 57-58.
83. Ibid., 71.

Later on, as the battle is depicted, Keogh not only makes his stand but also gives Comanche to the young hero so that he can deliver a last message to Custer then make his get away:

> A brief, crooked smile lifted the corners of Captain Keogh's mouth, and then he was shouting to his men to dismount, to throw their reins to those who had already lost their horses, and take cover behind rocks or sage brush, or whatever they could find. 'Here, catch!' he called to Jim, and Comanche's reins sailed through the air toward him. 'If anything happens to me, Peters, Comanche is yours.'
>
> Jim was about to stammer his thanks when Sergeant Schultz broke in with a warning cry. 'Look down there, sir!' he called. 'There are hundreds more Indians comin' to join the first lot! It'd be suicide for the Colonel to attack now.'
>
> Captain Keogh's face was lined with strain. He nodded briefly. 'Peters,' he ordered, putting his mouth to Jim's ear to make himself heard. 'Tell the Colonel what we've seen. Tell him I will hold this position with the aid of Lieutenant Calhoun and "L" company for as long as I can. Then I will retire to the crown of the bluff where he is.'
>
> 'Yessir,' Jim stepped up into Comanche's saddle and was away.
>
> Before he was halfway across the slope Captain Keogh was dead.[79]

Consequently, the "sole" survivors of the battle were Jim Peters and Comanche, thanks to Keogh's selfless act.

Another 1959 juvenile-oriented book looked at the story through the eyes of *Grant March-Steamboat Captain*. There are some brief mentions of Keogh in this small publication by A. M. Anderson. One demonstrates the main character's opinion of the "young Captain Myles Keogh" in these words:

> There was something about him Grant liked at once. Maybe it was his laughing eyes, the quick, easy way he had of making friends. Maybe it was the proud way he spoke of his buckskin horse, Comanche.
>
> 'I have the best horse in the Seventh,' he told Grant. 'He can smell an Indian a mile away.'[80]

The second reference to Keogh is after the battle when March anguishes over the news of the disaster. He especially mourns the loss of Keogh.[81]

These points are important in that Anderson would publish another work a half dozen years later entitled, *Comanche and His Captain*. Here Keogh befriends a young boy, Jeff Daniels, who eventually becomes a bugler, while Keogh is depicted as the most competent officer in the regiment, even when he is temporarily replaced as commander of Company I:

> 'I am turning over Company I to another officer,' Custer told him. 'You are to head north. You will get your new orders at Fort Hays and—.'
>
> Keogh broke in, 'Fort Hays! Turn over my company to someone else!'
>
> Custer took a paper from his table and handed it to Keogh. 'Here are your orders.' Without a word Keogh took the paper. Yes, here were his orders, all down in black and white.
>
> 'If all goes well, the Seventh should be back at Fort Hays sometime in the spring,' Custer said. 'Your company will be waiting for you there. Any questions?'
>
> 'No, sir.'
>
> 'I am a little surprised, Myles. I was sure you would question my orders.'
>
> 'I train my men to carry out orders. As a soldier I will carry out yours. But man to man, I sure would like to say something.'
>
> 'Sure.' Custer was all smiles. 'Go ahead.'
>
> Keogh stood straight and tall. His blue eyes flashed. 'Company I is my company. If need be, I will fight to be its captain again. No one, not even you, will stop me sir.'[82]

Keogh now becomes the model of a dutiful subordinate while, at the same time, being not afraid to speak his own mind. His strength of character continues as he rejoins the regiment later in the story. He will not be caught in the divided loyalties that are found in the Seventh, and he tells Benteen, "I am a soldier. As long as Custer is in command, I will carry out his orders. If I cannot, I shall tell him so to his face. I shall not talk about him behind his back."[83]

During much of the story Keogh and Company I are separated from Custer and the remainder of the unit. Keogh longs to rejoin his comrades, finally doing so in time for the last campaign. In an interesting turn, Custer asks Keogh to reassure Libbie that her fears about the impending dangers are unfounded:

> Keogh laughed. 'If I have time! Why, Mrs. Custer is second in command, sir.'
> Custer took a quick look around. Then he said in a low voice, 'Try to cheer her up, Myles. She has a feeling that I am not coming back.'
> Keogh could not help thinking of his last letter from the girl he loved. She had told him almost the same thing.
> Yet all he said was, 'You know women. Sometimes they let their feelings get the best of them.'
> 'Will you talk to her?' Custer asked.
> 'Of course, but I will be surprised if she has not already changed her mind. She is a good soldier, maybe the best in all the Seventh.'
> By the time Keogh went with Custer to the Boy General's house, it had started to rain. Mrs. Custer met them with a bright smile. She made Keogh stay to eat with them. All the while she talked and laughed, seeming to be as happy as ever.
> But when she said good-bye to Keogh, there were tears in her dark eyes. 'Take care, Captain.' she said quietly. 'And watch out—watch out for my Boy General.'
> Keogh smiled down at young, pretty Mrs. Custer. He took her small hand in his, 'Forget your fears. Think only of the day when the Seventh rides home again. Think only of that day, and all will be well.'[84]

Even though he gives words of encouragement to Mrs. Custer, Keogh later expresses his own sense of gloom to Nowlan. He asks the Lieutenant to make sure that a last letter reaches the girl he loves in case "there is a redskin out there with an arrow for me . . . ."[85]

Despite the foreboding, the author does not describe Keogh's death, although readers are assured of his heroism. In an unusual twist from earlier fictional interpretations, it is Keogh's gallantry which causes the Indians to spare Comanche:

> In the battle there had been little or no order in the way the soldiers had tried to fight. There had been no time to set up their lines. From the signs it was clear that Keogh had held Company I together. When all his men had been killed, he had gone on to fight with another company. It was Keogh, they [the Indians] said, who had been the finest soldier in the battle. Many were sure that Comanche's captain had been the last to die.[86]

While *Comanche and His Captain* represents a high watermark for juvenile fiction related to this historical figure, Keogh does not receive the same attention in subsequent youth-directed publications. For instance, Will Henry's *Custer's Last Stand* and Dale White's *The Boy Who Came Back*, both make but passing references to Keogh. In the former, Keogh is mentioned briefly as he and Cooke follow Reno to the crossing.[87] In the latter book, the young hero is asked to keep Keogh's horse in shape by riding him for exercise. More noteworthy, however, is the mention of a "Mrs. Keogh" who is found conversing with Mrs. Custer and Mrs. Yates.[88] Although Keogh loses his life in fact, as well as fiction, he at least gains a wife in this last story.

Keogh thus obtained a certain stature as a stand-alone character in "Last Stand" fiction, but he appears only infrequently in poetry, and usually only in relation to his horse. For instance, in "The Second Departure of Custer" by Mary Boyton Cowdrey, Keogh's name does not appear, but as the expedition marches from Fort Lincoln, "A captain spurs Comanche's sides."[89] Another early effort, this time by G.T. Lanigan, was printed in the *United States Army and Navy Journal* in 1878. It included the following verses related to Keogh and his mount:

> Honor to Keogh's charger!
>   Only his flashing eye
> Saw the Three Hundred fighting—
>   Saw the Three Hundred die!
>
> His was the place of honor,
>   Where his Irish rider fell
> When the Seventh rode into the valley
>   That blazed like the mouth of hell!

THE LEGEND CONTINUES

84. Anderson, *Comanche*, 169-171.
85. Ibid., 184-185.
86. Ibid., 204.
87. Will Henry, *Custer's Last Stand: The Story of the Battle of the Little Big Horn* (Philadelphia, PA: Chilton Book Co., 1966), 139.
88. Dale White, *The Boy Who Came Back* (New York, NY: Criterion Books, 1966), 54.
89. Lawrence, *His Very Silence Speaks*, 262.

90. Brian Dippie and John Carroll, compilers, *Bards of the Little Big Horn* (Bryan, TX: Guidon Press, 1978), 233. While Dippie and Carroll speculate that this poem's anonymous author may have been a member of Keogh's Company I, Lawrence, *His Very Silence Speaks*, 262 gives the author as G. T. Lanigan.

91. Dippie and Carroll, *Bards of the Little Big Horn*, 234-235.

92. Ibid., 223.

93. Lawrence, *His Very Silence Speaks*, 264.

94. Dippie and Carroll, *Bards of the Little Big Horn*, 236.

95. Ibid., 237-238.

96. Ibid., 239.

97. Lawrence, *His Very Silence Speaks*, 266-267.

> Honor to old Comanche,
> While strength and life remain!
> But, O to see the Captain
> Upon his back again![90]

Still more telling is John Hay's "Miles [sic] Keogh's Horse" which appeared in *The Atlantic Monthly* in 1880. The fifth and sixth stanzas reflect Keogh's memory:

> And of all that stood at noonday
> In that fiery scorpion ring.
> Miles [sic] Keogh's horse at evening
> Was the only living thing.
> Alone from that field of slaughter
> Where lay the three hundred slain,
> The horse Comanche wandered,
> With Keogh's blood on his mane.[91]

Nearly a decade later, Emma Rood Tuttle provided her "Comanche" poem for the *Banner of Light* in November 1891. This piece, similar in many ways to Hay's, appeared not long after the horse had died. It spoke of "Custer's brave three hundred," and how after the battle,

> . . . the horse, Comanche
> Splashed with Miles [sic] Keogh's blood,
> Utterly lone and riderless,
> Wounded and hungry stood.[92]

Tuttle went on to recount how the mount was treated thereafter:

> Discharged with honor was he,
> The Seventh Cavalry
> Kept him, a royal tribute
> To Custer's memory.
> On all display occasions,
> Comanche, draped in black,
> Paraded with the soldiers,
> But none might stride his back.
> Never might living rider
> Across his neck draw rein,
> Since Keogh's crimson life-blood
> Had stained his sweeping mane.[93]

Likewise, Wilbur Edgerton Sanders' thrilling "On Custer's Hill", from the 1910 edition of the *Contributions to the Historical Society of Montana*, provided this image:

> Still Crazy Horse sent forth his might
> To swell the thick'ning fray,
> Where in their last heroic fight
> Stood Custer's ranks at bay.
> Where Gall's fierce warriors breathe
> The combat's fiery breathe,
> From bloody work with brave Calhoun
> And gallant Keogh's death.[94]

By 1926, to honor the fiftieth anniversary of the battle, Minnie Carrell published "Comanche" as part of *Winners of the West*. The piece includes the sad picture of the horse standing his lonely vigil over Keogh.

> There a sorrel horse is standing,
> Bending o'er a form so still.
> 'Tis Comanche o'er his master
> The only life to greet the day,
> Keeping there his lonely vigil,
> As the long hours crept away . . . .
> Not because your feet were fleeter
> Nor was it for your form so grand,
> But that you were always faithful
> To the one who held command.[95]

Another poem of the same title was part of the 1945 edition, *Wigwam Smoke*. Here, poet James McGregor refers only to "Comanche, the noted war horse, That Captain Keough [sic] rode that day."[96] But a later poem, Ben Mayfield's "Talk T' Me," elaborates on the bond between man and beast. He wrote:

> Tell us why they left you there standin' all alone
> With them bullets an' them arr'ers stickin' in yer bones
> I kin' smell yer ev'ry fear and feel yer ev'ry woe
> I take me cap right off t' you—ol' buddy Keogh—[97]

Following a similar course, "Comanche" by Audrey J. Hazell, specially commissioned as part of the reprint of Charles King's description of the Little Big Horn, included the pair once more:

> There he stood, the battle over,
> Wounded, without his rider,
> His comrades lying all around,
> Comanche, the sole survivor.
>
> The smell of death was everywhere.
> He waited, sad, forlorn.
> But he'd done his best, stood his ground.
> The battle? Little Big Horn.
>
> Where's his faithful soldier friend
> Who was Irish, like the Banshee?
> They'd served together in the 7th,
> Captain Keogh and Comanche.[98]

Yet still one more poem titled "Comanche," this time by Gary Gildner, takes the story from the point of view that the horse is now a "museum display."[99] Gildner makes a fairly sarcastic point about Comanche's rider, "Fine. No more Keogh's kicking my guts (rugged Capt. Myles Keogh owned and rode me)."[100] In this instance, the warm relationship between the two is cut away for one of the few times in poetry.

F. A. Lydic has written a number of Custer-related poems which include references to Keogh. For example, in "The 'Far West's' Race With Death," published in 1979, the poet mentions Comanche as being on board the steamboat as it makes its way back toward Ft. Lincoln. Later, in *Comanche! Oh Comanche! A Narrative in Verse*, Lydic returns to the traditional interpretation, however. He also takes inspiration from David Dary's biography of the horse in this depiction of "Myles Keogh's peerless steed!"[101] Also, Lydic's description takes on additional significance in its ambiguity regarding Keogh's persona as:

> Keogh's reputation rests
> Upon which view to take.
> Some make him seem ascetic.
> Some claim he was a rake.
>
> Whatever were his foibles,
> Keogh was skilled in war.
> In the War Between The States,
> Was noted on that score.[102]

Not until 1987 does another twist take place when Keogh is mentioned in his own right, rather than in tandem with his mount. In a section of Howard (Hap) Wilson's *War Chiefs of the Northwest* contains the historically inaccurate lines:

> Captain Keogh is a name that lives on
> Though Captain Keogh died at the Little Bighorn
> An Adjutant to Custer was why he drew his pay
> And with all the troopers he died that day
> are found.[103]

Other verses go on to describe "Fort Keogh" and there is even a second "Fort Keogh" poem later in the volume.[104]

Finally, Bill O'Neill's 1989 "Little Big Horn" also includes Keogh as a figure separate from his horse. The brief passage reads:

> As the blue pants attack, Captain Keogh glances back
> an' sees lots of discouragin' looks.
> He knows these are men, let fate do them in,
> that will honor U.S. history books.[105]

Unlike his varied representations in fiction, then, Keogh receives little due in poetry. The emphasis, for the most part remains Comanche.

Even as there is less poetry devoted to Keogh the references in novels and short stories, there are even fewer occasions when he receives attention in films or television.[106] The first exception was the 1912 Bison production, *Custer's Last Fight*. Thomas H. Ince, the early Hollywood giant, at least included Keogh's mount in his picture. The charger is shown milling around in the background as Terry's column comes upon Custer and his decimated command. The audience is told, "The only thing found on the field is Comanche the horse of Captain Keogh; with many wounds, but saved by the care of the men—ever after the pet of the Seventh and never ridden." The image then cuts away to Comanche running wildly off camera, presumably toward Fort Lincoln and home, since a publicity still from the time shows the bloody animal back at the post surrounded by many of the distraught women of the garrison.[107] Incidently, the horse was pure white in this depiction, although this was not unusual since there had been some

THE LEGEND CONTINUES

98. Lawrence, *His Very Silence Speaks*, 267.
99. Ibid., 267.
100. F.A. Lydic, *Comanche! Oh Comanche! A Narrative in Verse* (Joliet, IL: Privately Printed, 1982), 3.
101. Howard (Hap) Wilson, *War Chiefs of the Northwest* (Helena, MT: Falcon Press, 1987), 45.
102. Ibid., 39.
103. Bill O'Neill, *Little Big Horn*, (Livingston, MT: Privately Printed, 1989).
106. For a brief synopsis on Custer and the Seventh Cavalry in film and television see Paul Andrew Hutton, "Hollywood's General Custer: The Changing Image of A Military Hero in Film," *Greasy Grass* (May, 1986), 15-21, and John P. Langellier, "Movie Massacre: The Custer Myth in Motion Picture and Television," *Research Review* (June, 1989), 20-31.
107. Lawrence, *His Very Silence Speaks*, 242. The 1925 reissue of *Custer's Last Fight*, available from Old Army Press of Fort Collins, Colorado on video tape (VHS) format, deleted this scene, perhaps in an effort to correct the inaccuracy of the original edition.

108. According to Lawrence, *His Very Silence Speaks*, 30-31, some sources as early as 1891 indicated that Comanche was a gray, which he was not.

109. A June 17, 1941 copy of an earlier version of the *They Died With Their Boots On* script exists in the main branch of the New York Public Library. For further information on the topic see Tom O'Neil, "The Making of *They Died With Their Boots On*," (unpublished MS, 1989 scheduled for publication in *Research Review* (June, 1990).

110. *She Wore A Yellow Ribbon*, Argosy Pictures, Released 1949 and distributed by RKO Radio. The film was based on James Warner Bellah's story, "War Party."

111. Ford, of course, featured other Irish characters in his "Cavalry Trilogy" including Sergeant Major O'Rourke (Ward Bond) in *Fort Apache* (1948), a Medal of Honor winner who had held a field grade rank with the Irish Brigade in the Civil War, and Sergeant Quincannon (Victor McLaglen) from *She Wore a Yellow Ribbon* and *Rio Grande* (1950) and the same character by Dick Foran in *Fort Apache*, as well as Sergeant Mulcahy (also McLaglen in Fort Apache) to name but a few examples. J. A. Place, *The Western Films of John Ford* (Secaucus, N.J.: Citadel Press, 1974), 74-91; 108-127; 146-159.

confusion about the color in early writings.[108] More to the point, the illusion to the animal as the only living survivor of the battle illustrates just how far that concept had become entrenched, even at such an early date.

Thereafter, no further mention of Keogh or Comanche was made in the numerous western motion pictures which followed in the late silent and early sound years, although some thought had been given to including a character in an original version of the script for *They Died With Their Boots On*.[109] At first, casting called for a fictional composite of the regimental adjutant, the Canadian William W. Cooke, and Keogh. The original concept was dropped and an Englishman, "Queens Own" Butler (George Huntley, Jr.), was substituted, in the spirit of strengthening Anglo-American relations during World War II. Even then, when Custer (Errol Flynn) takes command of the Seventh, he calls his officers together to tell them of his plan to turn the unit into the finest regiment in the Army. He says that there will be a great deal of work but the key will be to find something to build *esprit* and morale. At this point Butler enters, while several of the other officers are in the process of introducing themselves to the new commander. Having served with Custer in the Civil War, he is recognized immediately. Custer also remembers hearing a haunting tune that Butler once sang in a Monroe, Michigan saloon. He asks the lieutenant to play the song and soon all join in the strains of "Garry Owen," which, according to popular tradition, was introduced to the unit by Keogh. Additionally, an actor who bears more than a passing resemblance to Keogh stands behind Butler as he plays the piano and teaches the words to his comrades.

Not until *She Wore A Yellow Ribbon*, in 1949, was a more concrete reference made to Keogh. Early in the script, Captain Nathan Briddles (John Wayne) reads the list of officers killed with Custer. When he comes to the name Keogh, he repeats it for emphasis, then looks up at his commanding officer, Major Allshard (George O'Brien), and halts, moved by emotion. Later that evening, Briddles visits the grave of his wife, Mary. There he speaks of the news that just has been received of Custer's defeat and the death of many of his men, including Keogh, that "happy-go-lucky Irishman" with whom she used to "waltz so well."[110] This bitter-sweet reference may well have stemmed from director John Ford's affection for the sons and daughters of Erin, a sympathy which came out time and time again in his productions. In Ford's view then, Keogh represented the epitome of this group and their role within the American military on the frontier.[111]

A decade passed before Keogh surfaced once more. This time, Walt Disney brought him out of retirement for *Tonka*, a feature typical of that studio where an animal, in this case Comanche, played the main part. Nonetheless, Captain Keogh (Philip Carey, who interestingly enough, would take the part of George Custer in the 1965 Columbia release, *The Great Sioux Massacre*) assumed a major role while even his old friend Lieutenant Nowlan (Jerome Courtland) is depicted.

The story opens with a young Lakota, White Bull (Sal Mineo), as he is approaching manhood. He captures a wild mustang, which he calls "Tonka", then trains the mount to perfection. This ultimate war pony is the envy of all, including White Bull's older, influential cousin, Yellow Bull (H.M. Wynant). The senior warrior claims the steed for his own, but mistreats the horse.

This is too much for White Bull. White Bull decides to let Tonka go free rather than suffer from the cruelty of the brave. Afterwards, an Army patrol finds the horse and captures it. Bringing it back to the fort, Keogh sees the animal and buys it for himself. In the meantime, White Bull learns that Tonka, who by now has been renamed Comanche, is with the soldiers. He slips into the company stables one night to visit his former companion. While there, Keogh discovers him. Rather than turn the youth in, the kindly officer befriends White Bull.

Despite this positive step, tensions mount between the Indians and whites. The Sioux attack a wagon train and carry off two women. Custer (Britt Lomond, who also played the heavy-handed *comandante* in Disney's

"Zorro" series), "sporting a ludicrous bleach-blond coiffure . . . , seems more a shrewish Old West barmaid than a cavalry officer. . . ."[112] He reacts to the raid by attacking White Bull. Now, he is ready to carry the fight to those responsible for the kidnapping, telling Keogh, "It is more important to teach these red savages a lesson than to rescue the white women. They [the Indians] must be exterminated." Keogh, while not in concert with his commander, must follow orders.

Using White Bull as a messenger, Custer sends an ultimatum to the Indians who have left their reservation. He tells them that the troops "will march and burn every Sioux village to the ground" if they do not return to their agencies. Custer also quips to Keogh that there is "no way to separate the good from the bad. They burn-pillage-they're all bad." With this belief, he prepares to take to the field.

Custer's threat backfires. He rides off toward the Greasy Grass and the fate which awaits him and the Seventh Cavalry. Once more, Keogh obeys his leader and follows. Approaching the encampment, the column moves forward toward the final scene, one of only two serious attempts "to re-create the Last Stand on film between 1941 and the middle 1960's [sic]."[113] As the battle opens, the bluecoats face overwhelming odds. Rather than standing heroically in the center of his command, Long-Hair seats himself. He soon falls as an early casualty. Keogh then takes charge, fighting bravely to the end. This increases his stature from prior movie depictions and takes away the usual honors from the Seventh's stricken Lieutenant Colonel.

From these lofty heights, the Captain disappears from the screen, although his name at least is used in *The Great Sioux Massacre*, Columbia's 1965 entry into the Custer saga. At one point during the Battle of the Little Big Horn, an officer sends a trooper called Keogh to deliver a message that reinforcements are needed. Other than this reference, no more is said in the film or any subsequent ones thereafter.[114]

Although, Keogh exited the big screen, David Weisbert's proposed *The Day Custer Fell* (1965) did give the commander of Company I a number of scenes.[115] While actual filming never took place, the script called for an actor to use a strong Irish accent, and to have a certain sense of fatherly humor. Early in the story he teases young Lieutenant Sturgis who has just sprouted his first "mustache." Later, he is on board the *Far West* with Custer where he breaks up a fight between two enlisted men with the words, "All right, you've had your fun. Now get along with you. There'll be fighting enough without knocking the brains out of each other." He then turns to a cavalryman, McIlhargey, who had started the brawl with an infantryman over his bagpipes. Keogh tells McIlhargey, "You can mend your blathering pipes. The trouble with this regiment is it's got too many quarrelsome Irishmen in it. Now scatter it, boys, break it up, I say." The trooper makes an aside to the effect that, "Too many Irishmen, he says, and him with the dirt of Country Cork still under his fingernails."

As the days go by, the men have left the *Far West* and begin their final ride. McIlhargey, behind Keogh in column, asks his superior, "Captain, darlin', will you tell me what we're doing ten thousand miles from Ireland, where the rain damps the dust and there's Englishmen to be shot at instead of naked heathens." Keogh's reply is short, "Because a fight's a fight, McIlhargey, and thirteen dollars is more'n you were ever paid to shoot at Englishmen."

Towards the end, McIlhargey adopts a different tone. As the force meets the enemy head on, he turns to Keogh and requests, "Captain, darlin', if they lift me hair today will you write me old mother I died like a king." Soon thereafter, Keogh has a more weighty mission given to him, this time from Custer who calls the Captain to his side. Seeing what is ahead, he instructs, "Keogh, I'm going down this coulee. You'll hold your companies in reserve and support me if I'm attacked. If the way is clear as it looks you'll join me when we cross the river." Keogh acknowledges this order and turns his horse to the side for Custer's troops to pass. Keogh cannot carry out his objective, since he is cut off and forced to signal to Custer for help rather than provide

THE LEGEND CONTINUES

112. Dippie, *Custer's Last Stand*, 112.

113. For reactions to *Tonka* see "Injun Sal," *Newsweek* (January 5, 1959), 69; Howard Thompson, New York *Times* (March 26, 1959), 28; *Monthly Film Bulletin*, (May, 1959), 62, and "Tonka," *Screen Stories* (February, 1959), 63.

114. Michael R. Pitts, *Western Movies: A TV and Video Guide to 4200 Genre Films* (Jefferson, NC: McFarland & Co., Inc., 1986), 160.

115. In 1965 a wave of "Custer-mania" infected movie makers on both sides of the Atlantic. For example one article, "Slicing Custer Pie Thin," *The Hollywood Reporter* for March 11, 1965, 3, noted that "Besides the Leon Fromkess production on Gen. Custer already filmed for early release, [*The Great Sioux Massacre*, Columbia] and the 20th Century Fox "The Day Custer Fell," starting in June, comes word now an Italian Custer Epic, "General Custer's Trumpeter," which is a long-broached Dino DeLaurentis project that Robert Haggiage has just taken over. It will star Alberto Sordi. Here's the payoff: the Italian version will shoot on location in the U.S." Also see the Rome Column, *The Hollywood Reporter* (March 23, 1965). For more on this state of affairs, as well as the March 30, 1965, 4 issue article titled "Big Year for Gen. Custer" which noted that David Weisbert had advance plans with Fox for "The Day Custer Died."
While only *The Glory Guys* and *The Great Sioux Massacre* actually made it to the theaters (along with *Due Sergenti Del Generale Custer*) in 1965. There are also two references to Keogh in *The Great Sioux Massacre*. In one scene he assists Tom Custer in taking a drunken Reno (Joseph Cotten) back to his quarters and in another scene he is sent by Custer with a message during the final battle, although not actually seen in this segment. The Weisbert script, written by Wendell Mayes, was most interesting. Quotations are taken from Mayes, "The Day Custer Fell, "final script (April 2, 1965), 15, 50-51, 68, 100, and 118-122.

Grant Woods (right) would portray Keogh in the short-lived 1967 ABC television series "The Legend of Custer." Wayne Maunder was Custer, Peter Palmer played Sergeant James Bustard, and Slim Pickens took the part of trail scout Joe Miller. *Courtesy of Neil Summers.*

support. Wounded in the leg and arm, he fires a carbine, while McIlhargey and about forty of Keogh's battalion fight on. Captain Yates asks Custer for permission to reinforce Keogh, but is denied. At Keogh's side, one of the enlisted men, who has been waving a guidon to get Custer's attention realizes, " The General ain't comin' to help us, Captain." Limping over to McIlhargey, Keogh wants to know if the soldier has mended his bagpipes. "Yes, sir, I did that, sir," comes the reply. In response, Keogh has McIlhargey "pump them up," as he calls to the survivors, "Lads, when I give you the word we're marching to join the General."

With a revolver in each hand, Keogh sets out in front of the remaining members of his command, and shouts above the bagpipes, "Now, lads, march." The Indians allow them to move forward, for the moment unnerved or unsure of what the strange sound is that comes from the contingent. The "ragged formation" thus starts its strange march. Seeing this valiant effort, Custer tells Cooke to shift the men to cover Keogh if he "gets into range . . . ." That never happens, however, since one of the warriors, Two Moon, lifts his lance. Then comes a war cry. Two Moon and his followers ride down on "Keogh's brave Irishmen" who "are lost among the charging savages." This same fate will befall Custer as the scenario ends with the Sioux, Cheyenne, and Arapaho winning the day.

The project absorbed Weisbert for two and a half years, costing the studio a million dollars in development, only to be shelved. Weisbert managed to salvage the idea to some degree with the creation of the television series, "Legend of Custer," a short-lived ABC entry into the 1967 season.[116] In the series' premiere, on September 6, Custer (Wayne Maunder) arrives at Fort Hays, Kansas after the Civil War. According to the synopsis in *TV Guide*, " . . . the mustachioed fellow with Shirley Temple curls and the arrogant air" had been "reduced in rank and suspended on a charge of deserting his post; he has returned to duty to shape up the 7th Cavalry." His men are "the scum of the earth," in the words of General Alfred Terry (Robert F. Simon). To whip this rag-tag outfit into shape, Custer draws upon

Keogh (Grant Woods), a "brawny Irishman," as well as Sergeant James Bustard (Peter Palmer), portrayed as an ex-Confederate.[117] Keogh would play a part in at least four subsequent episodes. For example, in this first show, after entering the post, Custer finds the sentry asleep and the enlisted men gambling in the stables. The ringleader is a muscular, tough private who has no love for Yankees, nor officers. This is Bustard. Custer removes his shoulder straps and challenges the man to a fight. He beats the trooper but rather than making him go to the guard house, promotes him to a sergeant. With new stripes, Bustard becomes a Custer-man. Meanwhile, Captain Keogh has come in during the fight. He departs and says nothing. Bustard tells Custer that the cigar-chomping Irishman was Captain Keogh, who "doesn't carry any tales."

The next day Keogh, crossing the parade ground, stops and gives a man, who is spread-eagled for robbery, some water. He runs into Custer and introduces himself. Custer is puzzled since he states that he thought he saw Keogh the night before. Keogh says he never had the pleasure of meeting the General, thus indicating that the events in the stables during the prior evening never had happened as far as he was concerned. Custer responds that he is now a lieutenant colonel and not a general, despite Keogh referring to him in that grade.

Then, Reno, who is still a captain, comes up. He was at West Point ahead of Custer and is bitter about Yellow Hair's rank. He tells Keogh that the twenty-eight year-old Custer is conceited and a trouble-maker. Reno indicates that Keogh soon will find this out for himself. Keogh replies in his brogue, "I'm looking forward to it."

In subsequent episodes, Keogh becomes a Custer supporter. He even takes Custer's wolf hounds like some domestic when handed their leashes. Later, he joins Custer and works side by side with the enlisted men on a fatigue detail, cutting timber.

At the end of the day, Keogh is in the enlisted barracks, and Custer says that officers are not suppose to be there. The Captain acknowledges this but replies that, since he has to share his bachelor quarters with Reno, it is his only refuge. Custer understands, not being a Reno fan, but retorts at least the Captain could play something besides "dirges" on his harmonica. Keogh responds that he has something better in his repertoire and that it could make a "smashing song" for the regiment. He then breaks into "Garry Owen," thereby once again giving credence to the story that it was he who introduced the song to the unit.

Some time later, California Joe (Slim Pickens), Keogh, and Custer obtain permission from General Terry to go bear hunting. Keogh spots one, and gives his rifle an extra charge of powder. The recoil knocks him over. Custer goes in after the wounded bear. During the pursuit, the bear manages to cause a rock slide which traps Custer. At just that time, a band of Blackfeet come by with a prisoner, Crazy Horse. Seeing this, California Joe and Keogh head back to Fort Hays to report Custer's loss.

Keogh wants permission to take the regiment on "maneuvers" so he can search for Custer's body. Terry says that would possibly stir up the Blackfeet and perhaps even cause them to ally with their enemy the Sioux since the presence of so many soldiers in their area would be taken as a sign of hostility. Keogh essentially ignores this prohibition.

Eventually, he is allowed to go on patrol with a few men, however, and tells California Joe that he thinks the General Terry would not be too surprised if the detachment got "accidentally lost" in the area where they last saw Custer. So, with Bustard, California Joe, and a few men they set out, eventually coming upon some Blackfeet trackers. This makes Keogh reflect that the Indians might be looking for Custer too, and that the Colonel might still be alive. The patrol presses on, but with no success. Finally, Keogh concedes that Custer is lost for good and they should turn back the next day rather than "stir up a hornet's nest," as Terry had warned. Soon, Custer finds his way into camp, which is just across the Rosebud. He startles Keogh and orders the detachment to get saddled and mounted to follow Crazy Horse and his small band who only have about a 20 minute lead. Keogh gladly responds. The troops close in on the enemy. With drawn sabers, Custer, Keogh and the command let fly. They kill a number of Lakota but

THE LEGEND CONTINUES

116. Dave Kaufman, "Custer Rides Again: On TV," *Variety* (May 23, 1967), 7 discusses Weisbert's efforts to revive his project for television.

117. *TV Guide* (NY Metropolitan Edition), (September 9, 1967), 42.

MYLES KEOGH

118. According to a survey of the series as listed in *TV Guide* for 1967, Woods was mentioned in the credits for five of the episodes. Filmways also put together several of the episodes for a TV movie of the same title for release in 1968, but Woods was not featured in this 94 minute show. Michael R. Pitts, *Western Movies*, 229. The synopsis of the series is taken from this made-for television movie.

119. As indicated in Lawrence, *His Very Silence Speaks*, 256-279 only a few songs and pieces of art refer to Keogh, and even then they are in the context of his horse Comanche rather than the man himself.

Crazy Horse gets away. Keogh asks Custer if he is disappointed and also indicates that he is certain Custer and Crazy Horse will meet again.

At Fort Hays, Custer makes his report but is told by Terry that the Seventh will not be allowed to take to the field. They are to continue their training and garrison details, while the Fifth Cavalry goes out to do the fighting.

California Joe accompanies the Fifth and Terry. The outfit is pinned down. Terry sends a scout with orders to find Custer, who is to alert the post then come with help after the fort is secure from possible attack. Custer is found. Two troopers are dispatched to carry word to the fort, then Custer rides to the sound of the guns with Company B under Reno and Company C led by Keogh.

When they reach the siege they find the Indians have been supplied with new shotguns by a white trader. Custer sends out Keogh to mark the range of the pieces so that they can draw the Indians' fire then, as the Sioux reload, they will charge. Keogh enthusiastically responds, and asks if Bustard wants to accompany him. The answer positive and the two daredevils gallop out with guidons to mark the range. The tactic works. Custer, Keogh and the long knives strike the enemy and inflict a number of casualties, but again Crazy Horse eludes them.

At the fort, Terry dresses down Custer for being insubordinate. He says this pervades the Seventh, and Keogh especially is infected with Custer's attitude. Nevertheless, he has commended the unit for their actions but thereafter the Seventh would stick to foraging and garrison details. This disappointing news reaches Keogh who slumps in his saddle and bits down on his cigar. The troops are about to ride out on another fatigue and look none too soldierly. Then, the band strikes up "Garry Owen" as the unit is heading out. Keogh straightens his hat and sits upright. The men follow suit and pass in review with pride. As the film comes to a close, they have become a unit.[118] With that, Captain Keogh once more departed from the Hollywood scene. Despite his flowing locks, a dashing Custer was not a figure for Viet Nam era television.

In examining the character of Myles Keogh as portrayed in fiction, poetry, and occasional theatrical representations, the following conclusions can be reached. While it is true that Keogh, at first, was known because of Comanche, this association never limited his unique role within the larger drama of the Little Big Horn. Indeed, fiction tends to portray him apart from his mount, or places the horse in a lesser role, in most cases. Of course, the opposite situation is true in poetry, while film and television representation are almost equally divided.

Regardless, novelists, poets, playrights, and screenwriters have shared certain common traits, most notably the repeating of numerous inaccuracies caused by subscribing to faulty historical research. In turn, many an historical narrative seemed to draw on the romantic fictional image of Keogh, who thereby came to hold a special place in the Little Big Horn legend. He remains a relative constant in an otherwise ever-changing drama. While other aspects of this saga have altered with time, Keogh stands alone as the brave foreigner who gave his life for his adopted country. Keogh's characteristic Irish wit and charm represents a strongly rooted stereotype found in many depictions of the frontier military by artists, authors, and directors.[119] The portrait of Keogh as a colorful personality at times overshadows even those of Reno, Benteen, and Custer himself. As such, Myles Keogh seems assured of a continued niche in creative interpretations of the American West.

Finally, because of new scholarship, more information is available about Keogh than ever before. This material could serve to inspire future novels, poems, and media productions. Even if that is not the case, Keogh's stature has merged with the larger body of literature associated with "Custer's Last Stand," and far surpasses his own heroic vision of "The Irish Dragoon."

"Reconnaissance"

Henry Inman's Keogh: Fiction or Fact?

In modern historical works the emphasis is on fact and objective interpretation based upon sources. In earlier writing, reality and fancy often came together in the same piece with little or no distinction. For this reason, much of what had been published about Myles Keogh during the 19th-Century, and even into the 20th-Century, fell into this category where license was common. The work of Henry Inman offers a perfect example of that approach.

Inman had enlisted in 1857 as a soldier with the Ninth U.S. Infantry. After duty in Oregon and California, he transferred to the Seventeenth Infantry for Civil War service and obtained a commission in the regiment. After the war ended, he returned to the West where he had become the quartermaster officer at Fort Harker. Dismissed from the service in 1872, Inman turned to other pursuits to make a living. In 1878 he became a journalist.[1] As an author, he often concentrated on Western themes, with Keogh surfacing in several instances as one of his characters.

It appears that he knew Keogh from his days in Kansas but how much of his presentation came from actual exploits and how much of his story was fictional cannot be determined with complete certainty. For instance, in Inman's first book, *The Old Santa Fe Trail*, an incident supposedly related by Keogh described an exciting skirmish with Indians a few days after General Sully's abbreviated expedition of September 1868. After leaving Camp Supply, Keogh's command was harassed by Indians, until they reached Mulberry Creek. There, the incessant charges compelled the troops to expend their small amount of ammunition, leaving them nearly defenseless. At that point, the Indians launched another attack on the virtually helpless group.

Boldly riding toward the squadron of cavalry, they discharged "the shots from their revolvers, and then, in their rage, threw them at the skirmishers on the flanks of the supply train, while the latter, nearly out of ammunition, were compelled to sit quietly in their saddles, idle spectators of the extraordinary scene."[2] With the situation reaching a crucial point, Keogh sent out a messenger to Fort Dodge for a supply of cartridges. When the ammo arrived, it kept the engagement from becoming "a veritable last ditch." According to Inman, the Indians were repelled and Comanche received his first wound in the fray.

While there are enough references in the story to ground it in reality, numerous errors and nonsequiturs exist to call the whole episode into question. First of all, no official report has been found of the event. Next, Camp Supply was not established as yet, it being founded in November, after the period of the supposed fire-fight. Finally, by all accounts, Comanche was wounded during the Sully Expedition, not after that foray.

An article Inman wrote in 1892 provided another tantalizing vignette about Keogh, that may or may not have been true. In the Kansas City *Journal* "A Hunt With Custer," related events which Inman stated took place in March 1868. Generals Sheridan, Custer, and Sully, along with Keogh, Yates, Weir, Cooke, and

1. Dan L. Thrapp, *Encyclopedia of Frontier Biography* (Glendale, CA: Arthur H. Clark Company, 1988), 704.
2. Colonel Henry Inman, *The Old Santa Fe Trail: The Story of a Great Highway* (Minneapolis, MN: Ross & Haines, Inc., 1966), 478-479.

3. Henry Inman, "A Hunt With Custer," Kansas City *Journal* (October 23, 1892).

4. Henry Inman, *The Ranche on the Ox Hide* (New York, NY: MacMillian Company, 1898).

Hale joined Inman on a wolf hunt near Fort Harker, Kansas. The story again offered rich detail of "the limestone bluffs of the Smokey Hill," and even mentioned Sheridan's greyhound, Cinch. This dog was among "nearly the whole contingent of hounds" at the post which went out with the "little cavalcade" to give chase to the prey.

They located the wolves and started out after them at a dead run, with Sheridan giving a "characteristic" yell when he saw them and dashed on "like a tornado as if leading a charge." Then, Inman continued the narrative with exciting images:

> We were at various distances from each other; Captain Keogh and I were the only ones riding close together. Right in our path was the long trunk of an immense cottonwood tree that had been blown down by the wind, over which we must jump to make time. I cleared it in a bound, but as the Captain's horse, a magnificent sorrel, rose to make the leap, the effort so distended his belly that the saddle girth broke and the rider was incontinently tumbled off.
>
> Keogh landed on his feet, was not hurt in the least, and fortunately, having held on to the saddle reins, his horse did not get away. An orderly who was near rode up, saddlers were exchanged in a moment and we were after the wolves again, though much distance was lost in the mishap.³

After much research, it seems certain that the event could not have taken place, at least at the time Inman said it did. The fact is, at that date, Keogh was on leave in New York. Assuming that Inman erred by a few months, the possibility does exist to have Custer and Sheridan together since, prior to Yellow Hair's return to Monroe after his court martial, Custer was Sheridan's guest at Fort Leavenworth. But, the excursion from that post to Fort Harker was hardly a short one. Even if the party had gone there, it seems unlikely that Keogh, nursing a broken leg suffered during the previous February, would have agreed to such an expedition as a lark. It is even less likely that upon being thrown from his horse in the scene depicted by Inman that he would land on his feet and sustain no further injury.

To complicate matters, Inman related the same event some six years later in his book, *The Ranche on the Ox Hide*. This time, however, Sheridan was not present, and the "magnificent sorrel" now became Comanche. Written for juvenile readers, the text nonetheless contained many references which can be substantiated. Indeed, much attention was given to the kidnapping of two white women by Indians on May 30, 1869. Here Keogh appeared in the narrative to give credence to the story, arriving at the site of the raid where the women had been captured. He had orders to set up base camp in the area and to follow the Elkhorn on a scout, accompanied by Company I on their "fine bay horses," and by Custer's pack of dogs.⁴

Once in place, Keogh invited the book's young protagonist, sixteen-year old Joe Thompson, to join the camp. The lad was known not only to Keogh but also to Custer and Buffalo Bill, since both of these men figured into the story too. In fact, Keogh and Cody spent Thanksgiving with Joe's family after the Washita.

Although most of the publication smacks of a formula adventure for boys, the date May 30 does coincide with Keogh's only scout for 1869. Even the location of the action is set in the correct vicinity, although the companies which actually reported to the place of the kidnapping were A and/or D. The interweaving of known elements and colorful but imaginary scenarios then, contributed to much misinformation about Myles Keogh and added to his overall mystique. To this day, untangling fact from fiction remains one of the most difficult challenges for anyone setting out to understand Keogh as an historical figure rather than the characterization which has emerged from novels and short stories.

Afterword

In the summer of 1990, when I flew to the United States from Ireland to attend the symposium on Myles Keogh held at the Gene Autry Western Heritage Museum, my journey took me fourteen hours from Dublin to Los Angeles. When my great-granduncle sailed on the *Kangaroo*, arriving in New York from Liverpool on April 1, 1862, the journey took three weeks—and what a journey it must have been! Had he proceeded from the East to the West Coast of America, it would have taken him at least another three weeks. In fact, he would have been lucky to survive such a cross-country journey.

Having left the land of his birth, Myles, one of thirteen children, brought with him certain traits from his youth. For one thing, the horse had been a very dominant feature in his life—for working the farm, travelling, trading, fetching, and sporting (to a lesser degree). Strangely, the horse ultimately would bring him prominence in death.

As part of a rather well-to-do property-owning family, Myles did not feel the impact of the famine which struck his country when he was five in the same way as it did for so many others. The population diminished from eight million to four million over the next half decade. Perhaps this situation sowed the seed in Myles' mind and prompted him also to leave when he had completed his studies. Reading through his letters, it is very evident that he was well educated, that being somewhat unusual for a Roman Catholic in those times when you had to be wealthy, socially important, or Protestant to obtain advanced learning. It is because of this schooling that we are able to know so much of what we do about him since much of the correspondence remained in the family's possession for generations.

Indeed, it is interesting that "Clifden," the home of Myles' mother and the one he eventually inherited, is still owned and occupied by the Keoghs as is "Orchard House" where he was born and grew up. A Myles Keogh still lives there, while "Park House," where his favorite brother Tom lived, was sold in 1949 by my uncles when they moved to London. That home was bedecked with mementoes which Myles brought back in 1869. Indian headdresses, lances, bows and arrows all were there. I remember my father telling me that none of them were strong enough to pull the bows. There were also forage caps and Myles' Civil War sabre. My father and his brothers had a grand time playing cowboys and Indians with all these heirlooms.

As time went by, mice and moths took their toll on these items and my father broke the tip off the sabre, but it has survived. The saddest was the loss of the Papal blessing presented to Myles before he departed from Italy in 1861 in recognition for his services to Pope Pius IX. The Pope himself signed the document which hung in "Park" alongside a fine painting of Fort Keogh which the family was given in 1880. While the piece of art remains, unfortunately my late uncle, noted for his eccentricity, burnt the blessing and the pen it was signed with in a fit of anti-Catholicism. Perhaps he felt as Myles did about the Italian clergy.

In the small parish church in Tinryland, County Carlow, is a lovely stained glass window dedicated to Myles' memory. My uncle recently had it repaired and restored to its former glory as it was beginning to suffer from the ravages of time. It is the only memorial to him in Ireland. It is fortunate, however, that he has been given a fitting final resting place in Auburn, New York as a tribute to a great soldier. As each year passes, interest in him seems to grow and grow both in Ireland and the United States.

The Battle of the Little Big Horn played a very small part in his life but had such dire consequences. Myles was not the only member of the family to die at the hands of others, though. The previous generation saw his uncle Patrick hanged for his part in the 1798 Rebellion. Later, a grandniece, Margaret, was killed in the 1916 Rising, while a grandnephew, Blanchfield, was killed in Sicily during 1943. The family motto, *resistite usque ad sanguinem,* which translates "resist until bloodshed," was heeded by these family members. Perhaps nobody told them that their resistance did not have to conclude in death.

But with Myles, so much of his fame stemmed not just from his falling in battle but also from his association with Comanche, who survived where others died. If only this charger could have broken his silence and told the world what happened that day! But that would have taken away the mystery which seems to attract so many to his story, along with other romantic notions, such as Nelly Martin's association with the fallen Irish dragoon. This side of the grave, we will never know all we seek to learn about the matter. Perhaps this book will raise as many questions as it provides answers. If so, other generations may follow to take up where we left off.

GARY KEOGH
July 30, 1990
Blackrock, County Dublin
Ireland

Contributors

PEGGY CHAMPLIN, formerly a reference librarian at California State University, Los Angeles, recently received her Ph.D. in history from UCLA. Her dissertation was written about the American geologist, Raphael Pumpelly. Presently, Dr. Champlin serves as the administrator of the Gene Autry Western Heritage Museum's Research Center.

KURT HAMILTON COX attended UCLA's undergraduate program in film and television production. As a hobby, he became interested in the horse equipment of the U.S. Cavalry. From there he began to study other aspects of U.S. Army history in the West, and found Myles Keogh an interesting figure for a proposed one-man theatrical production which he presented to the Little Big Horn Associates at their annual meeting in 1990. Work on this play took Cox to Ireland and served as the stimulus for this book.

RICHARD A. FOX, JR., earned his B.A. and M.A. in anthropology at the University of Montana. He received his Ph.D. in archaeology from the University of Calgary in 1988. Dr. Fox has been involved in western frontier military research since 1983 when he began archaeological studies at the Custer Battlefield which led to new insights regarding the nature of the Battle of the Little Big Horn. Recently, Fox has directed archaeological investigations at Custer's home at Fort Lincoln, North Dakota. Now an archaeologist at the University of North Dakota, currently he is continuing his efforts at Fort Lincoln, while also preparing the final draft of his new book for the University of Oklahoma Press reporting his findings at the Custer Battlefield.

PATRICK D. GLEASON is Head Radio and Television Archivist for Ralph Edwards Productions in Hollywood, California. Graphology is one of his ongoing interests, as well as researching his own Keogh ancestry for possible ties to the Keoghs of Leighlinbridge.

REVEREND VINCENT A. HEIER, a Roman Catholic priest of the Archdiocese of St. Louis, has been interested in the Custer story since his childhood. He has chaired the editorial board of the Little Big Horn Associates', as well as serving on that organization's board of directors. Currently, Fr. Heier is on the book review committee of the Custer Battlefield. In addition, he has continued to gather materials for a bibliographic project which will cover items published about Custer from 1973 to the present.

ELIZABETH ATWOOD LAWRENCE, a veterinarian as well as an anthropologist, received her A.B. degree from Mount Holyoke College, her V.M.D. degree from the University of Pennsylvania School of Veterinary Medicine, and her Ph.D. in cultural anthropology from Brown University. She is an Associate Professor in the Department of Environmental Studies at Tufts University School of Veterinary Medicine, where she teaches and carries out research in the field of animal-human relationships. Dr. Lawrence is the author of three books: *Rodeo: An Anthropologist Looks at the Wild and the Tame*; *Hoofbeats and Society: Studies of Human-Horse Interactions*; and *His Very Silence Speaks: Comanche—the Horse Who Survived Custer's Last Stand*, as well as numerous journal articles dealing with human-animal relationships. She has been an enthusiastic scholar of the Battle of the Little Big Horn for a number of years, focusing particularly on Comanche and the cavalry horses, and on the clash of cultures underlying the battle. Dr. Lawrence is a member of many professional and historical organizations, including the American Anthropological Association, the American Ethnological Society, the American Veterinary Society of Animal Behavior, the (international) Equine Behavouir Study Circle, the U.S. Horse Cavalry Association, the Western History Association, the Custer Battlefield Historical and Museum Association, and the Western Writers of America, Inc.

JOHN P. LANGELLIER received his B.A. and M.A. in history and historical archaeology from the University of San Diego. His master's thesis, "Custer's Celluloid Image: A History of Custer and the Little Big Horn in Motion Pictures," served as his introduction into this field. He obtained his Ph.D. from Kansas State University with a concentration on military history and the history of the American West. For fourteen years he served in various positions as a museum director and historian for the United States Army and for the Wyoming State Archives, Museum, and Historical Department. Since 1987, he has been on the staff of the Gene Autry Western Heritage Museum as director of research and publications.

JOHN S. MANION was born in Sheridan, Wyoming, and raised in western Nebraska. He has had a lifetime interest in the Indian Wars, particularly the Battle of the Little Big Horn. He is a professional electrical engineer, a graduate of the University of Nebraska's College of Engineering. He spent his professional career with the General Electric Company in Syracuse, New York, near Auburn, New York, where Myles W. Keogh is interred. A visit to Captain Keogh's grave in 1967 sparked an insatiable desire on his part to learn all he could about this Irish Captain who died with Custer. Manion presently serves as Chairman of the Board of Directors of the Little Big Horn Associates. Previously he served as Chairman of the editorial board for that organization. His 1983 book, *Last Statement to Custer,* and subsequent sequels unraveled the long standing controversy over the Mary Adams affidavit.

KEVIN MULROY received his M.A. in U.S. History and Institutions and Ph.D. in American Studies from the University of Keele, Staffordshire, England, where he specialized in Indian-black relations on the frontier. He completed the M.L.S. degree at Rutgers before becoming assistant archivist and then reference librarian at the Getty Center for the History of Art and the Humanities. Dr. Mulroy recently became librarian and archivist at the Gene Autry Western Heritage Museum. He currently is working on a history of the Seminole blacks in Texas and Coahuila that is to be published by the Texas Tech University Press in the fall of 1991.

BRIAN C. POHANKA is a historian, writer, and consultant who lives in Alexandria, Virginia. He was a senior researcher and writer for Time-Life Books' twenty-eight volume history of the Civil War, and has written numerous articles and several books dealing with the history of that conflict and the Indian Wars. He is a contributing editor to *Military History* and *Military Images* magazines, and research consultant to *Civil War* magazine. Pohanka also holds memberships in numerous national organizations related to military history as well as the history of the American West. His interest in Myles Keogh dates to his childhood reading of "Landmark Books" biography of George Custer, and Walt Disney's *Tonka.*

LENORA A. SNEDEKER has taught English for three decades at Oxford Academy in New York State. For most of that time she has worked as a free-lance writer, focusing her interest on central New York history, which is how she discovered the Myles Keogh-Nelly Martin story. She did a feature on the couple in August 1989 at the time of the annual Myles Keogh Paddle, Wheel, and Run Race in Auburn, New York. She has established the Myles W. Keogh Memorial with the Custer Battlefield Preservation Committee, so that those who wish, may contribute to the fund in his name. Presently, she is working on a history of the Martin family.

FRANCIS B. TAUNTON of Bromley, Kent, England, was one of the earliest individuals to conduct research on Myles Keogh after the preliminary work of authors such as Edward Luce. During the course of his studies, he has unearthed considerable data on the subject and made his findings known in several publications, especially through the English Westerners' Society, an organization for which he currently serves as editor. Mr. Taunton also has shared the fruits of his labor with a wide number of people who are interested in the same field. In fact, many contributors to the present volume owe a debt to him for both making available information and providing encouragement over the years.

BIBLIOGRAPHY

PRIMARY SOURCES

Archives

Ayer Collection. Newberry Library. Chicago, Illinois.

Baptismal Records. Diocese: Kildare and Leighlin. Church of Jesus Christ, Latter-Day Saints Archives, Salt Lake City, Utah.

John G. Bourke Diaries. Library, United States Military Academy, West Point.

Custer Battlefield National Monument Files. Crow Agency, Montana.

Walter Camp Collection. Brigham Young University Library Special Collections, Provo, Utah.

Fort Wallace Microfilm. Fort Wallace Museum. Wallace, Kansas.

Lawrence Frost Collection. Monroe, Michigan.

Gray Family Collection.

Hagner Collection. New York Public Library. New York.

General Joseph Hooker Papers. Huntington Library, San Marino, California.

Myles Keogh Collection. Accession No. 89.218. Gene Autry Western Heritage Museum, Los Angeles, California.

Myles Keogh Collection. Manuscript No. 3885. National Library, Dublin.

Elizabeth Lawrence Collection. Westport Harbor, MA.

J. S. Manion Collection. Beverly Hills, Florida.

Memphis Public Library and Information Center. Archives.

National Archives. Washington, D.C. Records of the Adjutant General's Office. Record Group 94.

———. Records of the Bureau of Customs. Record Group 36.

———. Records of the Office of the Judge Advocate General (Army). Record Group 153.

———. Records of the United States Army Commands. Record Group 393.

———. Seventh U. S. Cavalry. Letters Sent. Record Group 391.

Regio Archivo di Stato. Ministero delle Armi Ponitificie. Rome.

Register of Baptisms, 1827-1844. Microfilm copy #928,118, Ireland, Carlow, Clonmelsh, Parish Church Leighlinbridge, Catholic Church, Dublin, 1773-1880.

Hugh Shick Collection. Burbank, California.

Seward Papers. Auburn Community College. Auburn, New York.

University of Kansas. Lawrence, Kansas. Archives.

Western History Collections. University of Oklahoma. Norman, Oklahoma.

Official Records and Reports

Annual Report of the Secretary of War. Vol. I. Washington, DC: Government Printing Office, 1876.

Coolidge, Richard H. *Statistical Report on the Sickness and Mortality in the Army of the United States Compiled from Records of the Surgeon General's Office Embracing a Period of Sixteen Years from January, 1839 to January, 1855.* Washington, DC: Government Printing Office, 1856.

Graham, William A. *The Official Record of a Court of Inquiry Convened by the President of the United States at Chicago, Ill., January 13, 1879, by Request of Major Marcus A. Reno to Investigate his Conduct at the Battle of the Little Big Horn, June 25-26, 1876.* Pacific Palisades, CA: W. A. Graham, 1951.

U.S. Congress. House. 44th Cong., 1st sess. *House Miscellaneous Document 105.*

War of the Rebellion: A Compilation of the Official Records of the Union and Confederate Armies. Washington, DC: Government Printing Office, 1885-.

Manuscripts

Hammer, Kenneth. "Camp Manuscript, Transcripts of Articles and Field Notes of Walter M. Camp."

Manion, John S., Jr. ed. "Correspondence Regarding the Death of Emily Norwood Martin Upton, March 30, 1870."

———. "The Diary of Mrs. Emily Norwood Martin Upton."

———. "The Life, Loves and Legends of Myles W. Keogh." Text of a speech given before Little Big Horn Associates, September 23, 1978.

Moore, M. B. "It Was a Day of Bravery: Eyewitness Accounts of the Custer Fight." 1987.

Mayes, Wendell. "The Day Custer Died." Draft script, April 1965.

Nichols, R. H., ed. "Reno Court of Inquiry." 1983.

Pohanka, Brian C. "Service Record of Myles Walter Keogh, Compiled and Edited from Post and Regimental Returns."

———., ed. "Papers in the Gary Keogh Collection."

Snedeker, Lenora A., ed. "The Martin-Seward Correspondence."

"Statement of Hollow Horn Bear." 1909.

"Statement of Two Eagles." 1908.

SECONDARY SOURCES

Books

Adams, William F. *Ireland and the Irish Emigration to the New World from 1815 to the Famine.* New Haven, CT: Yale University Press, 1932.

Agassiz, George A., ed. *Meade's Headquarters 1863-1865; Letters of Colonel Theodore Lyman from the Wilderness to Appomattox.* Salem, NH: Ayer Company, 1987. Reprint of 1922 edition.

Amory, Thomas C. *Military Services and Public Life of Major-General John Sullivan, of the American Revolutionary Army.* Boston: Wiggin and Lunt, 1868.

Annual Reunion of the Association of Graduates of the United States Military Academy, June 10, 1895.

Athearn, Robert F. *Thomas Francis Meagher.* Boulder, CO: University of Colorado Press, 1949.

Bards of the Little Big Horn. Brian Dippie and John Carroll, compilers. Bryan, TX: Guidon Press, 1978.

Battles and Leaders of the Civil War. 4 vols. New York: The Century Company, 1887-88.

Berkeley, G. F. H. *The Irish Battalion in the Papal Army.* Dublin and Cork: Talbot Press Limited, 1929.

Bourke, Marcus. *John O'Leary—A Study in Irish Separatism.* Dublin: Harcourt, 1968.

Brininstool, Earl A. *Troopers with Custer.* Harrisburg, PA: Stackpole Co., 1952.

Brown, Barron. *Comanche: The Sole Survivor of All the Forces in Custer's Last Stand, the Battle of Little Big Horn.* Kansas City, MO: Burton Publishing Company, 1935.

Burdick, Usher L., ed., *David F. Barry's Indian Notes on the Custer Battle.* Baltimore, MD: Wirth Brothers, 1949.

Burkey, Blain. *Custer, Come at Once!* Hays, KS: Thomas More Press, 1976.

Callahan, North. *Henry Knox, General Washington's General.* New York: Rinehart, 1958.

Carroll, John M. *A Bit of Seventh Cavalry History With All Its Warts.* Bryan, TX: J. M. Carroll, 1987.

———. *The Black Military Experience in the American West.* New York: Liveright, 1971.

———. *They Rode with Custer: A Biographical Directory of the Men that Rode with General George A. Custer.* Mattituck, NJ, and Bryan, TX: John M. Carroll and Co., 1987.

Carroll, John M., ed. *The Benteen-Goldin Letters on Custer and His Last Battle.* New York: John Carroll, 1974.

The Catholic Encyclopedia. New York: Robert Appleton Co., 1907.

Chandler, Melbourne C. *Of Garry Owen in Glory: The History of the 7th U. S. Cavalry.* Annandale, VA: Turnpike Press, 1960.

Coburn, Wallace David. *Battle of the Little Big Horn.* n.p.: Overland-Outwest Publications, 1936.

Coffman, Edward M. *The Old Army: A Portrait of the American Army in Peacetime, 1784-1898.* New York: Oxford University Press, 1986.

Condon, William H. *Life of Major-General James Shields, Hero of Three Wars and Senator from Three States.* Chicago: Blakely Printing Co., 1900.

Connell, Evan S. *Son of the Morning Star: Custer and the Little Big Horn.* New York: Harper and Row, 1985.

Convis, Charles L. *The Honor of Arms: A Biography of Miles W. Keogh.* Tucson: Westernlore Press, 1990.

Conyngham, D. P. *The Irish Brigade and Its Campaigns.* New York: W. McSorley and Co., 1867.

Croly, Herbert A. *The Promise of American Life.* New York: Macmillan, 1909.

Cunliffe, Marcus. *Soldiers and Civilians: The Martial Spirit in America, 1775-1865.* New York: Macmillan, 1973.

Curtis, George Ticknor. *McClellan's Last Service to the Republic.* New York: D. Appleton and Co., 1880.

Custer, Elizabeth. *Following the Guidon.* Norman, OK: University of Oklahoma Press, 1966.

———. *Tenting on the Plains, or General Custer in Kansas and Texas.* New York: Charles L. Webster, 1889, c. 1887.

Custer, George Armstrong. *My Life on the Plains.* Centennial ed. Norman, OK: University of Oklahoma Press, 1976.

D'Arcy, William. *The Fenian Movement in the United States, 1858-1886.* Washington, DC: Catholic University of America Press, 1947.

Dary, David. *Comanche.* Lawrence, KA: University of Kansas Museum of Natural History.

Davis, George Wesley. *Sketches of Butte: From Vigilante Days to Prohibition.* Boston: Cornhill Co., 1921.

Dippie, Brian W. *Custer's Last Stand: The Anatomy of an American Myth.* Missoula, MT: University of Montana Press, 1976.

Dixon, J. K. *The Vanishing Race.* Glorietta, NM: The Rio Grande Press, 1973.

Dolph, Edward A. *"Sound Off"; Soldier Songs from the Revolution to World War II.* 2nd ed. New York: Farrar and Rinehart, 1942.

Downey, Fairfax. *Fife, Drum and Bugle.* Ft. Collins, CO: privately printed, 1971.

Doyle, David Noel. *Ireland, Irishmen and Revolutionary America, 1760-1820.* Dublin and Cork: Mercier Press, 1981.

———. *Irish Americans, Native Rights and National Empires: The Structure, Divisions, and Attitudes of the Catholic Minority in the Decade of Expansion, 1890-1902.* New York: Arno Press, 1976.

Doyle, David Noel and Owen Dudley Edwards, eds. *America and Ireland, 1776-1976: The American Identity and the Irish Connection.* Westport, CT: Greenwood Press, 1980.

Du Picq, A. *Battle Studies.* Harrisburg, PA: Military Service Publishing Co., 1946.

Dustin, Fred. *The Custer Tragedy.* Ann Arbor, MI: Edwards Brothers, Inc., 1939.

Dyer, G. *War.* New York: Crown Publishers, 1985.

Eisenstadt, Abraham. *American History.* New York: Thomas Y. Cromwell Co., 1967.

Emmons, David M. *The Butte Irish: Class and Ethnicity in an American Mining Town.* Urbana, IL: University of Illinois Press, 1989.

Ernst, Robert. *Immigrant Life in New York City, 1825-1863.* New York: King's Crown Press, 1949.

Foner, Jack D. *Blacks and the Military in American History.* New York: Praeger, 1974.

Fowler, Arlen L. *The Black Infantry in the West, 1869-1891.* Westport, CT: Greenwood Press, 1971.

Friswold, Carroll. *Frontier Fighters and their Autograph Signatures.* (Publication no. 87) Los Angeles: Westernlore Press, 1968.

Frost, Lawrence A. *General Custer's Thoroughbreds.* Mattituck, N.J.: J.M. Carroll, 1986.

———. *The Custer Album: A Pictorial Biography of General George A. Custer.* Seattle, WA: Superior Publishing Company, 1964.

Gabriel, R. A. *No More Heroes: Madness and Psychiatry in War.* New York: Hill and Wang, 1987.

Gettysburg Papers. Ken Brandy and Florence Freeman, compilers. Dayton, OH: Press of Morningside Bookshop, 1978.

Gibson, Florence E. *The Attitudes of the New York Irish Toward State and National Affairs, 1848-1892.* New York: Columbia University Press, 1951.

Godfrey, Edward. *General George A. Custer and the Battle of the Little Big Horn.* New York: The Century Company, 1921.

Graham, William A. *The Custer Myth: A Source Book of Custeriana.* Harrisburg, PA: Stackpole Co., 1953.

———. *The Story of the Little Big Horn.* New York: Century Co., 1926.

Gray, John S. *Centennial Campaign: The Sioux War of 1876.* Fort Collins, CO: Old Army Press, 1976. Reprinted Norman, OK: University of Oklahoma Press, 1988.

Griffin, William D., ed. *The Irish in America, 550-1972: A Chronology and Fact Book.* Dobbs Ferry, NY: Oceana Pubs., 1973.

Grinnell, George B. *The Fighting Cheyennes.* Norman, OK: University of Oklahoma Press, 1956.

Hageman, E. R., ed. *Fighting Rebels and Redskins; Experiences in Army Life of Colonel George B. Sanford, 1861-1892.* Norman, OK: University of Oklahoma Press, 1969.

BIBLIOGRAPHY

Hammer, Kenneth. *Men with Custer: Biographies of the 7th Cavalry, 25 June 1876*. Fort Collins, CO: Old Army Press, 1972.

Hammer, Kenneth, ed. *Custer in '76: Walter Camp's Notes on the Custer Fight*. Provo, UT: Brigham Young Press, 1976.

Hammond, Harold Earl, ed. *Diary of a Union Lady, 1861-1865*. New York: Funk & Wagnalls, 1962.

Hardorff, Richard G. *Custer Battle Casualties: Burials, Exhumations, and Reinterments*. El Segundo, CA: Upton and Sons, Publishers, 1989.

———. *Markers, Artifacts and Indian Testimony: Preliminary Findings on the Custer Battle*. Short Hills, NJ: Don Horn Publications, 1985.

Hassard, John Rose Green. *Life of Archbishop John (Joseph) Hughes*. New York: D. Appleton and Co., 1866.

Hayes-McCoy, G. A. *Captain Myles Walter Keogh, United States Army, 1840-1876*. O'Donnell Lecture delivered at University College, Galway, on October 19, 1965. Galway: National University of Ireland, 1965.

Heitman, Francis B. *Historical Register and Dictionary of the United States Army, From its Organization, September 29, 1789, to March 2, 1903*. Washington, DC: Government Printing Office, 1903.

Hennessy, Maurice N. *The Wild Geese: The Irish Soldier in Exile*. Old Greenwich, CT: Devin-Adair, 1973.

Hergesheimer, Joseph. *Sheridan: A Military Narrative*. Boston and New York: Houghton-Mifflin, 1931.

Hernan, Joseph M. *Celts, Catholics and Copperheads: Ireland Views the American Civil War*. Columbus, OH: Ohio State University Press, 1968.

Higham, John. *Strangers in the Land: Patterns of American Nativism 1860-1925*. New York: Atheneum, 1971.

Holder, Robert. *You Can Analyze Handwriting*. New York: Signet, 1969.

Hurt, W. R. and W. E. Lass. *Frontier Photographer: Stanley J. Marrow's Dakota Years*. Lincoln, NE: University of Nebraska Press, 1956.

Hutton, Paul Andrew. *Phil Sheridan and His Army*. Lincoln, NE: University of Nebraska Press, 1985.

Johnston, J. Stoddard. *Memorial History of Louisville*. Louisville, KY: n.p., 1896.

Jones, Paul John. *The Irish Brigade*. Washington, DC: Robert Luce Inc., 1969.

Kaczmarek, Louis. *The Wonders She Performs*. Manassas, VA: Trinity Communications, n.d.

Kuhlman, Charles. *Legend into History: The Custer Mystery*. Harrisburg, PA: Stackpole Co., 1951.

Keegan, John and Andrew Wheatcroft, eds. *Who's Who in Military History*. New York: William Morrow, 1976.

Lamott, John H. *History of the Archdiocese of Cincinnati, 1821-1921*. New York: Frederick Pustet Company, Inc., 1921.

Lawrence, Elizabeth Atwood. *His Very Silence Speaks: Comanche—the Horse Who Survived Custer's Last Stand*. Detroit, MI: Wayne State University Press, 1989.

Leckie, William H. *The Buffalo Soldiers: A Narrative of the Negro Cavalry in the West*. Norman, OK: University of Oklahoma Press, 1967.

Lever, Charles James. *Charles O'Malley, The Irish Dragoon*. Dublin: W. Curry, 1841.

Lonn, Ella. *Foreigners in the Confederacy*. Chapel Hill, NC: University of North Carolina Press, 1940.

———. *Foreigners in the Union Army and Navy*. Baton Rouge, LA: Louisiana State University Press, 1951.

Lt. Fred H. Beecher—A Memorial of. Portland, OR: Stephen Berry, 1870.

Luce, Edward S. *Keogh, Comanche and Custer*. St. Louis: John S. Swift Co., 1939.

MCreight, M. I. *Firewater and the Forked Tongues: A Sioux Chief Interprets U.S. History*. Pasadena, CA: Trails End Publishing Co., 1947.

McEniry, Blanche Marie. *American Catholics in the War with Mexico*. Washington, DC: n.p., 1937.

McGee, James E. *Sketches of Irish Soldiers in Every Land*. New York: J.A. McGee, 1873.

McGuire, James F. *The Irish in America*. London: Longmans, Green and Co., 1868.

MacLysaght, Edward. *Irish Families, Their Names, Arms and Origins*. Dublin: Hodges, Figges & Company, 1957.

Mahon, John K. *Letters from the Frontiers by Major General George A. McCall*. Gainesville, FL: University of Florida Press, 1974. Facsimile of 1868 edition.

Marquis, T. B. *Custer on the Little Bighorn*. Lodi, CA: Marquis Custer Publications, 1967.

———. *Wooden Leg: A Warrior Who Fought Custer*. Lincoln, NE: University of Nebraska Press, 1931.

Martin, Cornelia Williams. *The Old Home*. 2 vols. Auburn, NY: privately published, 1894.

Martin, Edward S. *Some Account of Family Stocks Involved in Life at Willowbrook*. Privately published, 1933.

Menge, W. Springer and J. August Shimrak, eds. *The Civil War Notebook of Daniel Chisholm*. New York: Orion Books, 1989.

Merington, Marguerite, ed. *The Custer Story: The Life and Intimate Letters of General George A. Custer and his Wife Elizabeth*. New York: Devin-Adair, 1950. Reprinted, Lincoln, NE: University of Nebraska Press, 1987.

Miller, David H. *Custer's Fall: the Indian Side of the Story*. New York: Duell, Sloan and Pearce, 1957.

Miller, Kirby A. *Emigrants and Exiles: Ireland and the Irish Exodus to North America*. New York: Oxford University Press, 1985.

Miller, Robert Ryal. *Shamrock and Sword: Saint Patrick's Battalion in the U.S.-Mexican War*. Norman, OK: University of Oklahoma Press, 1989.

Moore, Frank, ed. *The Civil War in Song and Story*. New York: P.F. Collier, 1889.

Myres, Sandra L., ed. *Cavalry Wife: The Diary of Eveline M. Alexander, 1866-1867*. College Station, TX: Texas A&M University Press, 1977.

Neidhardt, W. S. *Fenianism in North America*. University Park, PA: Pennsylvania State University Press, 1975.

Nelson, Paul David. *Anthony Wayne, Soldier of the Early Republic*. Bloomington, IN: Indiana University Press, 1985.

Nevins, Allan, ed. *A Diary of Battle: The Personal Journals of Colonel Charles S. Wainwright, 1861-1865*. New York: Harcourt, Brace & World, Inc., 1962.

Nevins, Allan and Milton H. Thomas, eds. *The Diary of George Templeton Strong*. 2 vols. New York: Macmillan, 1952.

The New Catholic Encyclopedia. New York: McGraw-Hill, 1967.

The New Encyclopedia Britannica. 15th ed. Chicago: Encyclopedia Britannica, 1988.

O'Connor, Richard. *Sheridan the Inevitable*. Indianapolis and New York: Bobbs-Merrill, 1953.

O'Hart, John. *Irish Pedigrees*. Vol. I. New York: Murphy & McCarthy, 1923.

Perpetua, Sister M., Mary Synon, and Katherine Rankin. *These Are Our Freedoms*. Boston: Ginn & Company, 1959.

Perry, Bliss. *Life and Letters of Henry Lee Higginson*. Boston: Atlantic Monthly Press, 1921.

Pitts, Michael R. *Western Movies: A TV and Video Guide to 4200 Genre Films*. Jefferson, NC: McFarland & Co., Inc., 1986.

Place, J. A. *The Western Films of John Ford*. Secaucus, NJ: Citadel Press, 1974.

Potter, Woodbine. *The War in Florida, Being an Exposition of its Causes and an Accurate History of the Campaigns of General Clinch, Gaines and Scott*. Baltimore, MD: Lewis and Coleman, 1836.

Powell, J. W. *Fourth Annual Report of the Bureau of Ethnology*. Washington, DC: Government Printing office, 1883.

Prucha, Francis Paul. *Broadax and Bayonet: The Role of the United States Army in the Development of the Northwest, 1815-1860*. Lincoln, NE: University of Nebraska Press, 1967.

———. *The Sword of the Republic: The United States Army on the Frontier, 1783-1846*. Bloomington, IN: Indiana University Press, 1969.

Prucha, Francis Paul, ed. *Army Life on the Western Frontier: Selections from the Official Reports Made Between 1826 and 1845 by Colonel George Croghan*. Norman, OK: University of Oklahoma Press, 1958.

Reedstrom, Ernest Lisle. *Bugles, Banners and War Bonnets*. Caldwell, ID: Caxton Printers, 1977.

Report of the Kansas Board of World's Fair Managers. Topeka, KS: Hamilton Printing Co., 1894.

Robertson, James I., Jr. *The Stonewall Brigade*. Baton Rouge, LA: Louisiana State University Press, 1963.

Rosenberg, Bruce A. *Custer And the Epic of Defeat*. University Park, PA: Pennsylvania State University Press, 1974.

Russell, Ampthill O. W. L. *The Roman Question*. Noel Blakiston, ed. London: Chapman & Hill, 1962.

Russell-Killough, Le Count Frank. *Dix Annees au Service Pontifical*. Paris: Victor Palme Libraire-Editeur, 1871.

Ryan, J. C., ed. and comp. *Custer Fell First: The Adventures of John C. Lockwood*. San Antonio, TX: Naylor, 1966.

Rydell, Robert W. *All the World's a Fair*. Chicago: University of Chicago Press, 1984.

Santoy, Claude. *The ABC's of Handwriting Analysis*. New York: Paragon House, 1989.

Sarkesian, Sam C. *Combat Effectiveness: Cohesion, Stress and the Volunteer Military*. Beverly Hills, CA: Sage Publications, 1980.

Scott, D. D., R. A. Fox, M. A. Connor and D. Harmon. *Archaeological Perspectives on the Battle of the Little Bighorn*. Norman, OK: University of Oklahoma Press, 1989.

Spotts, David L. *Campaigning with Custer*. E. A. Brininstool, ed. Lincoln, NE: University of Nebraska Press, 1988.

Stands in Timber, John and Margo Liberty. *Cheyenne Memories*. New Haven, CT: Yale University Press, 1967.

Stanfer, Helen. *Mari Sandoz: Story Catcher of the Plains*. Lincoln, NE: University of Nebraska Press, 1982.

Steiner, Bernard Christian. *Life and Correspondence of James McHenry, Secretary of War Under Washington and Adams*. Cleveland, OH: Burrows Brothers Co., 1907.

Stewart, Edgar. *Custer's Luck*. Norman, OK: University of Oklahoma Press, 1955.

Styple, William B. *Letters from the Peninsula; The Civil War Letters of General Philip Kearny*. Kearny, NJ: Belle Grove Publishing Co., 1989.

Sumner, Merlin E., ed. *The Diary of Cyrus B. Comstock*. Dayton, OH: Morningstar House, Inc., 1977.

Taunton, Francis. *Custer's Field: A Scene of Sickening, Ghastly Horror*. London: Johnson-Taunton Military Press, 1986.

Taylor, Philip. *The Distant Magnet: European Emigration to the United States*. New York: Harper and Row, 1971.

Thrapp, Dan L. *Encyclopedia of Frontier Biography*. Glendale, CA: Arthur H. Clark Company, 1988.

Tillett, L. *Wind on the Buffalo Grass*. New York: Thomas Y. Cromwell Co., 1976.

Trevelyan, G. M. *Garibaldi and the Making of Italy*. New York: Longmans, Green & Company, 1928.

United States Bureau of the Census. *Historical Statistics of the United States, 1789-1945*. Washington, DC: Government Printing Office, 1949.

United States. War Department. *General Regulations for the Army; or, Military Institutes*. Philadelphia: M. Carey and Sons, 1821; Washington, DC: Davis and Force, 1825.

Upton, Emory. *Cavalry Tactics, United States Army*. New York: D. Appleton and Co., 1874.

———. *The Military Policy of the United States*. Washington, DC: Government Printing Office, 1912.

Upton, Richard, ed. and comp. *The Custer Adventure*. Fort Collins, CO: The Old Army Press, 1975.

Urwin, Gregory J. W. and Roberta Fagan, eds., *Custer and his Times: Book Three*. Conway, AK: University of Arkansas and the Little Big Horn Associates, 1987.

Utley, Robert M. *Cavalier in Buckskin: George Armstrong Custer and the Western Military Frontier*. Norman, OK: University of Oklahoma Press, 1989.

———. *Frontier Regulars: The United States Army and the Indian, 1866-1891*. New York: Macmillan, 1973.

———. *Frontiersmen in Blue: The United States Army and the Indian, 1848-1865*. New York: Macmillan, 1967.

———. *Life in Custer's Cavalry*. New Haven, CT: Yale University Press, 1977.

Van de Water, Frederick F. *Glory Hunter: A Life of General Custer*. New York: Bobbs-Merrill, 1934.

War Diary and Letters of Stephen Minot Weld, 1861-1865. Boston: Massachusetts Historical Society, 1979.

Whittaker, Frederick A. *A Complete Life of Gen. George A. Custer* New York: Sheldon & Co., 1876.

Wilson, James B. *The Life and Services of Brevet Brigadier General Andrew Jonathan Alexander*. New York: Privately published, 1887.

Wittke, Carl Frederick. *The Irish in America*. Baton Rouge, LA: Louisiana State University Press, 1956.

PERIODICAL ARTICLES

Allen, Theodore F. "Myles Keogh, Yesterday." *Journal of the United States Cavalry Association* 11 (March, 1898): 227-228.

Bailly, E. C. "Echoes from Custer's Last Fight." *Military Affairs* 17 (1953): 170-173.

"Big Year For Gen. Custer." *The Hollywood Reporter* (March 30, 1965): 4.

"Brevet Lieutenant Colonel Myles W. Keogh." *The Army and Navy Journal* 14 (September 2, 1876): 58.

Browne, Henry J., ed. "A Memoir of Archbishop Hughes, 1838-1858." *U. S. Catholic Historical Society, Historical Records and Studies* 39-40 (1952): 164-168.

Burton, William L. "Irish Regiments in the Union Army: The Massachusetts Experience." *Historical Journal of Massachusetts* 11 (1983): 104-119.

Campbell, Vern D. "Armor and Cavalry Music." *Armor* 80 (March-April, 1971): 26-41.

"Capt. Keogh's Will." *The Westerners Brand Book* (Chicago) IX (No. 6., August, 1952): 42.

Charles, Tom. "Why Comanche Survived." *The Graduate Magazine* (December 4, 1941): 4.

Cousens, S. H. "The Regional Pattern of Emigration during the Great Famine, 1846-1851." *Transactions of the Institute of British Geographers* 28 (1960): 119-134.

———. "The Regional Variations in Emigration from Ireland Between 1821 and 1841." *Transactions of the Institute of British Geographers* 37 (1965): 15-29.

Dowling, Catherine. "Irish-American Nationalism in Butte, 1900-1916." *Montana* 39 (Spring, 1989): 50-63.

Ege, Robert J. "Legend Was a Man Named Keogh." *Montana* 16 (Spring, 1966): 27-39.

Evertt, John P. Bullets, Boots, and Saddles Being the Personal Recollections of Men Who Took Part in the Battle of the Big Horn, Montana Territory, June 25, 1876, As Told to John P. Evertt." *Sunshine Magazine* 11 (September, 1930): 1-10.

Garland, Hamlin. "General Custer's Last Fight as Seen by Two Moon." *McClure's* 9 (September, 1898): 443-448.

Garland, J. L. "Irish Soldiers of the American Confederacy." *Irish Sword* 1 (1949-1952): 174-180.

Godfrey, Edward S. "Custer's Last Battle." *Century Magazine* 43 (January, 1892): 358-384.

Grada, C. O. "A Note on Nineteenth-Century Irish Emigration Statistics." *Population Studies* 29 (1975): 143-144.

Gwyther, Annie R. "Pioneer Days on Fort Rice Military Reserve." *North Dakota History* 26 (1959): 128-131.

Hardorff, Richard G. ("Dutch"). "Captain Keogh's Insurance Policy." *Research Review* 11 (1977-79): 17-19.

Hassler, William W. "The Irrepressible James Shields." *Lincoln Herald* 81 (1979): 187-191.

Hatch, K. "Saint Patrick's Battalion: Unlikely Victims of a Mexican War." *Ireland of the Welcomes* 26 (1977): 32-35.

Heffernan, John B. "Ireland's Contribution to the Navies of the American Civil War, 1861-1865." *Irish Sword* 3 (1957): 81-87.

Hutton, Paul Andrew. "Hollywood's General Custer: The Changing Image of a Military Hero in Film." *Greasy Grass* 2 (May, 1986): 15-21.

"Injun Sal." *Newsweek* 53 (January 5, 1959): 68-69.

Ireland, John de Courcy. "The Confederate States at Sea in the American Civil War: The Irish Contribution." *Irish Sword* 14 (1980): 73-94.

"Irish-Born Recipients of the U. S. Congressional Medal of Honor." *Irish Sword* 12 (1975): 149-151.

"Irish in the 7th U. S. Cavalry." *Irish Sword* 1 (1949-1952): 336-338.

"Journal of J. E. Bangs." *North Dakota State Historical Society Collections* 4 (1913): 219-234.

Kaufman, Dave. "Custer Rides Again: On TV." *Variety* (May 23, 1967): 7.

Langellier, John P. "Movie Massacre: The Custer Myth in Motion Picture and Television," *Research Review*, n.s. 3 (June, 1989): 20-31.

Luce, Edward S., ed. "The Diary and Letters of Dr. James M. DeWolf." *North Dakota History* 25 (1958): 33-81.

McClernand, E. J. "With Indians and Buffalo in Montana." *Cavalry Journal* 36 (January, 1927): 7-54.

McCormack, Jack. "The Irish at the Little Big Horn." *Research Review* 3 (June, 1986): 3-19.

Millbrook, Minnie Dubbs. "Fort Leavenworth Races." *Research Review* 12 (December, 1978): 18-20.

Miller, David Humphreys. "Echoes of the Little Bighorn." *American Heritage* 22 (June, 1971): 28-39.

Montgomery, Mrs. Frank C. "Fort Wallace and Its Relation to the Frontier." *Collections of the Kansas State Historical Society* 17 (1926-1928): 189-283.

Mooney, Michael J. " 'From Garry Owen in Glory'." *Army* 39 (February, 1989): 58-64.

Mullen, Thomas J., Jr. "The Fighting Sixty-Ninth." *Eire-Ireland* 4 (Winter 1969): 13-26.

Murphy, W. S. "Four American Officers of the War of 1812." *Irish Sword* 6 (1963): 1-12.

———. "Four Soldiers of the American Revolution." *Irish Sword* 5 (1962): 164-174.

———. "The Irish Brigade of France at the Seige of Savannah, 1779." *Georgia Historical Quarterly* 38 (1954): 307-321.

O'Neil, Tom. "The Making of They Died With Their Boots On." *Research Review* n.s. 4 (June, 1990): 22-30.

O'Ryan, William D. and Robert M. Gaynor. "Irish Recipients of Awards for Bravery in the United States Armed Forces, 1863-1963." *Irish Sword* 8 (1967-1968): 274-275.

Pohanka, Brian C. "Myles Keogh." *Military Images* 8 (September-October, 1986): 15-24.

———. "Myles Walter Keogh (1840-1876)." *Greasy Grass* 4 (May, 1988): 5-11.

———. "Lt. Wallingford's Court Martial." *Research Review* 11 (September, 1977): 9-12.

"Pope Pius IX. Expulsion of Protestant Worship from Rome." *Harper's Weekly* 11 (February 9, 1867): 84-85.

Porter, Kenneth Wiggins. "Louis Pachecho: The Man and the Myth." *Journal of Negro History* 28 (January 1943): 65-72.

Power, Wally. "The Enigma of the Patricios." *Eire-Ireland* 4 (1969): 7-12.

Power, Walter. "Facets of the Mexican War." *Recorder* 36 (1975): 135-143.

Prucha, Francis Paul. "The United States Army as Viewed by British Travellers, 1825-1860." *Military Affairs* 17 (Fall 1953): 113-124.

Purcell, R. J. "James Shields: Soldier and Statesman." *Studies: An Irish Quarterly Review.* 21 (1932): 73-87.

"Slicing 'Custer' Pie Thin." *Hollywood Reporter* (March 11, 1965): 3.

Sprague, Marshall. "The Dude from Limerick." *American West* 3 (Fall, 1966): 53-61, 91-93.

Strother, D. H. "Personal Recollections of the War by a Virginian." *Harper's New Monthly Magazine* 34 (December-May, 1866-1867): 423-449.

Sweeny, William M. "The Irish Soldier in the War with Mexico." *Journal of the American Irish Historical Society* 26 (1927): 256-259.

"Tonka." *Screen Stories* (February, 1959): 63.

Vestal, Stanley. "The Man Who Killed Custer." *American Heritage* 8 (February, 1957): 6-9.

NEWSPAPERS AND GUIDES

Army and Navy Chronicle
Army and Navy Journal
Cork Examiner
Daily Tribune (New York)
Fort Wallace Bugle
Hardin Tribune
Hollywood Reporter
Junction City Union
Irish American (New York)
Kansas City Journal
Kansas City Star
Leavenworth Times
Lawrence Journal-World
Louisville Courier-Journal
Monthly Film Bulletin
National Intelligencer (Washington)
National Tribune (Washington)
New York Herald
New York Times
Olathe Daily News
Philadelphia Inquirer
The Times (London)
TV Guide
University Daily Kansan (Lawrence, Kansas)
Washington Post

FICTION AND POETRY

Anderson, A. M. *Comanche and His Captain.* New York: Harper & Row, Publishers, 1965.

MYLES KEOGH

———. *Grant March-Steamboat Captain*. New York: Harper & Row, Publishers, 1959.

Appel, David. *Comanche: The Story of America's Most Heroic Horse*. New York: The World Publishing Co. 1951.

Beecher, Elizabeth, adapter. *Walt Disney's Tonka*. New York: Golden Press, 1959.

Berger, Thomas. *Little Big Man*. New York: Dial Press, 1964.

Birney, Hoffman. *The Dice of God*. New York: Henry Holt and Co., 1956.

Bonehill, Ralph. *With Custer in the Black Hills*. New York: Grossett and Dunlap Pubs., 1902.

Brady, Cyrus Townsend. *Britton of the Seventh*. New York: A. L. Burt Co., 1914.

Brooks, Eldridge S. *Master of the Strong Hearts: A Story of Custer's Last Rally*. New York: E. P. Dutton and Co., 1931.

Daly, Kathleen N. *Tonka*. New York: Pyramid Books, 1976.

Downey, Fairfax. *The Seventh's Staghound*. New York: Dodd, Mead and Co., 1948.

Fraser, George Macdonald. *Flashman and the Redskins*. New York: Alfred A. Knopf, 1982.

Haycox, Ernest. *Bugles in the Afternoon*. New York: Grossett and Dunlap Pubs., 1943.

Henry, Will. *Custer's Last Stand: The Story of the Battle of the Little Big Horn*. Philadelphia: Chilton Book Co., 1966.

———. *No Survivors*. New York: Random House, 1950.

Hunter, E. J. *White Squaw #8: Horn of Plenty*. New York: Kensington Publishing Co., 1985.

Inman, Henry. *The Old Santa Fe Trail: The Story of a Great Highway*. Minneapolis, MN: Ross & Haines, Inc., 1966.

———. *The Ranche on the Ox Hide*. New York: MacMillian Company, 1898.

Jefferies, Jeff. *Seventh Cavalry*. London: Collins, 1959.

Jones, Douglas C. *The Court-Martial of George Armstrong Custer*. New York: Charles Scribner's Sons, 1976.

Leighton, Margaret. *Comanche of the Seventh*. New York: Ariel Books, 1957.

Lydic, F. A. *Comanche! Oh Comanche! A Narrative in Verse*. Joliet, IL: Privately Printed, 1982.

MacKaye, Loring. *The Great Scoop*. New York: Thomas Nelson & Sons, 1956.

Miller, Jim. *That Damn Single Shot*. New York: Ballantine Books, 1988.

Mills, Charles K. *A Mighty Afternoon: A Novel of the Battle of the Little Big Horn*. Garden City, NY: Doubleday and Co., 1980.

O'Neill, Bill. *Little Big Horn*. Livingston, MT: Privately Printed, 1989.

Oliver, Chad. *Broken Eagle*. New York: Bantam Books, 1989.

Patten, Lewis B. *The Red Sabbath*. Garden City, NY: Doubleday and Company, 1968.

Randle, Kevin, and Cornett, Robert. *Remember the Little Bighorn!* New York: Charter Books, 1990.

Reynolds, Quinton. *Custer's Last Stand*. New York: Random Row, Publishers, 1968.

Sabin, Edwin L. *On the Plains With Custer*. Philadelphia, PA: J. B. Lippincott Co., 1913.

Sandoz, Mari. *The Battle of the Little Bighorn*. Philadelphia, PA: J. B. Lippincott Co., 1966.

Scofield, Jonathan. *The Frontier War*. New York, NY: Dell Publishing, 1981.

Shiflet, Kenneth. *The Convenient Coward*. Harrisburg, PA: Stackpole Co., 1961.

Utley, Steven and Waldrop, Howard. "Custer's Last Jump," in Terry Carr, ed., *Universe 6*. Garden City, NY: Doubleday and Co., 1968.

Van de Water, Frederic F. *Thunder Shield*. Indianapolis, IN: Bobbs-Merrill, Co., 1934.

Walt Disney's Tonka. New York: Dell Publishing Co., 1958.

White, Dale. *The Boy Who Came Back*. New York: Criterion Books, 1966.

Wilson, Howard (Hap). *War Chiefs of the Northwest*. Helena, MT: Falcon Press, 1987.

Films and Television

Mathison, Melissa. "Son of the Morning Star." Pts. 1 and 2. Teleplay, March 12, 1990. Gene Autry Western Heritage Museum.

Mayes, Wendell. "The Day Custer Fell", Final Script April 2, 1965. Vincent Heier Collection. St. Louis, MO.

She Wore A Yellow Ribbon. Argosy Pictures. 1949.

They Died With Their Boots On. Working Script. Main Branch, New York Public Library.

Index

Abell, Henry H: 117
Abingdon: 81
Adriatic Sea: 52
Akers, James: 41
Alabama: 39
Albany: 94
Alexander, Andrew: mention of, 15, 17, 71-74, 87, 91; and Evelina Martin, 88, 91; retirement and death, 99; and Upton, 99
Alexander, Evelina (Evy) Martin: mention of, 84, 86, 88, 91-92, 157; observations on Keogh and Upton, 98
Alexandria: 70, 109
Aldie: 76
Allen, Theodore: describes Keogh in Tennessee, 79
American Frontier: 24
American Revolution: 16, 29-30, 43
Ancona: mention of, 52, 55; siege of, 57; collapse of, 58
Anderson, A. M: 178
Andersonville: 80, 88
Andrews, Clinton: 117
Angel, W. W: 81
Antietam: battle of, 38, 46, 71, 176
Antwerp: 55
Appel, David: 173
Appomattox: 65, 103, 110, 174
Arapaho: 112, 184
Arkansas River: 113
Arikara scouts: See Ree scouts
Arickaree Fork: 113
Armstrong, Christie: 117
Army and Navy Journal: 179
Army of Northern Virginia: 76, 83
Army of the Potomac: 36, 64, 72, 76-77, 79, 166
Arthur, President Chester: 65
Artillery: Seventh New York Heavy, 37; First Ohio, Battery L, 68; First Connecticut Heavy, 78
Atlanta: 80

Atlantic Monthly, The: 179
Auburn: 18, 51, 88, 96, 157-160
Austria: 52, 57
Ayres, Romeyn: 64

Badger, Joseph M: 104
Badger, Rev. Norman: 104
Bailey, Henry Allen: 121, 135
Baker, Stephen: 130
Baldwin, George A: 117
Ball's Bluff: 72
Baltimore: 35
Bangs, J. E: 121
Bankhead, H. C: 110
Banks, Nathaniel P: 72
Bannon, Father John: 38, 61
Barclay, Clement Biddle: 112
Barnitz, Albert: 108-109, 112, 128
Barry, D. F: 145
Barry, John: 41
Barthelmess, Christian: 159-160
Battalion of St. Patrick: 57, 176
Battle of the Little Big Horn, The: 169
Beecher, Fredrick H: mention of 104, 113, 124; describes Keogh, 105; on drinking at Ft. Wallace, 129
Beecher, Henry Ward: 105
Belknap, William: 117
Bell, James M: 106, 117
Bell, William A: 102, 109
Begenalstown: 51
Benjamin Franklin: fictional airship, 170
Benteen, Frederick: mention of, 42, 113, 132-134, 138, 140, 155, 186; in fiction, 165-166, 168, 170-173, 175, 178
Berger, Thomas: 71, 169
Beverly's Ford: 75
Big Timbers: 108

Birney, Hoffman: 168
Bismark: 157, 176
Black Hills: gold exploration, 40
Black Kettle: 40
Black Man's Hand: 170
Blaine, Alice: 65
Blaine, James G: 65
Blaine, Walker: 65
Blair, Eliza Violet: 91
Blair, Frances Preston, Jr: 91
Blair, Frank: 80
Blanchfield, J. P: 51
Blanchfield, Margarete: 49
Blanchfield, Mary: 50, 121
Bobo, Edwin: 148-149, 155
Bonehill, Ralph: 166
Badger, Joseph M: 104
Badger, Rev. Norman: 104
Bailey, Henry Allen: 121, 135
Baker, Stephen: 130
Baldwin, George A: 117
Ball's Bluff: 72
Baltimore: 35
Bangs, J. E: 121
Bankhead, H. C: 110
Banks, Nathaniel P: 72
Bannon, Father John: 38, 61
Barclay, Clement Biddle: 112
Barnitz, Albert: 108-109, 112, 128
Barry, D. F: 145
Barry, John: 41
Barthelmess, Christian: 159-160
Battalion of St. Patrick: 57, 176
Battle of the Little Big Horn, The: 169
Beecher, Fredrick H: mention of 104, 113, 124; describes Keogh, 105; on drinking at Ft. Wallace, 129

199

MYLES KEOGH

Beecher, Henry Ward: 105
Belknap, William: 117
Bell, James M: 106, 117
Bell, William A: 102, 109
Begenalstown: 51
Benjamin Franklin: fictional airship, 170
Benteen, Frederick: mention of, 42, 113, 132-134, 138, 140, 155, 186; in fiction, 165-166, 168, 170-173, 175, 178
Berger, Thomas: 71, 169
Beverly's Ford: 75
Big Timbers: 108
Birney, Hoffman: 168
Bismark: 157, 176
Black Hills: gold exploration, 40
Black Kettle: 40
Black Man's Hand: 170
Blaine, Alice: 65
Blaine, James G: 65
Blaine, Walker: 65
Blair, Eliza Violet: 91
Blair, Frances Preston, Jr: 91
Blair, Frank: 80
Blanchfield, J. P: 51
Blanchfield, Margarete: 49
Blanchfield, Mary: 50, 121
Bobo, Edwin: 148-149, 155
Bonehill, Ralph: 166
Boston: 36
Bourke, John Gregory: 134
Bouyer, Mitch: 140
Boy Who Came Back, The: 179
Bradford, Dexter: 163
Brady, Cyrus Townsend: 166
Brainard, Rev: 160
Brandy Station: 75-78, 85-86
Brave Wolf: 143, 147
Briddles, Nathan: 182
Bristoe Station: 38, 74, 77
Bristol: 82
Britton of the Seventh: 166
Broken Eagle: 173
Brooklyn: 35
Brooks, Elbridge: first account of Keogh at Little Big Horn, 165
Brown, Barron: 24
Bruce, Sir Fredrick: 96
Bucephalers: 22

Buell, David H: 117
Buena Vista: 33
"Buffalo Bill" (William F. Cody): 187
"Buffalo Soldiers": 40
Buford, John: mention of, 70-73, 75, 77, 87; stand at Battle of Gettysburg, 76; diagnosed with typhoid, 78
Bugles in the Afternoon: 167
Bull Run: first battle, 36; second battle of, 64, 71, 85
Burnside, Ambrose: 71
Bustard, James: 41, 134, 148, 155; in fiction and film, 172, 184-185
Butler, William O: 34
Butte: 43
Byrne, C. C: 122
Byrnes, Richard: 37

Caddle, Michael: 41
Calhoun Coulee: 145
Calhoun, James: mention of, 118, 120, 132, 140, 143; in fiction, 167, 169, 178
Calhoun Ridge (Hill): 139, 143-146, 151-152, 155
Calhoun sector: 144
California Brigade (Philadelphia Brigade): 37
"California Joe": 185-186
Callan, Thomas J: 41
Camp Alfred Gibbs: 112
Camp Supply: 47, 113-114, 187
Camp Terry: 120
Camp, Walter: 160
Canby, Henry Seidel: 39
Capston, James L: 38
Carey, Joseph: 31
Carey, Patrick: 41
Carey, Philip: 164, 182
Carland, J. A: 130, 132
Carlow, County: 16, 43, 49, 51, 54, 160
Carrell, Minnie: 180
Carroll, Samuel S: 68
Carroll, William: 31
Cartwright Ridge: 139
Cashan, William: 41
Castle Garden: 36
Cavalry: mentioned, 16; Seventh U.S., 21-22, 40-41, 46-47, 86, 104, 108-110, 113-114, 117-121, 126, 132-134, 136 170, 173, 178, 183; Chief, 31, 78; Ninth and Tenth U.S., 40; Fifteenth New York, 64-65; First Virginia (Union), 68; Third U.S., 71; Cavalry Corps, 72, 75; Second U.S., 75, 85, 126, 134; Bureau, 78; Eleventh Kentucky, 83; Twelfth Kentucky, 83; Fourth U.S., 86, 104; Third U.S., 92; Eighteenth Kansas, 109: Eighteenth New York, 109; tactics, 134; Fifth U.S., 186

Cavour, Count Camillo Benso di: mention of, 52-53; and Napoleon, pact between, 54
Cedar Creek: 64
Cemetery Ridge: 151
Chalk Creek Station: 104
Chancellorsville: battle of, 74
Chapman, Mary: 96
Chapultepec: storming of, 33
Charles O'Malley: The Irish Dragoon: 16, 21, 45, 49, 67, 95, 103-104, 131
Chelsea: 35
Cheyennes: 47, 135, 138, 140, 143, 177, 184
Churubusco: battle of, 33
City of Brooklyn: 116
City of Chester: 122
City of Paris: 115
Civita: 55
Clary, Abby Grace: 85, 98
Clary, Robert Emmett, Jr: 85-86
Clay, Edward W: 30
Cleburne, Patrick Ronayne: 39
Clifden: 49-50, 157
Clinton: 80
Clinton, Sir Henry: 31
Cocoran, Colonel Michael: 36-37
Coffee, John: 31
Columbia: 109
Comanche: symbolism of, 15, 24; "only survivor", 21; General Orders No. 7, 23; wounds, 23, 119, 187; at Ft. Lincoln, 24; at Chicago Fair, 25; display of, 26-27; Indian-white relations, effect on, 28; posthumous career of, 28; mention of, 112, 138, 140, 165-166, 190; and "last stand," 173; in fiction, poetry, and film, 165, 173-177, 179-182
Comanche and His Captain: 179
Comanche of the Seventh: 176
Comanche! Oh Comanche! A Narrative in Verse: 181
Comanches: 110
Comes in Sight: 146
Companies at Little Big Horn: mention of, 134, 136, 139-140, 143; disintegration of, 143, 148
Company I, ("Wild I") Seventh U.S. Cavalry: mention of, 20, 108, 112-114, 117, 119-121, 132-134, 136, 138-139, 144, 146, 148, 154, 155, 157; in fiction and film, 168, 170-173, 177, 179
Company of St. Patrick, 48, 59
Comstock, Cyrus: 94-95
Comstock, William "Medicine Bill": mention of 104, 113; kills Wyatt, 126; death of, 127
Conelly, Patrick: 41
Connell, Evan S: mention of, 46; account of Keogh at Little BigHorn, 140

INDEX

Considine, Martin: 41
Conte di Cavour: 59
Contrary Belly: 146
Convenient Coward, The: 168
Cooke, William W: 117, 119, 134-135, 187; in fiction, 169, 172, 179, 182
Coolidge, Richard H: 32
Cooney, David: 41
Cooper, Herring: 115
Cooper, James Fenimore: 126
Coppinger, Alice B: 65
Coppinger, John Joseph: mention of, 55-56, 71, 176; as Union officer, 64 early life, 64; service in California, 65; death of, 65
Corcoran, Michael: 36
Cork, County: 54-55, 64
Costello, Michael J: 44
Courtland, Jerome: 182
Court Martial of George Armstrong Custer, The: 170
Cowdrey, Mary Boyton: 179
Cox, Charles: 108
Cox, Jacob: 84
Crabbe, Jack: 169
Crazy Horse: 138, 140, 144-146, 170, 185-186
Crew, Fleming: 173
Crittenden Hill: 155
Crittenden, John J: 120
Croghan, George: 32
Croley, Herbert: 44
Crook, George: 157
"Croquet Cottage": 84, 92-94, 96
Crow King: 145-146
Crow scouts: 157
Crimea: 37, 109
Culpepper: 77
Curtiss, William A: 134
Custer Battlefield National Monument: 26
Custer, Elizabeth: mention of, 45-46, 116-117, 131, 134, 170, 177, 179; on Keogh's drinking, 128
Custer, George A: mention of, 15-16, 24, 42, 75, 77, 91, 103, 107, 109, 112, 116, 123, 126, 131-133; "last stand," 21, 136, 139- 141, 143, 155; Irish ethnic background, 41; familiarity with "Garry Owen," 45-46; comments on Coppinger, 65; first meets Keogh, 71; letter to Libbie on Keogh's expected appointment to Sheridan's staff, 82; letter to Keogh on Indians, 108; on Keogh and "Miss Hf," 118; buys life insurance; 120, body found, 135; referred to as "Yellow Hair," 138, 170, 185, 188; in fiction, poetry, film, and television, 165-174, 178-179, 182-186
Custer Hill (Ridge): 138, 145-147, 153
Custer's Last Fight: 181

Custer's Last Stand: 175
Custer, Tom: 132, 134-135, 143; in fiction, 167-169

Dade, Francis L: 32
Dade Massacre: 32
Dallas, Georgia: 80
Dalton, Patrick: 33
Daly, Kathleen: 175
Dandy: 177
Daniels, Jeff: 178
D'Arcy, James: 60
Dary, David: 181
Davern, Edward: 42
Davis, Jefferson: 38
Davis, Nelson H: 113
Davis, Theodore R: 126
Day, Horace H: 63
Day Custer Fell, The: 29, 183
Decatur: 80
Deep Ravine (Coulee): 139, 143
De Lacy, Milton: 121
DeRudio, Charles: mentio of 42, 133; in fiction, 167, 169, 171, 174, 176
Deserters: 33, 106
Dewey Beard: 150
Dice of God, The: 168
Disney, Walt: 175, 182
Donahue, John: 42
Downey, Fairfax: 167
Downing, Thomas Patrick: 41, 121
Doyle, David Noel: 30
Drake, Daniel: 34
Driscoll, Edward C: 41, 121
Dublin: 35, 41-43, 44, 176
Dummel, William H: 108
Dungannon: 34
Dustin, Fred: 118, 129
Dyche, Lewis L: 24-25
Dyche Museum: 26, 28

Eagen, Thomas P: 41-42
Ebbitt House: 72, 76
Edgerly, W. S: 120, 133, 144
Ege, Robert: account of Keogh at Little Big Horn, 138-139
Elliott, Joel H: 112
Ellis Station: 112
Emerald Guards: 39
Emmet Guards: 35
England: 40, 62

Ethnic make-up of troops at Little Big Horn Battle: 41
Etna: 62

Farragut, Admiral David: 91
Far West: 131, 168-169, 181, 183
Favor, Nannie: mention of, 124; brings suit against Keogh and Beecher, 125
Favor, Warren: 125
Fifth Royal Lancers: 45, 49, 167, 174, 176
"Fighting Irish": Bull Run, 36
Finley, Jeremiah: 41
Finnegan, Joseph: 39
Fitzgerald, John: 31
Five Forks: 65, 83-84
Flanagan, James: 41-42
Flashman and the Redskins: 172
Flashman, Sir Henry: 172
Fleming, Miss: 90
Fletcher: 157
Flying Hawk: 145
Flynn, Errol: 182
Foolish Elk: 146, 151
Fort Abacrombie: 120
Fort Abraham Lincoln: frontpiece, 22, 24, 123, 157, 172-173, 177, 179, 181
Fort Custer: 157
Fort Dodge: 114, 187
Fort Harker: 112-113, 188
Fort Hays: 114, 178, 184, 186
Fort Hill: 98
Fort Keogh: 181, 189
Fort Leavenworth: 115-116, 188
Fort Laramie: 112
Fort Lyon: 109, 113
Fort Meade: 24-25
Fort Pembina: 120
Fort Riley: 24-26, 103, 109
Fort Totten: 24, 121
Fort Sumter: 60
Fort Reynolds: 113, 131
Fort Wallace: 103-107, 109, 124, 126, 129
Ford, John: 182
Foreign Enlistment Act: 54
France: 29, 57
Franco-Prussian War: 116

201

Fraser, George MacDonald: 172
Fredericksburg: battle of, 38
Frémont, John C: 63, 67-68
French, Thomas: 136
Friswold, Carroll: 100
The Frontier War: 172
Frost, Lawrence: 11, 138

Gaffney, George: 41
Gall: 138, 145-146, 150, 177
Gall, Alice: 173
Galway: 42
Garibaldi, Giuseppe: 52, 61, 116
Garland, Hamlin: 137
"Garry Owen": 40, 45-47, 167, 173-174, 176, 182, 185-186
Gatling gun: 132
George III: 30
George, Lloyd: 93
Georgia: mention of, 39; Home Guards and Militia, 80
Gettysburg: 38, 64, 76, 176
Gibbon, John: 132
Gibbs, Alfred: proposer of regimental band, Seventh Cavalry, 46; mention of 104, 112
Gildner, Gary: 181
Gillem, Alvan C: 83-84
Girard, F.F: 42
"Girl I Left Behind Me": 40, 46, 99, 113
The Glory Guys: 169, 183
Godfrey, Edward: 42, 47, 132
Goff, O. S: 122
Goosecreek Station: 104, 107
Gordonsville: 73-74
Graham, Hiram J: 124
Graham, William A: 40, 137
Grant, U. S: 91, 115
Grant Marsh - Steamboat Captain: 178
Great Scoop, The: 176
Great Sioux Massacre, The: 182-183
Gregg, David McMurtie: 75
Grinell, George B: 147
Grinell Springs: 107
Grover, Abner "Sharp": 127
Guiney, Patrick Robert: 36

Hagan, James: 39
Hale, Joseph: 104

Hamlin, William: 108
Hancock, Winfield S: expedition, 104, 109; mention of, 107
Hand, Edward: 31
Hardorff, Richard: 139-140
Harrison, Thomas W: 41
Hay, John: 180
Haycox, Ernest: 167
Hayes-McCoy, G. A: 128
Hays City: 114
Hazell, Audrey J: 180
He Dog: 146
Henry, E. E: 102
Henry, Will (Henry Allen Wilson): 167, 179
Hetesimer, Adam: 121
Higham, John: 35
Hofmann, Richard: 90
Hooker, Joseph: 72, 74, 76
Hood, John Bell: 81
Hughes, Archbishop John: 61, 64
Hughes, Robert: 41-42
Hull: 55
Hunter, E.J: 173
Huntley, George, Jr: 182

Illinois: 67
Ilsey, Captain Charles S: 25
Immigrants in U.S. Military: 40
Ince, Thomas H: 181
India-Rubber Poncho tent: 63
Indian Warfare: Fort Wallace, 106
Indianapolis: 116
Infantry: First U.S., 31; Fifth U.S., 33; Sixty-Ninth New York, 35-36, 46; Ninth Massachusetts, 37; Twenty-Eight New York, 37; Twenty-Ninth Massachusetts, 37; One hundred Sixteenth Pennsylvania, 37; Eighth Alabama, 39; Second Louisana Battalion (Louisiana Tiger or Irish Tartars), 39; First Georgia Volunteers, 39; First Irish Battalion (Virginia), 39; Twenty-Fourth and Twenty-Fifth U.S., 40; Fourteenth U.S., 54; Eighteenth U.S., 64-65; Tenth U.S., 65; Twenty-Third U. S., 65, Third U.S., 104, 108; Thirty-Seventh U.S., 104; Sixth U.S., Company B Officers, 130, 132; Fifth U.S., 110, 115; Fifteenth U. S., 117; Ninth U.S., 187; Seventeenth U.S., 187
Ingalls, Charles Henry: 130
Inman, Henry: 187
Inman, William: 62
Internal Revenue: 118
Ireland: 16, 29, 31, 34, 189
Irish Brigade: 29-30, 36, 39, 50
Irish: immigrants and immigration, 30, 34-35, 44; during Civil War, 31, 35; prejudice against, 31-33, 35, 39; in U.S. military, 32, 36, 38; religious problems, 33; potato famine, 34; vs. Know nothings, 35; New York militia, 35; recruitment of, 36, 61; Confederate military, 39; in Seventh U.S. Cavalry, 40; at Little Big Horn, 40; narrow escapes in battle, 42; mention of, 43; ranks, 43; poverty of, 44; in Papal service, 56, 59; defense of Ancona, 57; military at Monte Pelago, 58
Irish-American Guards: 35
Irish Rifles: 35
Italy: 16, 52
Iverson, Alfred: 80

Jackson, Andrew: 31
Jackson, Thomas J. "Stonewall": 67, 70-71
Jackson, William: 42
Jasper Greens: 35
Jeffries, Jeff: 177
Johnson, Andrew: 91
Johnston, Joseph E: 79
Jones, Douglas: 170
Joyce, J. M: 127
Judge, Robert P: 159

Kangaroo: ship, 62, 189
Kanipe, Daniel: 139
Kansas, University of: 22, 24-28
Kearny, Philip: body retrieved from Confederates, 71
Kearney, S. W: 34
Kehoe, Richard J: 61, 77
Keily, Daniel J: mention of, 54-55, 59, 62, 67, 86-87; bravery in battle of Port Republic, 69; wounded at Port Republic, 70; petitions to reenter active service, 72; death of, 110-111
Kelly's Ford: 74
Kelly, Patrick: 41
Kenny, Michael: 41
Kentucky: 70-71, 83, 123
Kenyon College: 104
Keogh, Alice: 160
Keogh, Bridget: 50
Keogh, Catherine: 50
Keogh, Ellen: 50
Keogh Family: money problems, 50; home, 189; political involvements, 190
Keogh, Fanny: 50
Keogh, Gary: 190
Keogh, James: 50
Keogh, Joanna: 50
Keogh, John: 49-50
Keogh, Julia: 50
Keogh, Margaret: 50, 157

Keogh, Mary: 50
Keogh, Myles Walter: mention of, 15, 48, 66, 85, 187; relationship to Ireland, 16, 41, 43; in Papal Wars, 16, 29, 62; description of, 52, 95; post Civil War, 17; death of, 18; "soldier of fortune," 21, 29; bond with Comanche, 22-23; fame related to Comanche, 28; influence of Arthurian legend on, 44; and regimental band, Seventh Cavalry, 46; birthplace of, 49; siblings of, 50; relations with family, 50; interest in women, 51; breaks leg, 51; European military career, 52; in Papal States, 54; travel to Papal States, 55; medal of Spoleto, 56; at battle of Castelfidardo, 57; life in post-war Rome, 59-60; joins Union Army, 61; and Daniel Keily passage to America, 62-63; Civil War, 67; and Keily in Port Republic battle, 68-69; and horse "Tom," 70; and O'Keefe at Second battle of Manassas, 71; and O'Keefe at Rappahannock encampment, 72; at Thompson's Crossroads, 74; and O'Keefe lauded by Buford, 75; travel to Washington to meet two cousins, 77; problems with cousins O'Sullivan and Kehoe, 78; at death of Buford, 78; and Stoneman, 79, 88; letter to sister on horses, 80; capture by Confederates 80-81; winter at Knoxville, 83; achieves rank of brevet lt. col., 83; on war and peace, 84; thoughts on marriage, 84, 97; link to Abby Grace Clary, 86, 94; assigned to Company I, Seventh U.S. Cavalry, 86; and Martin family, 87- 88, 91-92, 94-95, 97-99; Andersonville, 88; handwriting, 100; arrives at Fort Riley, 103; letter about Seventh Cavalry, 104; at Fort Wallace, 104-106; thoughts on troops at Fort Wallace, 105; on deserters, 106; on Indian trouble at Fort Wallace, 107; on fighting Indians, 108; on killing of Wylliams, 109; hunting with Nowlan, 110; desire to visit Ireland, 110; broken leg, 111-112; goes to Fort Harker, 112-113; desire for advancement, 113; at Camp Supply, 114; on board of courts martial, 114-115; in Europe 1869, 116; capture of rustlers, 117; at Fort Leavenworth, 117; and "Miss Hf," 118; relationship with Custer, 119; purchases life insurance, 120, 132; generosity, 121; return to Ireland in 1874, 121-122; period of illness, 122; in Kentucky, 123; at home of Dr. John Arvid Ouchterlony, 123; at Little Big Horn, 123, 134-137; backs Beecher against Favor, 124; praise for Comstock, 126; as a drinker, 128-129; on route to Little Big Horn, 131, 133; commands Companies I, B, & C, 132; body of, 135, 155; Little Big Horn, 140; and final struggle of troops at Custer Battle, 147-148; memorials, 160; medals worn at Little Big Horn, 162; in novels, 165-168; in films and television, 181-186; wolf hunting, 188; memorabilia in Ireland, 189
Keogh, Patrick: 50
Keogh sector: panic of troops in, 144, 148, 152; lack of firearms use, 150; lack of intense fighting, 151
Keogh, Thomas: 50, 160
Keogh's Company: discovery and burial, 155
Kilkenny, County: 49
Kilpatrick, Judson: 77
Kimball, Nathan: 70
King, Charles: 180

Kiowas: 110
Know-nothingism: 36
Knox, Henry: 31
Knoxville: 82-83, 92
Korean War: 43
Korn, Gustave: 20
Kuhlman, Charles: 136-138, 140
Ku Klux Klan: 118

Lake Station: 109
Lame White Man: 138, 145-146
Lamoriciére, Louis Christophe León Juchault de: 56-59
Lane, Walter Paye: 39
Lanigan, G. T: 179
Lawrence, KS: 22
Lawrence, MA: 35
Lawrence, Elizabeth: 173
Lebanon: 119
Lee, D. Mortimer: 104
Lee, Henry: 30
Lee, Robert E: 71, 76-77
Lee, W. H. F. "Rooney": 75-76
Leighlinbridge: 51
Leighton, Margaret: 176
Lever, Charles: 15, 21, 45, 49, 67, 103, 131
Limerick, County: 45, 49
Lincoln, Abraham: mention of, 60, 72-73; duel with James Shields, 67
Little Big Heart River: 131
Little Big Horn, battle of: mention, 15-18, 22, 24, 26-27, 29, 33, 40, 42-44, 75, 87, 121, 123, 132, 134, 136, 138, 142-153; battalion configuration, 134, 136, 138-139, 143; alleged Indian oral accounts, 136; in fiction, poetry, and film, 165- 166, 168-170, 175, 179, 181, 183
Little Big Man: 36
Little Missouri River: 131
Little Soldier, 140
Liverpool: 62
Logan, Will A: 135
Lomond, Britt: 182
London: 54, 189
Lone Bear: 147
Long, David Burton: 128
Long-Hair: 183
Longstreet, James: 71
Louisville: 118-120, 123, 155, 163
Loyd, George: 41, 43
Luce, Edward: mention, 15, 26, 49, 165, 172-173; on relationship of Keogh and Nelly Martin, 99; account of Little Big Horn battle, 136
Lydic, F. A: 181

Lyman, Theodore: 70, 78
Lynch, Patrick: 38
Lynch, Bishop Patrick: 61

Macon & Western Railroad: 80
Madden, Michael P: 42
Madison, Mira: 91
Maguire, Edward G: 157
Mallery, Garrick: 135
Malory, Sir Thomas: 15
Mangum, Neil: 160
Maguire, Edward: 144, 157
Manassas: 70, 77
Maroney, Mathew: 41
Marseilles: 55
Marsh, Grant: 167
Marston, John J: 114
Martin, Cornelia Eliza: 87, 90-91
Martin, Edward: 90, 93, 96
Martin, Eliza Williams: 94
Martin, Emily: see Emily Martin Upton
Martin, Enos Thompson Throop: mention of, 90-91; death of, 98; real estate lot, 159
Martin, Evelina: see Evelina Martin Alexander
Martin family: mention of, 17, 89-93; Keogh's body, 157
Martin, George Bliss: 93
Martin, James: 41
Martin, John (Jack): 92, 99
Martin, Lylie: 91
Martin, Mary: 90
Martin, Michael: 41
Martin, Nelly: 17, 95, 97-98, 160, 190
Martin, Samuel: 117
Martin, Throop: 92, 94
Martin, Violet Blair: marries Wilbur Elliott Wilder, 94
Massachusetts: 35,37
Maunder, Wayne: 184
Mayes, Wendell: 29
Mayfield, Ben: 180
Mayo, County: 33
Mazzini, Giuseppe: 52
McCall, George A: 32
McClellan, George: 67, 70-71, 87, 92
McClernand, Edward J: 135
McCormack, John: 41
McKibbin, Chambers: 117

MYLES KEOGH

McDermott, Father John: 57
McDermott, George M: 41-42
McDougall, Thomas M: 117, 165, 171
MacDonough, Thomas: 31
McGlone, John: 41
McGregor, James: 180
McGuigan, Patrick: 62
McHenry, James: 31
McIlhargey, Archibald: 29, 42, 183-184
McIlhargey, Josie: 42
MacKaye, Loring: 176
McKeown, Mike: 168
McKibben, Chambers: 117
MacLoughlin, Chaplain Edward: 60
McNally, James P: 41
Meade, George Gordon: 76-77
Meagher, Thomas Francis: 36
Medal of Honor: 41, 94
Medals: given to Irish, 41-42; *Medalaglia Pro Petri Sede* (For the Chair of Peter), 55, 66, 155, 162, 172, 176; *Ordine di San Gregorio* (Order of St. Gregory), 64, 66, 111, 163; *Ordine di Piano*, 64; Papal, mention of, 78, 110, 165; *Agnus Dei*, 155, 162
Medicine Tail Coulee: 143
Meigs, Montgomery: 117
Merrill, Lewis: 114-115
Merritt, Wesley: 76
Metcalf, Mr. & Mrs. George: 88
Metropolitan Hotel: 115
Mexican War: 33-34, 43
Mexico: 33-34
Mexico City: 33
Michigan: 182
Middleburg: 76
Middleton: 64
Miles, Nelson A: 114
Miller, David Humphreys: 137
Miller, Jim: 173
Mills, Charles: 170
Mineo, Sal: 182
Minnesota: 67
Mississippi River: 72
Missouri: 39
Mitchel Light Guards: 35
Mix, John: 76
Modena: 52-53
Montgomery Guards: 35

Monument Station: 107
Moore, Patrick Theodore: 39, 105
Morrow, Robert: 75, 83, 85
Morrow, Stanley J: 160
Moseby, John S: 170
Moylan, Myles: mention of, 100, 102, 139; letter to Keogh, 107; commands Company A, Seventh Cavalry, 132
Moylan, Stephen: 31
Mulberry Creek conflict: 187
Mulholland, St. Clair Augustin: 36
Munns, Thurmena: 100
Murphy, Lawrence: 41-42
My Life on the Plains: 177

Naples: 53
Napper Tandy Light Artillery: 35
Napoleon III: 53
Nashville: 82, 86
Native American Narratives on Little Big Horn: 141, 145-146
Nave, Andrew: 120, 158
Nelaton, August: 116
New York: 30, 35-36, 61, 65, 188
New York City: 33-37, 51, 62-63, 111, 115-116, 118, 122, 189
New York Rifles: 35
Nichols, Andrew: 129
Nice: 53
Nolan, John: 42
North Dakota: 42
North River: 68
Northern Boundary Survey: 120
No Survivors: 167
Nowlan, Bessie: 51
Nowlan, Henry: mention of, 41, 54, 97, 102, 117; career of, 109; and Keogh's will, 132, 157; in fiction and film, 167, 169, 174-177, 182

Oak Grove Plantation: 111
Oak Hill Cemetery: 84-85
Oberlin: 93
O'Brien, George: 182
O'Brien, Michael J: 30
O'Flynn, Surgeon P: 60
Ohio: 69
O'Keefe, Joseph: mention of, 54-55, 59, 67, 70, 176; in Whiting's Brigade, 75; released in prisoner exchange, 78; letter about Sherian's desire to have Keogh on staff, 81; dies in Providence Hospital in 1865, 83-84
Old Santa Fe Trail: 187
O'Mahony, John: 35
O'Meara, Thomas: 115

O'Neill, Bill: 181
O'Neill, Thomas: 42-43
On The Plains With Custer: 166
Orange and Alexandria Railroad: 73
Orchard: 49, 51, 189
Oregon: 34, 187
O'Rielly, Myles: 56
O'Sullivan, Daniel Keogh: 77
Ouchterlony, John Arvid: 119, 123, 158
Owasco Lake: 90
Owens, Eugene: 41
Owens Garden: 45

Pachecho, Louis: 32
Palmer, Peter: 184
Papal States: 38, 52-54; 59
Papal Zouaves: 59, 174
Papal Wars: 16, 29, 61
Park House: 189
Parma: 52-53
Patten, Lewis: 169
Patton, John W: 148, 155, 172
Peninsula Campaign: 70
Penn-Gaskell, Peter: 74-75
Pennsylvania: 30-31, 37
Perugia: 52
Peters, Jim: 177
Philadelphia: 35, 37, 62
Piedmont-Sardinia: 52-53
Pius IX: 38, 52, 54-55, 189
Plesanton, Alfred: 71, 75, 77
Poetry on Comanche and Keogh: 180-181
Pohanka, Brian: 160
Pointe Coupee Parrish: 111
Polk, James K: 33
Pope, John: 70, 166
Port Hudson: 72, 109
Port Republic: 68-69
Porter, Eliza: 132
Porter, James E: 120, 132-133
Powder River: 47, 131
Powell, James W: 131
Prior, Charles: 121, 129
Purcell, Archbishop John Baptist: 61

Quebec: 46
Queenstown: 115, 122

Rapidan River: 77

Rappahannock: 74, 77
Red Feather: 144, 150
Red Horse: 135-137, 141, 147
Ree scouts: 131, 138
Reed, Joseph: 31
Reilly, John: 33
Remember the Little Big Horn: 173
Reno Creek: 134
Reno, Marcus: retreat, 42; mention of, 120, 131-132, 134, 140; in fiction and television, 165, 168-171, 185-186
Reserve brigade: 72
Reynold, Quentin: 175
Reynolds, Charley: 131, 139
Reynolds, John: 76
Robinson, William E: 33
Romagna: 52-53
Rome: 16, 52-53, 55, 59-60, 62, 163, 168, 176
Rosebud: 132
Rosenberg, Bruce A: 15
Rossiter, Thomas: 72, 77
Royal Military College: 109
Runs the Enemy: 145-147
Russell, Frank: 57-58
Ryan, Sgt. John: 16

Sabin, Edward: 166
Saint Louis: 35
Saint Patrick's College: 51
Saint Paul: 133
Saint Paul and Pacific Railroad: 120
Saline River: 109, 117
Salisbury: 83
Saltville: 82
San Patricios: 33
Sanders, Wilbur Edgerton: 180
Sanderson, George Kaiser: 156
Sandoz, Mari: 169
Sandringham Military Academy: 54
Savannah: siege of, 30
Savoy: 53
Schofield, John: 79, 82
Scofield, Jonathan: 172
Scott, Hugh: 25
Scott, W: 25
Scott, Sir Walter: 15
Scott, Winfield: 31; defense of Irish-American soldiers, 33;
Seminole: 32
Seven Days Campaign: 38
Seventh Cavalry: 177

Seventh's Staghound, The: 167
Seward, William H: 61, 64, 87, 91, 97
Shelbyville: 119
Shellabarger, Jacob Henry: 114-115
Shenandoah Valley: 67, 81
Sheridan, Michael V: 103, 112, 157
Sheridan, Philip H: mention of, 43, 81-82, 113, 187-188; letter to Nelly Martin on remains of Keogh, 157-158
Sherman, William Tecumseh: 79-80, 109, 113, 157
She Wore A Yellow Ribbon: 182
Shields, James: Keogh's commanding officer, 34; mention of, 36, 63, 68; early military career, 67; on Keily's bravery at Port Republic, 70
Simon, Robert F: 184
Sioux: 21, 23, 42-43, 112, 137, 140, 146, 169, 172, 177, 182, 184
Sitting Bull: 140, 150, 157, 170, 177
Smith, A. E: 143
Smith, A. J: 112
Smyth, Thomas Alfred: 36
Snake Creek engagement: 42
Snedeker, Lenora: 160
"Song of the Camp": 161
South Carolina Irish Artillery: 39
South River: 68
Spanish-American War: 43
Spellman, John Francis: 49
Spoleto: 52, 56, 64
Stafford, William F: 60
Stanley, David S: 40
Stanton, Edwin: 61, 72
Staples, Samuel Frederick: 121
Stephens, James: 35
Stone, Charles P: 72, 86
Stoneman, George: 72-75, 82, 87, 92
Stoneman's Raid: 73
Stowe, Harriet Beecher: 105
Strong, George Templeton: 34
Strother, David H: 63
Stuart, James Ewell Brown: 75
Studdart, I. F. A: 120
Sturgis, Samuel D: 23, 79, 116
Sullivan, John: 31
Sully, Alfred: mention of 47, 113; expedition: 187
Sumner, E.V., Jr: 74
Sunshine Church: 81
Sweeny, Thomas William: 36
Sweeny, William M: 34

Tactical stability in Custer Battle: 143
Tasmania: 36

INDEX

Taunton, Francis: 49
Taylor Barracks: 119
Taylor, Bayard: 155, 161
Taylor, Richard: 69
Taylor, Zachary: 33
Tennessee: 39
Tennyson, Alfred Lord: 15
Terry, Alfred: 120, 131-132, 157, 184-186
Texas: 39
"Thaddy O'Brien": 40
That Damn Single Shot: 173
They Died With Their Boots On: 46, 182
Thirteenth (Duke of Cabridge's) Regiment: 49
Thompson, Joe: 188
Thompson, John: 125
Thompson, William: 114
Thompson's Crossroads: 74
Throop, Enos Thompson: 88-89
Throop family name: 96
Throop, William: 96
Thuder Shield: 166
Tinryland: 189
Tipperary: 42
Tongue River: 132, 157
Tonka: 175, 182
Torbert, Alfred: 64
Townsend, E. D: 115
Traveller: R. E. Lee's horse, 22
Tremain, Greville: 94
Trevilian's Station: 64, 74
Trieste: 55
Tuscany: 52-53
Turner, Theophilus H: 104
Turkey Leg: 127
Turtle Mountain: 120
Turtle Rib: 145-146; 151
TV Guide: 184
Two Eagles: 145-147, 151
Two Moon: 136, 138, 140-141, 143-146, 177, 184
Tyler, Erastus B: 69
Tyrone, County: 34
Tyrrhenian Sea: 52

Umbria: 52-53
Uniforms: United States, 35, 39, 64, 66, 70, 74, 80, 102, 111, 114, 119-120; Papal, 54-56

MYLES KEOGH

Union College: 92
United States: need for experienced foreign military, 61
United States Military Academy: 17, 33, 70, 73, 92
United States Naval Academy: 92
United States Sanitary Commission: 35
University of Oklahoma Press: 25
Upperville: 76
Upton, Daniel: 93
Upton, Elicha Randall: 93
Upton, Emily Martin: 84, 91, 93, 95-96
Upton, Emory: mention, 17, 84, 88, 93, 111; marries Emily Norwood Martin, 93; military career of, 93-94; suicide, 98
Utley, Robert M: 41

Vatican City: 59, 176
Van Buren, Martin: 88-89
Van de Water, F. F: 128, 166
Van Tine, Charles: 89
Varden, Frank E: 121, 149, 155, 172
Varnum, Charles A: 131
Vecchia: 55
Vestal, Stanley: 145-146
Victor Emmanual II: 52-53

Vienna: 55
Viet Nam: 43
Virginia: mention of, 39, 67; Home Guards, 82

Wadsworth, Craig "Tic": 75, 77
Wadsworth, Emma and Nellie: frontpiece, 122
Wadsworth, James S: 72, 77
Wainwright, Charles S: 70
Wainwright, Jonathan: 25
Walker, Leicester: 74
Wallingford, David: 114-115
War Chiefs of the Northwest: 181
War of 1812: 31, 43
Warrenton: 74
Washington, D.C: 63, 65, 72, 74, 111, 113, 116
Washington, George: 30
Washita: battle of, 40, 47, 113, 188
Wayne, Anthony: 31
Wayne, John: 182
Weir, Thomas: mention of, 120, 128, 131, 187; in fiction, 171-172
Weisbert, David: 183-184
Weld, Stephen Minot: 77
West Point: See United States Military Academy
White Bull: 144-146, 150, 175, 182-183
White Cow Bull: 147
White, Dale: 179

White Squaw, Horn of Plenty: 173
Whiting, Charles J: 75
Whittaker, Frederick: 134, 169
"Wild Geese": 29
Wild, John: 148, 155
Wilder, Wilbur Elliott: 94
Williams, Cornelia: 90
Williams, John: 90
Willowbrook: 16, 92, 96, 99, 112, 157-158
Wilson, Howard (Hap): 181
Wilson, James H: 84
With Custer in the Black Hills: 166
Wooden Leg: 136, 141, 146
Woods, Grant: 184-185
World's Columbian Exposition at Chicago, 1893: 24
Wounded Knee, South Dakota: 27, 43
Wright, Horatio G: 108-109
Wylliams, Frederick: 109
Wynant, H. M: 182
Wytheville: 82

"Yankee Doodle": 77
Yates, George: 75, 114, 134, 143, 155, 173, 187
Yellow Bull: 175, 182
Yellow Nose: 146
Yellowstone: 40, 175